Itsuwaribito 空

The Imperial Capital Palace Onkado
Assassination Incident
Who will live through it?!

YUUKI IINUMA

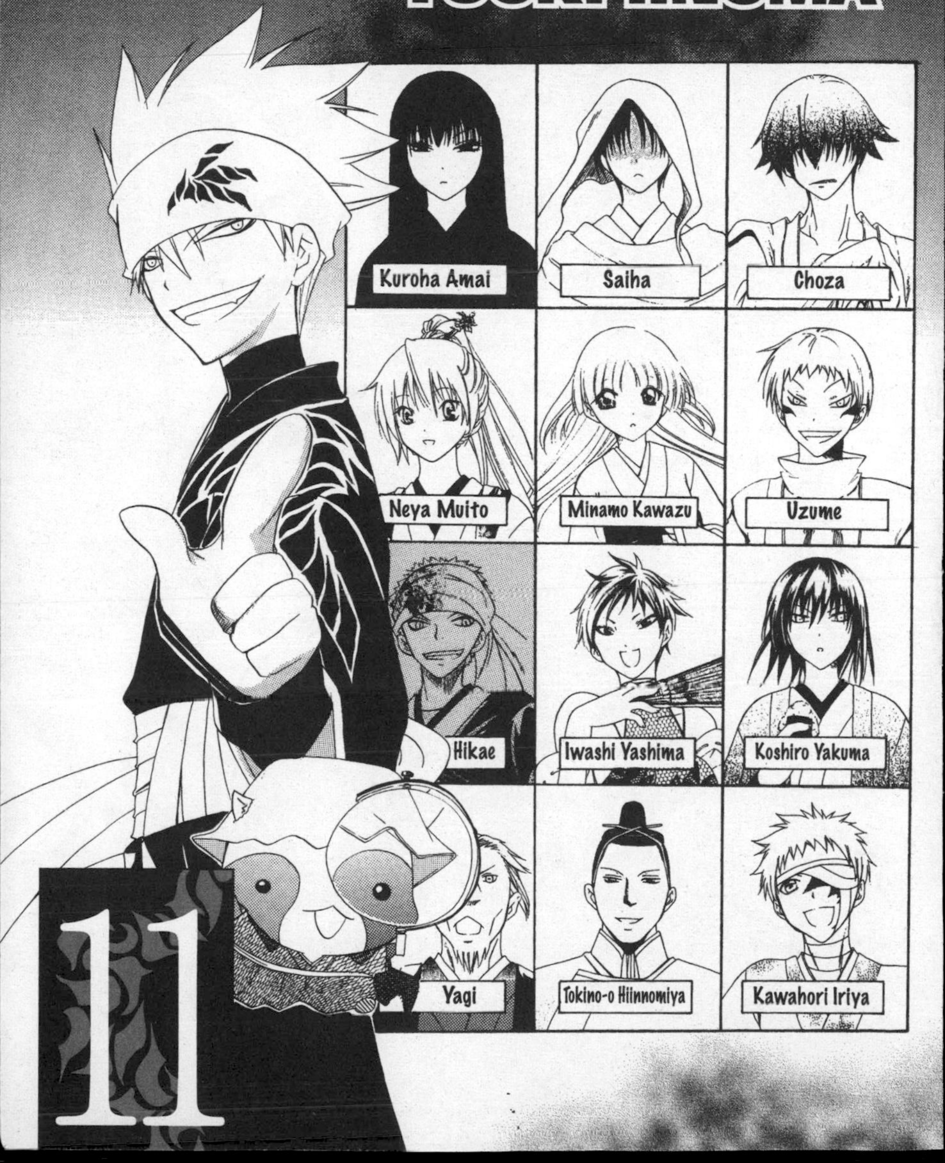

Kuroha Amai
Saiha
Choza
Neya Muito
Minamo Kawazu
Uzume
Hikae
Iwashi Yashima
Koshiro Yakuma
Yagi
Tokino-o Hiinnomiya
Kawahori Iriya
11

Contents

Chapter 98 Strategy

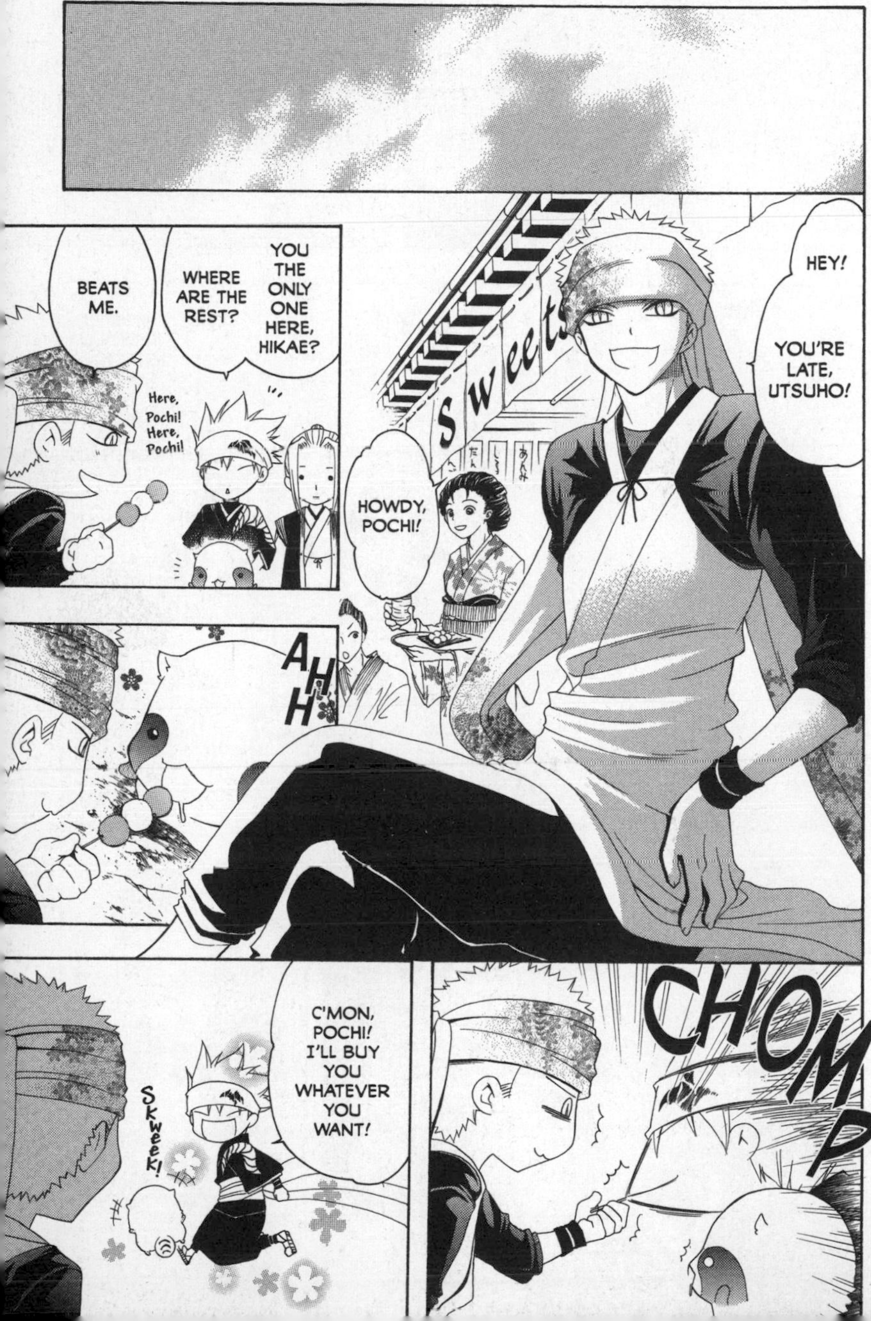
HEY!
YOU'RE LATE, UTSUHO!
HOWDY, POCHI!
YOU THE ONLY ONE HERE, HIKAE?
WHERE ARE THE REST?
BEATS ME.
Here, Pochi! Here, Pochi!
AHH
CHOMP
C'MON, POCHI! I'LL BUY YOU WHATEVER YOU WANT!
SKWEEK!

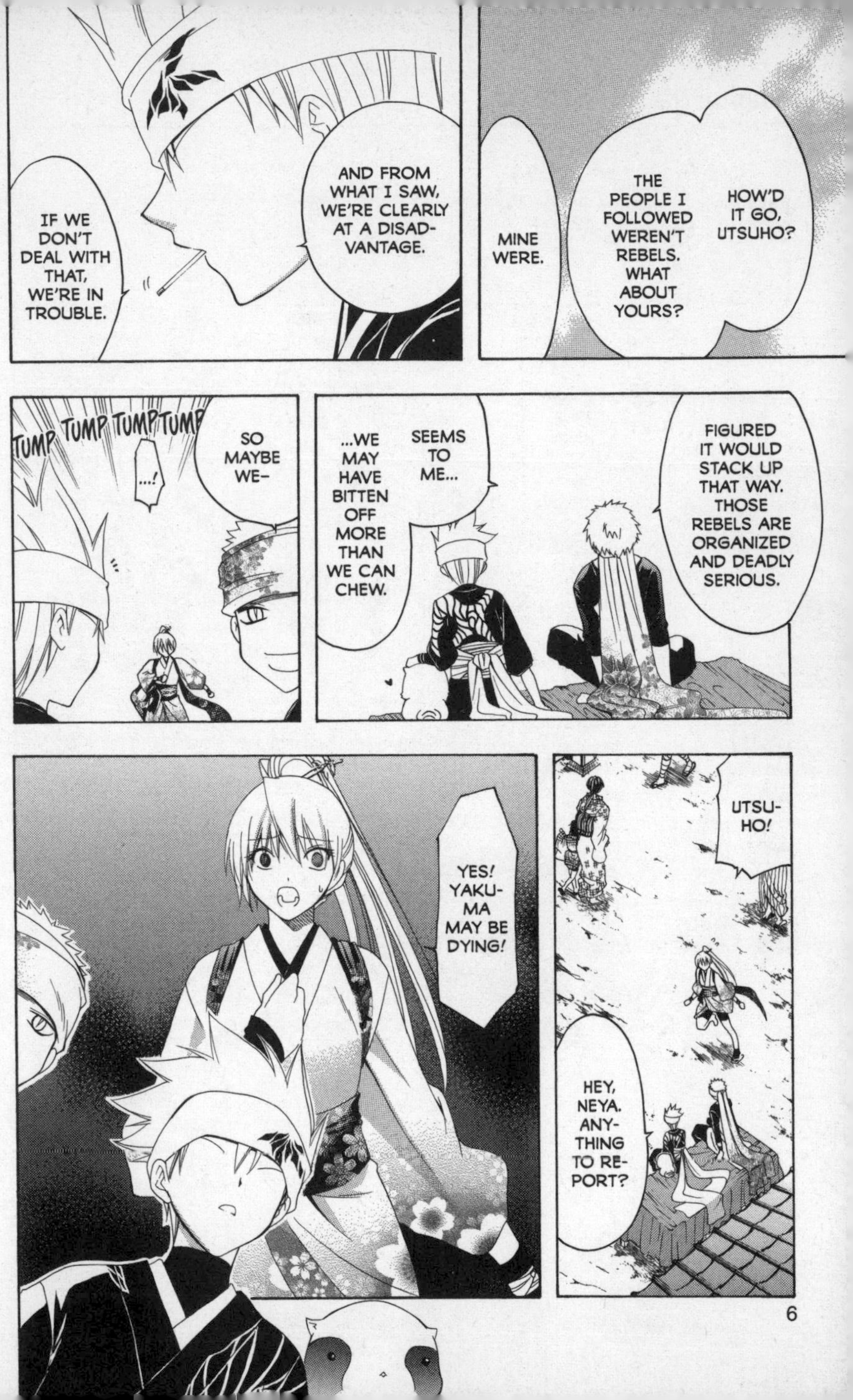
HOW'D IT GO, UTSUHO?
THE PEOPLE I FOLLOWED WEREN'T REBELS. WHAT ABOUT YOURS?
MINE WERE.
AND FROM WHAT I SAW, WE'RE CLEARLY AT A DISAD-VANTAGE.
IF WE DON'T DEAL WITH THAT, WE'RE IN TROUBLE.
FIGURED IT WOULD STACK UP THAT WAY. THOSE REBELS ARE ORGANIZED AND DEADLY SERIOUS.
SEEMS TO ME...
...WE MAY HAVE BITTEN OFF MORE THAN WE CAN CHEW.
SO MAYBE WE–
TUMP TUMP TUMP TUMP
...!
UTSU-HO!
HEY, NEYA. ANY-THING TO RE-PORT?
YES! YAKUMA MAY BE DYING!

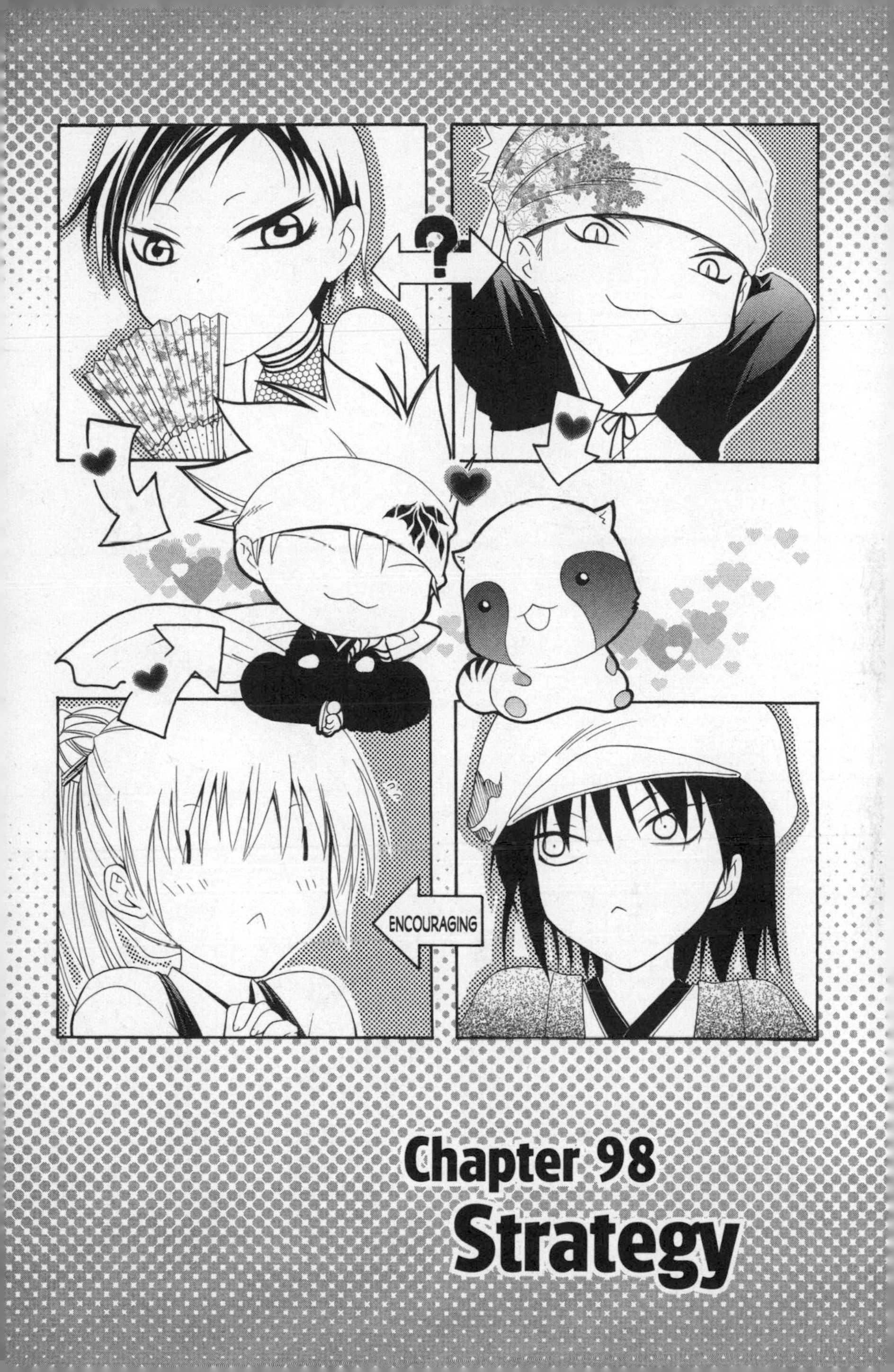
?
ENCOURAGING

Chapter 98
Strategy

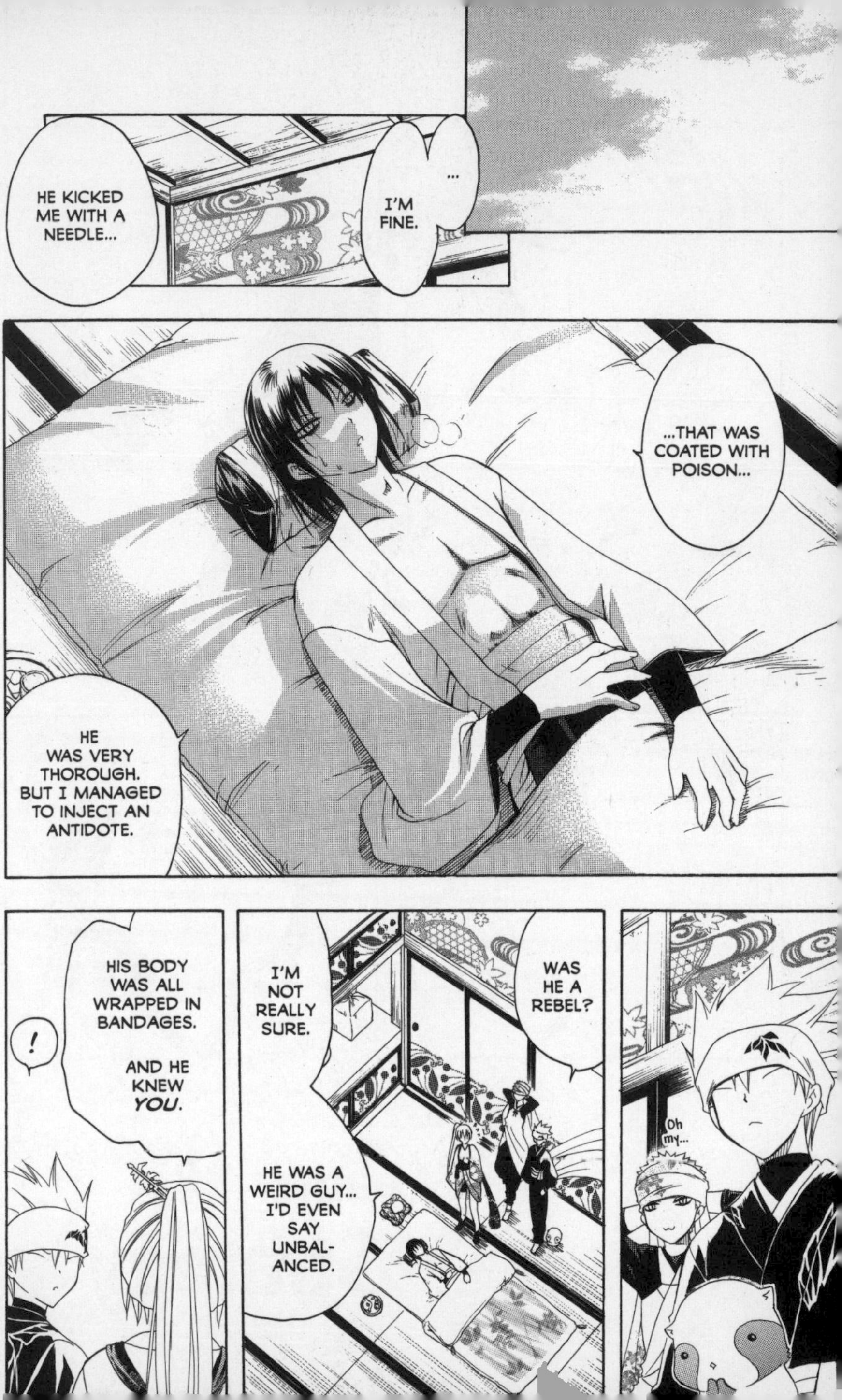
...
I'M FINE.
HE KICKED ME WITH A NEEDLE...
...THAT WAS COATED WITH POISON...
HE WAS VERY THOROUGH. BUT I MANAGED TO INJECT AN ANTIDOTE.
Oh my...
WAS HE A REBEL?
I'M NOT REALLY SURE.
HE WAS A WEIRD GUY... I'D EVEN SAY UNBAL-ANCED.
HIS BODY WAS ALL WRAPPED IN BANDAGES.
AND HE KNEW *YOU*.
!

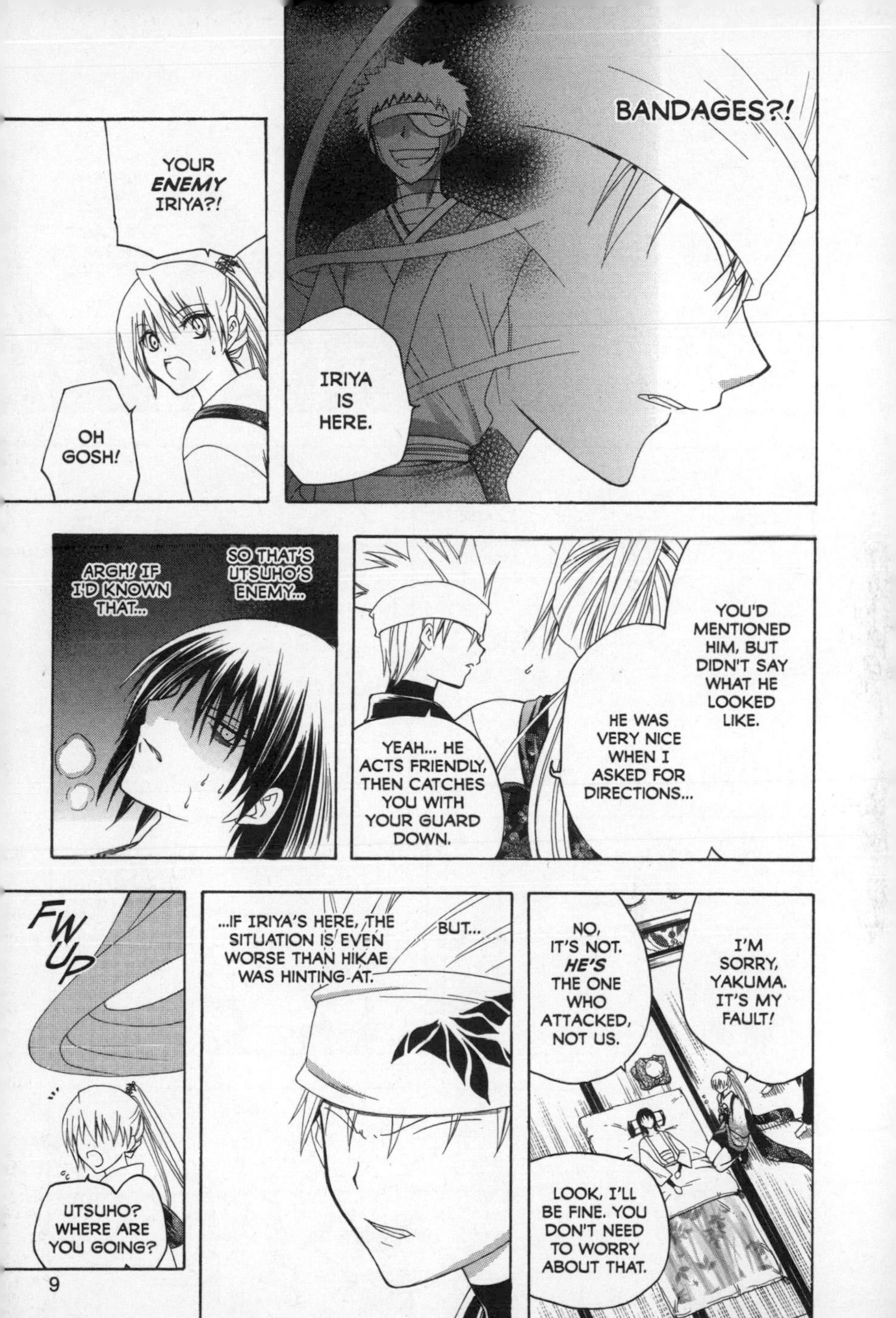
BANDAGES?!
IRIYA IS HERE.
YOUR *ENEMY* IRIYA?!
OH GOSH!
YOU'D MENTIONED HIM, BUT DIDN'T SAY WHAT HE LOOKED LIKE.
HE WAS VERY NICE WHEN I ASKED FOR DIRECTIONS...
YEAH... HE ACTS FRIENDLY, THEN CATCHES YOU WITH YOUR GUARD DOWN.
SO THAT'S UTSUHO'S ENEMY...
ARGH! IF I'D KNOWN THAT...
I'M SORRY, YAKUMA. IT'S MY FAULT!
NO, IT'S NOT. *HE'S* THE ONE WHO ATTACKED, NOT US.
LOOK, I'LL BE FINE. YOU DON'T NEED TO WORRY ABOUT THAT.
BUT...
...IF IRIYA'S HERE, THE SITUATION IS EVEN WORSE THAN HIKAE WAS HINTING AT.
FWUP
UTSUHO? WHERE ARE YOU GOING?

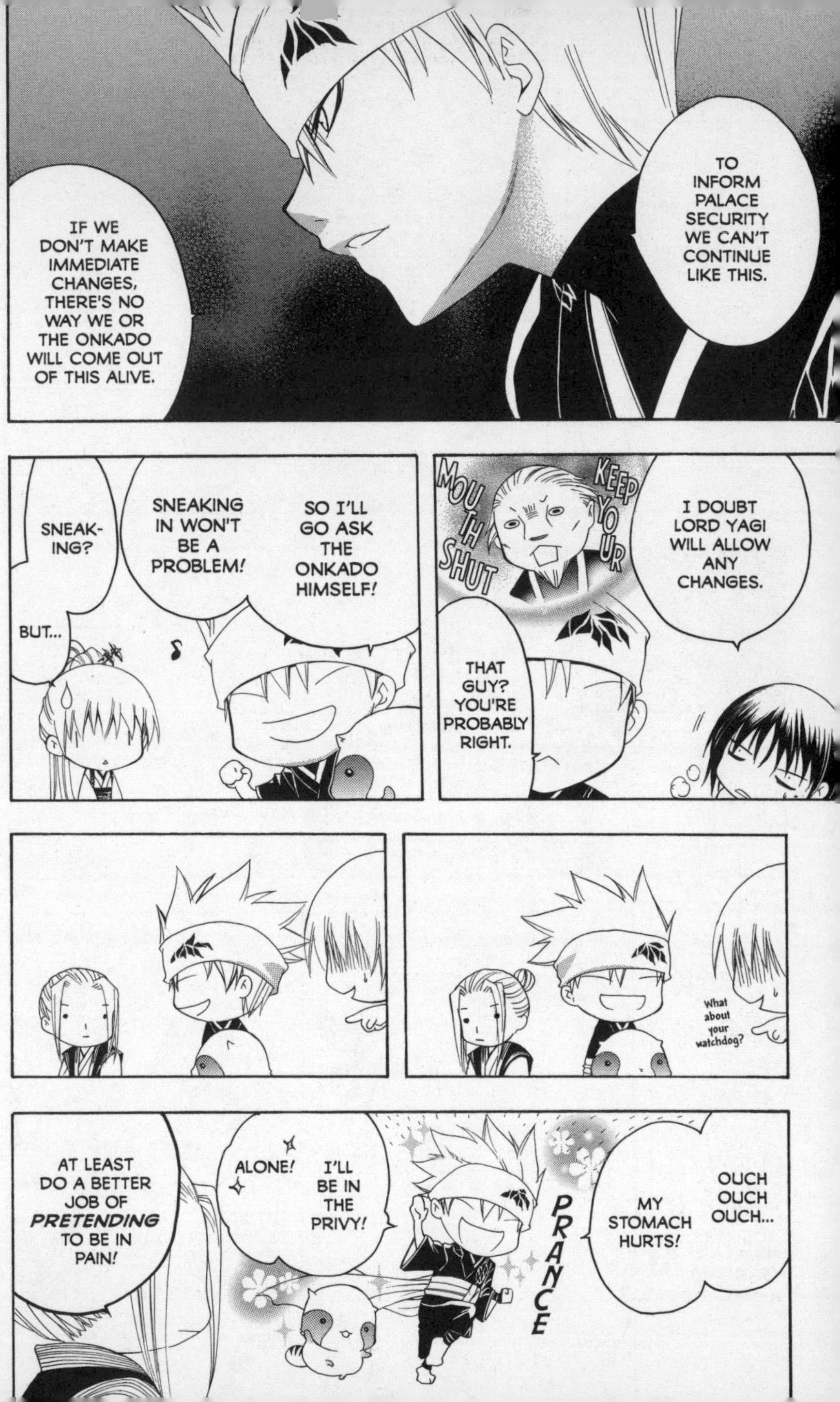
TO INFORM PALACE SECURITY WE CAN'T CONTINUE LIKE THIS.
IF WE DON'T MAKE IMMEDIATE CHANGES, THERE'S NO WAY WE OR THE ONKADO WILL COME OUT OF THIS ALIVE.
I DOUBT LORD YAGI WILL ALLOW ANY CHANGES.
KEEP YOUR MOUTH SHUT
THAT GUY? YOU'RE PROBABLY RIGHT.
SO I'LL GO ASK THE ONKADO HIMSELF!
SNEAKING IN WON'T BE A PROBLEM!
SNEAK-ING?
BUT...
What about your watchdog?
OUCH OUCH OUCH...
MY STOMACH HURTS!
PRANCE
I'LL BE IN THE PRIVY!
ALONE!
AT LEAST DO A BETTER JOB OF *PRETENDING* TO BE IN PAIN!

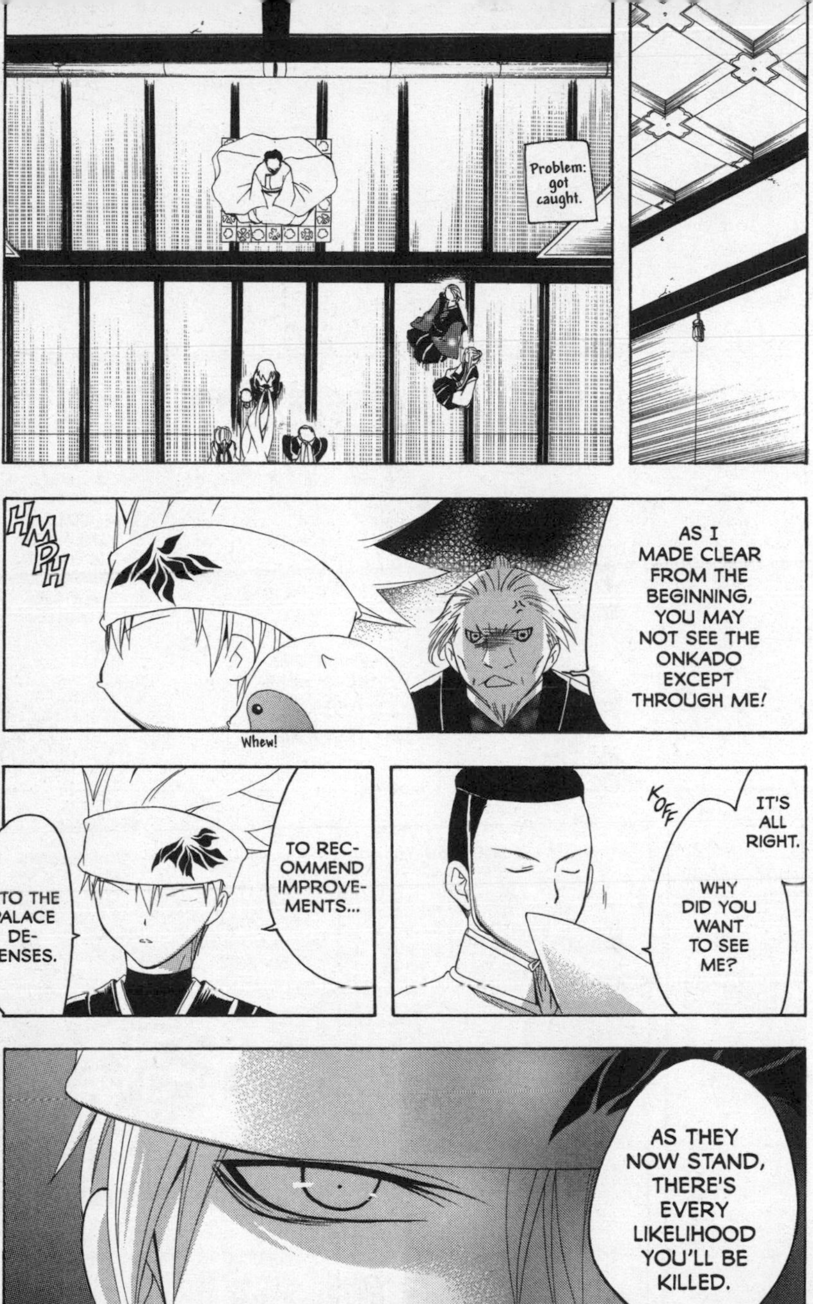
Problem: got caught.
AS I MADE CLEAR FROM THE BEGINNING, YOU MAY NOT SEE THE ONKADO EXCEPT THROUGH ME!
HMPH
Whew!
KOFF
IT'S ALL RIGHT.
WHY DID YOU WANT TO SEE ME?
TO RECOMMEND IMPROVEMENTS...
...TO THE PALACE DEFENSES.
AS THEY NOW STAND, THERE'S EVERY LIKELIHOOD YOU'LL BE KILLED.

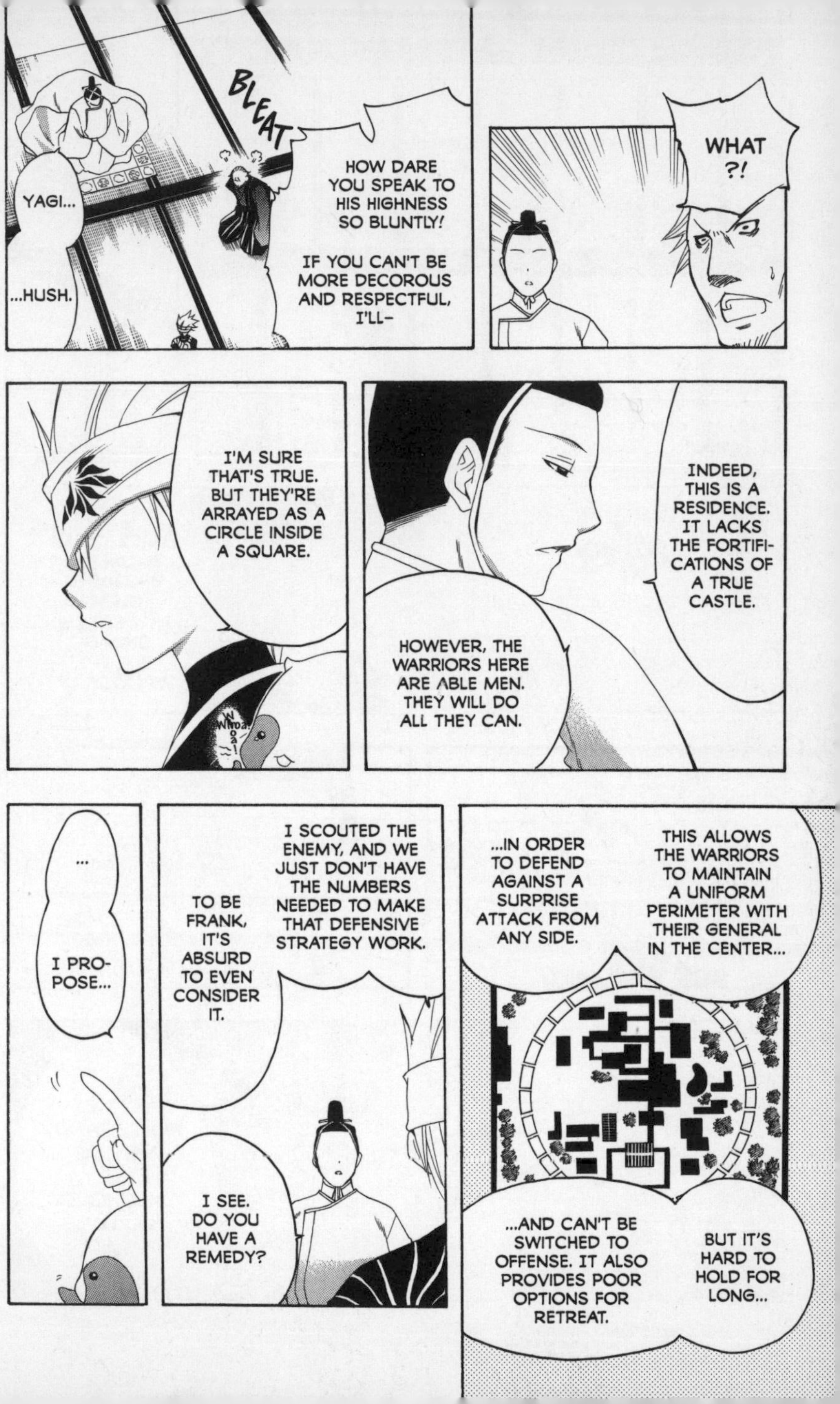
WHAT ?!
BLEAT
HOW DARE YOU SPEAK TO HIS HIGHNESS SO BLUNTLY!
IF YOU CAN'T BE MORE DECOROUS AND RESPECTFUL, I'LL–
YAGI...
...HUSH.
INDEED, THIS IS A RESIDENCE. IT LACKS THE FORTIFI- CATIONS OF A TRUE CASTLE.
HOWEVER, THE WARRIORS HERE ARE ABLE MEN. THEY WILL DO ALL THEY CAN.
I'M SURE THAT'S TRUE. BUT THEY'RE ARRAYED AS A CIRCLE INSIDE A SQUARE.
Whoa!
THIS ALLOWS THE WARRIORS TO MAINTAIN A UNIFORM PERIMETER WITH THEIR GENERAL IN THE CENTER...
...IN ORDER TO DEFEND AGAINST A SURPRISE ATTACK FROM ANY SIDE.
BUT IT'S HARD TO HOLD FOR LONG...
...AND CAN'T BE SWITCHED TO OFFENSE. IT ALSO PROVIDES POOR OPTIONS FOR RETREAT.
I SCOUTED THE ENEMY, AND WE JUST DON'T HAVE THE NUMBERS NEEDED TO MAKE THAT DEFENSIVE STRATEGY WORK.
TO BE FRANK, IT'S ABSURD TO EVEN CONSIDER IT.
I SEE. DO YOU HAVE A REMEDY?
...
I PRO- POSE...

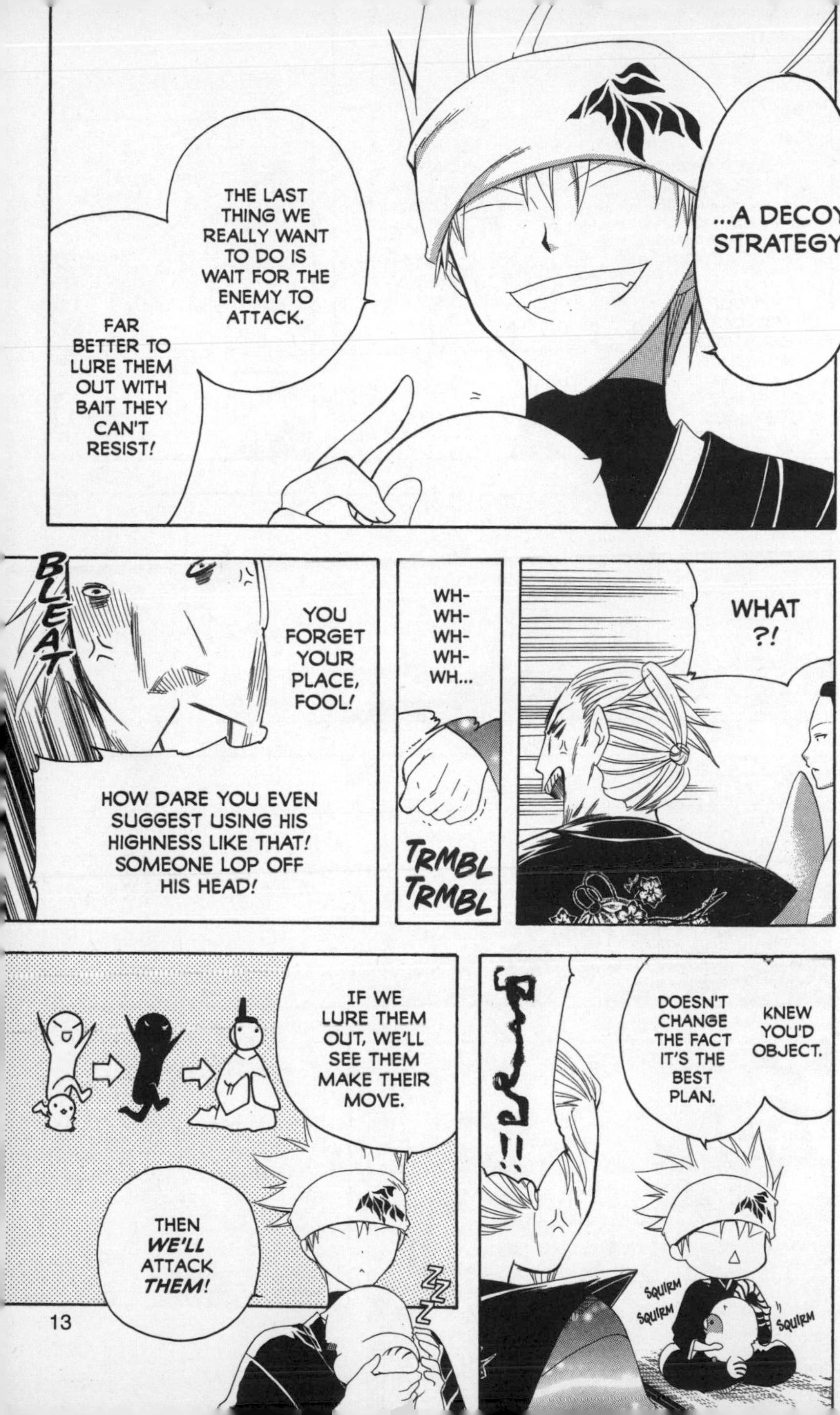
...A DECOY STRATEGY.
THE LAST THING WE REALLY WANT TO DO IS WAIT FOR THE ENEMY TO ATTACK.
FAR BETTER TO LURE THEM OUT WITH BAIT THEY CAN'T RESIST!
WHAT ?!
WH-WH-WH-WH-WH...
TRMBL TRMBL
BLEAT
YOU FORGET YOUR PLACE, FOOL!
HOW DARE YOU EVEN SUGGEST USING HIS HIGHNESS LIKE THAT! SOMEONE LOP OFF HIS HEAD!
KNEW YOU'D OBJECT.
DOESN'T CHANGE THE FACT IT'S THE BEST PLAN.
SQUIRM SQUIRM
SQUIRM
!!
IF WE LURE THEM OUT, WE'LL SEE THEM MAKE THEIR MOVE.
THEN *WE'LL* ATTACK *THEM*!
ZZZ

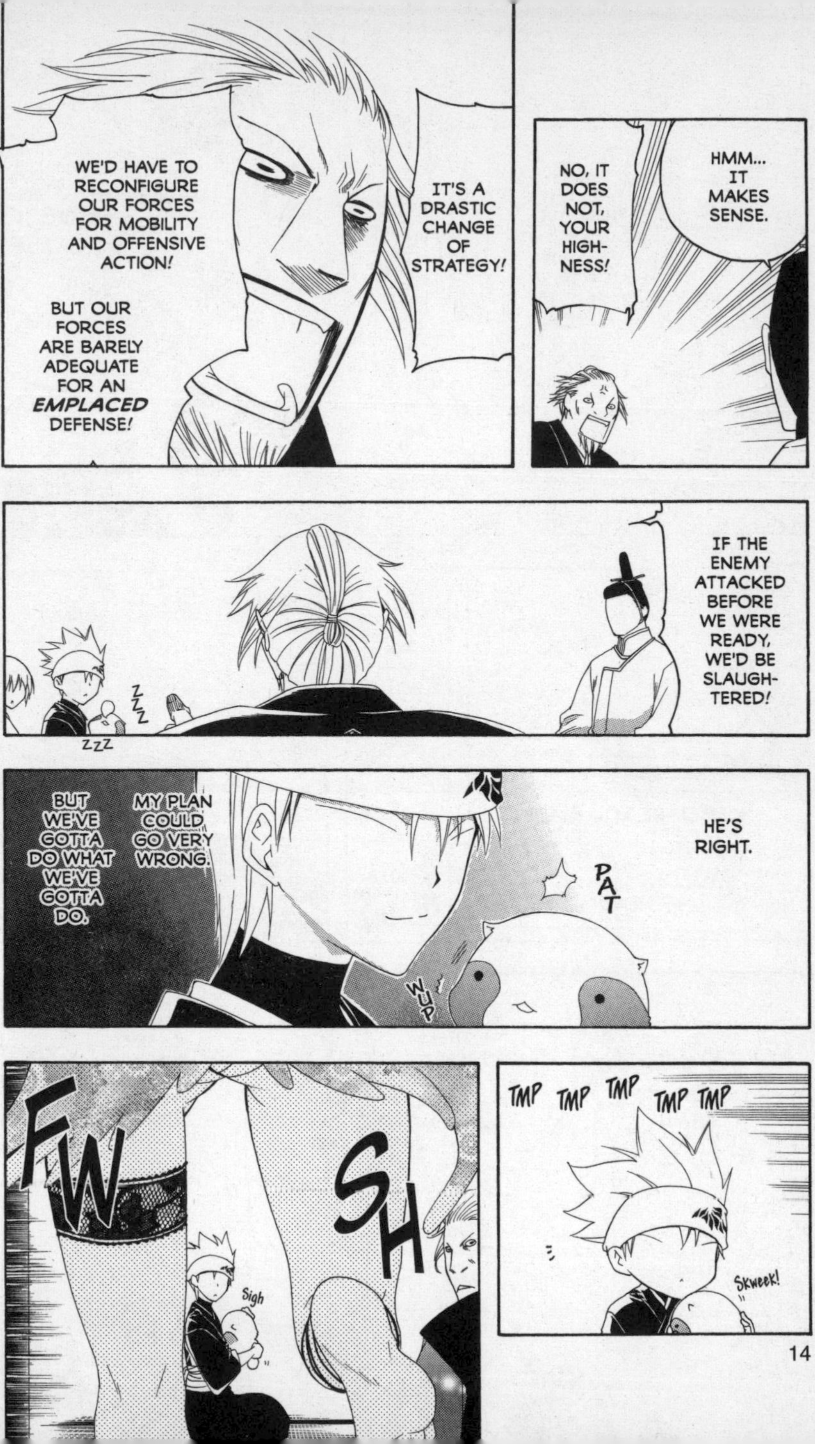
HMM... IT MAKES SENSE.
NO, IT DOES NOT, YOUR HIGHNESS!
IT'S A DRASTIC CHANGE OF STRATEGY!
WE'D HAVE TO RECONFIGURE OUR FORCES FOR MOBILITY AND OFFENSIVE ACTION!
BUT OUR FORCES ARE BARELY ADEQUATE FOR AN *EMPLACED* DEFENSE!
IF THE ENEMY ATTACKED BEFORE WE WERE READY, WE'D BE SLAUGHTERED!
ZZZ
ZZZ
HE'S RIGHT.
PAT
WUP
MY PLAN COULD GO VERY WRONG.
BUT WE'VE GOTTA DO WHAT WE'VE GOTTA DO.
TMP TMP TMP TMP TMP
Skweek!
FW
SH
Sigh

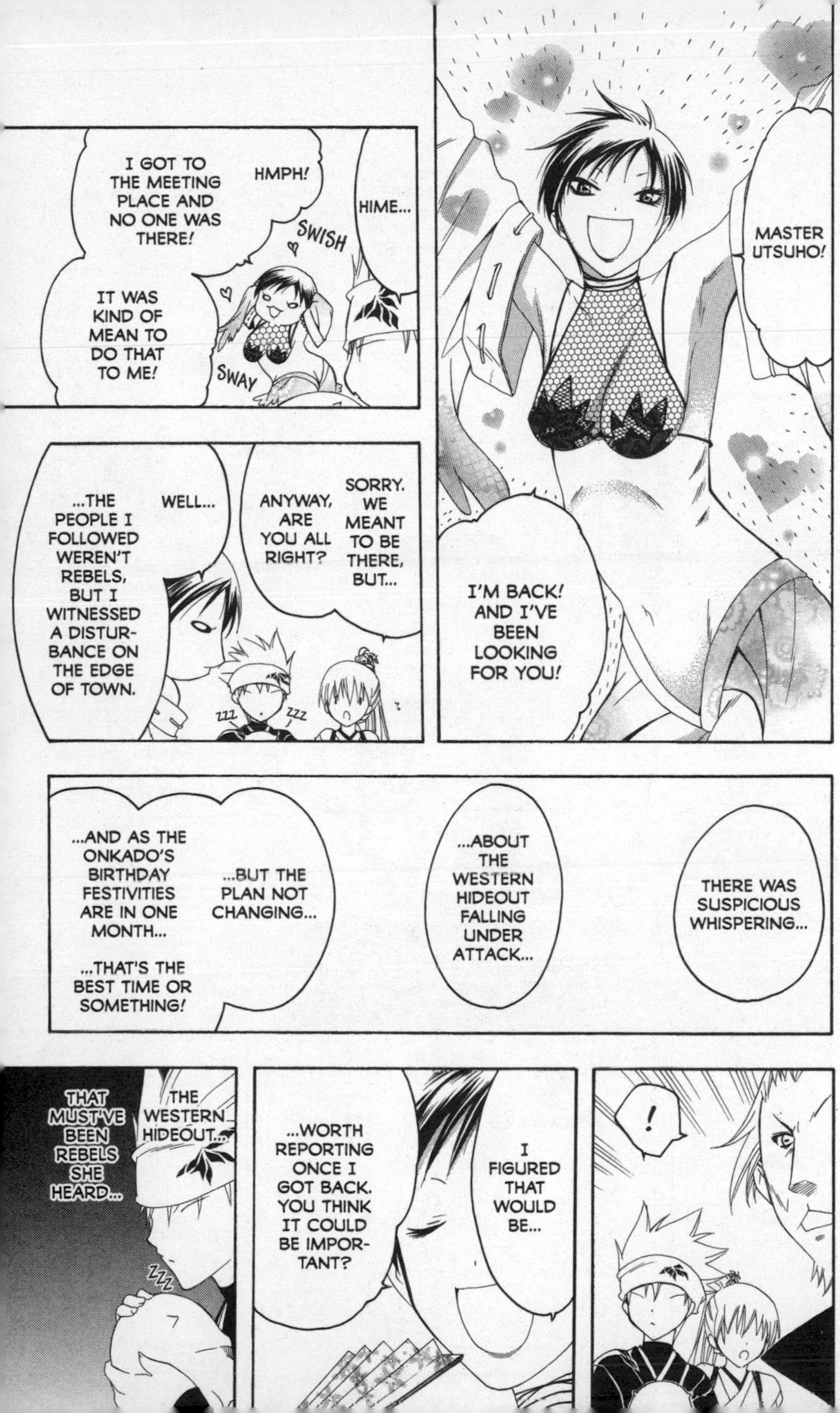
MASTER UTSUHO!
I'M BACK! AND I'VE BEEN LOOKING FOR YOU!
HIME...
HMPH!
I GOT TO THE MEETING PLACE AND NO ONE WAS THERE!
SWISH
IT WAS KIND OF MEAN TO DO THAT TO ME!
SWAY
SORRY. WE MEANT TO BE THERE, BUT...
ANYWAY, ARE YOU ALL RIGHT?
WELL...
...THE PEOPLE I FOLLOWED WEREN'T REBELS, BUT I WITNESSED A DISTUR-BANCE ON THE EDGE OF TOWN.
ZZZ
ZZZ
THERE WAS SUSPICIOUS WHISPERING...
...ABOUT THE WESTERN HIDEOUT FALLING UNDER ATTACK...
...BUT THE PLAN NOT CHANGING...
...AND AS THE ONKADO'S BIRTHDAY FESTIVITIES ARE IN ONE MONTH...
...THAT'S THE BEST TIME OR SOMETHING!
!
I FIGURED THAT WOULD BE...
...WORTH REPORTING ONCE I GOT BACK. YOU THINK IT COULD BE IMPOR-TANT?
THE WESTERN HIDEOUT...
THAT MUST'VE BEEN REBELS SHE HEARD...
ZZZ

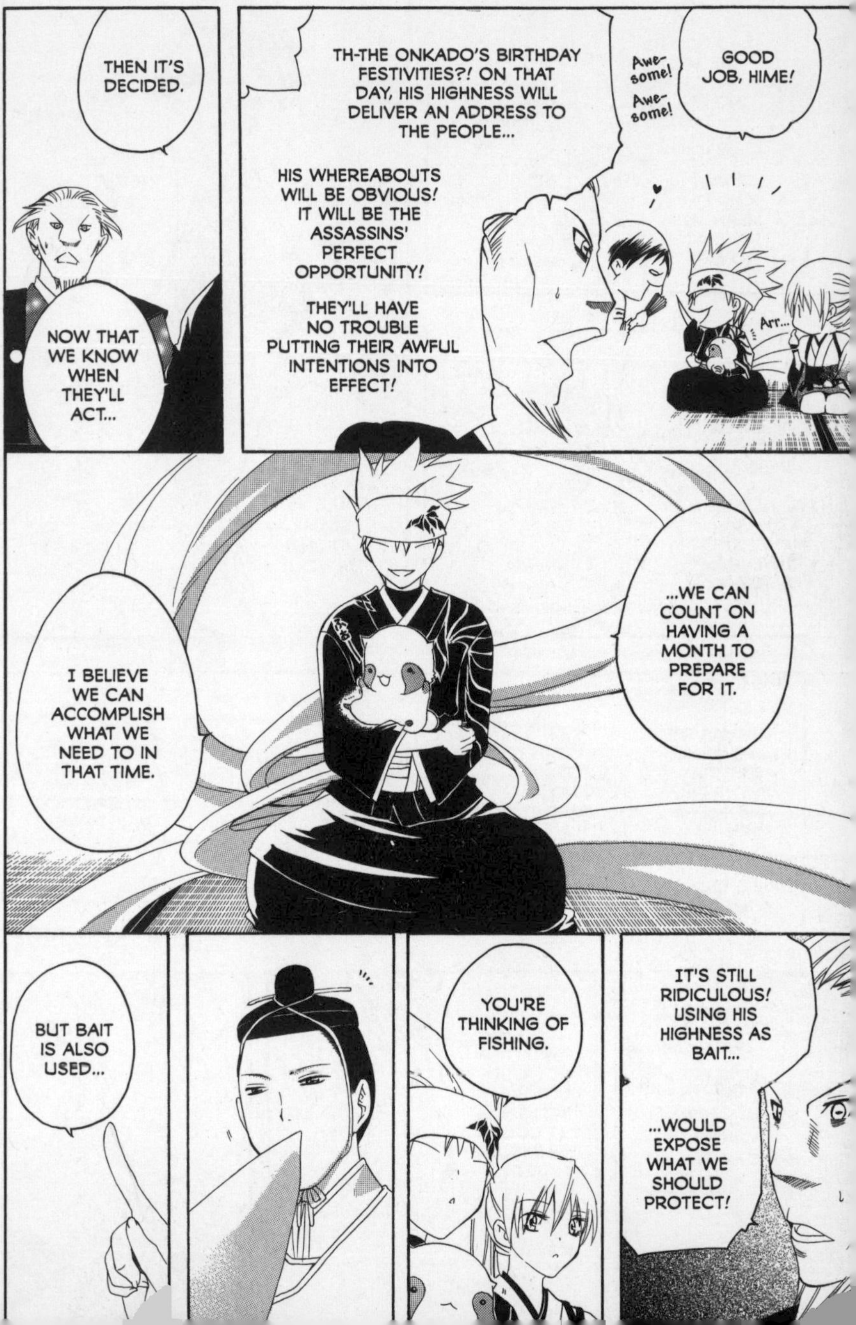
GOOD JOB, HIME!
Awe-some!
Awe-some!
TH-THE ONKADO'S BIRTHDAY FESTIVITIES?! ON THAT DAY, HIS HIGHNESS WILL DELIVER AN ADDRESS TO THE PEOPLE...
HIS WHEREABOUTS WILL BE OBVIOUS! IT WILL BE THE ASSASSINS' PERFECT OPPORTUNITY!
THEY'LL HAVE NO TROUBLE PUTTING THEIR AWFUL INTENTIONS INTO EFFECT!
Arr...
THEN IT'S DECIDED.
NOW THAT WE KNOW WHEN THEY'LL ACT...
...WE CAN COUNT ON HAVING A MONTH TO PREPARE FOR IT.
I BELIEVE WE CAN ACCOMPLISH WHAT WE NEED TO IN THAT TIME.
IT'S STILL RIDICULOUS! USING HIS HIGHNESS AS BAIT...
...WOULD EXPOSE WHAT WE SHOULD PROTECT!
YOU'RE THINKING OF FISHING.
BUT BAIT IS ALSO USED...

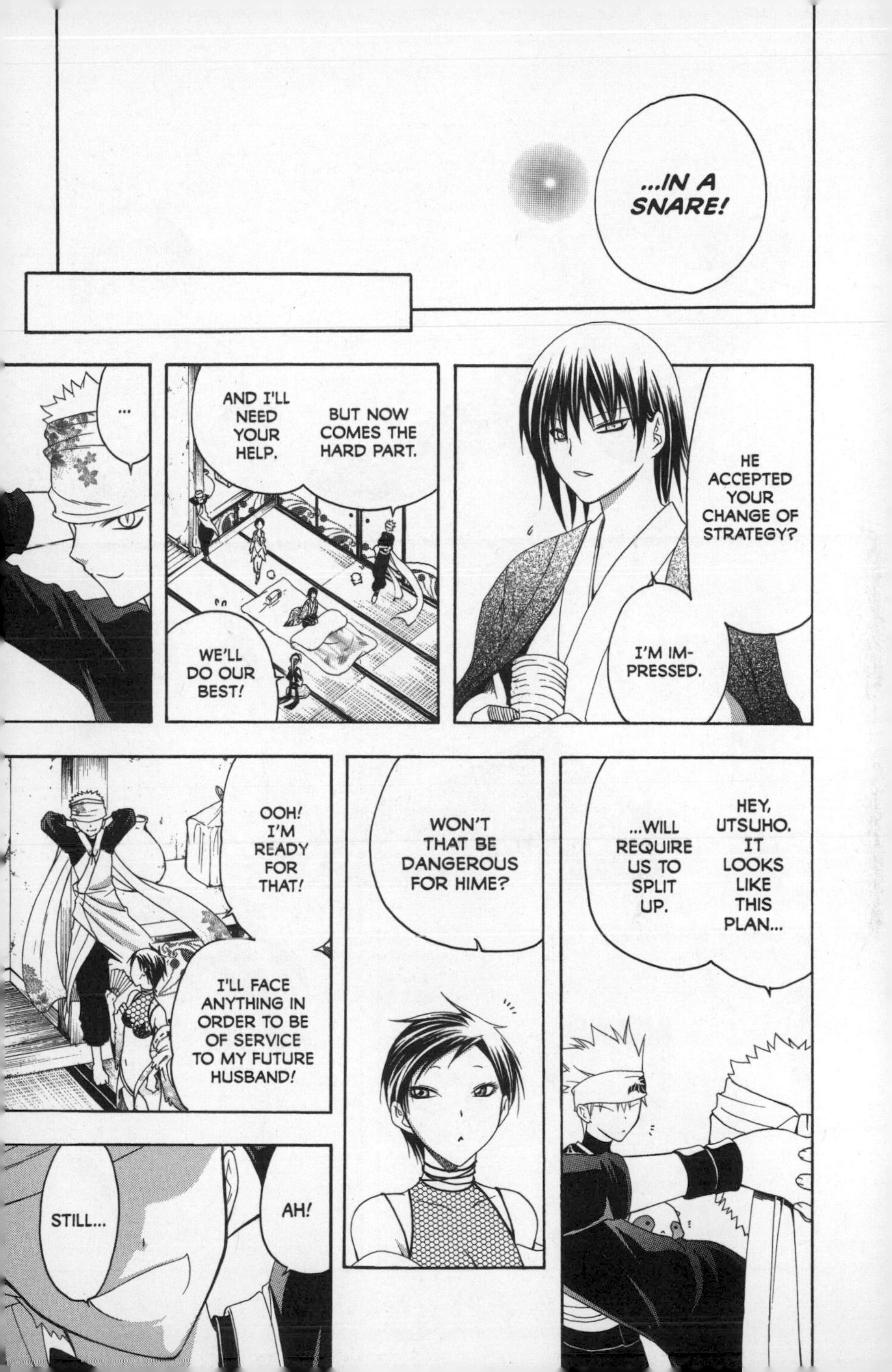
...IN A SNARE!
HE ACCEPTED YOUR CHANGE OF STRATEGY?
I'M IM-PRESSED.
BUT NOW COMES THE HARD PART.
AND I'LL NEED YOUR HELP.
WE'LL DO OUR BEST!
...
HEY, UTSUHO. IT LOOKS LIKE THIS PLAN...
...WILL REQUIRE US TO SPLIT UP.
WON'T THAT BE DANGEROUS FOR HIME?
OOH! I'M READY FOR THAT!
I'LL FACE ANYTHING IN ORDER TO BE OF SERVICE TO MY FUTURE HUSBAND!
AH!
STILL...

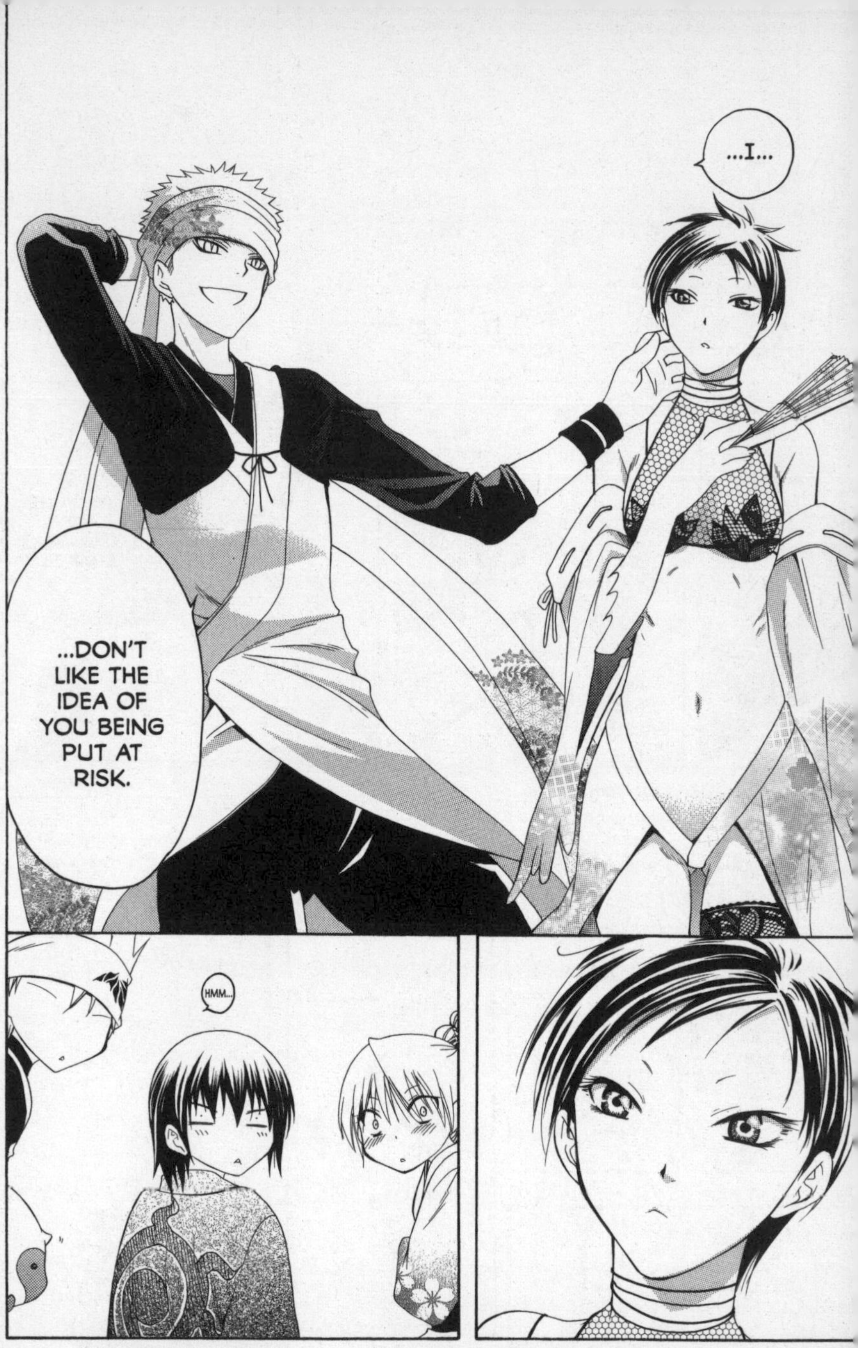
...I...
...DON'T LIKE THE IDEA OF YOU BEING PUT AT RISK.
HMM...

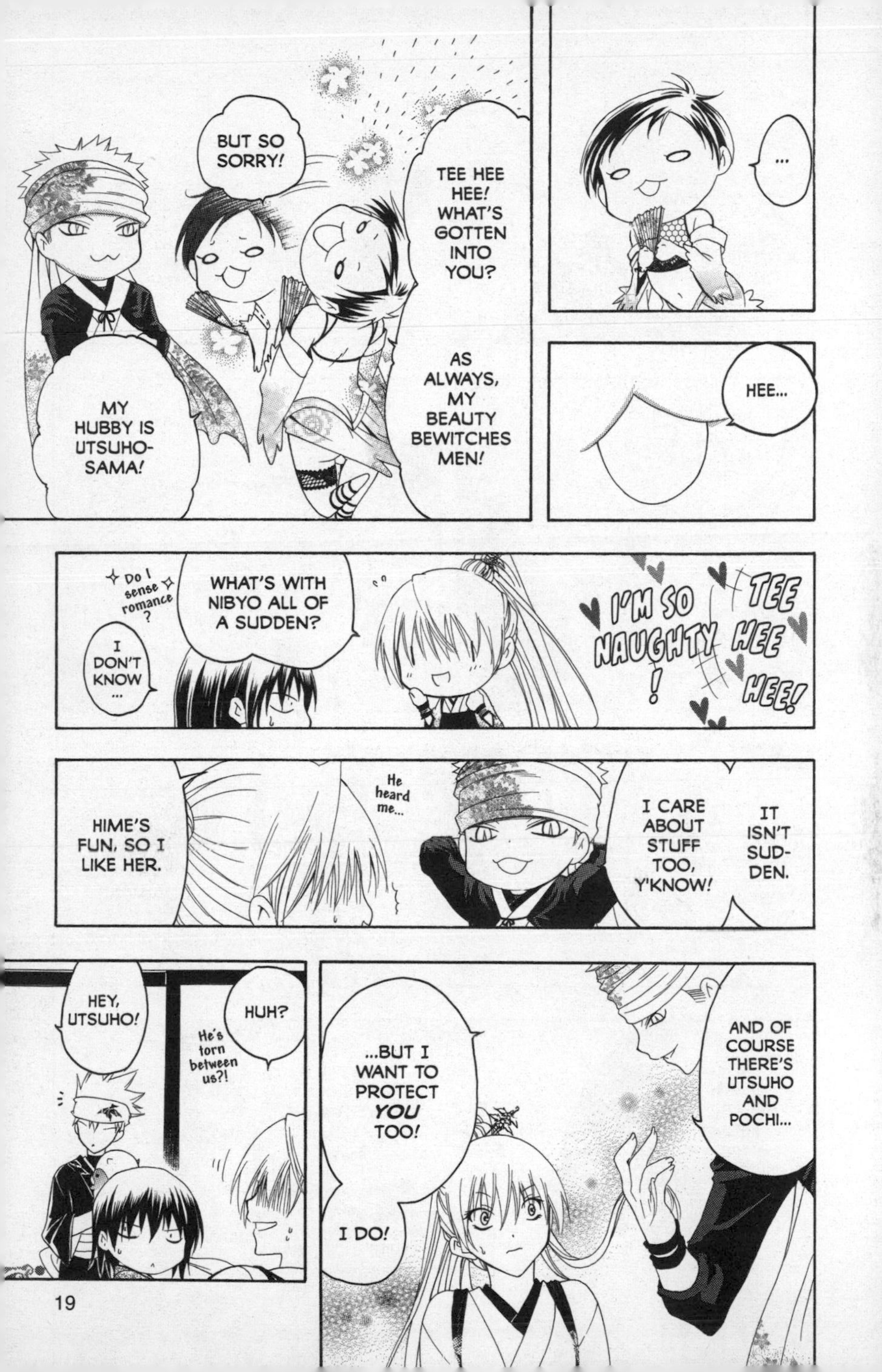
...
HEE...
TEE HEE HEE! WHAT'S GOTTEN INTO YOU?
BUT SO SORRY!
AS ALWAYS, MY BEAUTY BEWITCHES MEN!
MY HUBBY IS UTSUHO-SAMA!
TEE HEE HEE!
I'M SO NAUGHTY!
WHAT'S WITH NIBYO ALL OF A SUDDEN?
Do I sense romance?
I DON'T KNOW...
IT ISN'T SUD-DEN.
I CARE ABOUT STUFF TOO, Y'KNOW!
He heard me...
HIME'S FUN, SO I LIKE HER.
AND OF COURSE THERE'S UTSUHO AND POCHI...
...BUT I WANT TO PROTECT YOU TOO!
I DO!
HEY, UTSUHO!
HUH?
He's torn between us?!

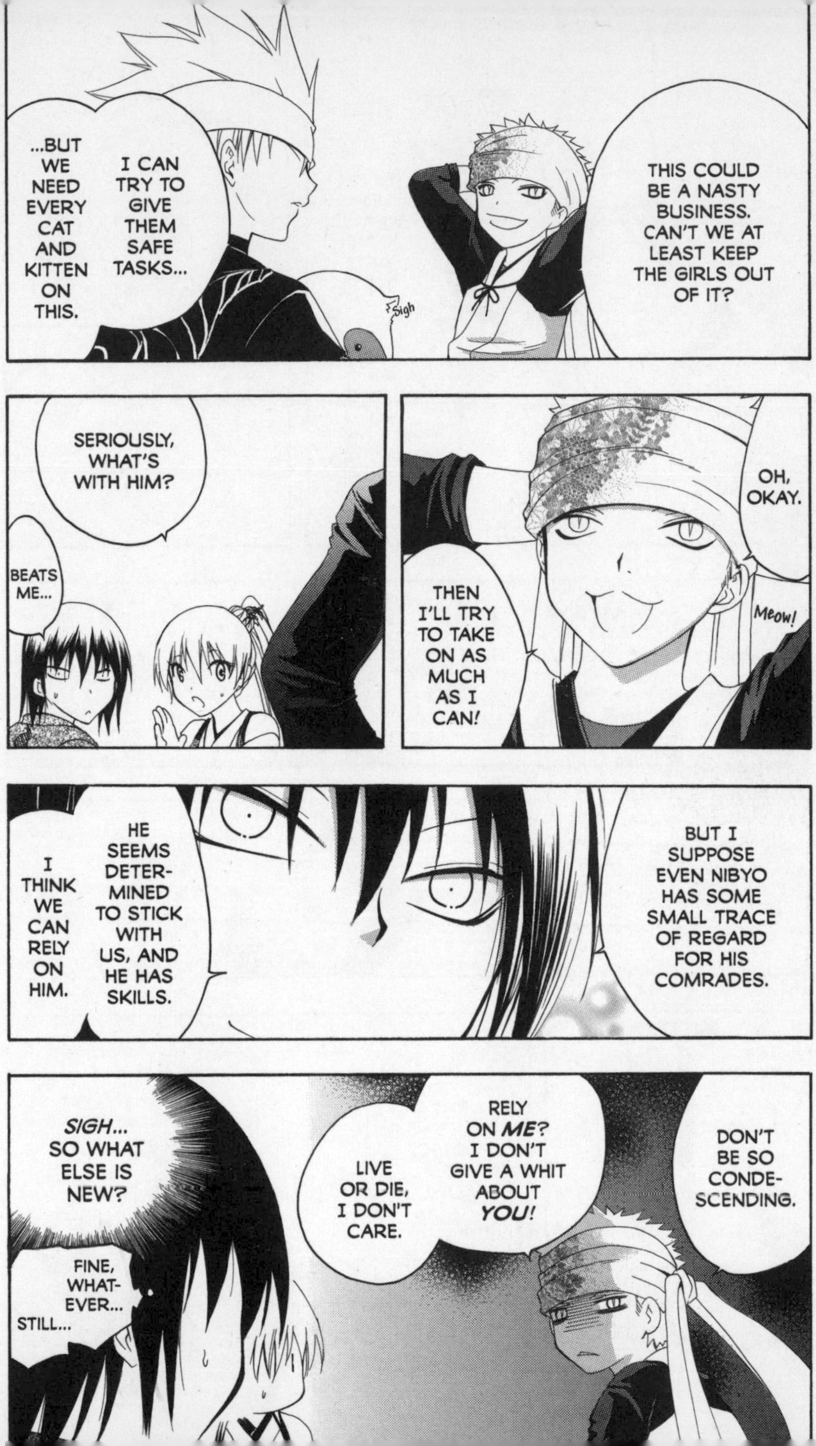
THIS COULD BE A NASTY BUSINESS. CAN'T WE AT LEAST KEEP THE GIRLS OUT OF IT?
Sigh
I CAN TRY TO GIVE THEM SAFE TASKS...
...BUT WE NEED EVERY CAT AND KITTEN ON THIS.
OH, OKAY.
THEN I'LL TRY TO TAKE ON AS MUCH AS I CAN!
Meow!
SERIOUSLY, WHAT'S WITH HIM?
BEATS ME...
BUT I SUPPOSE EVEN NIBYO HAS SOME SMALL TRACE OF REGARD FOR HIS COMRADES.
HE SEEMS DETERMINED TO STICK WITH US, AND HE HAS SKILLS.
I THINK WE CAN RELY ON HIM.
DON'T BE SO CONDESCENDING.
RELY ON ME? I DON'T GIVE A WHIT ABOUT YOU!
LIVE OR DIE, I DON'T CARE.
SIGH... SO WHAT ELSE IS NEW?
FINE, WHATEVER... STILL...

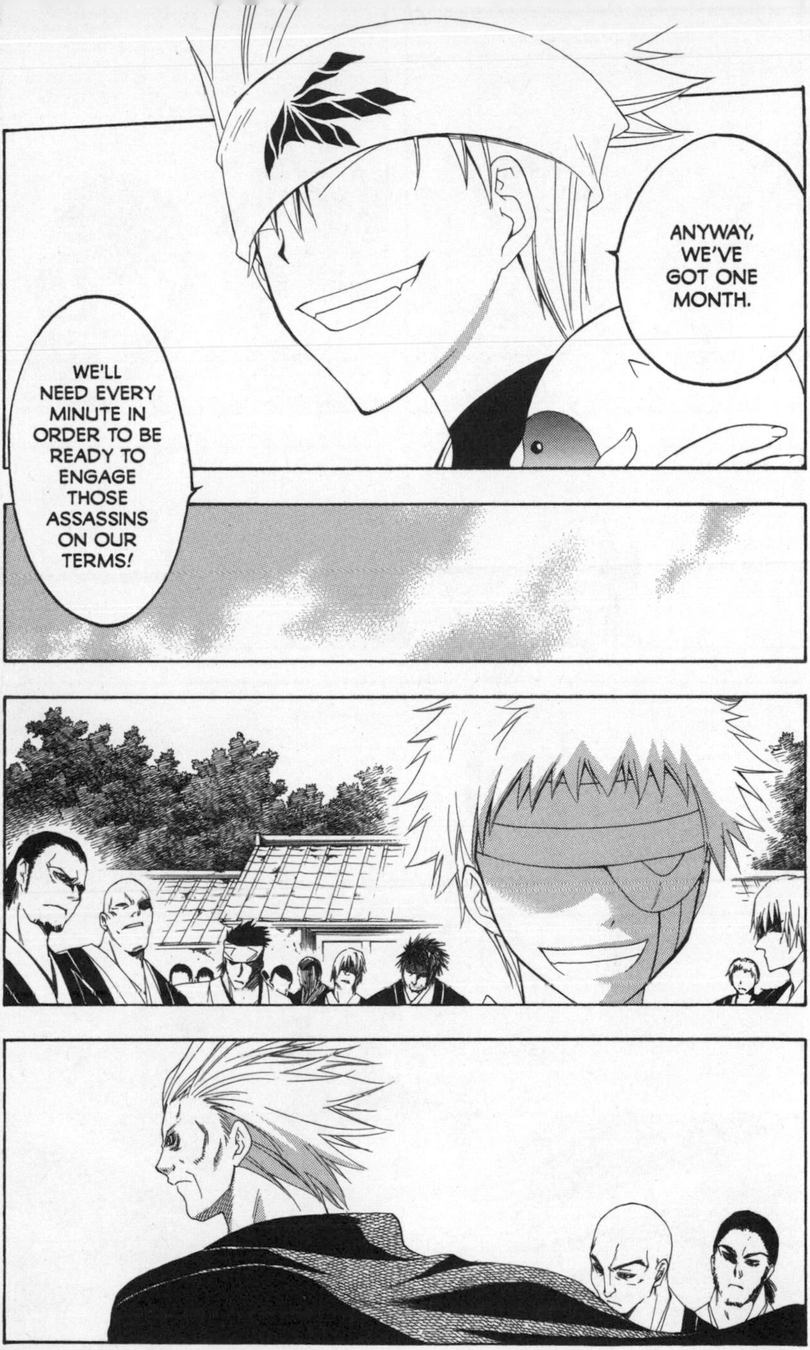
ANYWAY, WE'VE GOT ONE MONTH.
WE'LL NEED EVERY MINUTE IN ORDER TO BE READY TO ENGAGE THOSE ASSASSINS ON OUR TERMS!

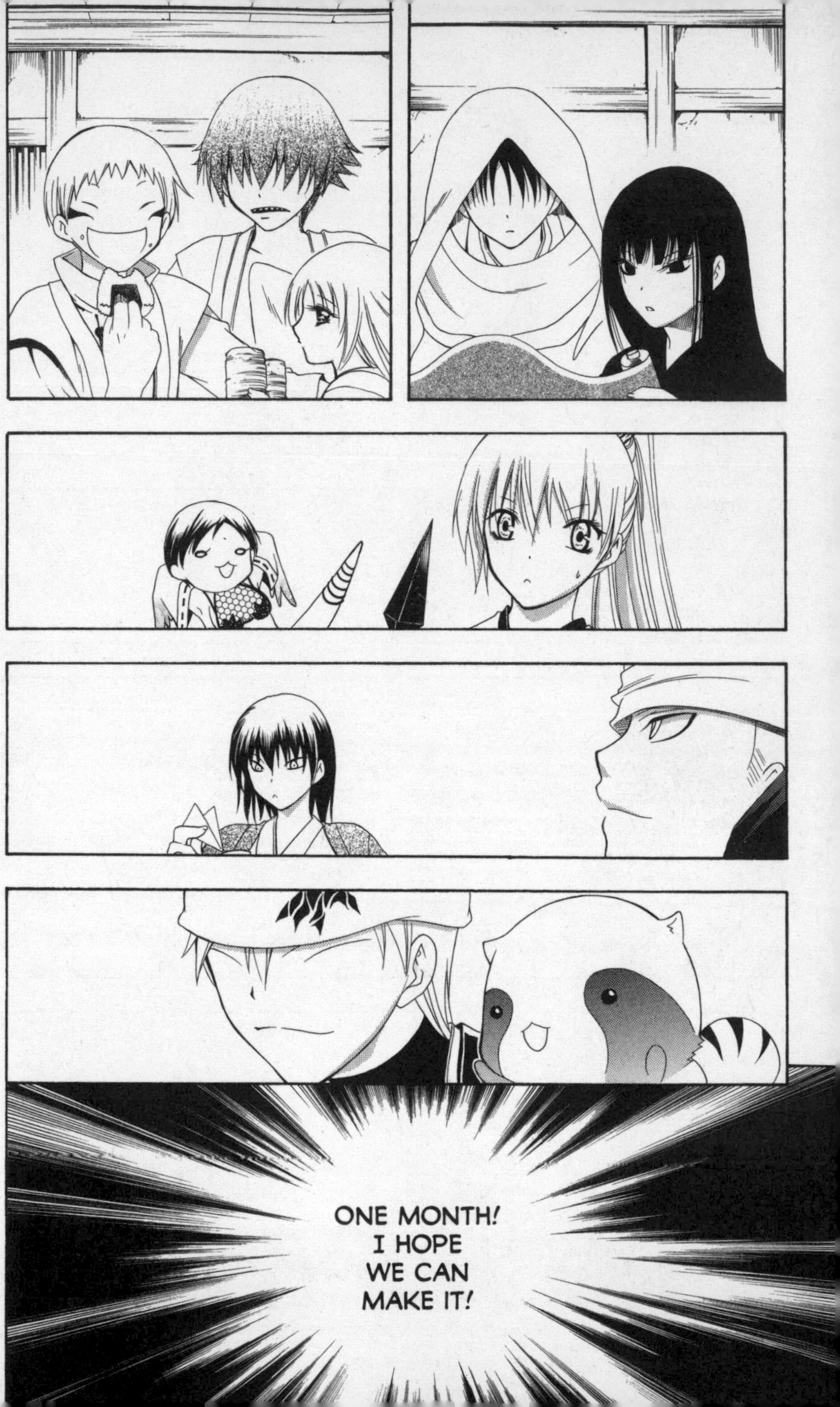
ONE MONTH!
I HOPE
WE CAN
MAKE IT!

Chapter 100
The Onkado's Birthday Festivities

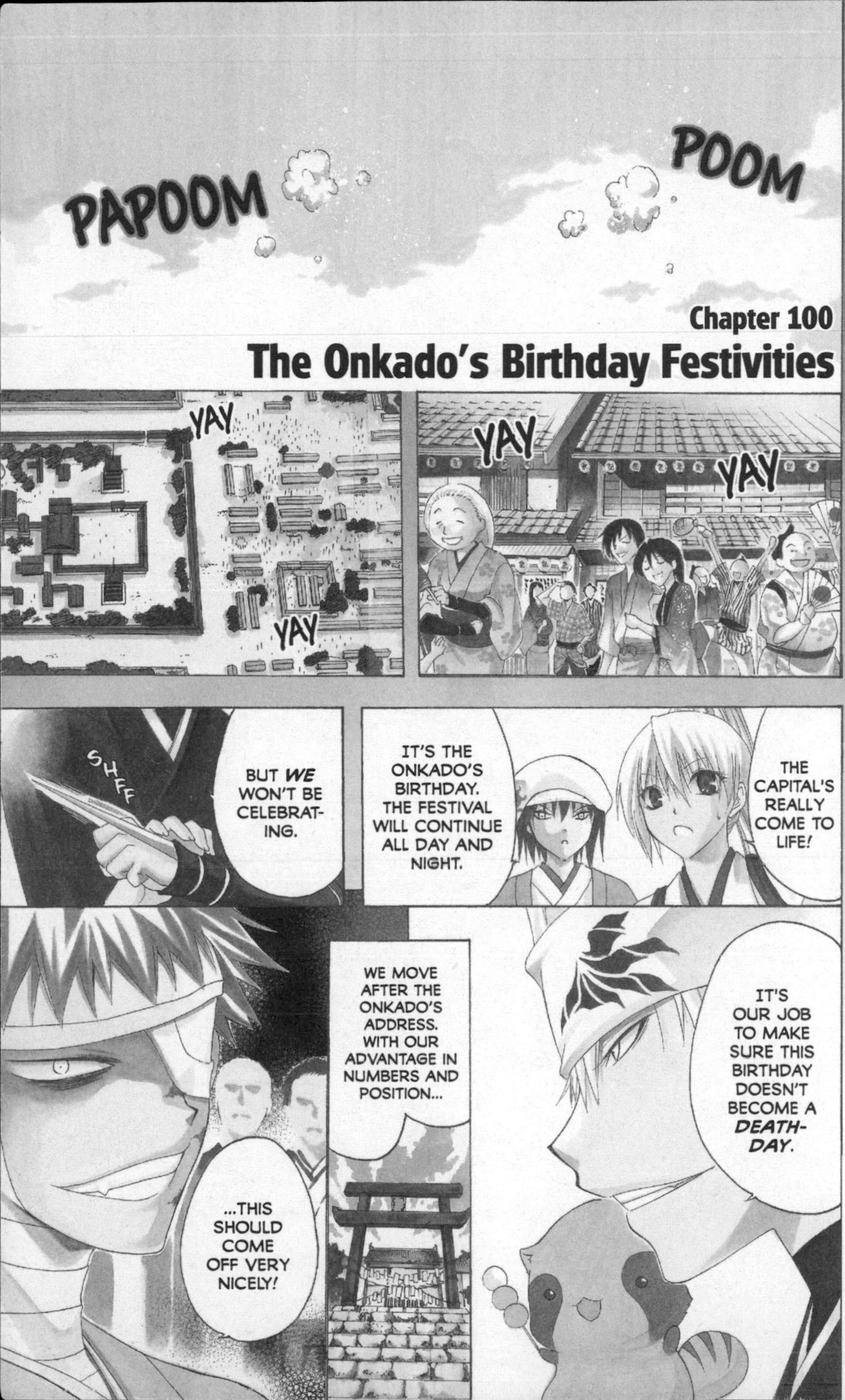
POOM
PAPOOM
YAY
YAY
YAY
YAY
THE CAPITAL'S REALLY COME TO LIFE!
IT'S THE ONKADO'S BIRTHDAY. THE FESTIVAL WILL CONTINUE ALL DAY AND NIGHT.
BUT *WE* WON'T BE CELEBRATING.
SHFF
IT'S OUR JOB TO MAKE SURE THIS BIRTHDAY DOESN'T BECOME A *DEATH-DAY*.
WE MOVE AFTER THE ONKADO'S ADDRESS. WITH OUR ADVANTAGE IN NUMBERS AND POSITION...
...THIS SHOULD COME OFF VERY NICELY!

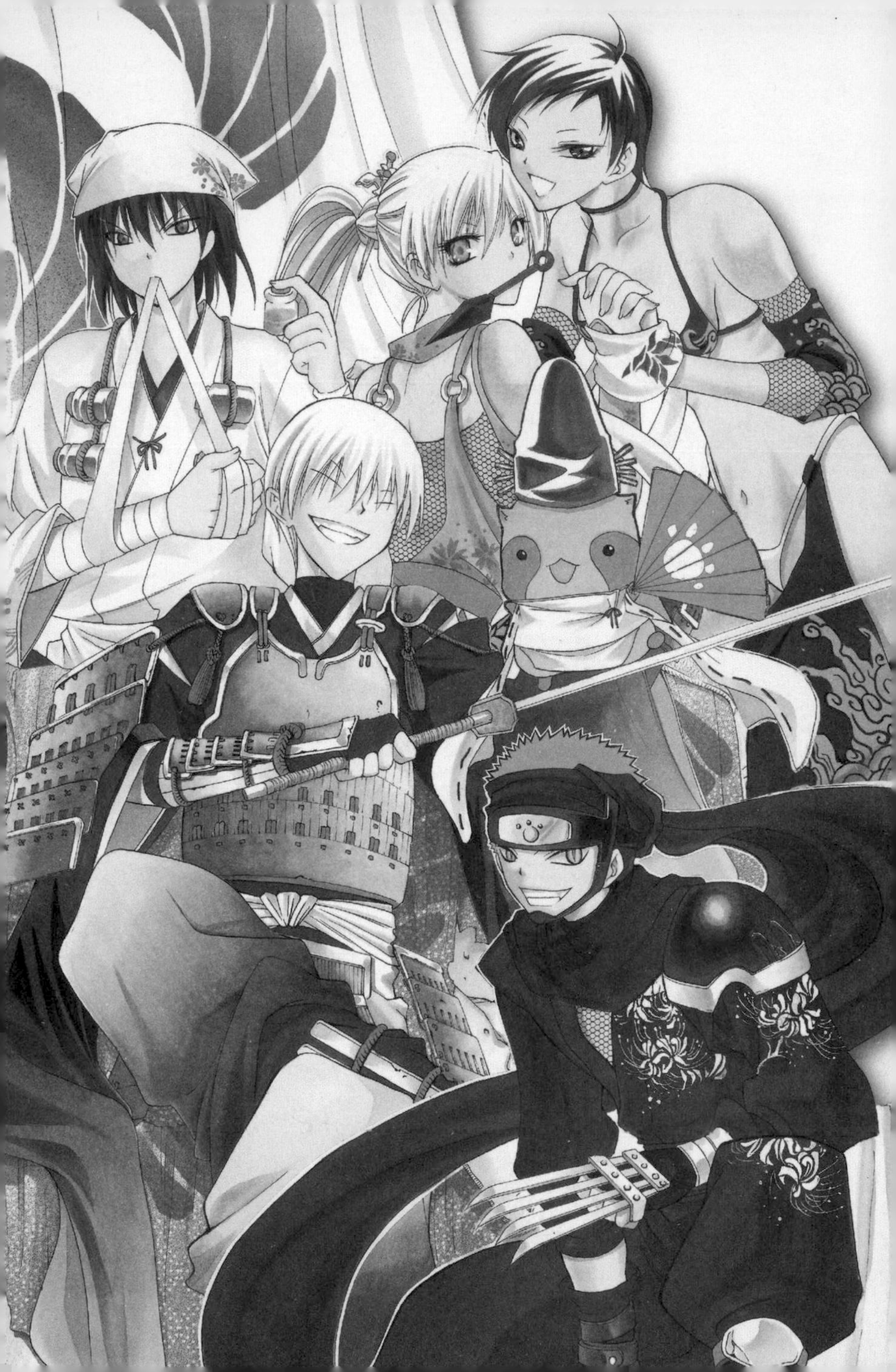

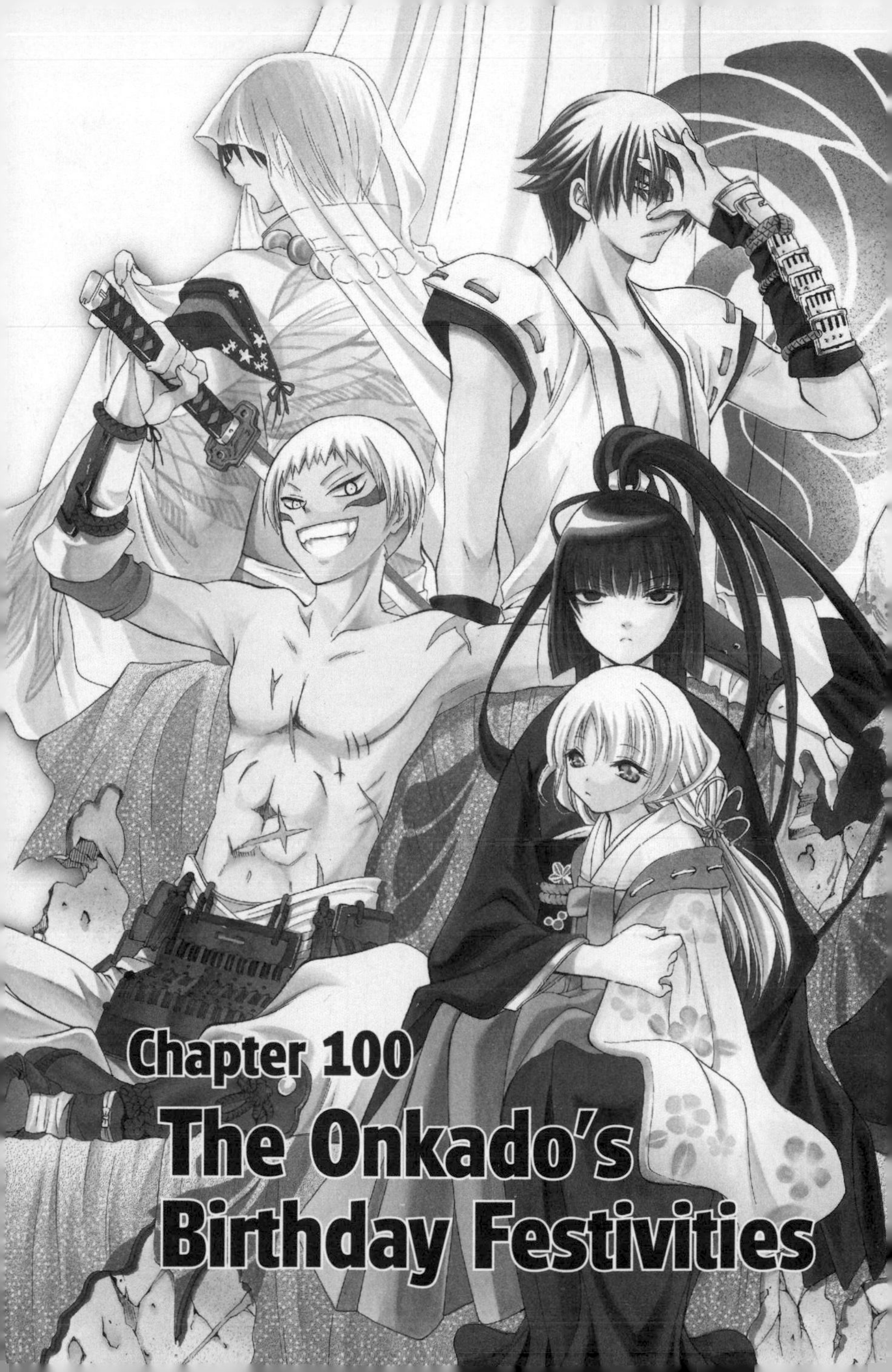
Chapter 100
The Onkado's Birthday Festivities

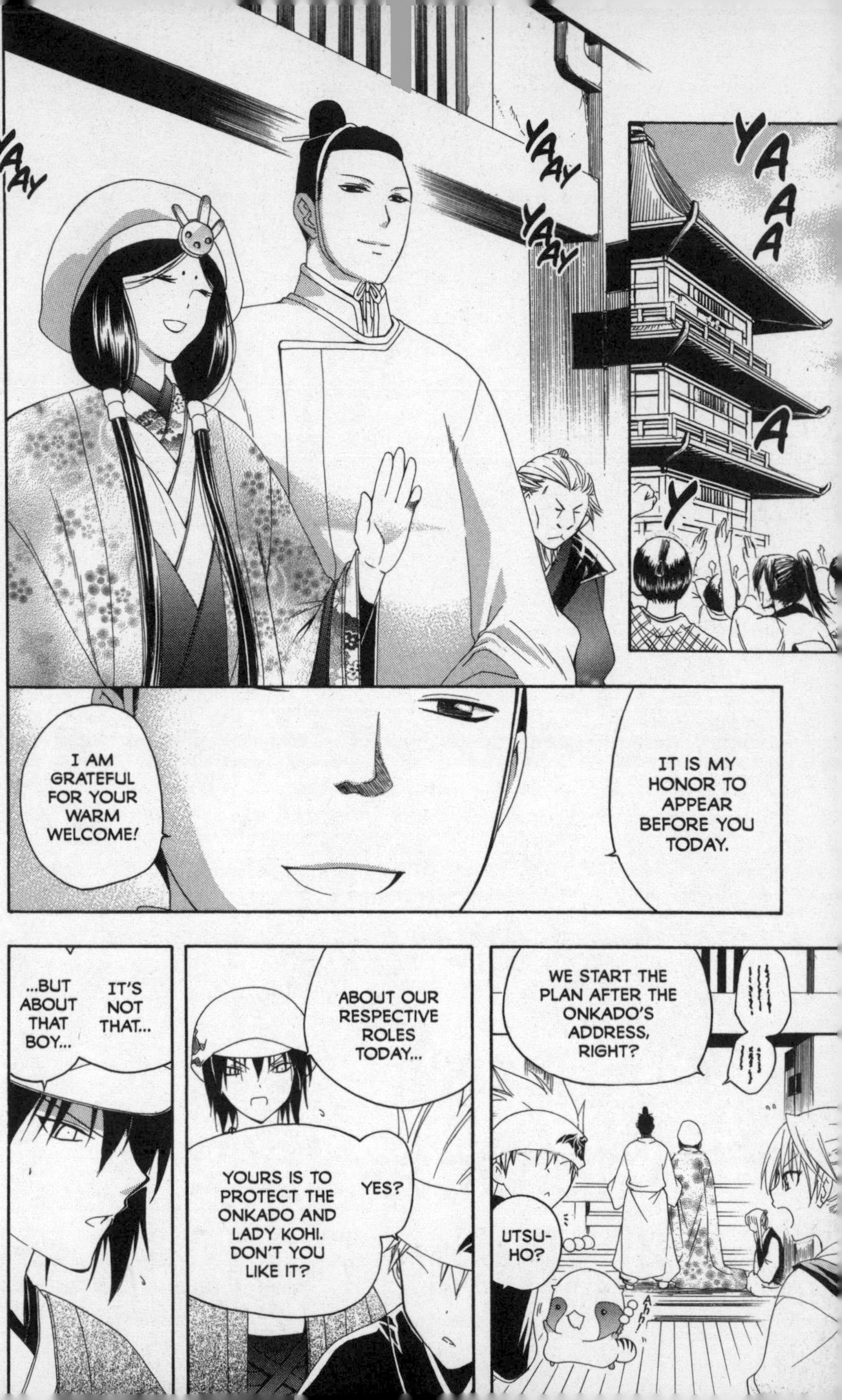
YAAAAY
YAAY
YAAY
YAAY
IT IS MY HONOR TO APPEAR BEFORE YOU TODAY.
I AM GRATEFUL FOR YOUR WARM WELCOME!
WE START THE PLAN AFTER THE ONKADO'S ADDRESS, RIGHT?
UTSU-HO?
Ahh!
ABOUT OUR RESPECTIVE ROLES TODAY...
YES?
YOURS IS TO PROTECT THE ONKADO AND LADY KOHI. DON'T YOU LIKE IT?
IT'S NOT THAT...
...BUT ABOUT THAT BOY...

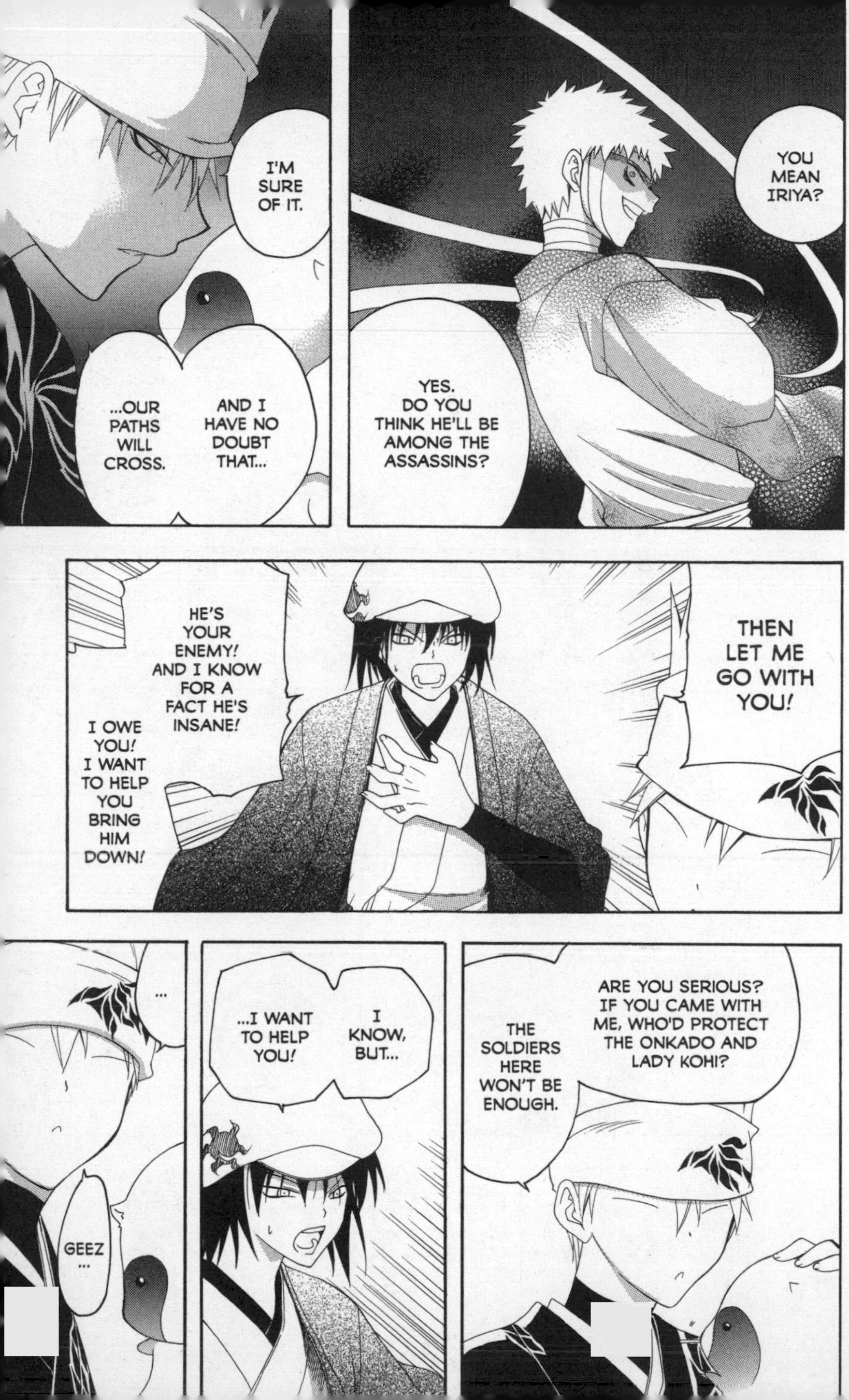
YOU MEAN IRIYA?
YES. DO YOU THINK HE'LL BE AMONG THE ASSASSINS?
I'M SURE OF IT.
AND I HAVE NO DOUBT THAT...
...OUR PATHS WILL CROSS.
THEN LET ME GO WITH YOU!
HE'S YOUR ENEMY! AND I KNOW FOR A FACT HE'S INSANE!
I OWE YOU! I WANT TO HELP YOU BRING HIM DOWN!
ARE YOU SERIOUS? IF YOU CAME WITH ME, WHO'D PROTECT THE ONKADO AND LADY KOHI?
THE SOLDIERS HERE WON'T BE ENOUGH.
I KNOW, BUT...
...I WANT TO HELP YOU!
...
GEEZ...

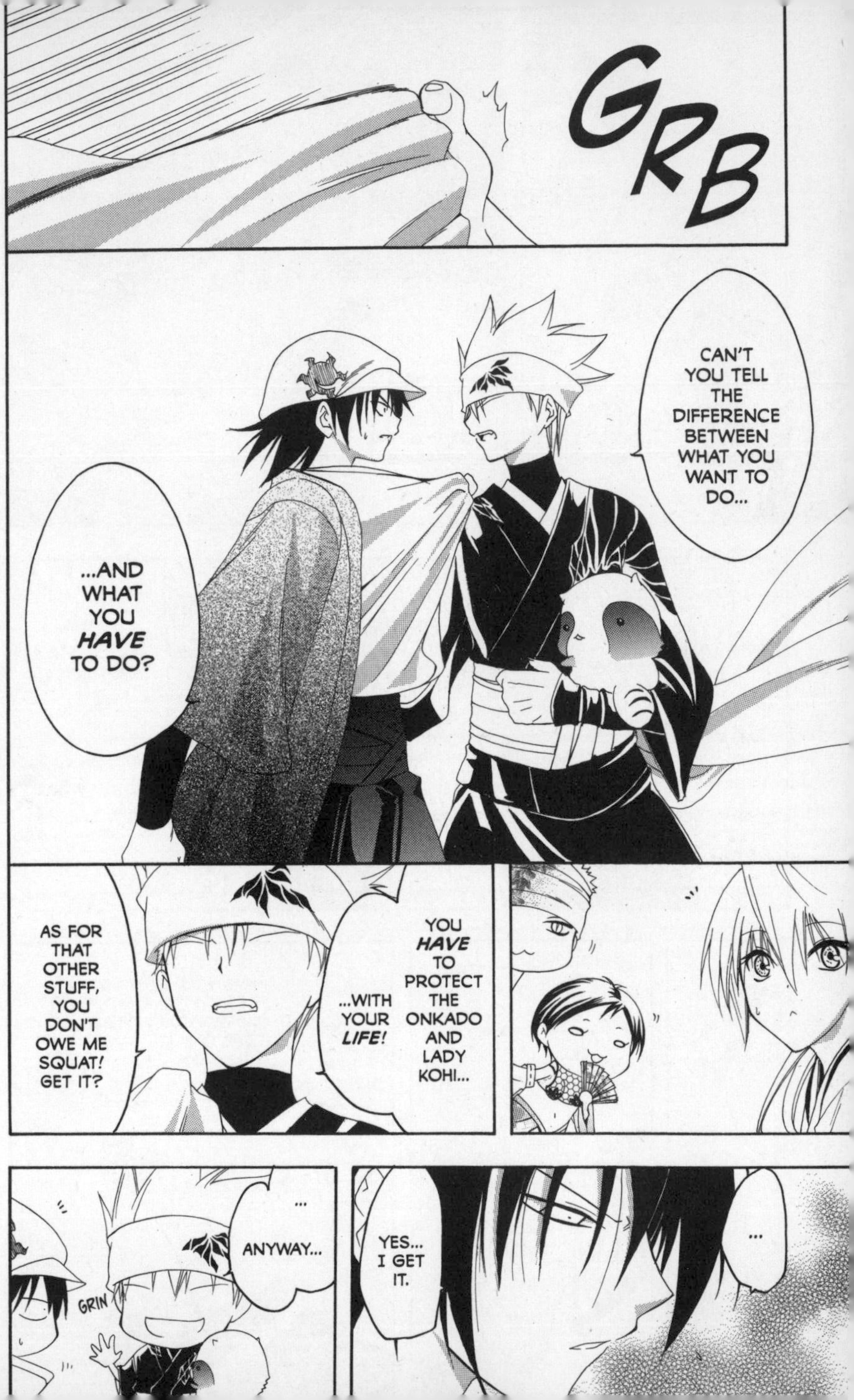
GRB
CAN'T YOU TELL THE DIFFERENCE BETWEEN WHAT YOU WANT TO DO...
...AND WHAT YOU HAVE TO DO?
YOU HAVE TO PROTECT THE ONKADO AND LADY KOHI...
...WITH YOUR LIFE!
AS FOR THAT OTHER STUFF, YOU DON'T OWE ME SQUAT! GET IT?
...
YES... I GET IT.
...
ANYWAY...
GRIN

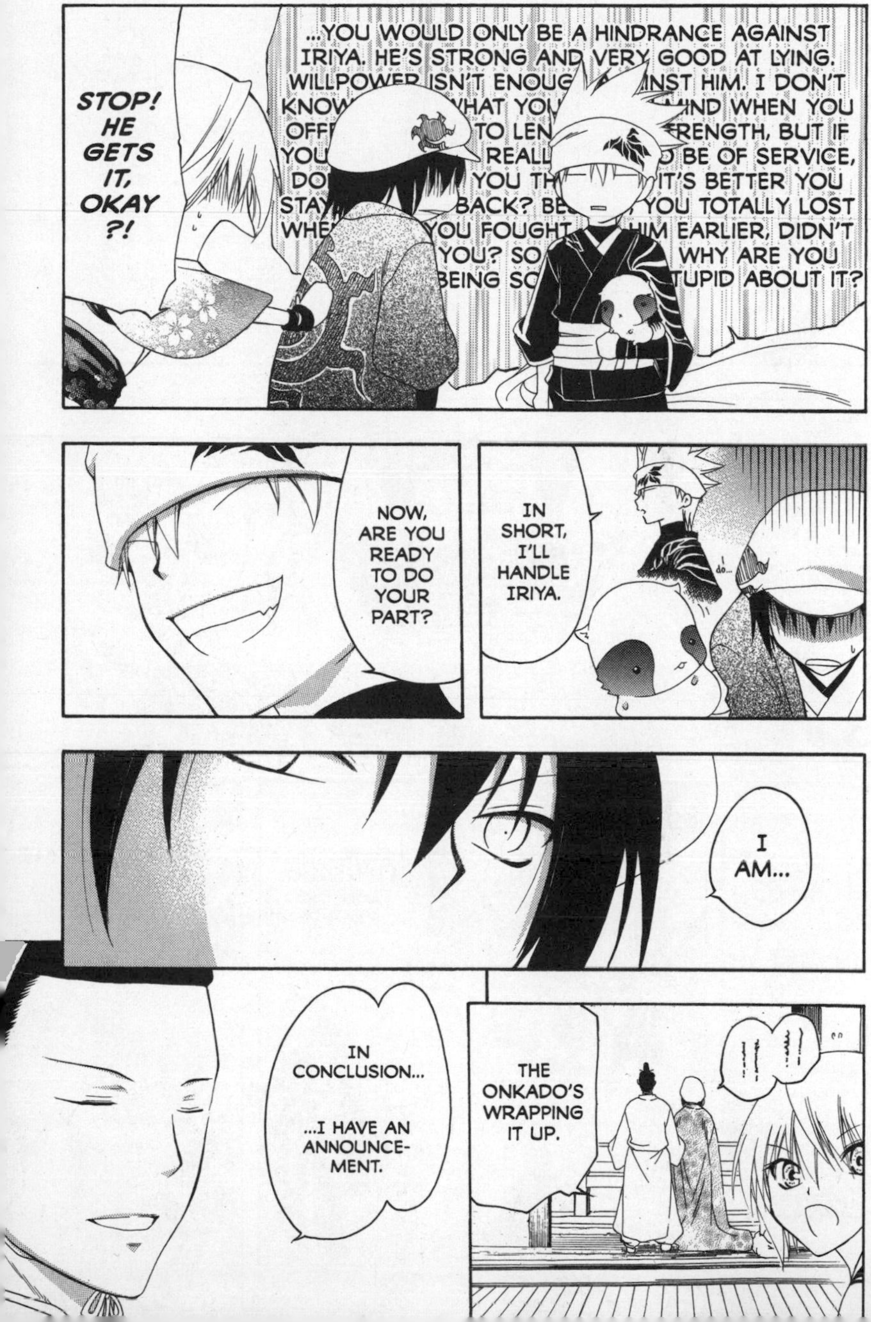
...YOU WOULD ONLY BE A HINDRANCE AGAINST IRIYA. HE'S STRONG AND VERY GOOD AT LYING. WILLPOWER ISN'T ENOUG INST HIM. I DON'T KNOW WHAT YOU MIND WHEN YOU OFF TO LEN RENGTH, BUT IF YOU REALL BE OF SERVICE, DO YOU TH IT'S BETTER YOU STAY BACK? BE YOU TOTALLY LOST WHE YOU FOUGHT HIM EARLIER, DIDN'T YOU? SO WHY ARE YOU BEING SO TUPID ABOUT IT?
STOP! HE GETS IT, OKAY?!
IN SHORT, I'LL HANDLE IRIYA.
NOW, ARE YOU READY TO DO YOUR PART?
I AM...
THE ONKADO'S WRAPPING IT UP.
IN CONCLUSION...
...I HAVE AN ANNOUNCE-MENT.

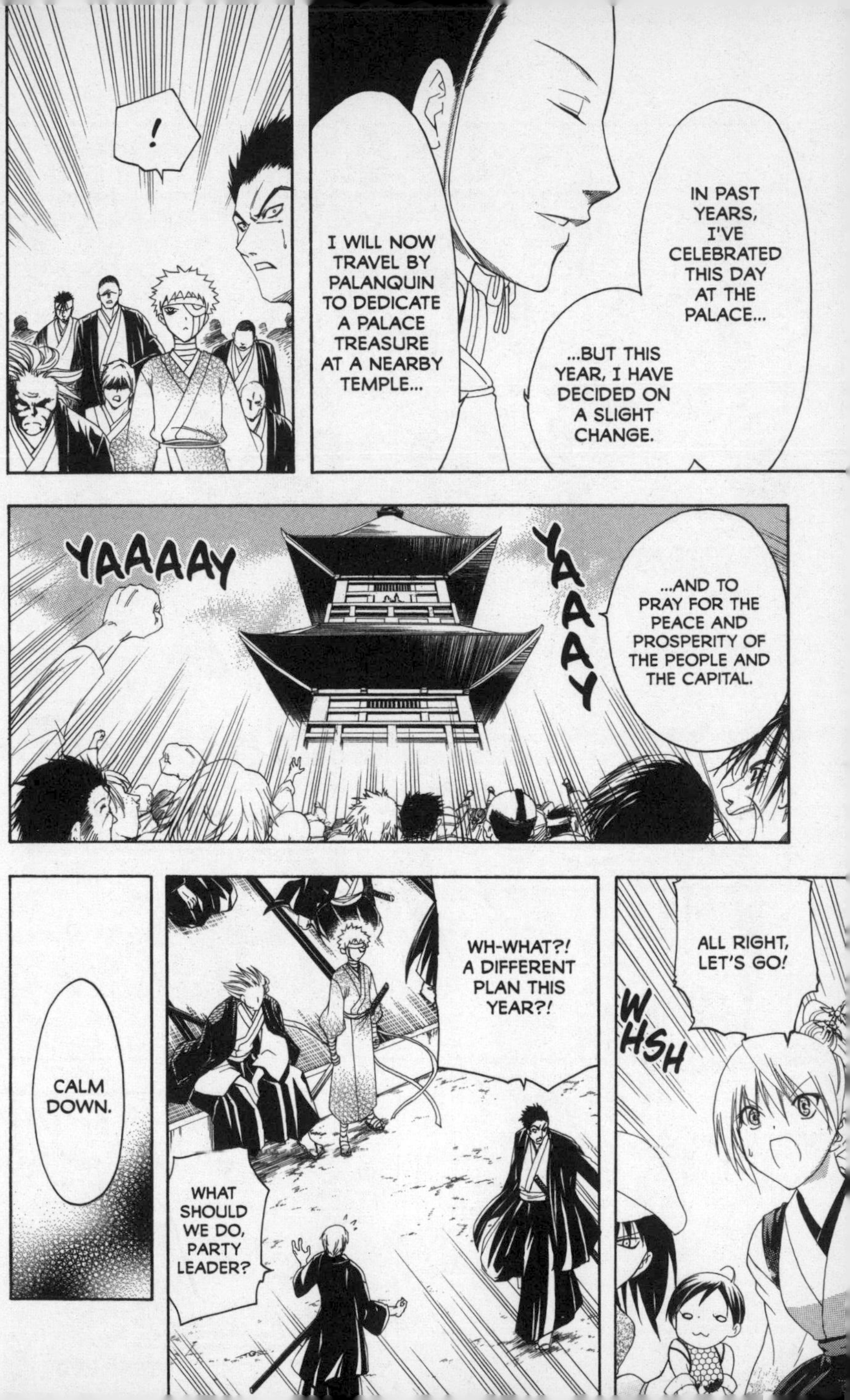
IN PAST YEARS, I'VE CELEBRATED THIS DAY AT THE PALACE...
...BUT THIS YEAR, I HAVE DECIDED ON A SLIGHT CHANGE.
I WILL NOW TRAVEL BY PALANQUIN TO DEDICATE A PALACE TREASURE AT A NEARBY TEMPLE...
!
...AND TO PRAY FOR THE PEACE AND PROSPERITY OF THE PEOPLE AND THE CAPITAL.
YAAAY
YAAAAY
ALL RIGHT, LET'S GO!
WHSH
WH-WHAT?! A DIFFERENT PLAN THIS YEAR?!
WHAT SHOULD WE DO, PARTY LEADER?
CALM DOWN.

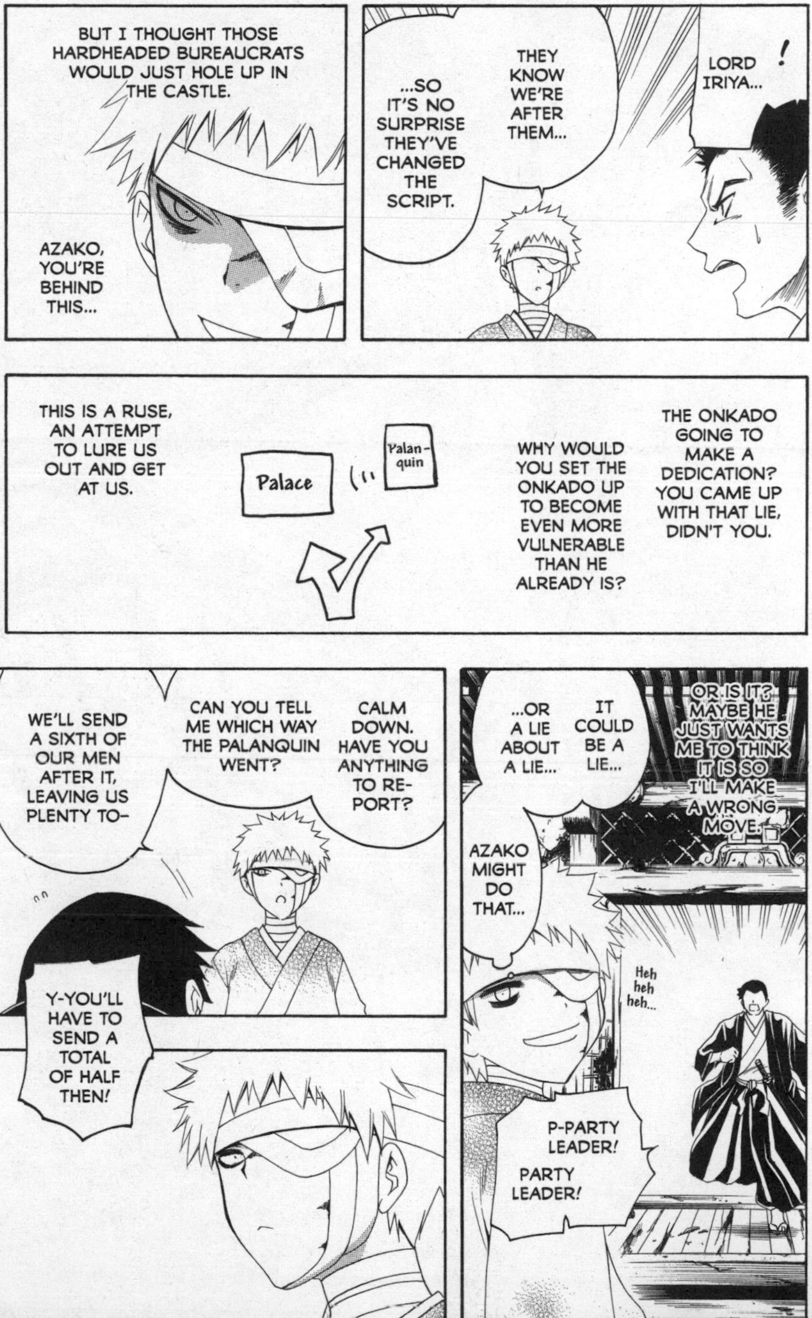
LORD IRIYA...
!
THEY KNOW WE'RE AFTER THEM...
...SO IT'S NO SURPRISE THEY'VE CHANGED THE SCRIPT.
BUT I THOUGHT THOSE HARDHEADED BUREAUCRATS WOULD JUST HOLE UP IN THE CASTLE.
AZAKO, YOU'RE BEHIND THIS...
THE ONKADO GOING TO MAKE A DEDICATION? YOU CAME UP WITH THAT LIE, DIDN'T YOU.
WHY WOULD YOU SET THE ONKADO UP TO BECOME EVEN MORE VULNERABLE THAN HE ALREADY IS?
Palanquin
Palace
THIS IS A RUSE, AN ATTEMPT TO LURE US OUT AND GET AT US.
OR IS IT? MAYBE HE JUST WANTS ME TO THINK IT IS SO I'LL MAKE A WRONG MOVE.
IT COULD BE A LIE...
...OR A LIE ABOUT A LIE...
AZAKO MIGHT DO THAT...
Heh heh heh...
P-PARTY LEADER!
PARTY LEADER!
CALM DOWN. HAVE YOU ANYTHING TO RE-PORT?
CAN YOU TELL ME WHICH WAY THE PALANQUIN WENT?
WE'LL SEND A SIXTH OF OUR MEN AFTER IT, LEAVING US PLENTY TO–
Y-YOU'LL HAVE TO SEND A TOTAL OF HALF THEN!

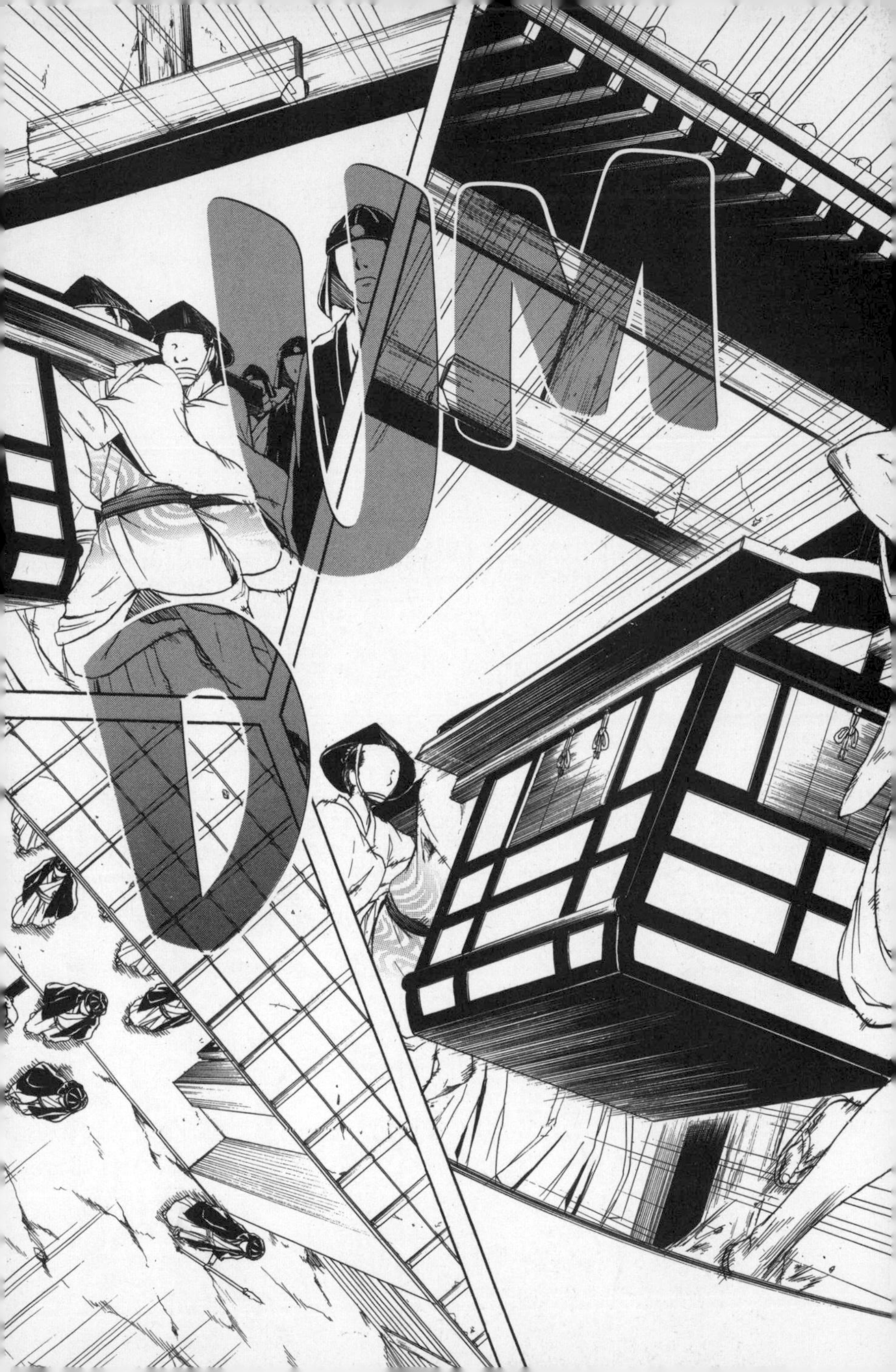
DUM

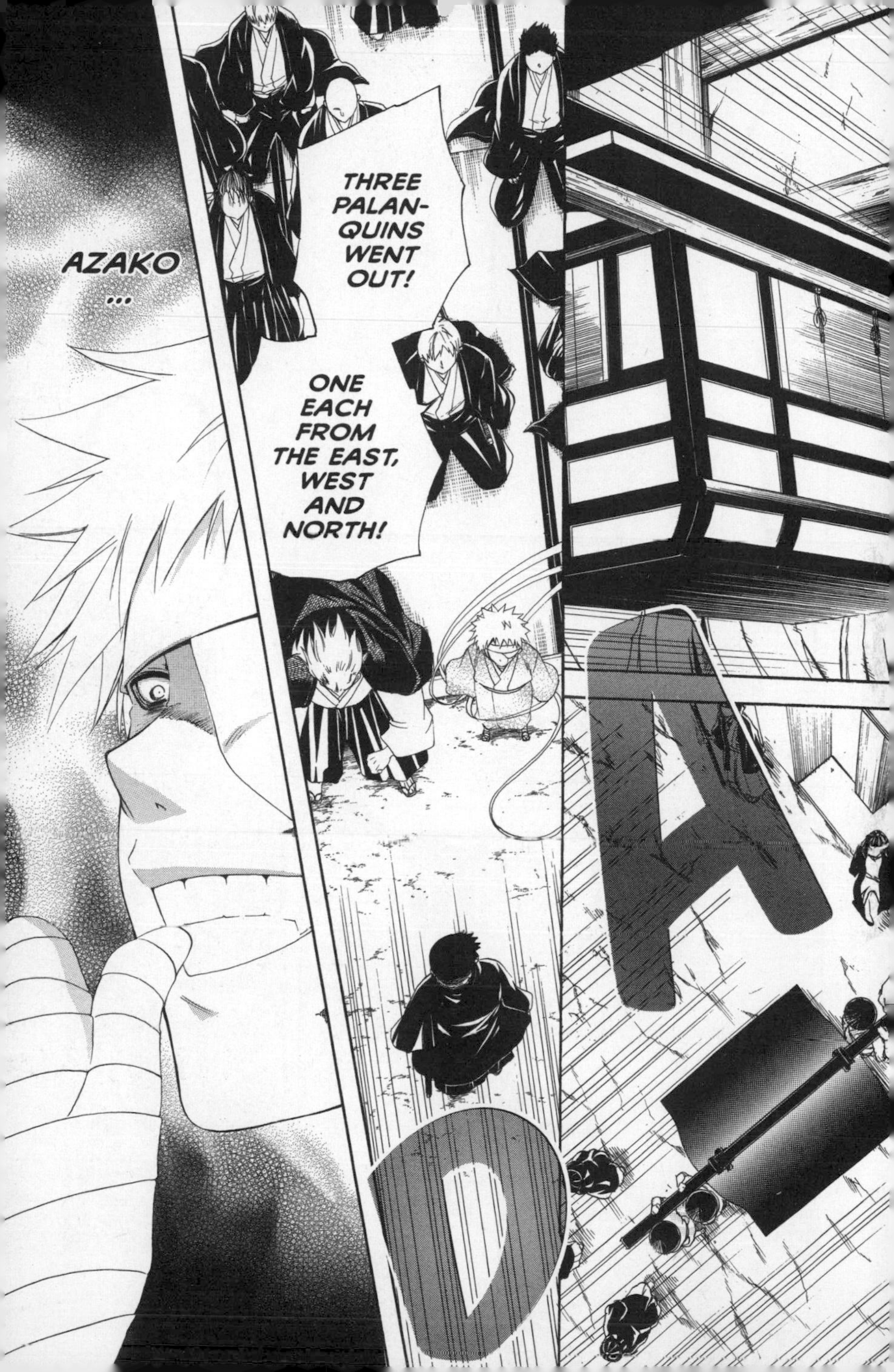
THREE PALAN-QUINS WENT OUT!
ONE EACH FROM THE EAST, WEST AND NORTH!
AZAKO ...

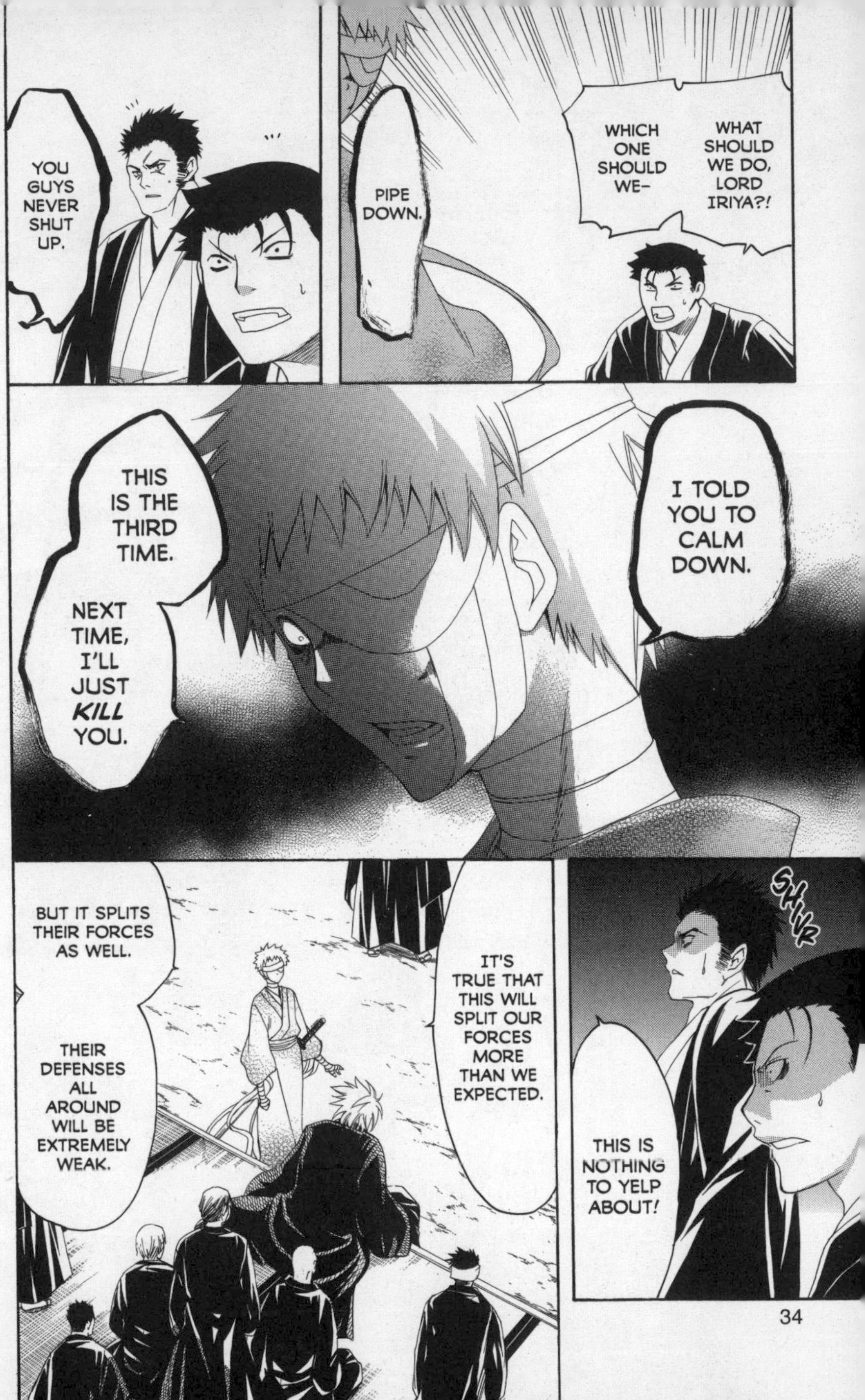
WHAT SHOULD WE DO, LORD IRIYA?!
WHICH ONE SHOULD WE–
PIPE DOWN.
YOU GUYS NEVER SHUT UP.
I TOLD YOU TO CALM DOWN.
THIS IS THE THIRD TIME.
NEXT TIME, I'LL JUST *KILL* YOU.
SHIVR
THIS IS NOTHING TO YELP ABOUT!
IT'S TRUE THAT THIS WILL SPLIT OUR FORCES MORE THAN WE EXPECTED.
BUT IT SPLITS THEIR FORCES AS WELL.
THEIR DEFENSES ALL AROUND WILL BE EXTREMELY WEAK.

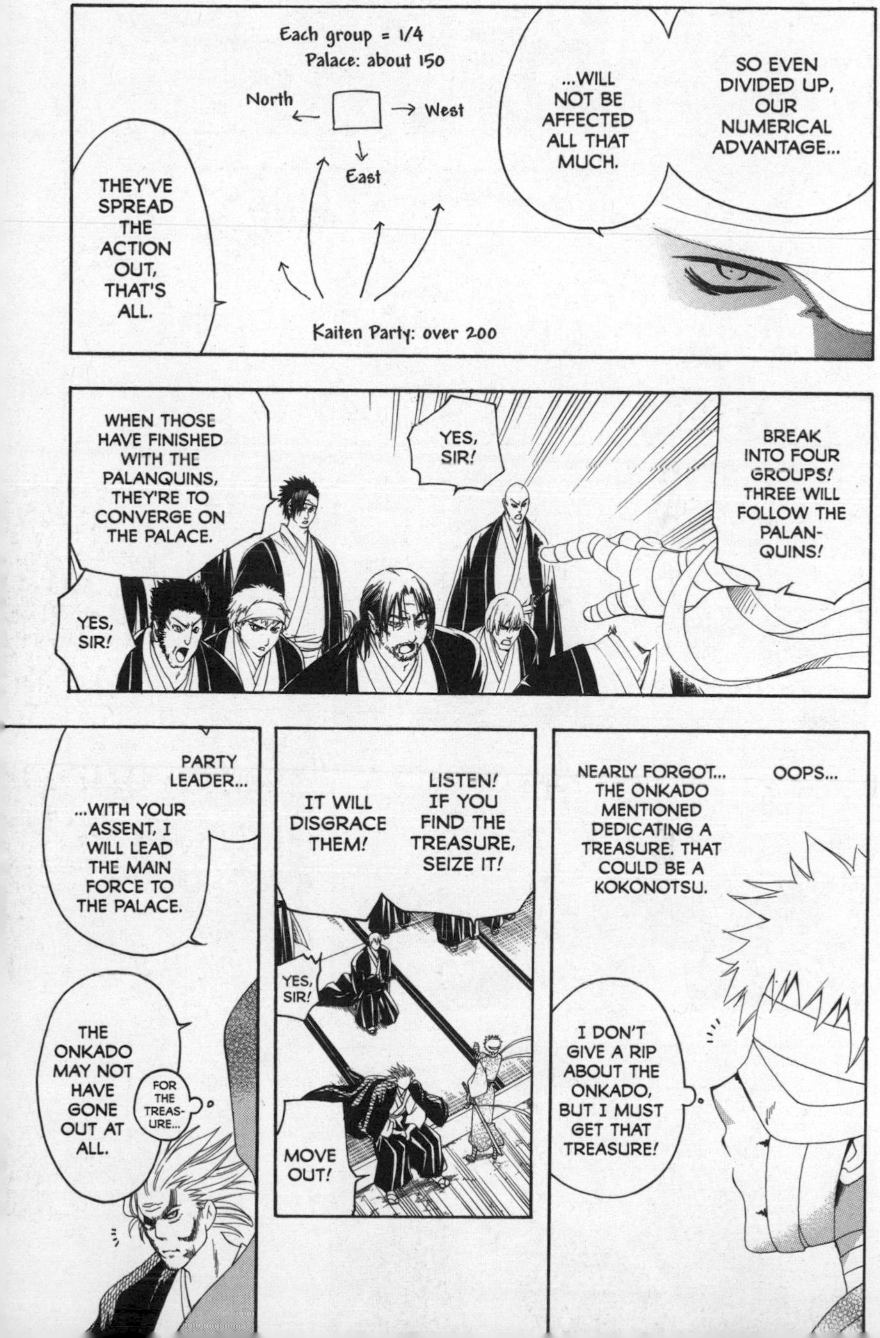
SO EVEN DIVIDED UP, OUR NUMERICAL ADVANTAGE...
...WILL NOT BE AFFECTED ALL THAT MUCH.
Each group = 1/4
Palace: about 150
North
West
East
Kaiten Party: over 200
THEY'VE SPREAD THE ACTION OUT, THAT'S ALL.
BREAK INTO FOUR GROUPS! THREE WILL FOLLOW THE PALAN-QUINS!
YES, SIR!
WHEN THOSE HAVE FINISHED WITH THE PALANQUINS, THEY'RE TO CONVERGE ON THE PALACE.
YES, SIR!
OOPS...
NEARLY FORGOT... THE ONKADO MENTIONED DEDICATING A TREASURE. THAT COULD BE A KOKONOTSU.
I DON'T GIVE A RIP ABOUT THE ONKADO, BUT I MUST GET THAT TREASURE!
LISTEN! IF YOU FIND THE TREASURE, SEIZE IT!
IT WILL DISGRACE THEM!
YES, SIR!
MOVE OUT!
PARTY LEADER...
...WITH YOUR ASSENT, I WILL LEAD THE MAIN FORCE TO THE PALACE.
THE ONKADO MAY NOT HAVE GONE OUT AT ALL.
FOR THE TREASURE...

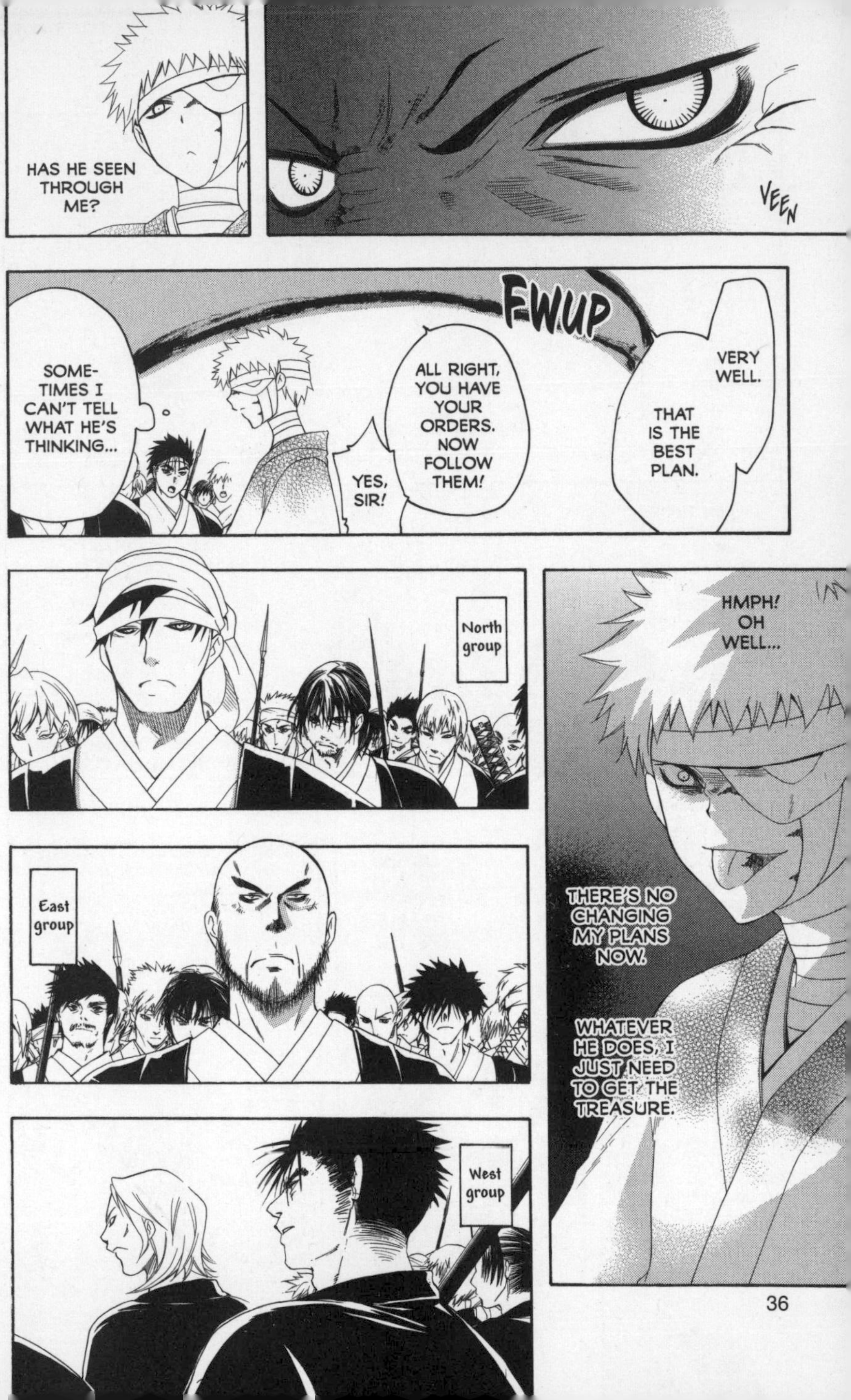
VEEN
HAS HE SEEN THROUGH ME?
VERY WELL.
THAT IS THE BEST PLAN.
FWUP
ALL RIGHT, YOU HAVE YOUR ORDERS. NOW FOLLOW THEM!
YES, SIR!
SOME-TIMES I CAN'T TELL WHAT HE'S THINKING...
HMPH! OH WELL...
THERE'S NO CHANGING MY PLANS NOW.
WHATEVER HE DOES, I JUST NEED TO GET THE TREASURE.
North group
East group
West group

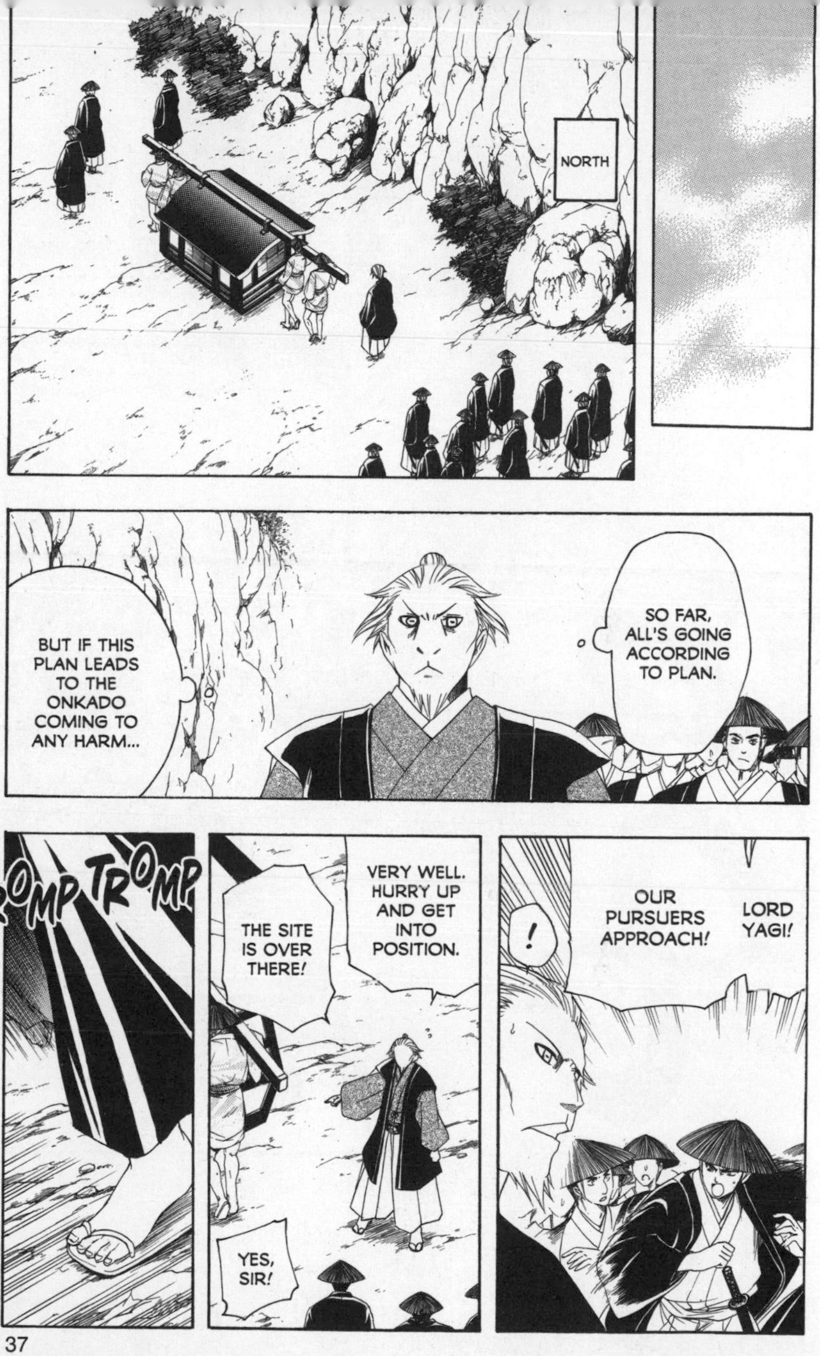
NORTH
SO FAR, ALL'S GOING ACCORDING TO PLAN.
BUT IF THIS PLAN LEADS TO THE ONKADO COMING TO ANY HARM...
LORD YAGI!
OUR PURSUERS APPROACH!
!
VERY WELL. HURRY UP AND GET INTO POSITION.
THE SITE IS OVER THERE!
YES, SIR!
TROMP TROMP

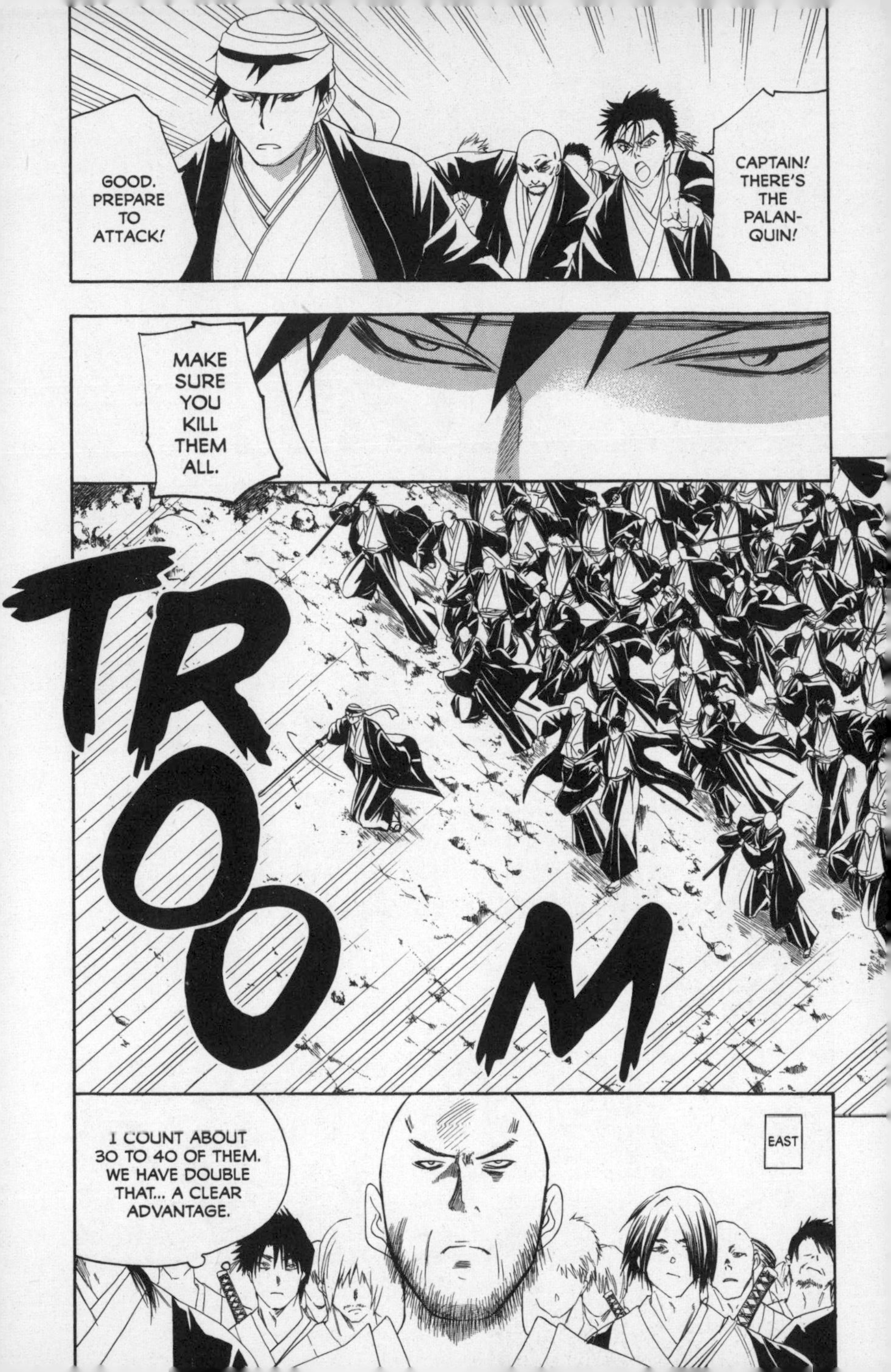
CAPTAIN! THERE'S THE PALAN-QUIN!
GOOD. PREPARE TO ATTACK!
MAKE SURE YOU KILL THEM ALL.
TROOM
EAST
I COUNT ABOUT 30 TO 40 OF THEM. WE HAVE DOUBLE THAT... A CLEAR ADVANTAGE.

TROMP TROMP TROMP

YES, SIR!

WIPE THEM OUT!

WEST

TMP

BACK GATE

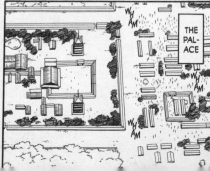

WHAM

WHAM

WHAM

THE PALACE

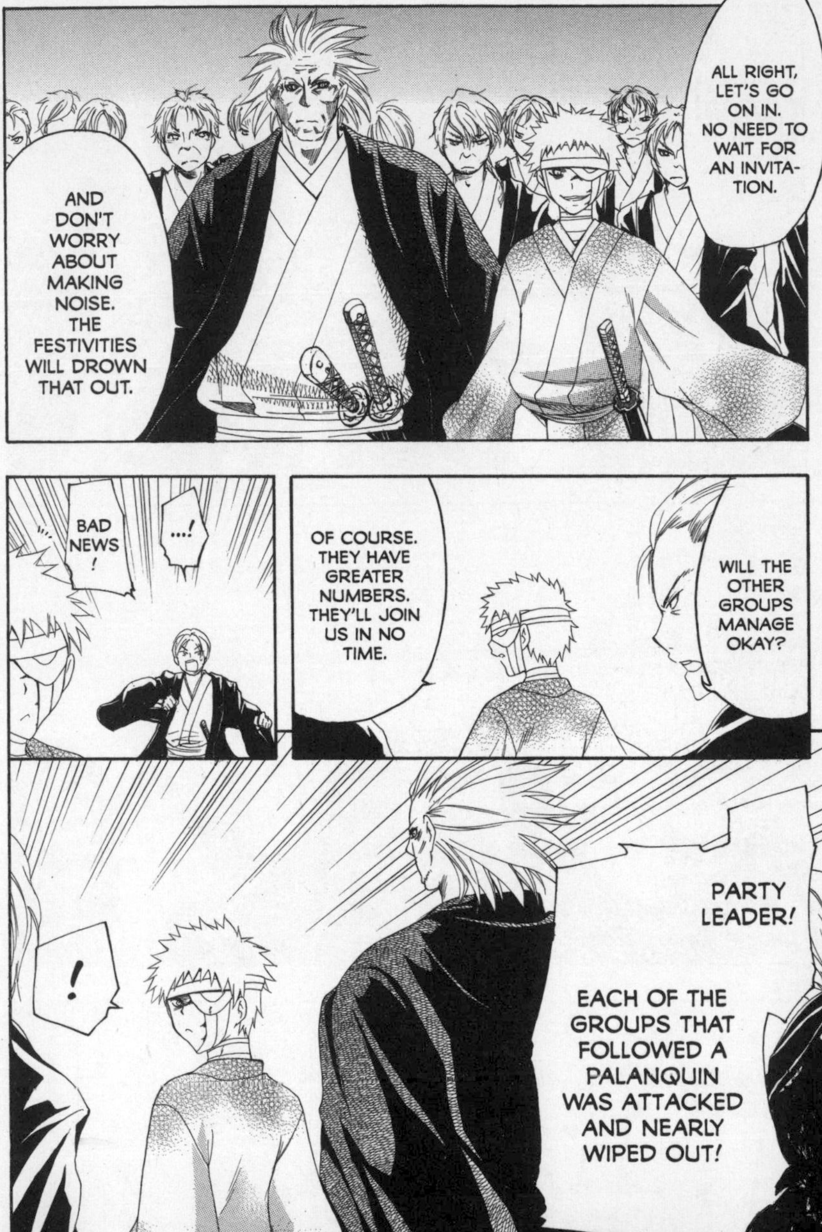
ALL RIGHT, LET'S GO ON IN. NO NEED TO WAIT FOR AN INVITATION.
AND DON'T WORRY ABOUT MAKING NOISE. THE FESTIVITIES WILL DROWN THAT OUT.
WILL THE OTHER GROUPS MANAGE OKAY?
OF COURSE. THEY HAVE GREATER NUMBERS. THEY'LL JOIN US IN NO TIME.
...!
BAD NEWS!
PARTY LEADER!
EACH OF THE GROUPS THAT FOLLOWED A PALANQUIN WAS ATTACKED AND NEARLY WIPED OUT!
!

Chapter 101 Luring Out

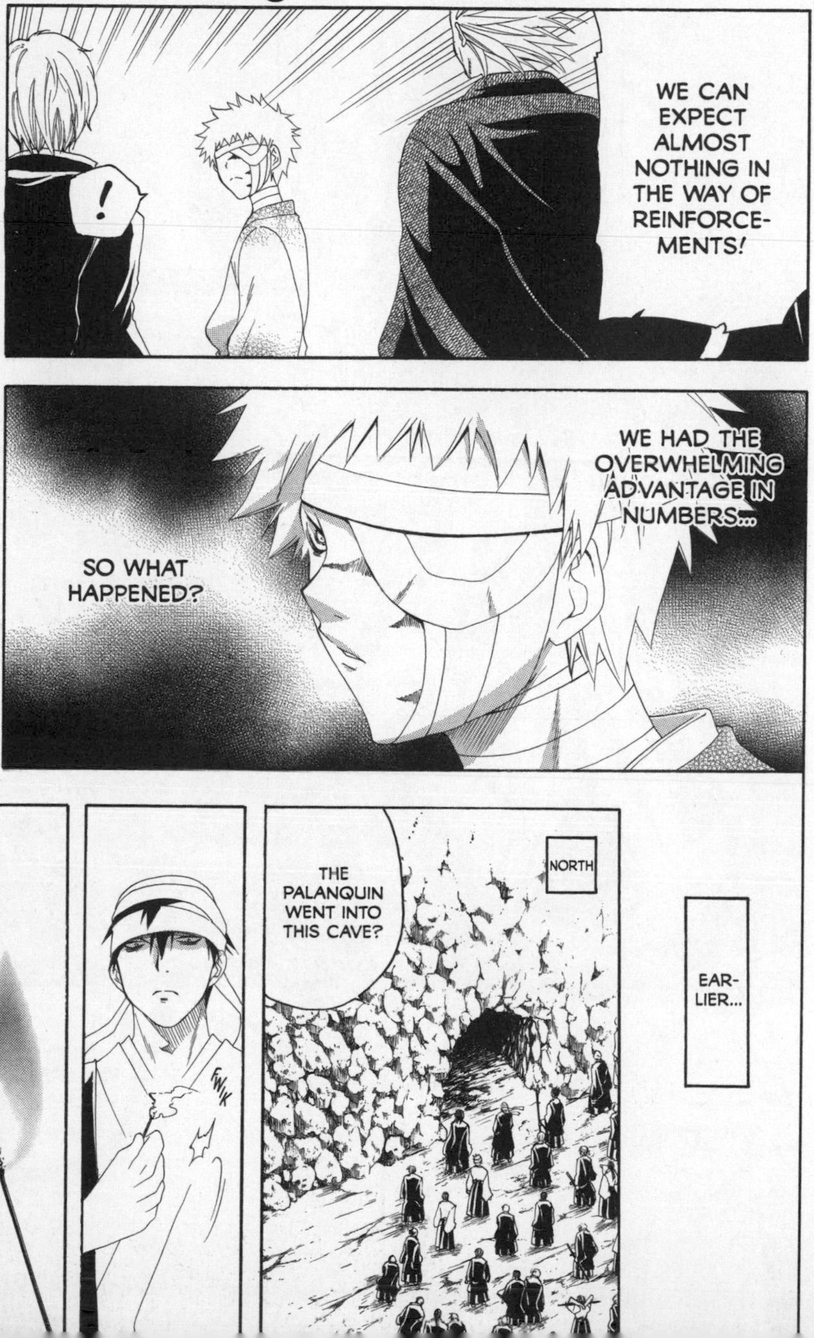

WE CAN EXPECT ALMOST NOTHING IN THE WAY OF REINFORCE-MENTS!
!
WE HAD THE OVERWHELMING ADVANTAGE IN NUMBERS...
SO WHAT HAPPENED?
EAR-LIER...
NORTH
THE PALANQUIN WENT INTO THIS CAVE?
FWIK

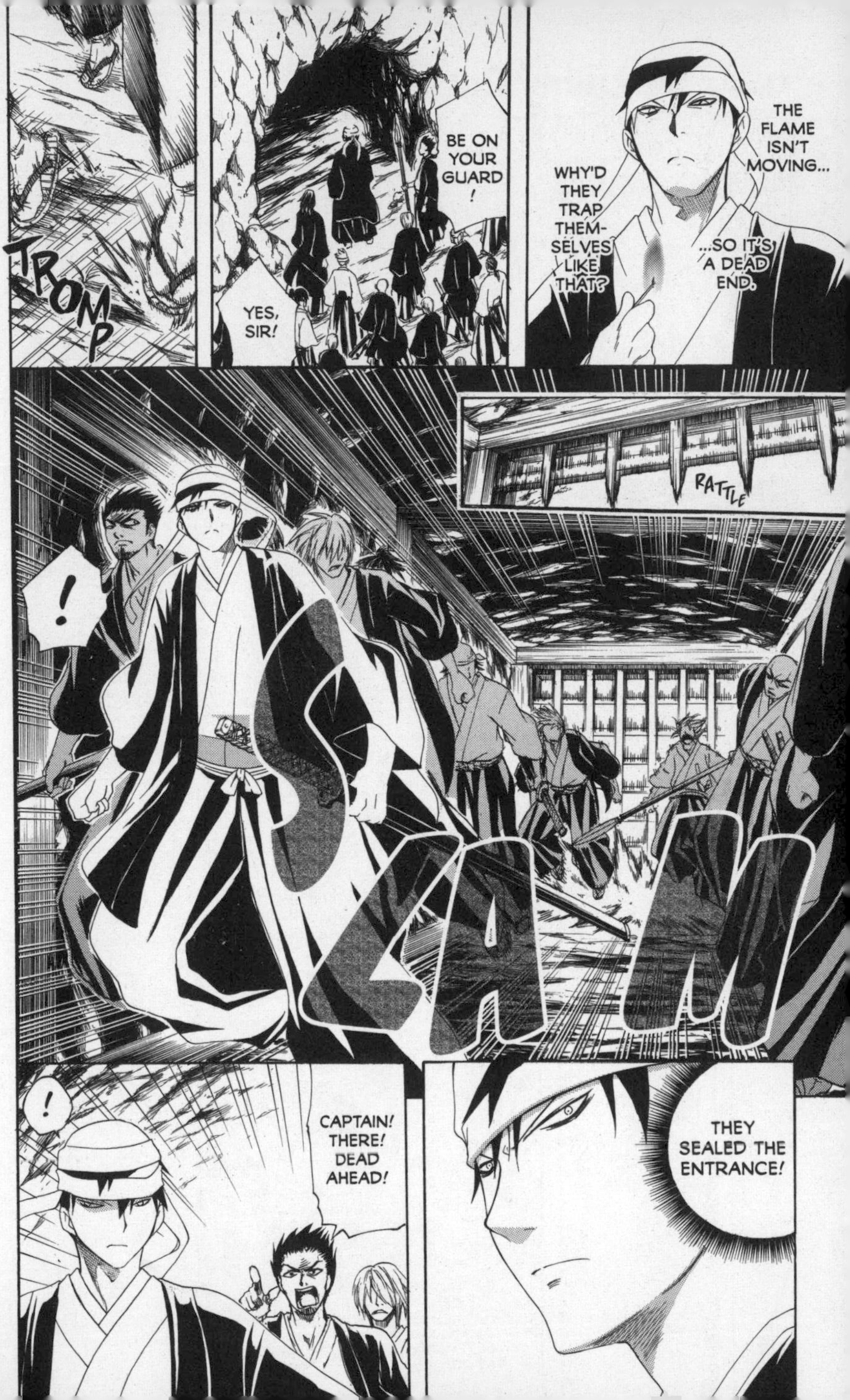
THE FLAME ISN'T MOVING...
...SO IT'S A DEAD END.
WHY'D THEY TRAP THEM-SELVES LIKE THAT?
BE ON YOUR GUARD!
YES, SIR!
TROMP
RATTLE
!
SLAM
THEY SEALED THE ENTRANCE!
!
CAPTAIN! THERE! DEAD AHEAD!

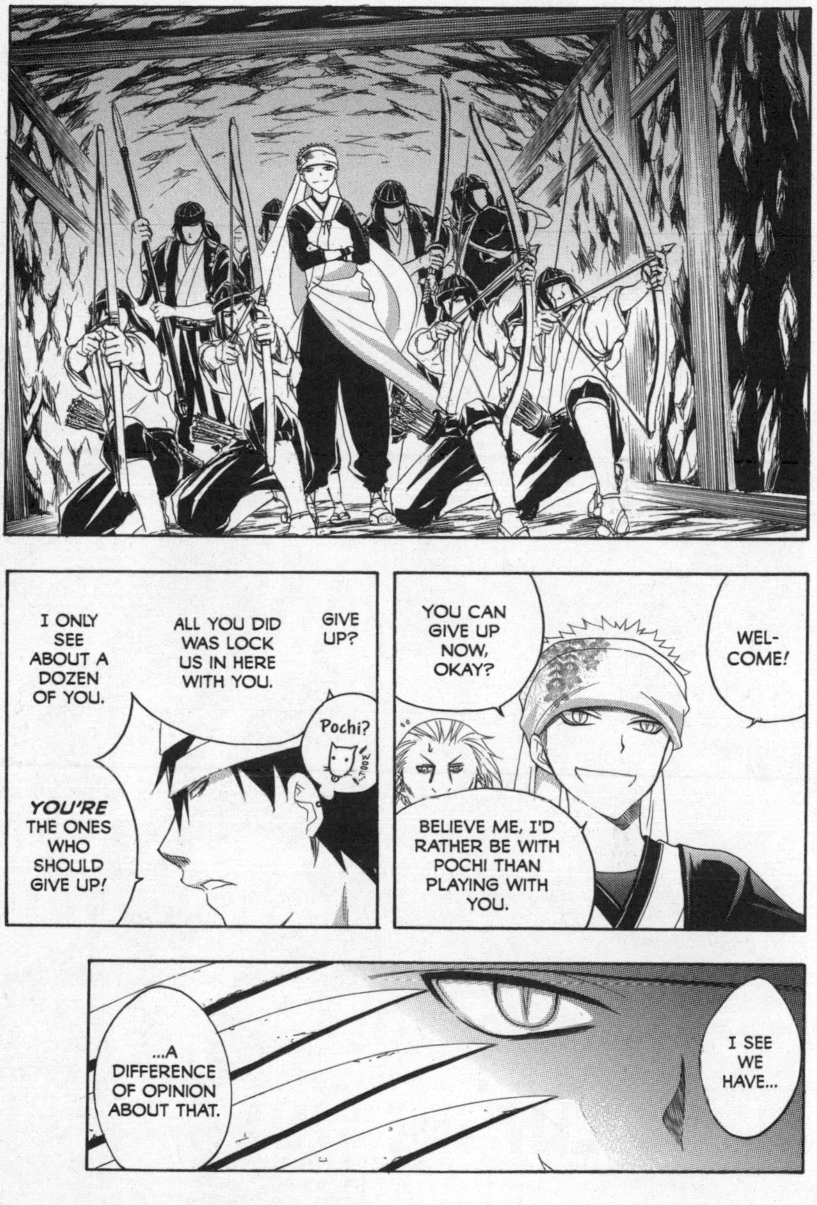
WEL-COME!
YOU CAN GIVE UP NOW, OKAY?
BELIEVE ME, I'D RATHER BE WITH POCHI THAN PLAYING WITH YOU.
GIVE UP?
Pochi?
ALL YOU DID WAS LOCK US IN HERE WITH YOU.
I ONLY SEE ABOUT A DOZEN OF YOU.
YOU'RE THE ONES WHO SHOULD GIVE UP!
I SEE WE HAVE...
...A DIFFERENCE OF OPINION ABOUT THAT.

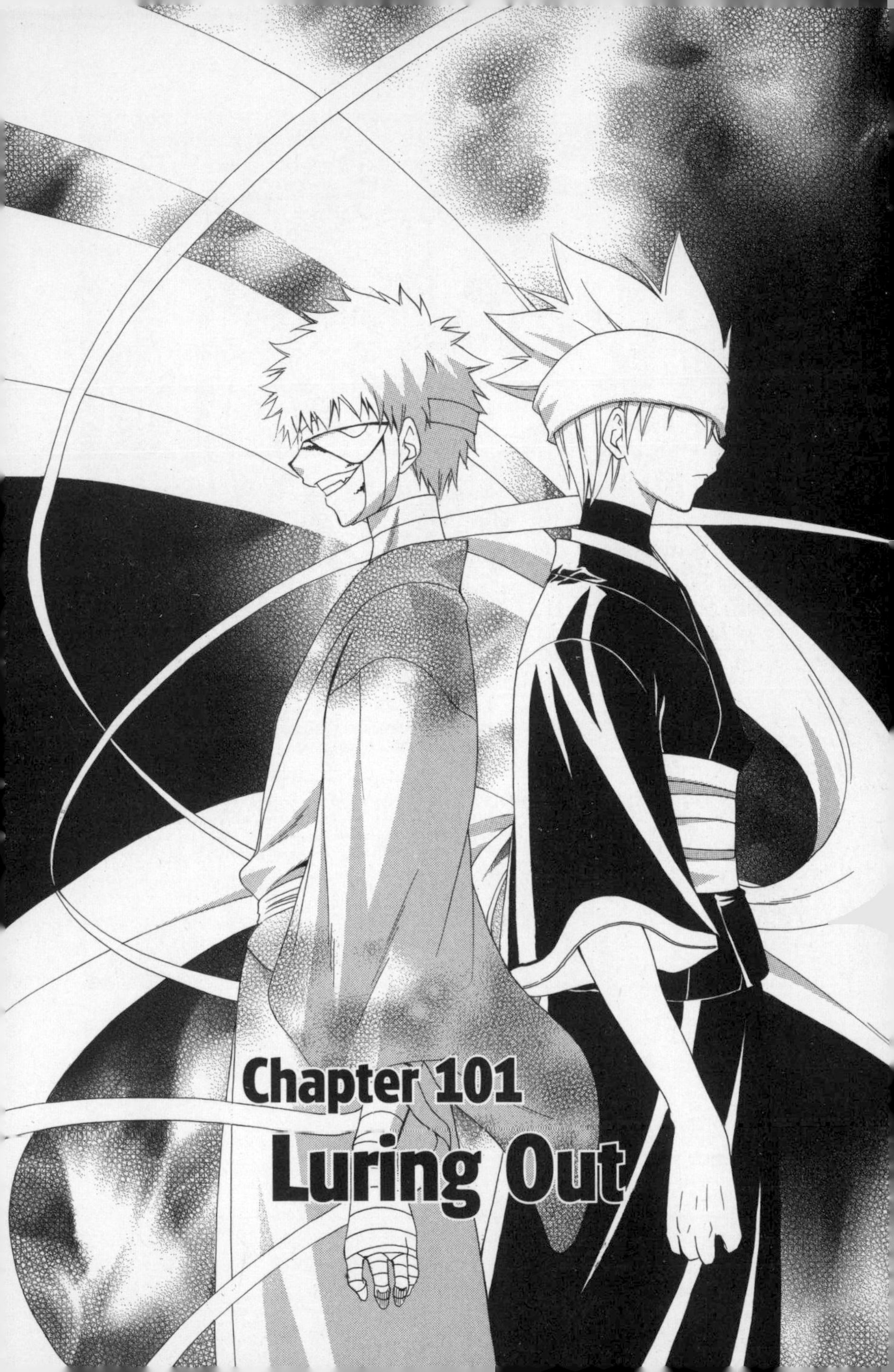
Chapter 101
Luring Out

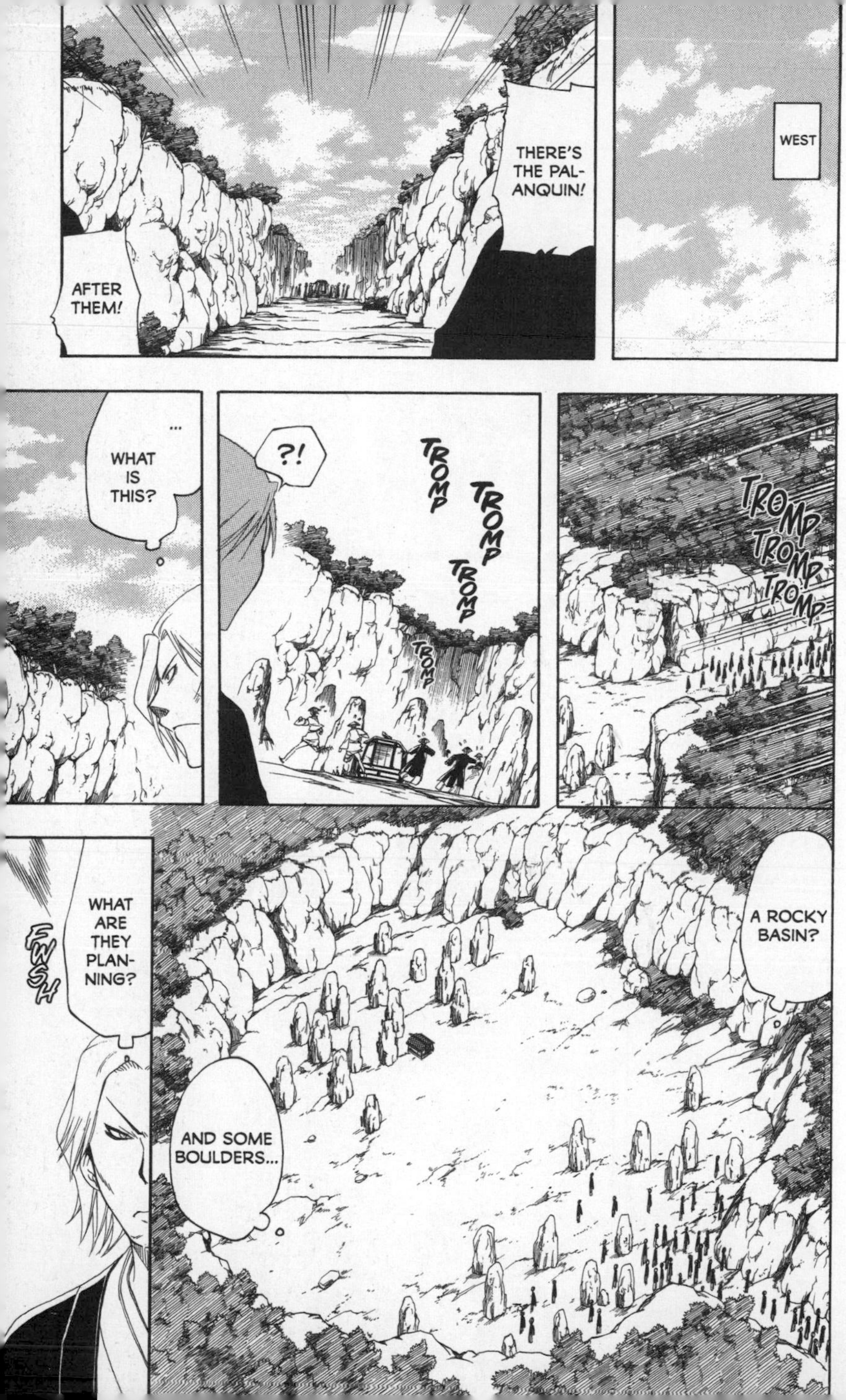
WEST
THERE'S THE PAL-ANQUIN!
AFTER THEM!
TROMP TROMP TROMP
TROMP
TROMP
TROMP
TROMP
?!
... WHAT IS THIS?
A ROCKY BASIN?
WHAT ARE THEY PLAN-NING?
FWSH
AND SOME BOULDERS...

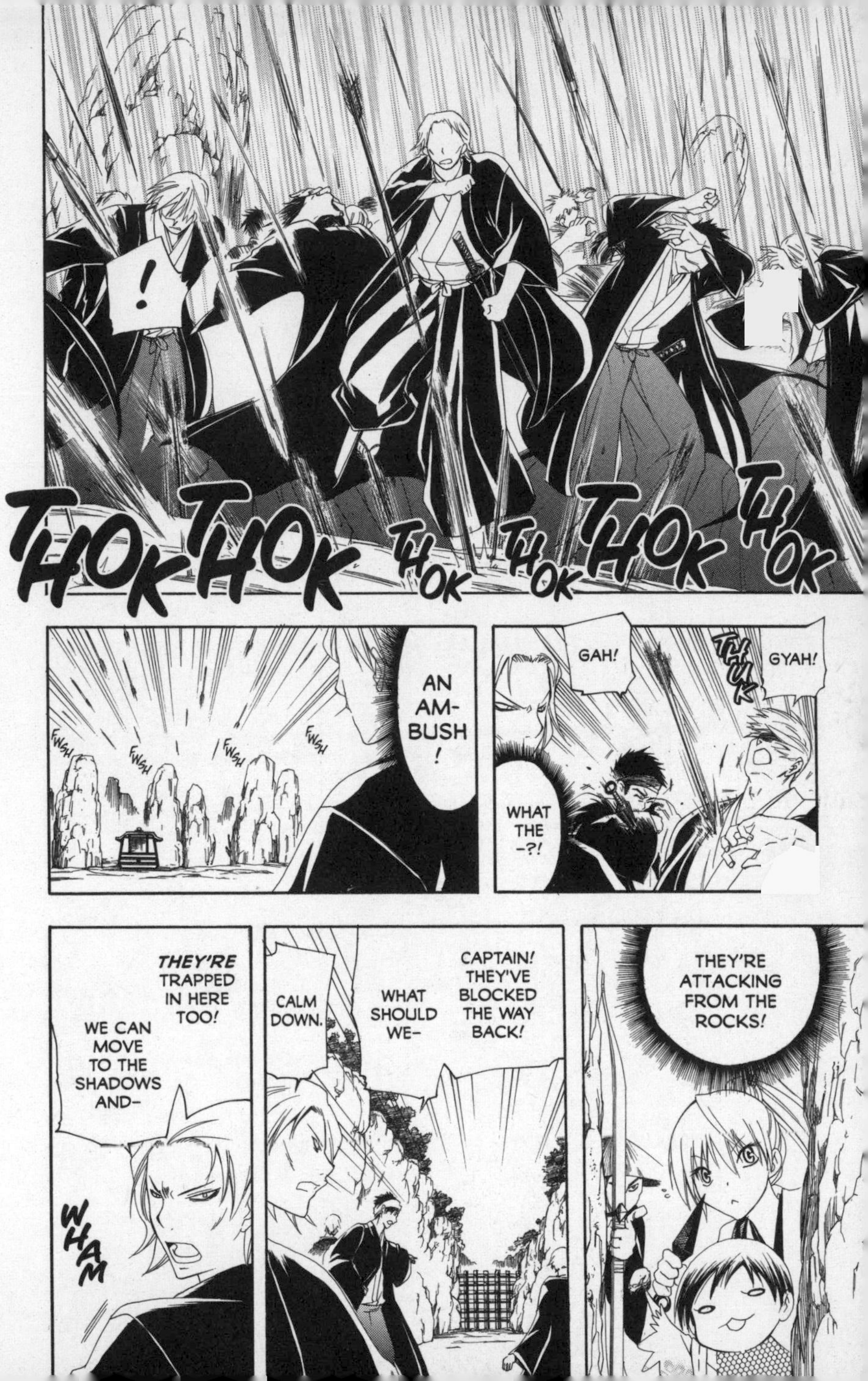
!
THOK
THOK
THOK
THOK
THOK
THOK
GAH!
THUK
GYAH!
WHAT THE -?!
FWSH
FWSH
FWSH
FWSH
AN AM-BUSH!
THEY'RE ATTACKING FROM THE ROCKS!
CAPTAIN! THEY'VE BLOCKED THE WAY BACK!
WHAT SHOULD WE-
CALM DOWN.
THEY'RE TRAPPED IN HERE TOO!
WE CAN MOVE TO THE SHADOWS AND-
WHAM

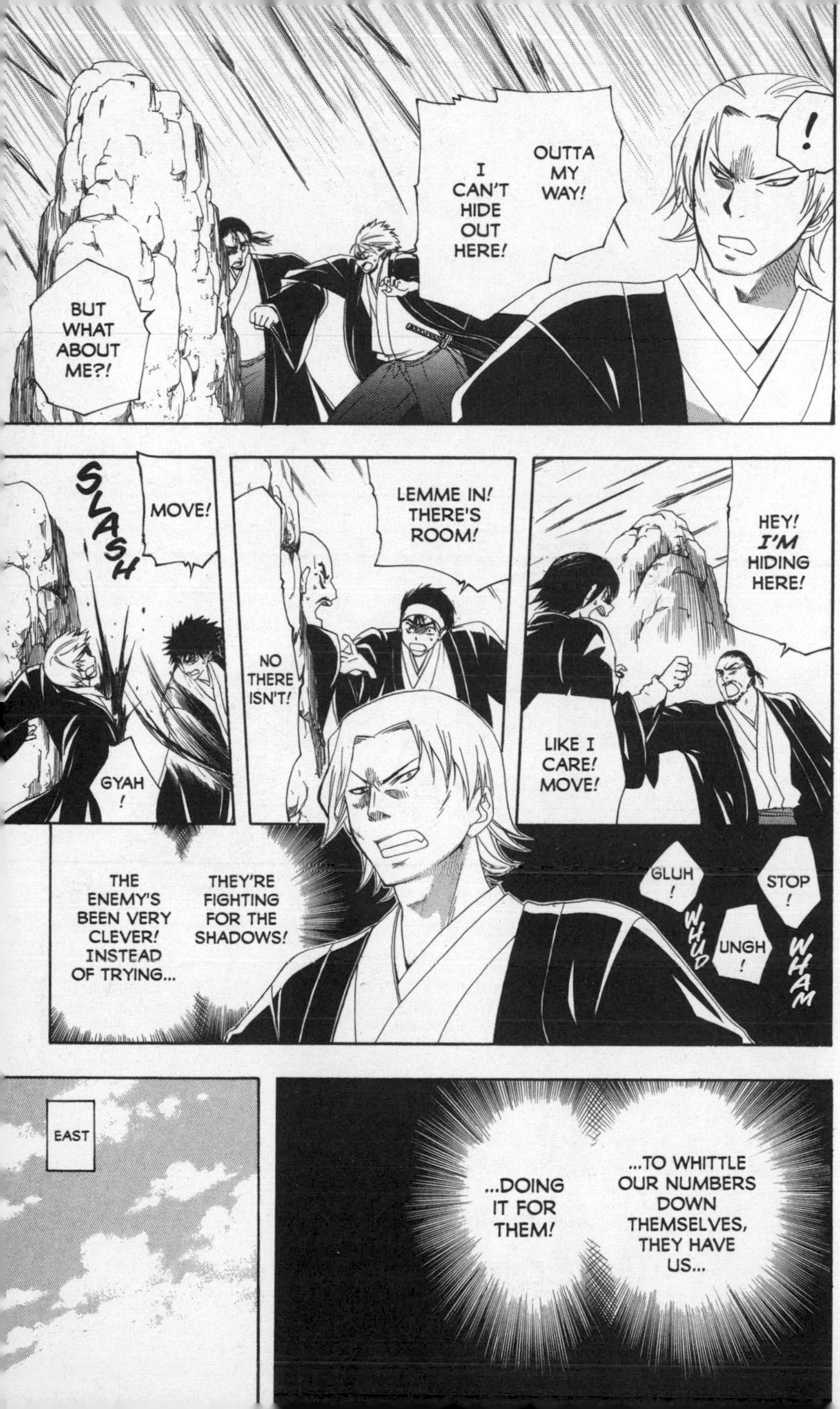
!
OUTTA MY WAY!
I CAN'T HIDE OUT HERE!
BUT WHAT ABOUT ME?!
HEY! I'M HIDING HERE!
LIKE I CARE! MOVE!
LEMME IN! THERE'S ROOM!
NO THERE ISN'T!
MOVE!
SLASH
GYAH!
STOP!
WHAM
UNGH!
GLUH!
WHUD
THEY'RE FIGHTING FOR THE SHADOWS!
THE ENEMY'S BEEN VERY CLEVER! INSTEAD OF TRYING...
...TO WHITTLE OUR NUMBERS DOWN THEMSELVES, THEY HAVE US...
...DOING IT FOR THEM!
EAST

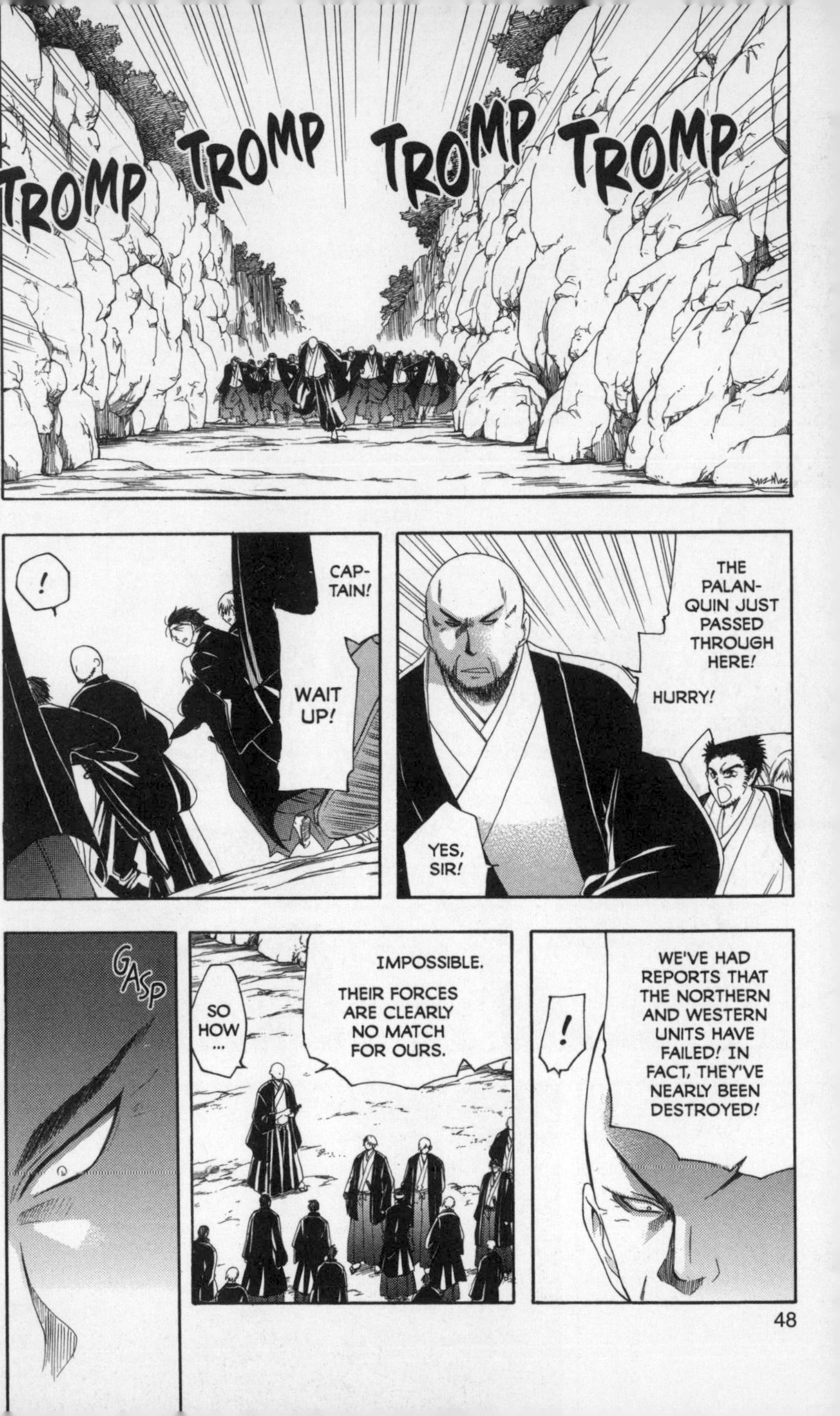
TROMP TROMP TROMP TROMP
THE PALAN-QUIN JUST PASSED THROUGH HERE!
HURRY!
YES, SIR!
CAP-TAIN!
WAIT UP!
!
WE'VE HAD REPORTS THAT THE NORTHERN AND WESTERN UNITS HAVE FAILED! IN FACT, THEY'VE NEARLY BEEN DESTROYED!
!
IMPOSSIBLE.
THEIR FORCES ARE CLEARLY NO MATCH FOR OURS.
SO HOW ...
GASP

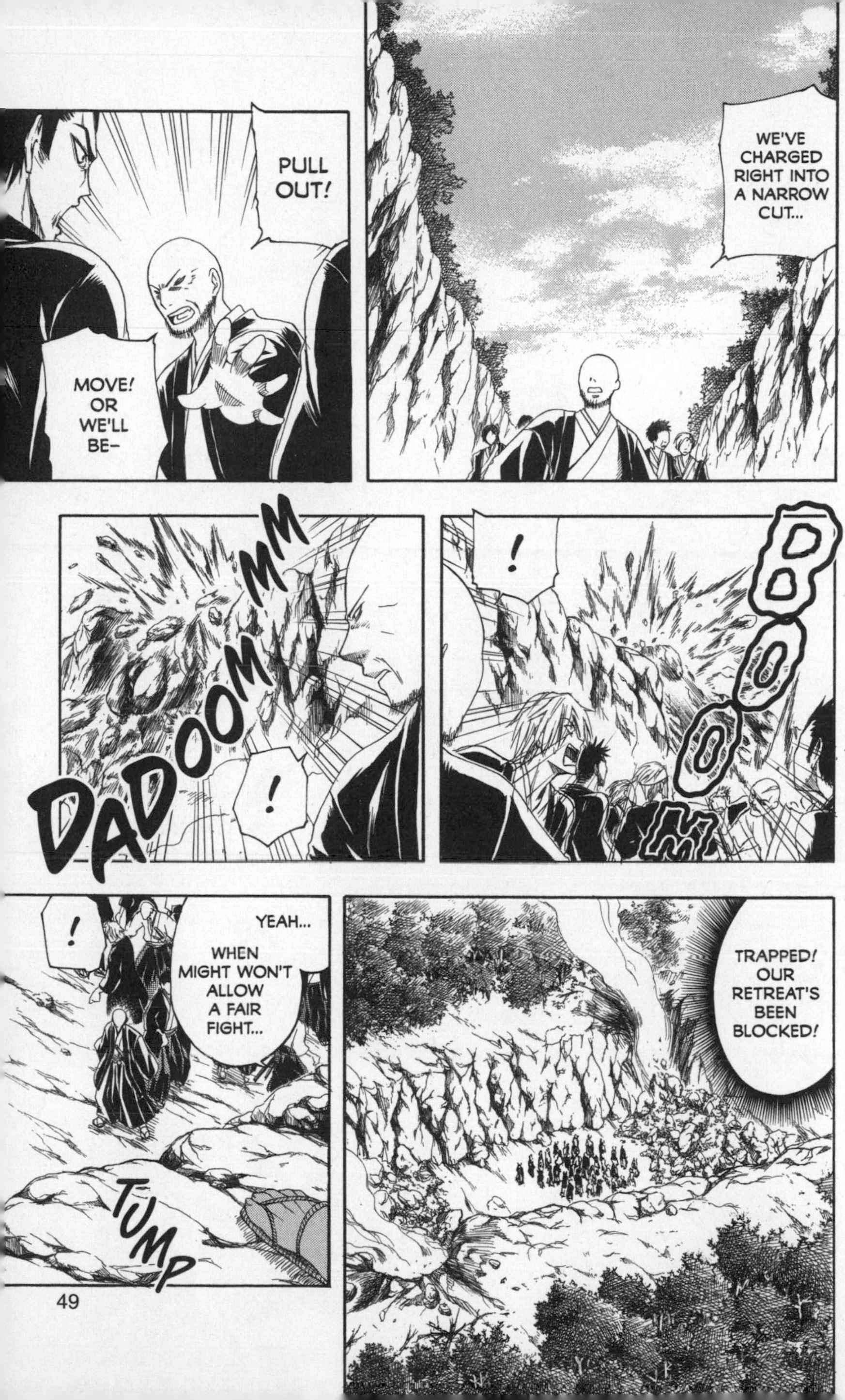
WE'VE CHARGED RIGHT INTO A NARROW CUT...
PULL OUT!
MOVE! OR WE'LL BE–
!
BOOOM
DADOOMM
!
TRAPPED! OUR RETREAT'S BEEN BLOCKED!
!
YEAH...
WHEN MIGHT WON'T ALLOW A FAIR FIGHT...
TUMP

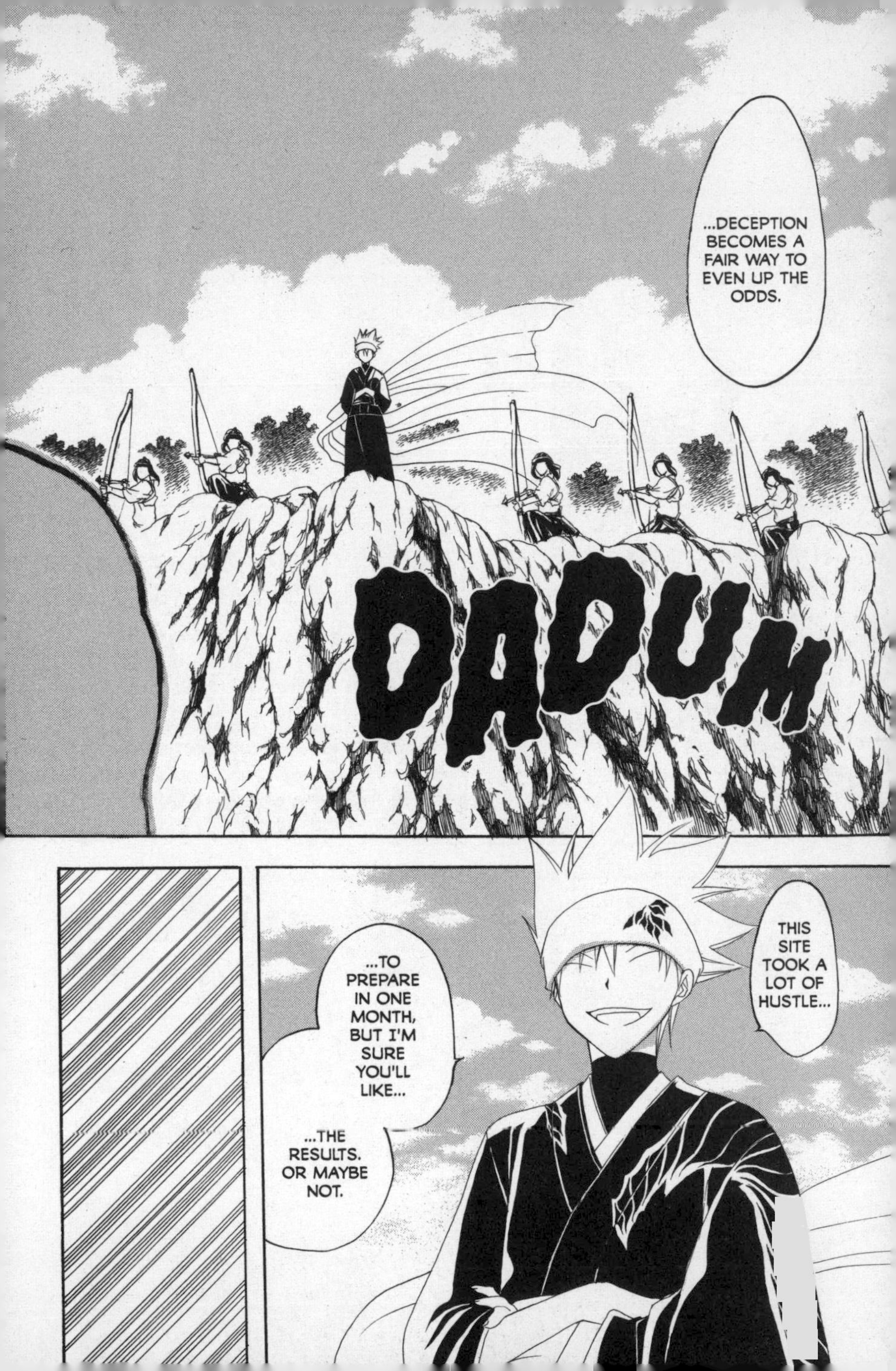
...DECEPTION BECOMES A FAIR WAY TO EVEN UP THE ODDS.
DADUM
THIS SITE TOOK A LOT OF HUSTLE...
...TO PREPARE IN ONE MONTH, BUT I'M SURE YOU'LL LIKE...
...THE RESULTS. OR MAYBE NOT.

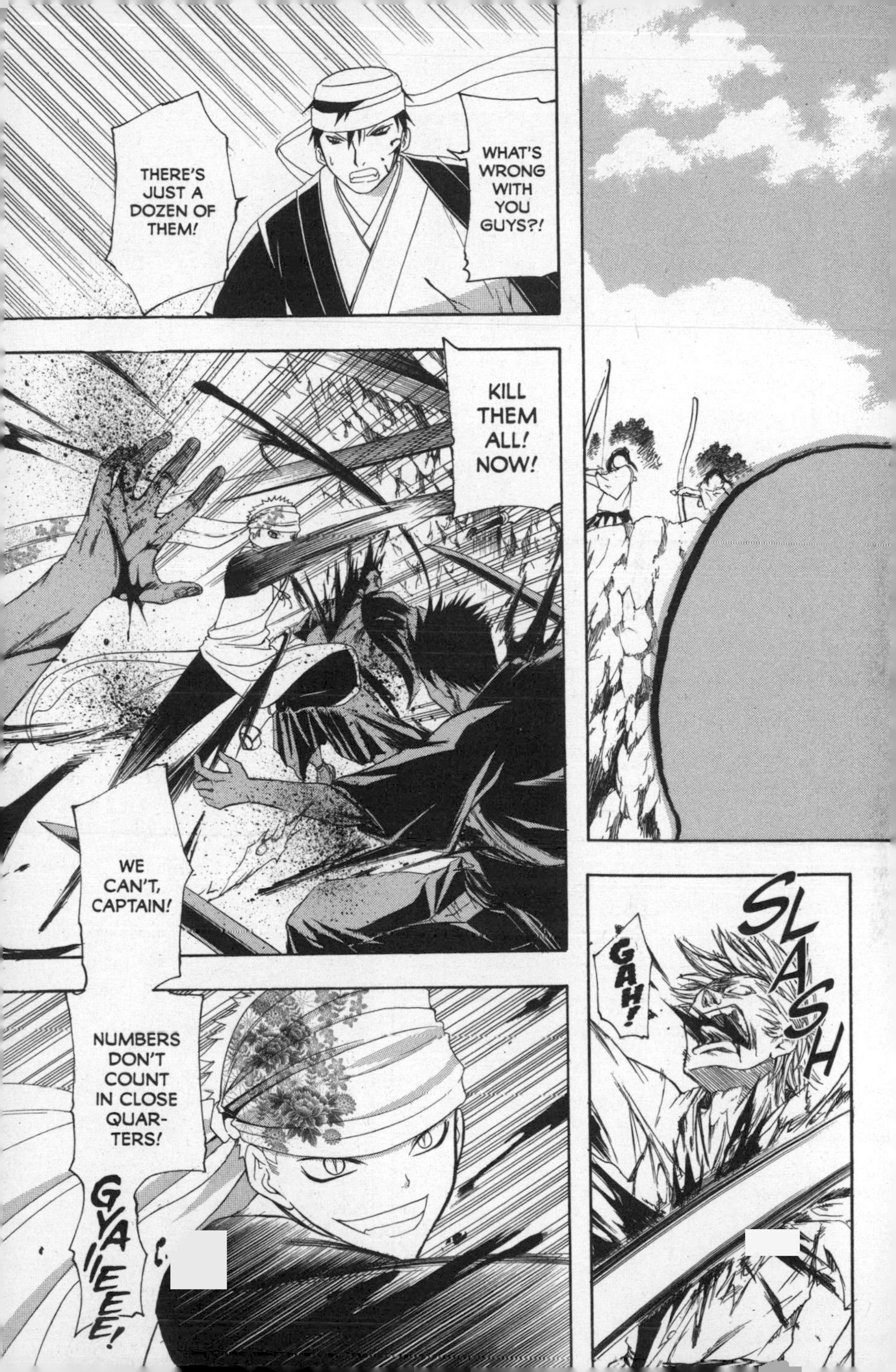
WHAT'S WRONG WITH YOU GUYS?!
THERE'S JUST A DOZEN OF THEM!
KILL THEM ALL! NOW!
WE CAN'T, CAPTAIN!
GAH!
SLASH
NUMBERS DON'T COUNT IN CLOSE QUAR-TERS!
GYAIIEEE!

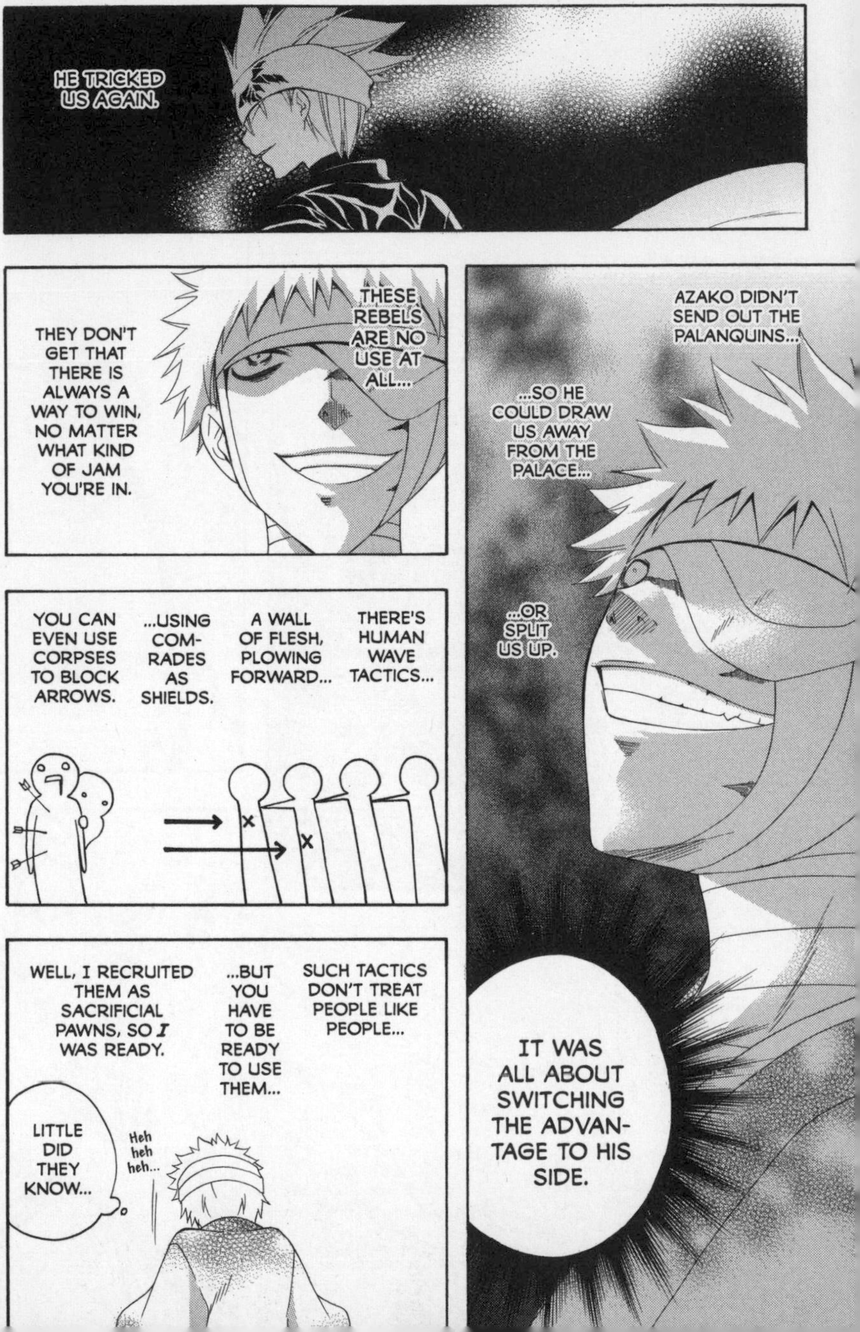

HE TRICKED US AGAIN.
AZAKO DIDN'T SEND OUT THE PALANQUINS...
...SO HE COULD DRAW US AWAY FROM THE PALACE...
...OR SPLIT US UP.
IT WAS ALL ABOUT SWITCHING THE ADVANTAGE TO HIS SIDE.
THESE REBELS ARE NO USE AT ALL...
THEY DON'T GET THAT THERE IS ALWAYS A WAY TO WIN, NO MATTER WHAT KIND OF JAM YOU'RE IN.
THERE'S HUMAN WAVE TACTICS...
A WALL OF FLESH, PLOWING FORWARD...
...USING COMRADES AS SHIELDS.
YOU CAN EVEN USE CORPSES TO BLOCK ARROWS.
SUCH TACTICS DON'T TREAT PEOPLE LIKE PEOPLE...
...BUT YOU HAVE TO BE READY TO USE THEM...
WELL, I RECRUITED THEM AS SACRIFICIAL PAWNS, SO *I* WAS READY.
Heh heh heh...
LITTLE DID THEY KNOW...

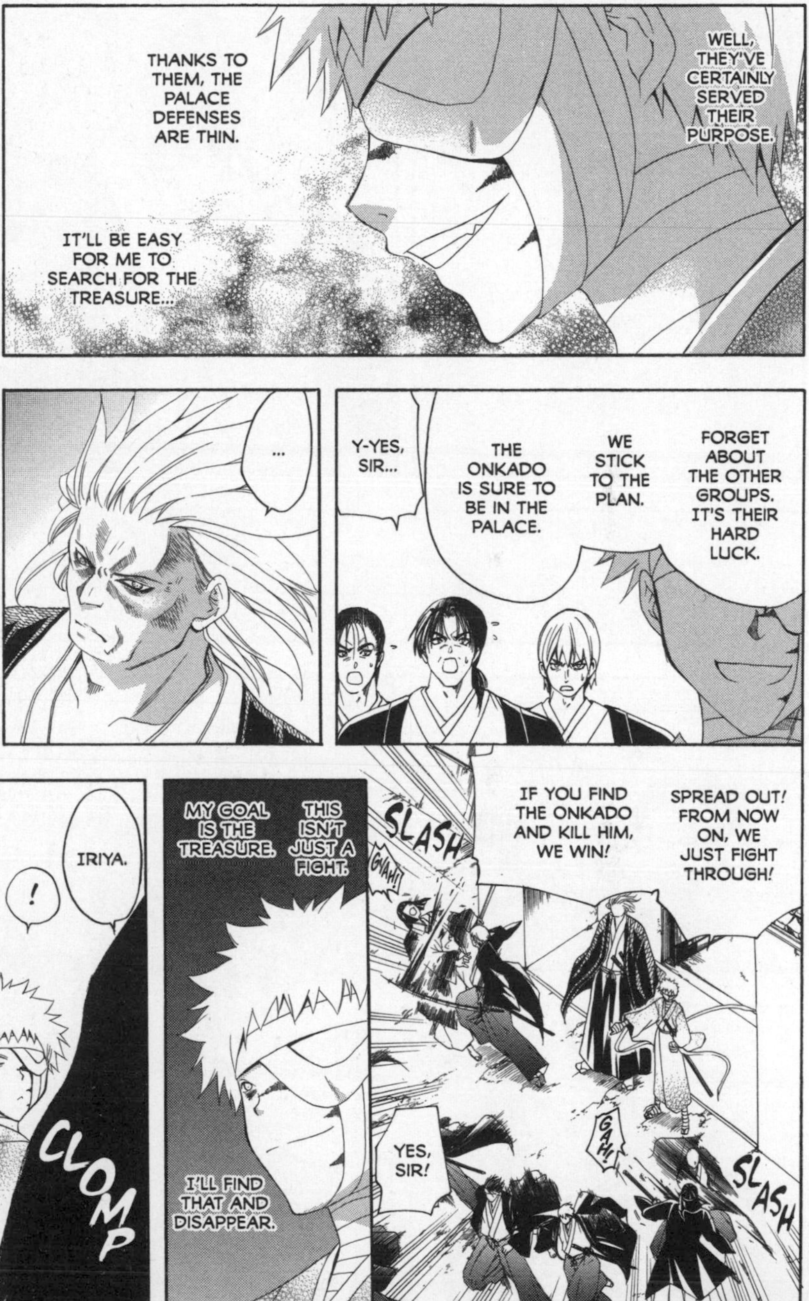
WELL, THEY'VE CERTAINLY SERVED THEIR PURPOSE.
THANKS TO THEM, THE PALACE DEFENSES ARE THIN.
IT'LL BE EASY FOR ME TO SEARCH FOR THE TREASURE...
FORGET ABOUT THE OTHER GROUPS. IT'S THEIR HARD LUCK.
WE STICK TO THE PLAN.
THE ONKADO IS SURE TO BE IN THE PALACE.
Y-YES, SIR...
...
SPREAD OUT! FROM NOW ON, WE JUST FIGHT THROUGH!
IF YOU FIND THE ONKADO AND KILL HIM, WE WIN!
SLASH
GYAH!
GAH!
SLASH
YES, SIR!
THIS ISN'T JUST A FIGHT.
MY GOAL IS THE TREASURE.
I'LL FIND THAT AND DISAPPEAR.
IRIYA.
!
CLOMP

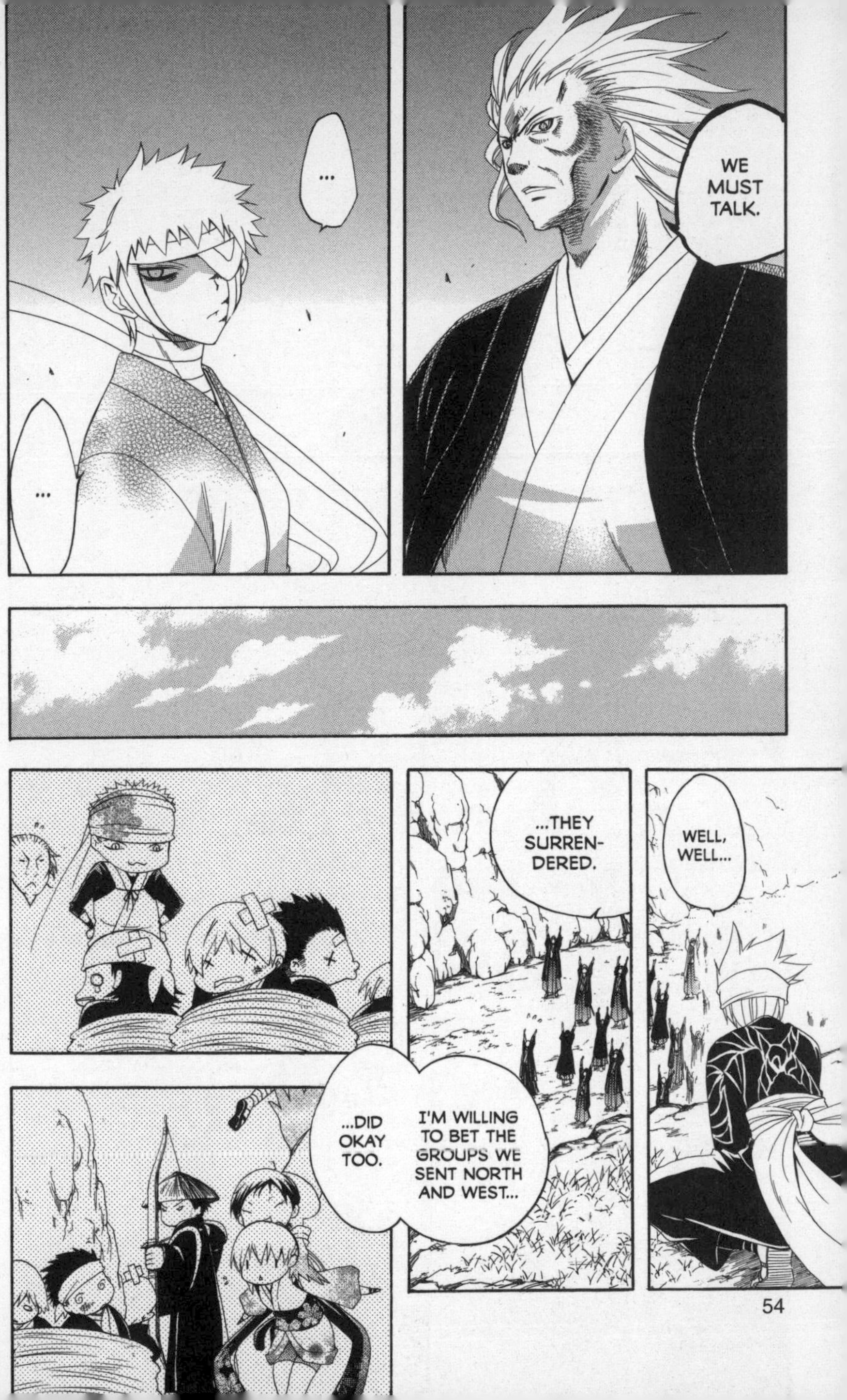
WE MUST TALK.
...
...
WELL, WELL...
...THEY SURREN-DERED.
I'M WILLING TO BET THE GROUPS WE SENT NORTH AND WEST...
...DID OKAY TOO.

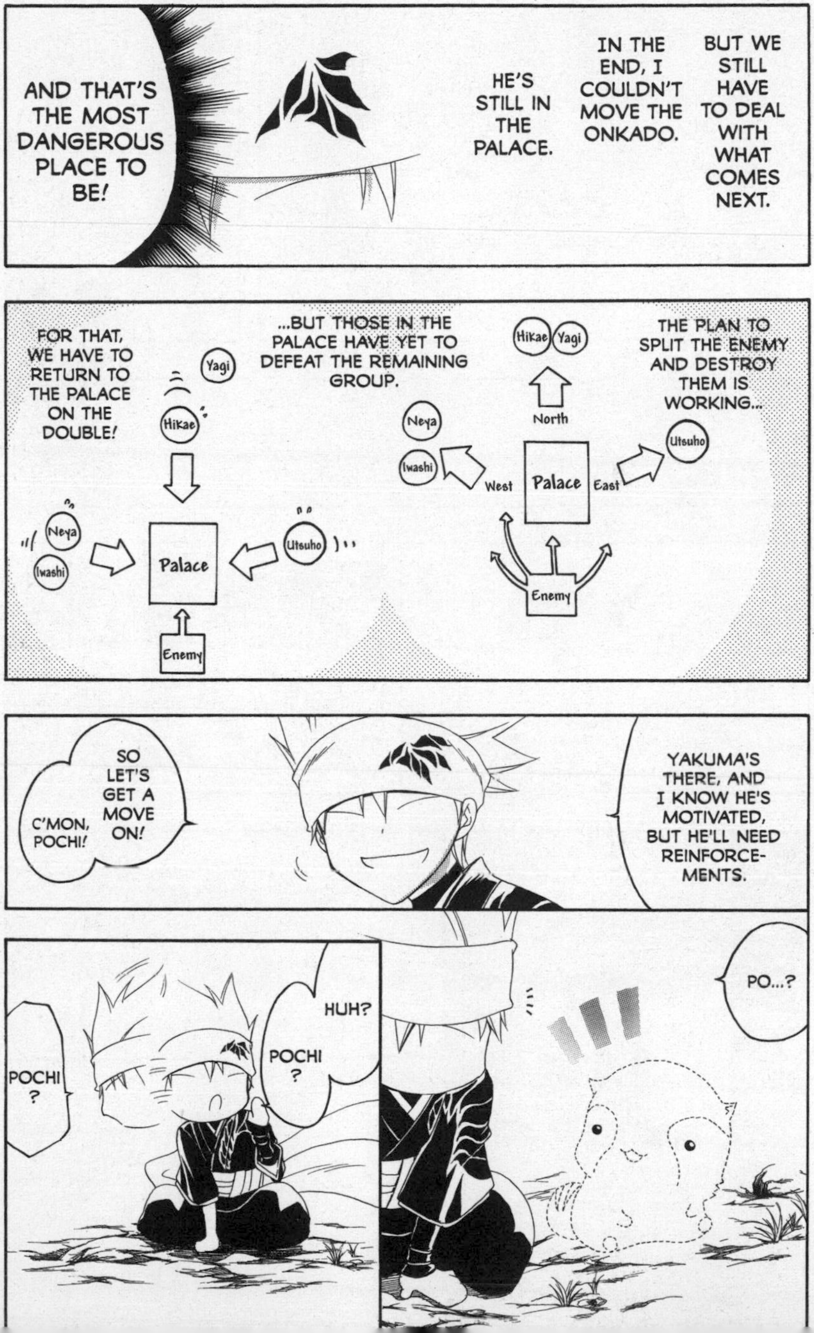
BUT WE STILL HAVE TO DEAL WITH WHAT COMES NEXT.
IN THE END, I COULDN'T MOVE THE ONKADO.
HE'S STILL IN THE PALACE.
AND THAT'S THE MOST DANGEROUS PLACE TO BE!
THE PLAN TO SPLIT THE ENEMY AND DESTROY THEM IS WORKING...
Hikae
Yagi
North
Neya
Iwashi
West
Palace
East
Utsuho
Enemy
...BUT THOSE IN THE PALACE HAVE YET TO DEFEAT THE REMAINING GROUP.
FOR THAT, WE HAVE TO RETURN TO THE PALACE ON THE DOUBLE!
Yagi
Hikae
Neya
Iwashi
Palace
Utsuho
Enemy
YAKUMA'S THERE, AND I KNOW HE'S MOTIVATED, BUT HE'LL NEED REINFORCE-MENTS.
SO LET'S GET A MOVE ON!
C'MON, POCHI!
PO...?
HUH?
POCHI?
POCHI?

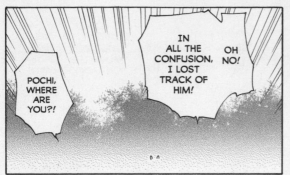

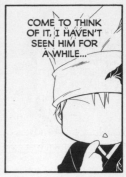

COME TO THINK OF IT, I HAVEN'T SEEN HIM FOR A WHILE...
OH NO!
IN ALL THE CONFUSION, I LOST TRACK OF HIM!
POCHI, WHERE ARE YOU?!
PAL-
ACE
TMP
TMP

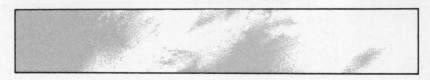

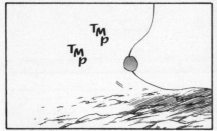

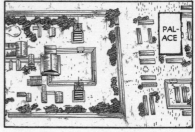

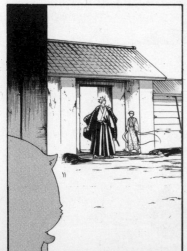

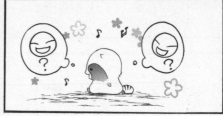

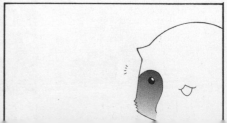

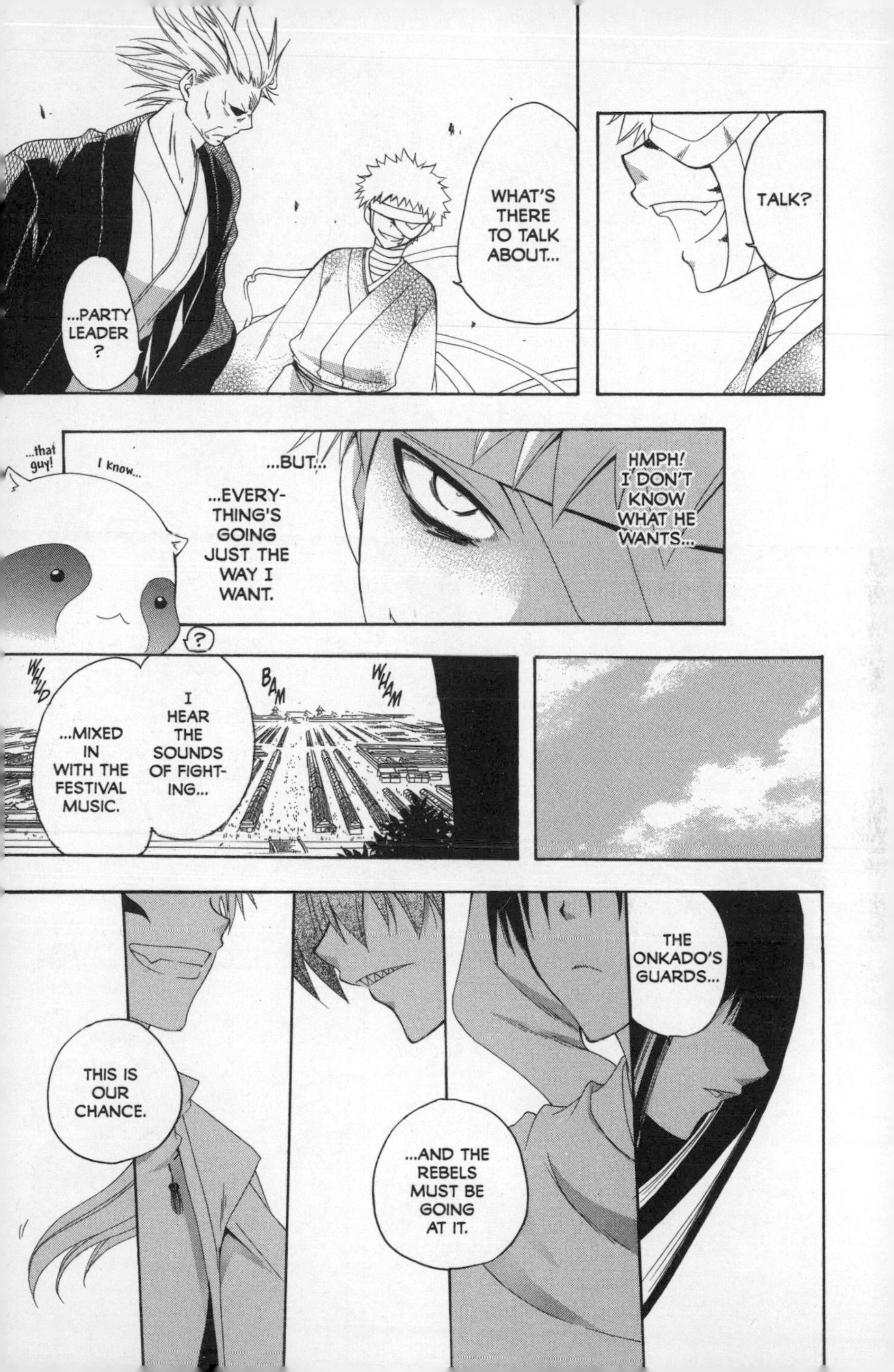
TALK?
WHAT'S THERE TO TALK ABOUT...
...PARTY LEADER ?
HMPH! I DON'T KNOW WHAT HE WANTS...
...BUT...
...EVERY-THING'S GOING JUST THE WAY I WANT.
I know...
...that guy!
?
WHAM
BAM
I HEAR THE SOUNDS OF FIGHT-ING...
...MIXED IN WITH THE FESTIVAL MUSIC.
THE ONKADO'S GUARDS...
...AND THE REBELS MUST BE GOING AT IT.
THIS IS OUR CHANCE.

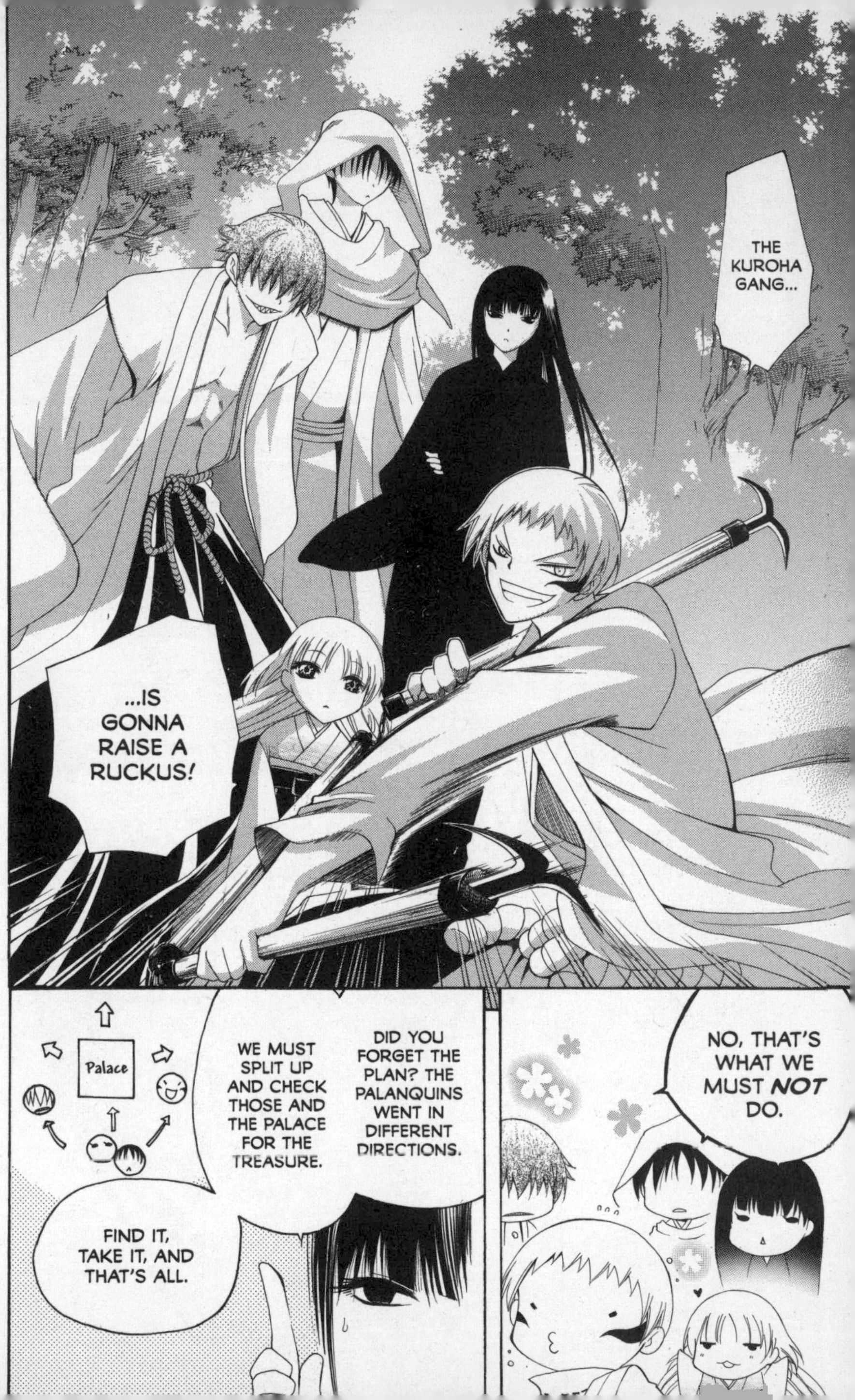
THE KUROHA GANG...
...IS GONNA RAISE A RUCKUS!
NO, THAT'S WHAT WE MUST ***NOT*** DO.
DID YOU FORGET THE PLAN? THE PALANQUINS WENT IN DIFFERENT DIRECTIONS.
WE MUST SPLIT UP AND CHECK THOSE AND THE PALACE FOR THE TREASURE.
Palace
FIND IT, TAKE IT, AND THAT'S ALL.

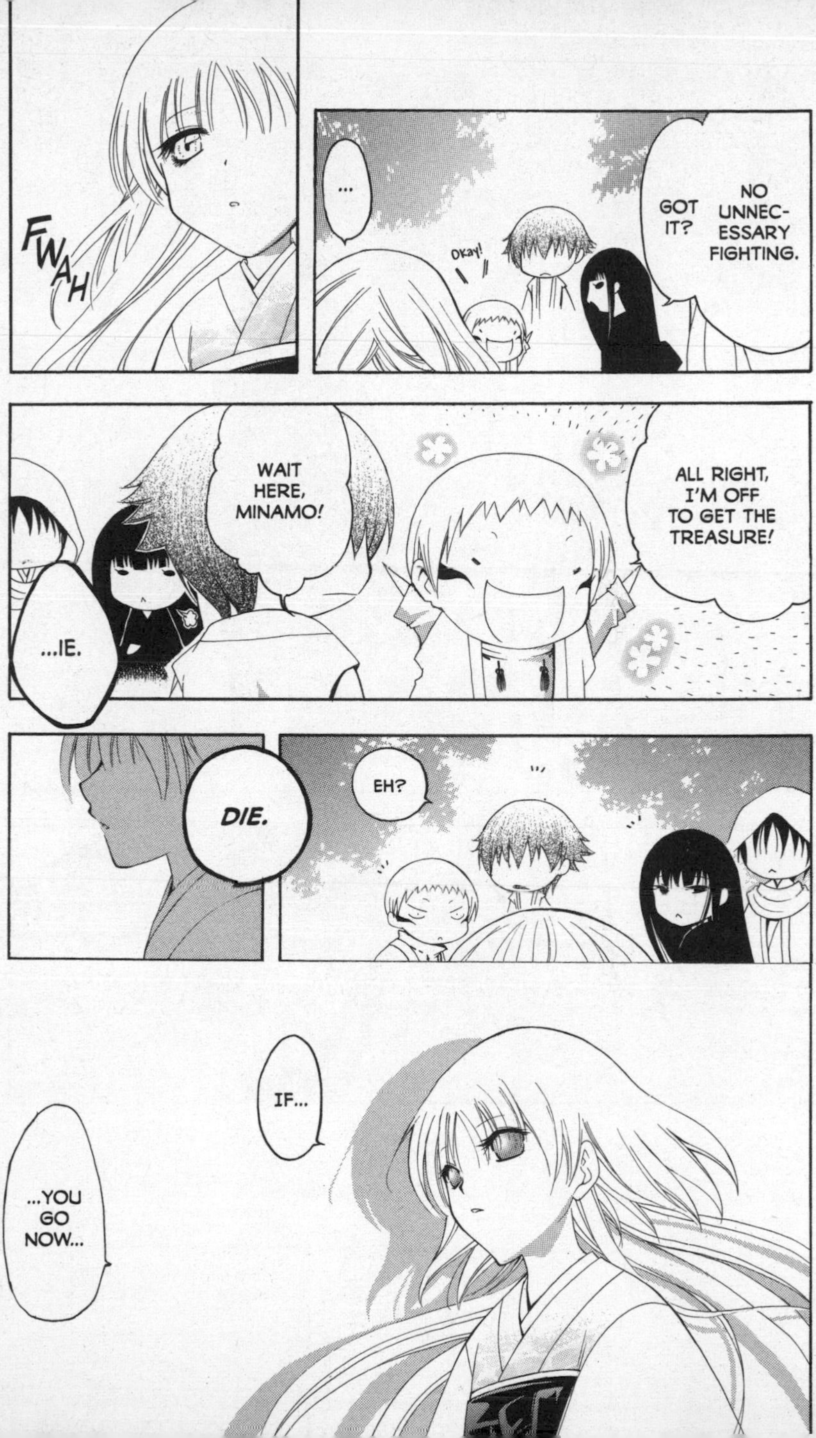
NO UNNECESSARY FIGHTING.
GOT IT?
Okay!
...
FWAH
ALL RIGHT, I'M OFF TO GET THE TREASURE!
WAIT HERE, MINAMO!
...IE.
DIE.
EH?
IF...
...YOU GO NOW...

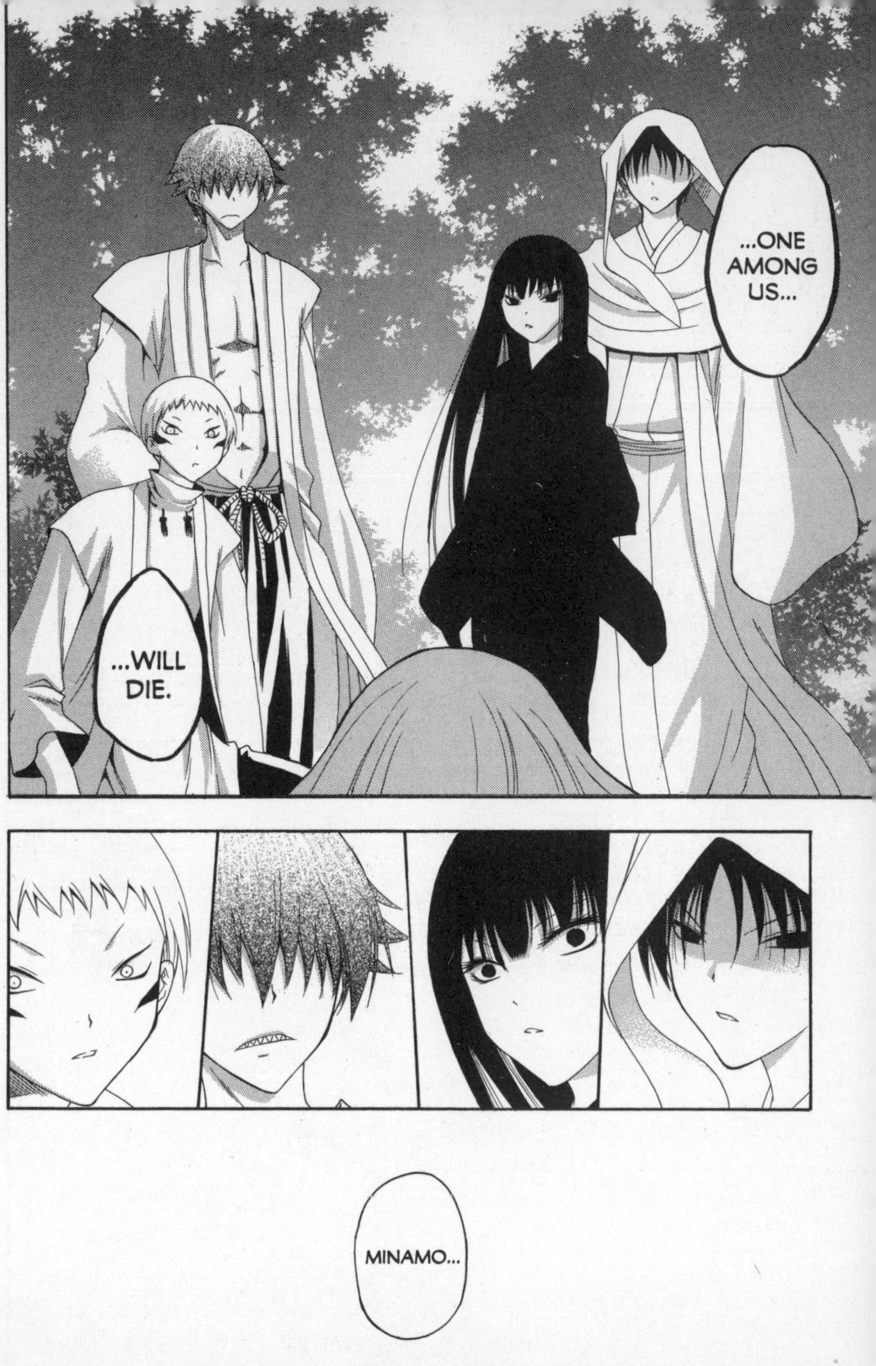
...ONE AMONG US...
...WILL DIE.
MINAMO...

Chapter 102 A Bad Feeling

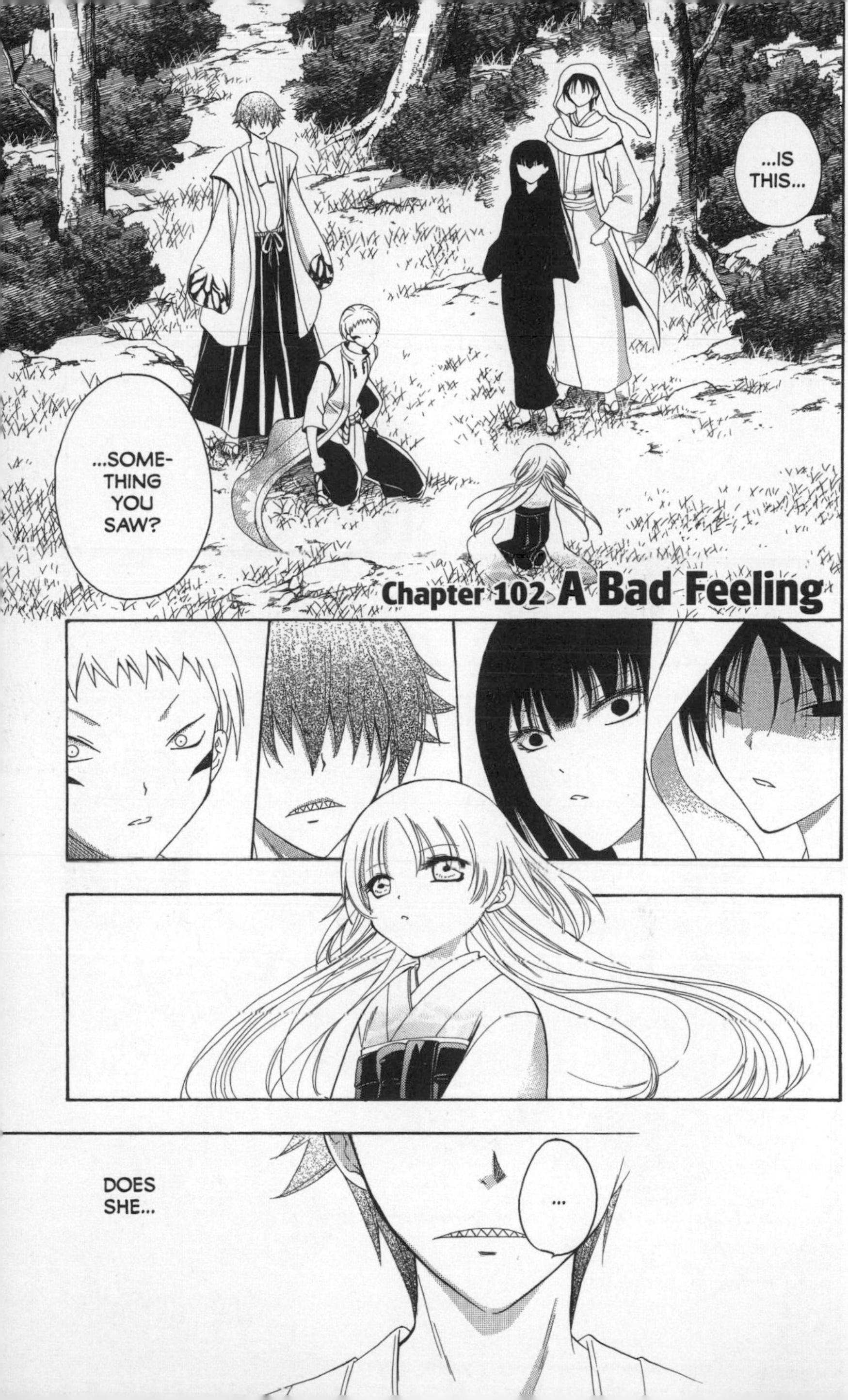
...IS THIS...
...SOME-THING YOU SAW?
...
DOES SHE...

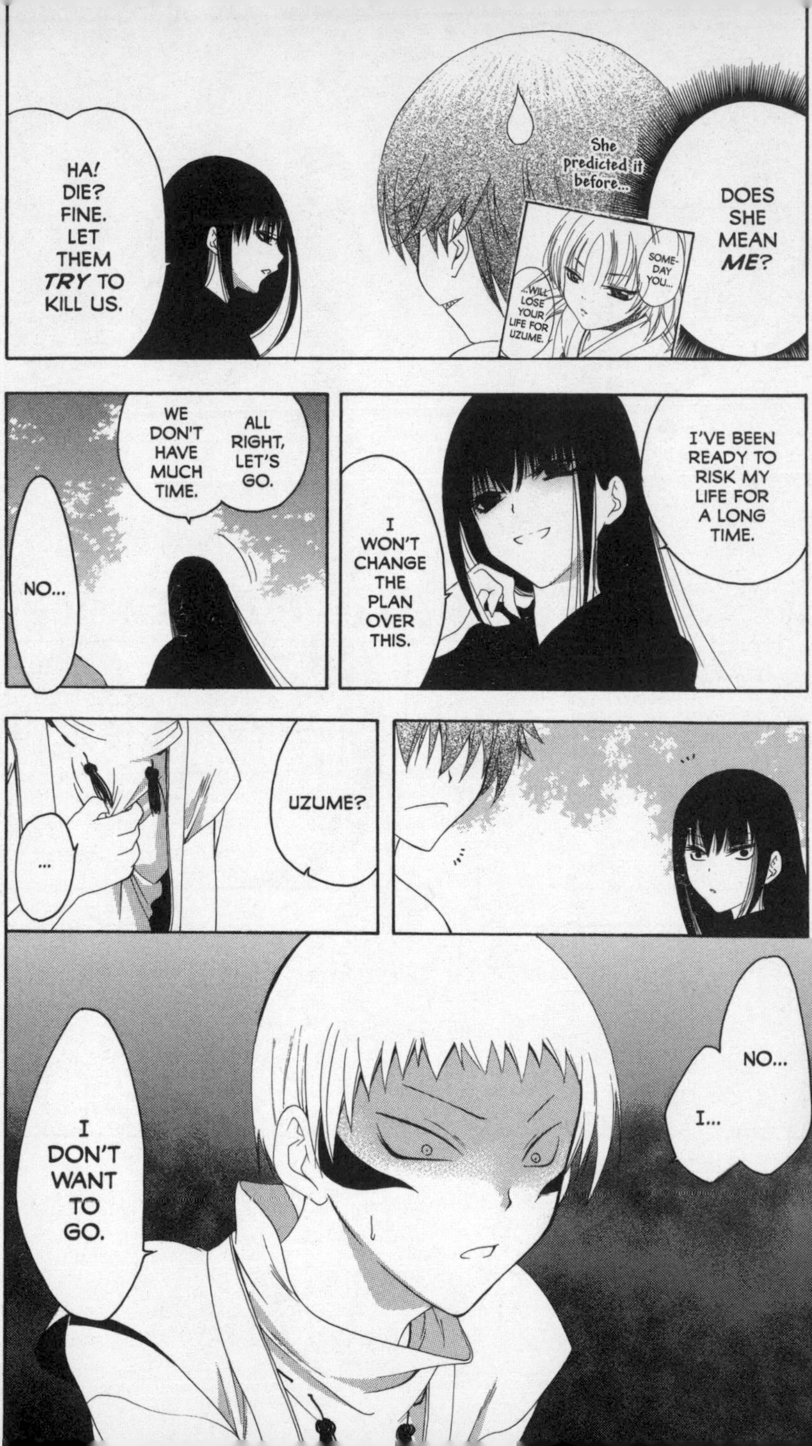
DOES SHE MEAN *ME*?
She predicted it before...
SOME-DAY YOU...
...WILL LOSE YOUR LIFE FOR UZUME.
HA! DIE? FINE. LET THEM *TRY* TO KILL US.
I'VE BEEN READY TO RISK MY LIFE FOR A LONG TIME.
I WON'T CHANGE THE PLAN OVER THIS.
ALL RIGHT, LET'S GO.
WE DON'T HAVE MUCH TIME.
NO...
UZUME?
...
NO... I...
I DON'T WANT TO GO.

Chapter 102
A Bad Feeling

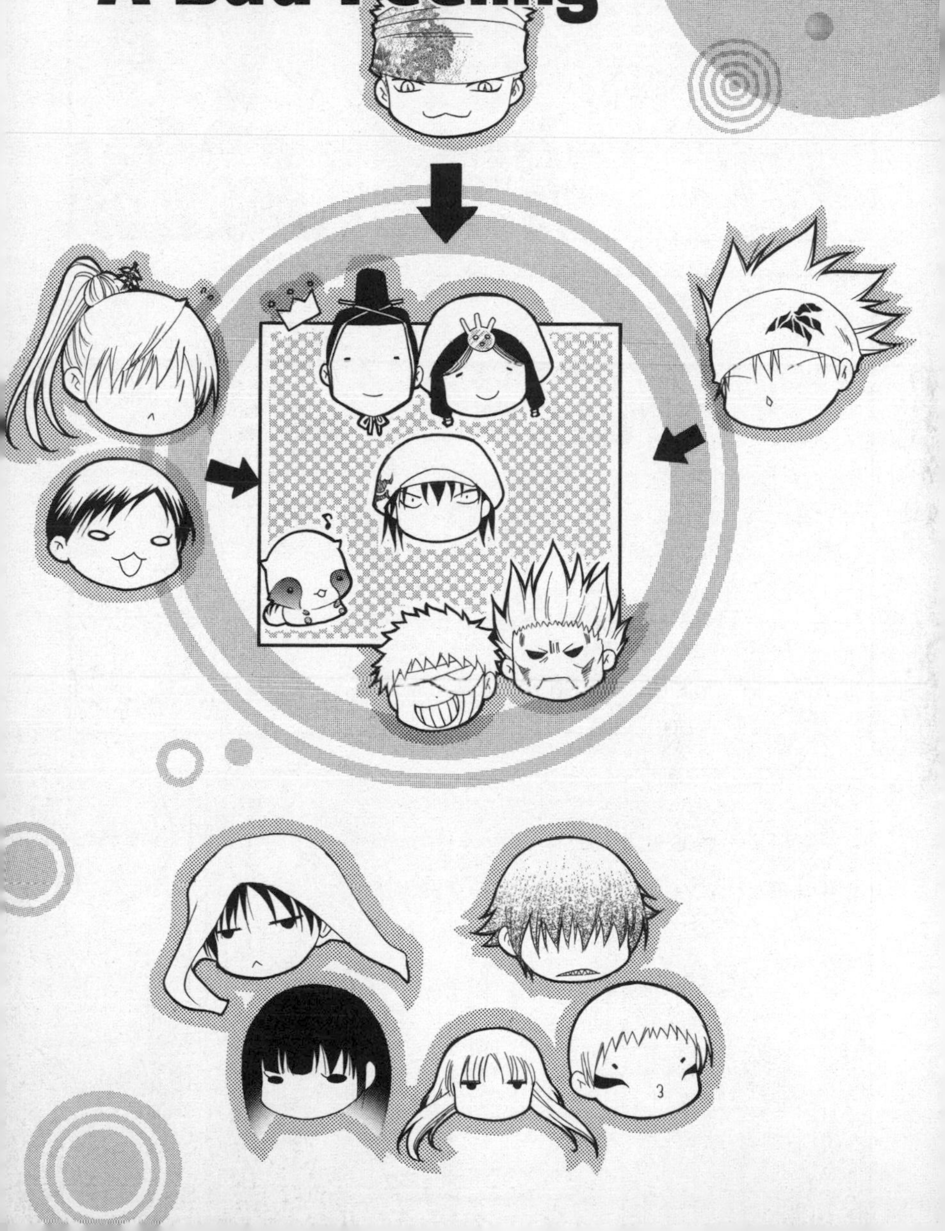

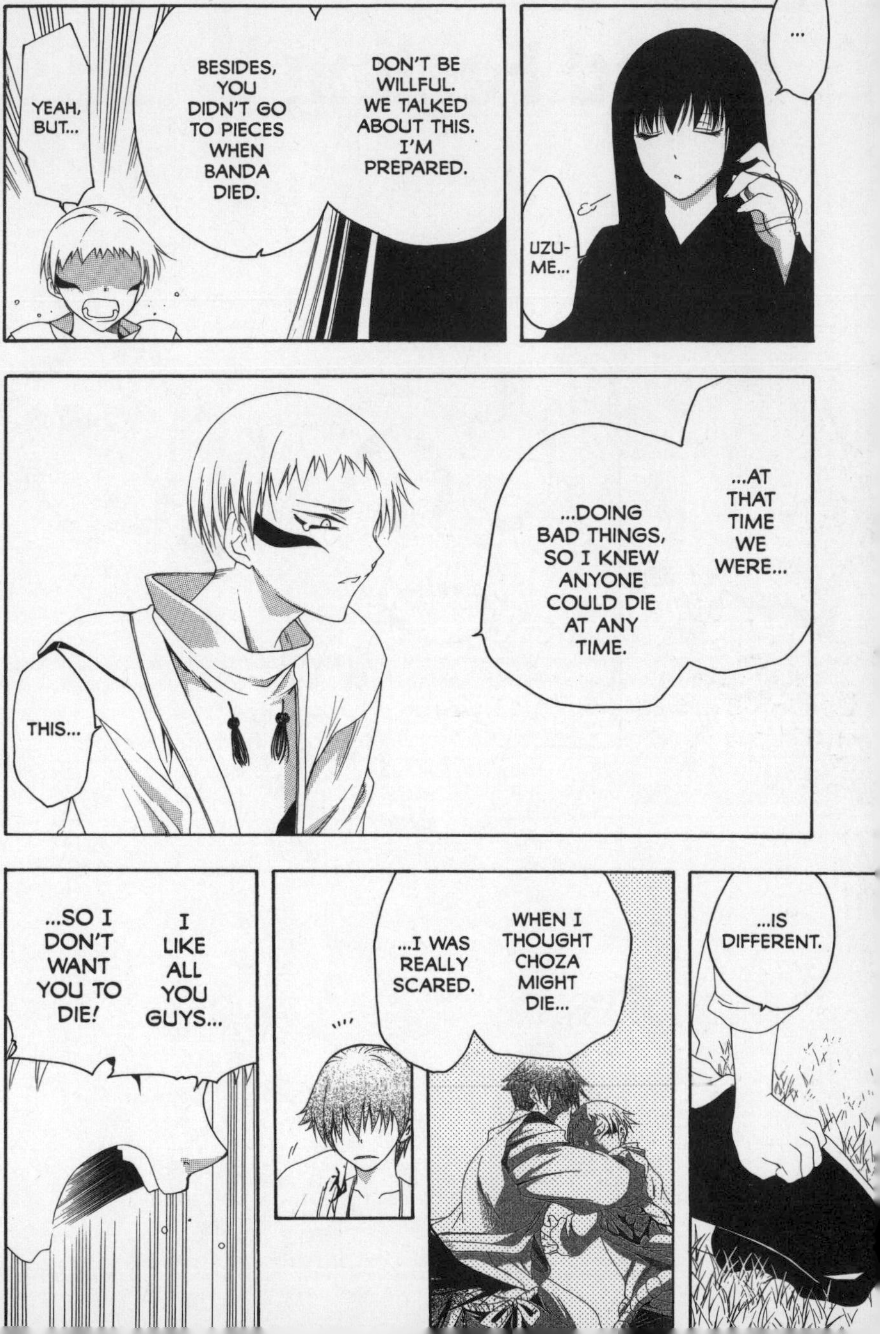
...
UZU-ME...
DON'T BE WILLFUL. WE TALKED ABOUT THIS. I'M PREPARED.
BESIDES, YOU DIDN'T GO TO PIECES WHEN BANDA DIED.
YEAH, BUT...
...AT THAT TIME WE WERE...
...DOING BAD THINGS, SO I KNEW ANYONE COULD DIE AT ANY TIME.
THIS...
...IS DIFFERENT.
WHEN I THOUGHT CHOZA MIGHT DIE...
...I WAS REALLY SCARED.
I LIKE ALL YOU GUYS...
...SO I DON'T WANT YOU TO DIE!

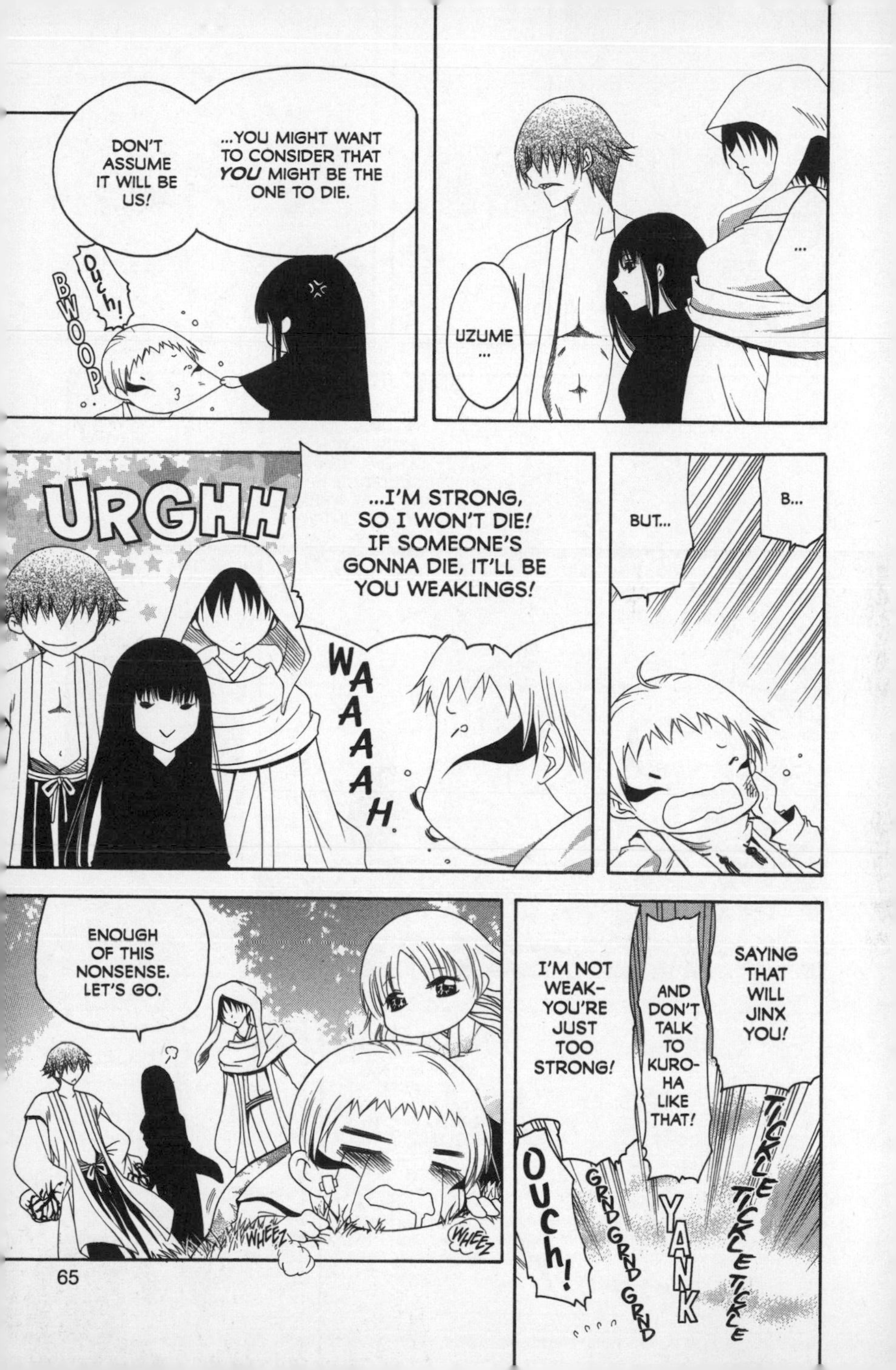
...
UZUME ...
...YOU MIGHT WANT TO CONSIDER THAT *YOU* MIGHT BE THE ONE TO DIE.
DON'T ASSUME IT WILL BE US!
Ouch!
BWOOP
B...
BUT...
...I'M STRONG, SO I WON'T DIE! IF SOMEONE'S GONNA DIE, IT'LL BE YOU WEAKLINGS!
URGHH
WAAAAH.
SAYING THAT WILL JINX YOU!
AND DON'T TALK TO KURO-HA LIKE THAT!
I'M NOT WEAK- YOU'RE JUST TOO STRONG!
TICKLE TICKLE TICKLE
YANK
GRND GRND GRND
OUCH!
ENOUGH OF THIS NONSENSE. LET'S GO.
WHEEZ
WHEEZ

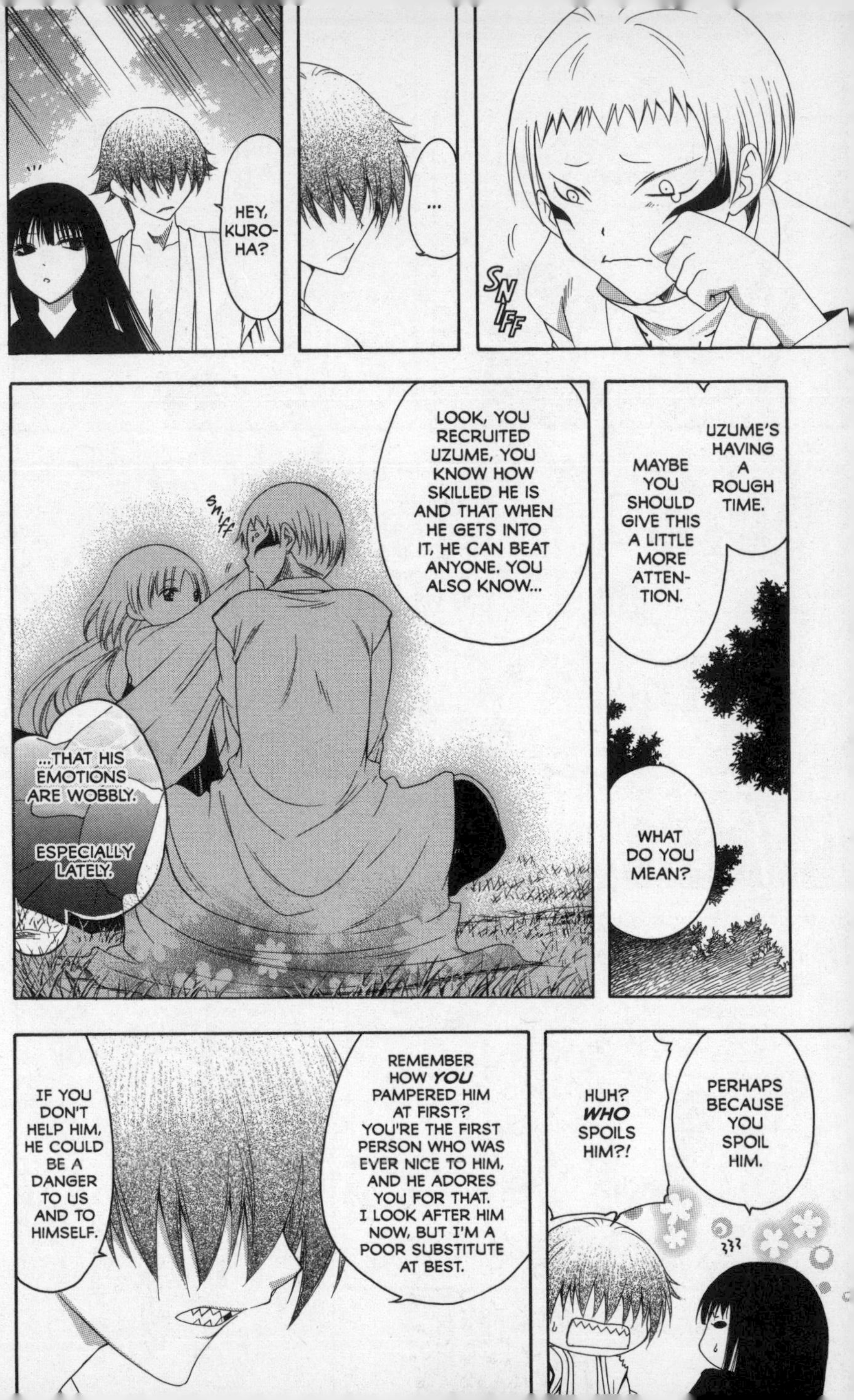
SNIFF
...
HEY, KURO-HA?
UZUME'S HAVING A ROUGH TIME.
MAYBE YOU SHOULD GIVE THIS A LITTLE MORE ATTEN-TION.
WHAT DO YOU MEAN?
LOOK, YOU RECRUITED UZUME, YOU KNOW HOW SKILLED HE IS AND THAT WHEN HE GETS INTO IT, HE CAN BEAT ANYONE. YOU ALSO KNOW...
sniff
...THAT HIS EMOTIONS ARE WOBBLY.
ESPECIALLY LATELY.
PERHAPS BECAUSE YOU SPOIL HIM.
HUH? *WHO* SPOILS HIM?!
REMEMBER HOW *YOU* PAMPERED HIM AT FIRST? YOU'RE THE FIRST PERSON WHO WAS EVER NICE TO HIM, AND HE ADORES YOU FOR THAT. I LOOK AFTER HIM NOW, BUT I'M A POOR SUBSTITUTE AT BEST.
IF YOU DON'T HELP HIM, HE COULD BE A DANGER TO US AND TO HIMSELF.

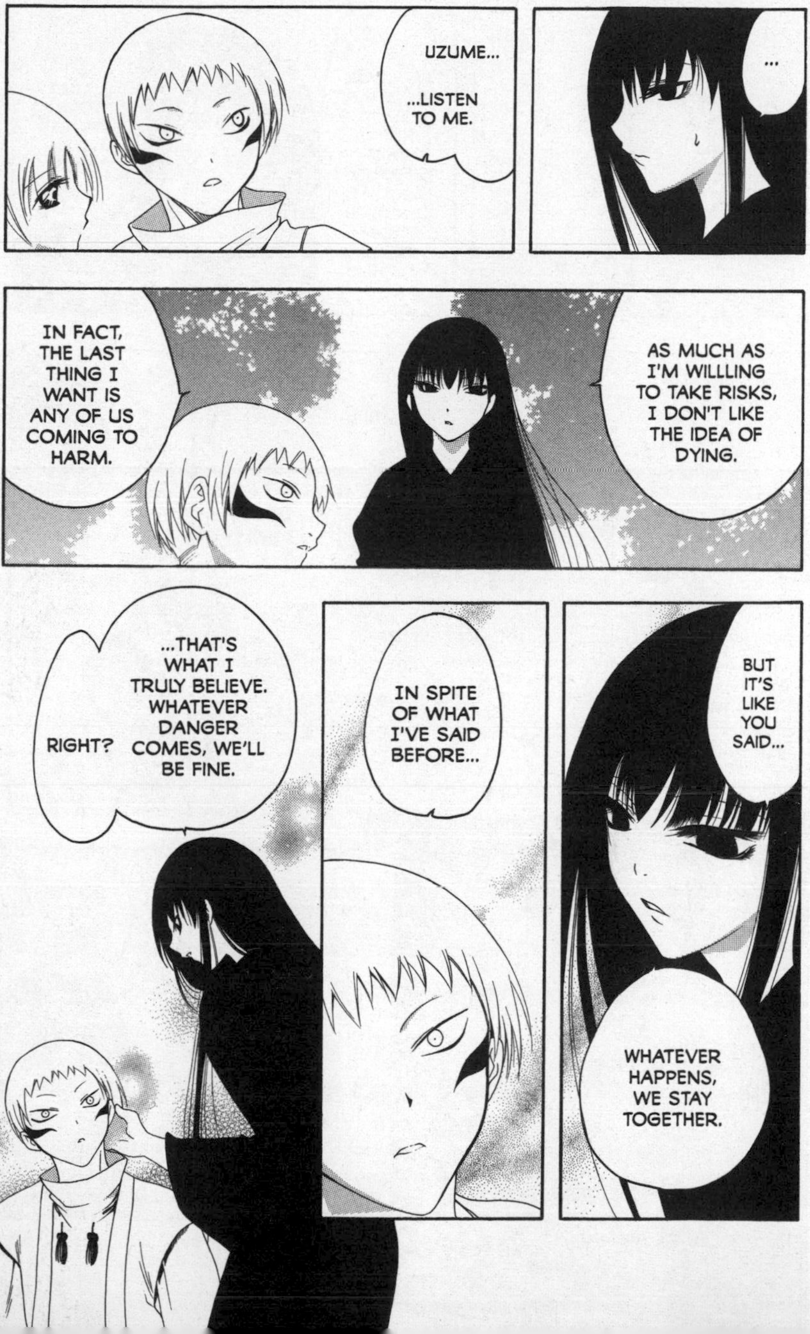
...
UZUME...
...LISTEN TO ME.
AS MUCH AS I'M WILLLING TO TAKE RISKS, I DON'T LIKE THE IDEA OF DYING.
IN FACT, THE LAST THING I WANT IS ANY OF US COMING TO HARM.
BUT IT'S LIKE YOU SAID...
WHATEVER HAPPENS, WE STAY TOGETHER.
IN SPITE OF WHAT I'VE SAID BEFORE...
...THAT'S WHAT I TRULY BELIEVE. WHATEVER DANGER COMES, WE'LL BE FINE.
RIGHT?

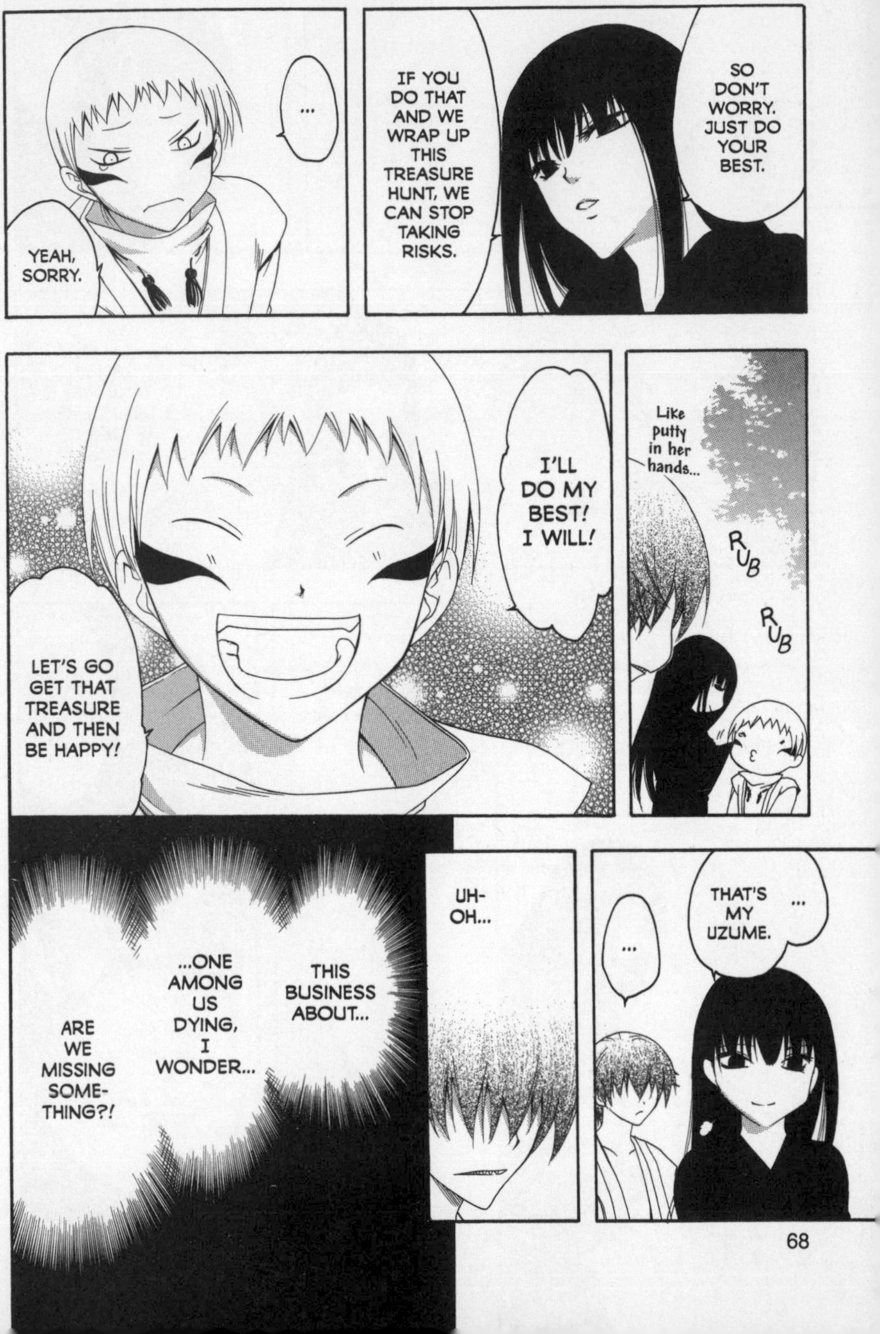
SO DON'T WORRY. JUST DO YOUR BEST.
IF YOU DO THAT AND WE WRAP UP THIS TREASURE HUNT, WE CAN STOP TAKING RISKS.
...
YEAH, SORRY.
Like putty in her hands...
RUB
RUB
I'LL DO MY BEST! I WILL!
LET'S GO GET THAT TREASURE AND THEN BE HAPPY!
THAT'S MY UZUME.
...
...
UH-OH...
THIS BUSINESS ABOUT...
...ONE AMONG US DYING, I WONDER...
ARE WE MISSING SOME-THING?!

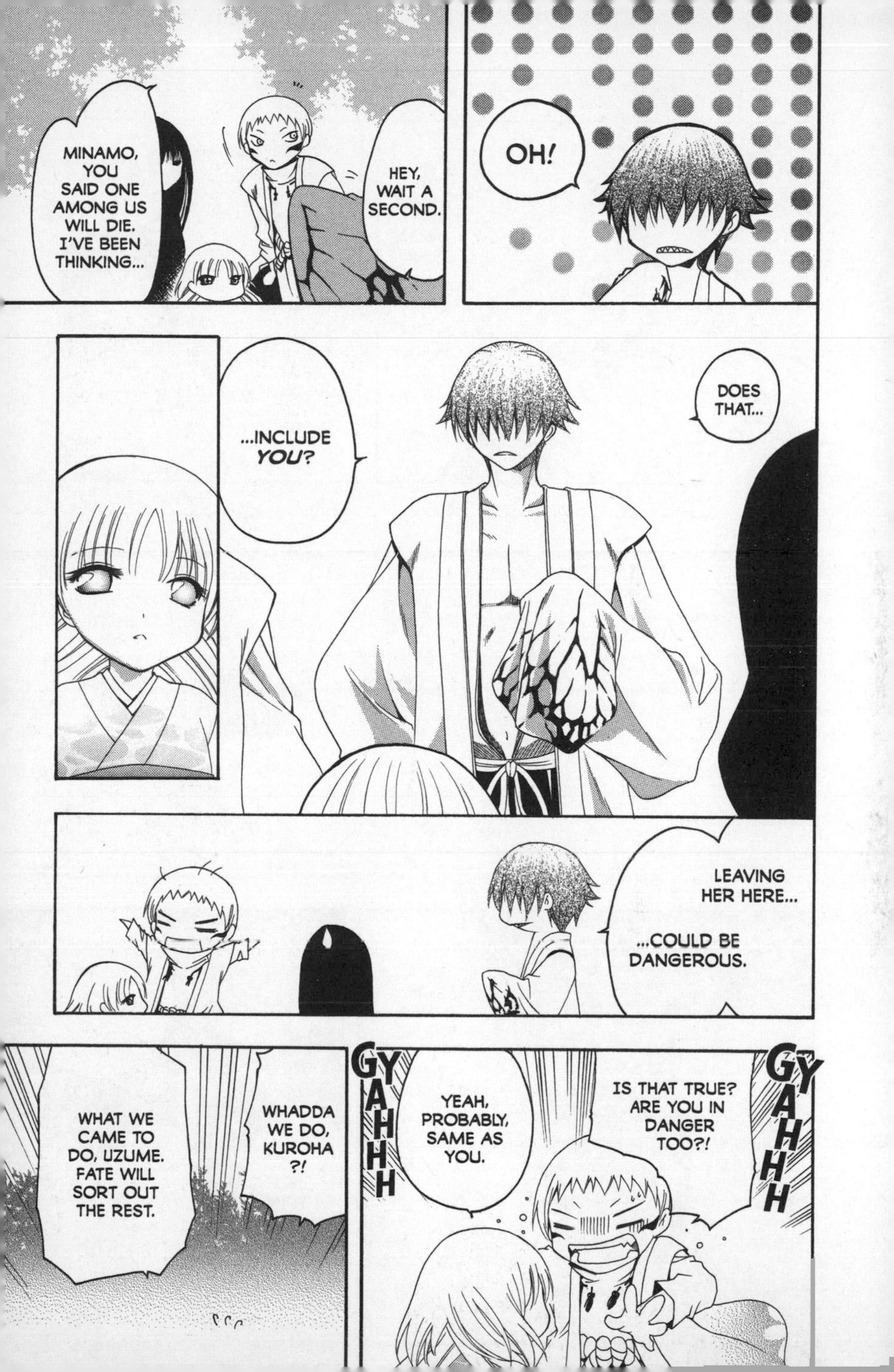
OH!
HEY, WAIT A SECOND.
MINAMO, YOU SAID ONE AMONG US WILL DIE. I'VE BEEN THINKING...
DOES THAT...
...INCLUDE *YOU*?
LEAVING HER HERE...
...COULD BE DANGEROUS.
GYAHHH
IS THAT TRUE? ARE YOU IN DANGER TOO?!
YEAH, PROBABLY, SAME AS YOU.
GYAHHH
WHADDA WE DO, KUROHA?!
WHAT WE CAME TO DO, UZUME. FATE WILL SORT OUT THE REST.

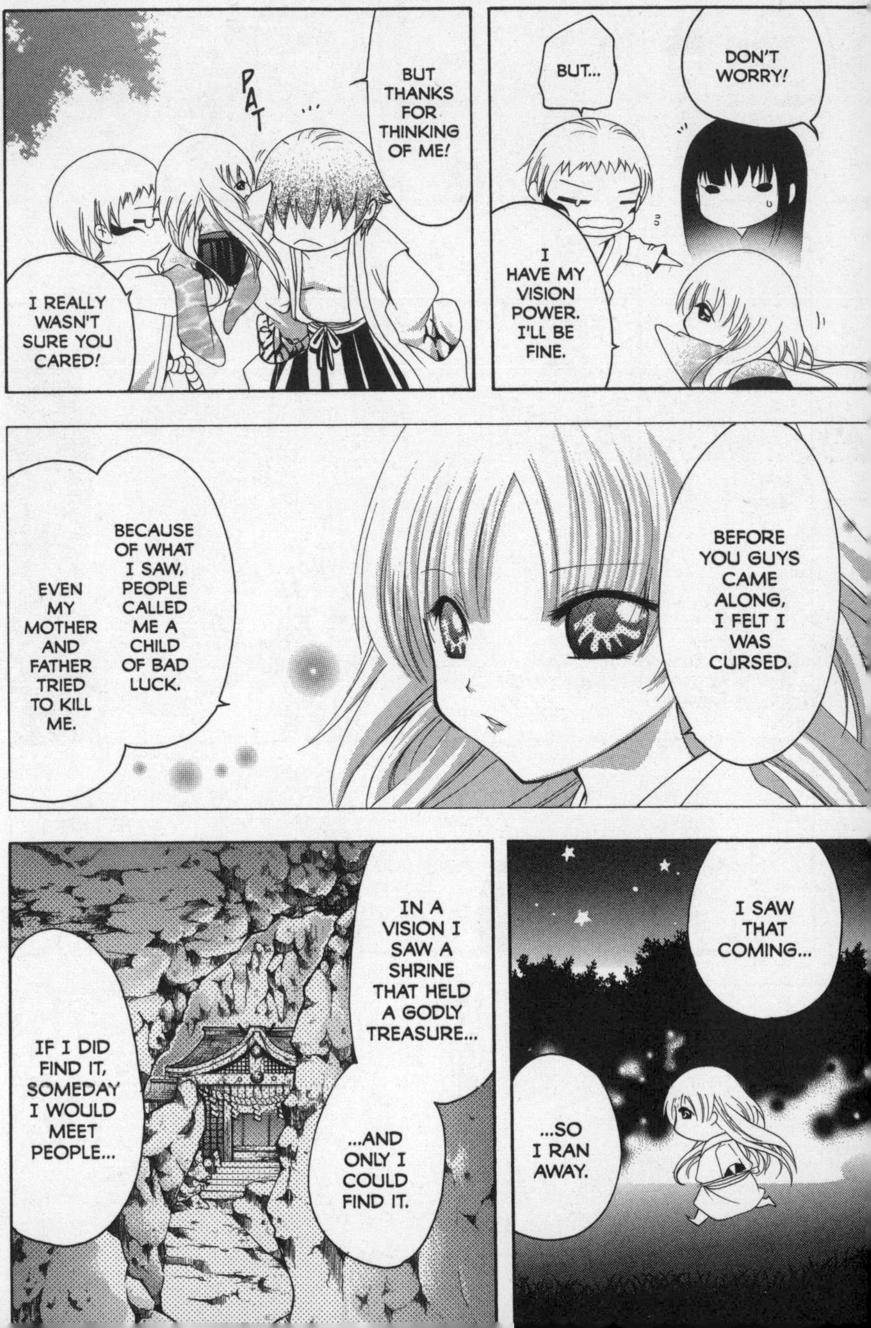
DON'T WORRY!
BUT...
I HAVE MY VISION POWER. I'LL BE FINE.
BUT THANKS FOR THINKING OF ME!
PAT
...
I REALLY WASN'T SURE YOU CARED!
BEFORE YOU GUYS CAME ALONG, I FELT I WAS CURSED.
BECAUSE OF WHAT I SAW, PEOPLE CALLED ME A CHILD OF BAD LUCK.
EVEN MY MOTHER AND FATHER TRIED TO KILL ME.
I SAW THAT COMING...
...SO I RAN AWAY.
IN A VISION I SAW A SHRINE THAT HELD A GODLY TREASURE...
...AND ONLY I COULD FIND IT.
IF I DID FIND IT, SOMEDAY I WOULD MEET PEOPLE...

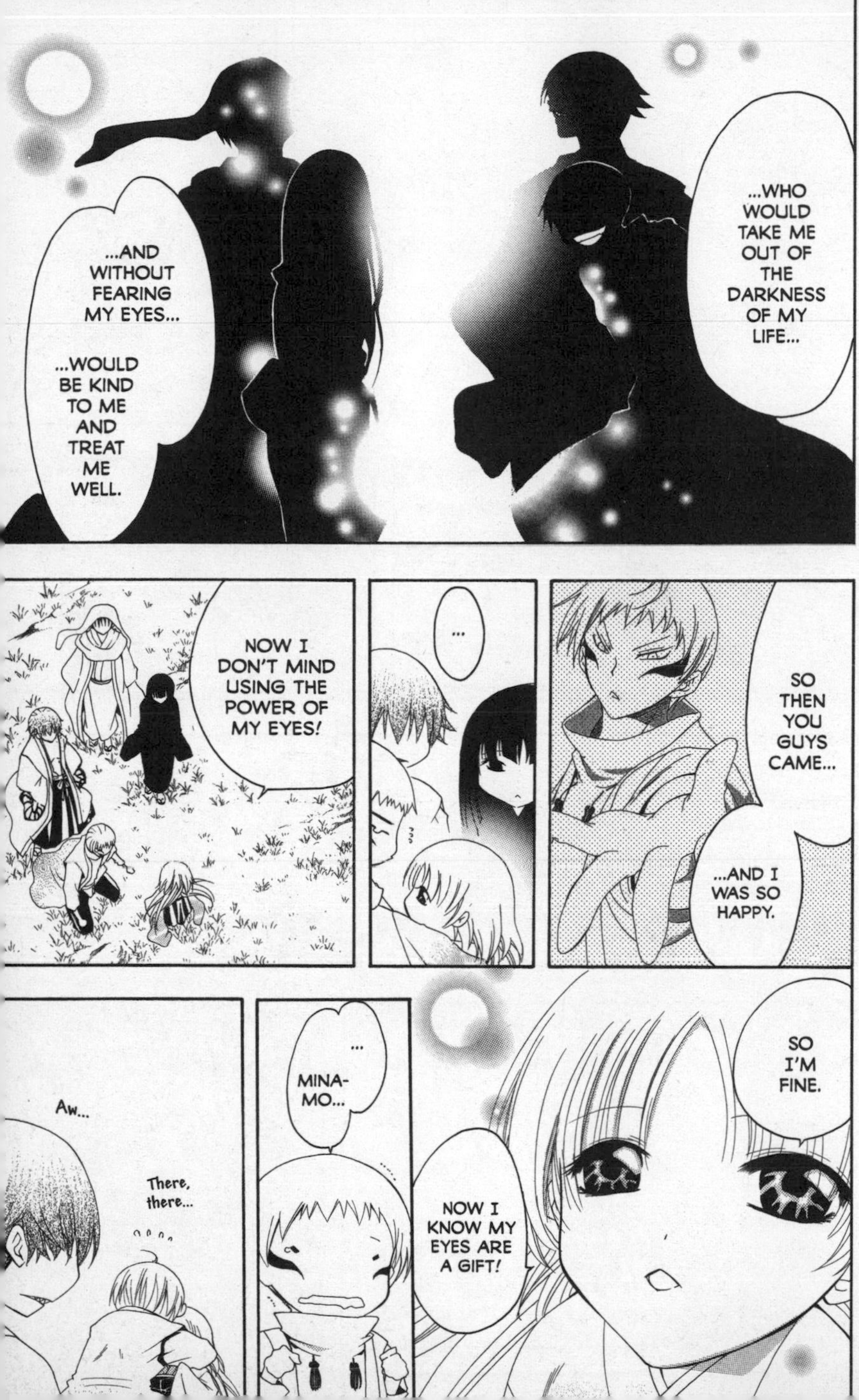
...WHO WOULD TAKE ME OUT OF THE DARKNESS OF MY LIFE...
...AND WITHOUT FEARING MY EYES...
...WOULD BE KIND TO ME AND TREAT ME WELL.
SO THEN YOU GUYS CAME...
...AND I WAS SO HAPPY.
...
NOW I DON'T MIND USING THE POWER OF MY EYES!
SO I'M FINE.
NOW I KNOW MY EYES ARE A GIFT!
...
MINA-MO...
Aw...
There, there...

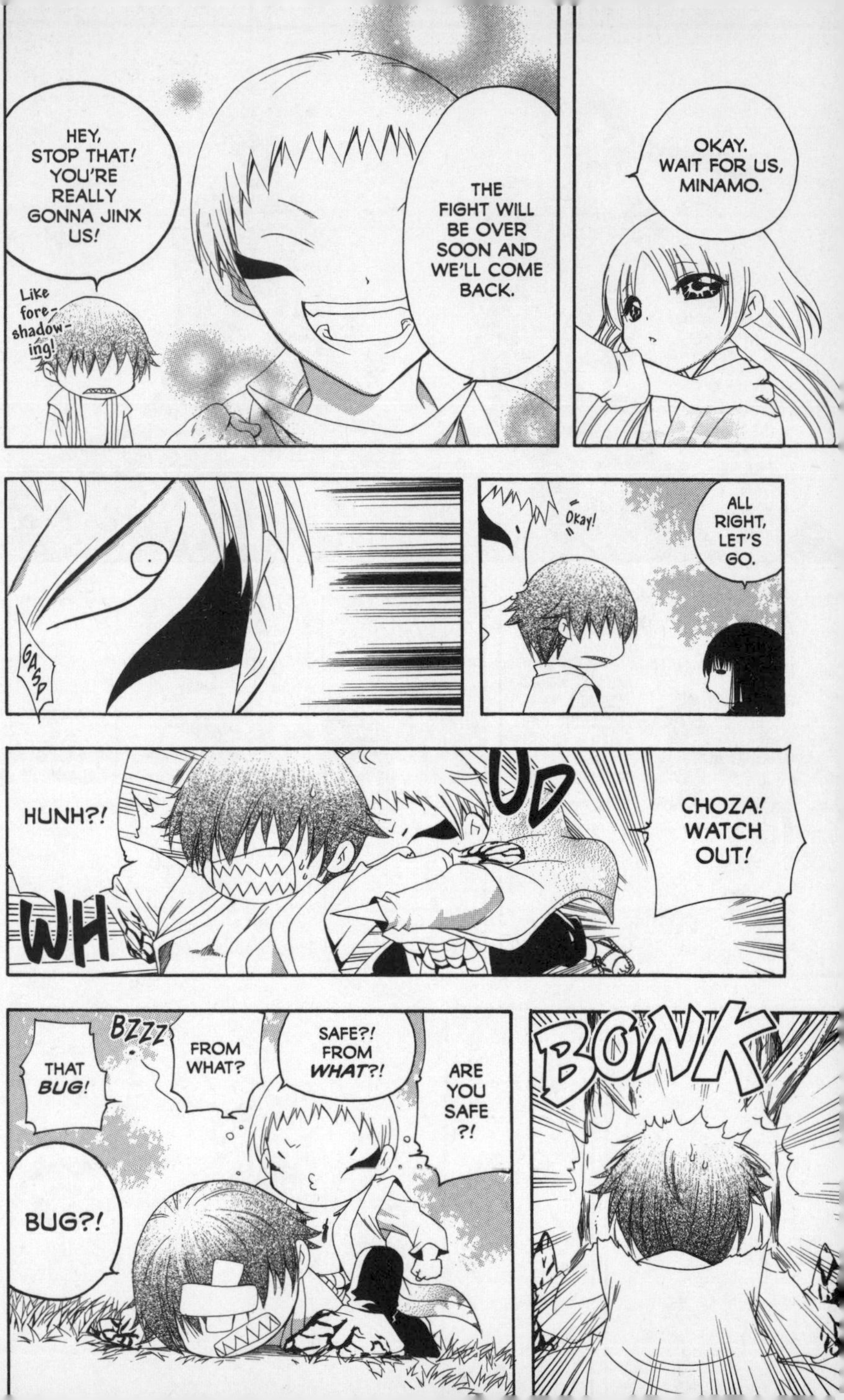
OKAY. WAIT FOR US, MINAMO.
THE FIGHT WILL BE OVER SOON AND WE'LL COME BACK.
HEY, STOP THAT! YOU'RE REALLY GONNA JINX US!
Like fore-shadow-ing!
ALL RIGHT, LET'S GO.
Okay!
GASP
CHOZA! WATCH OUT!
OD
HUNH?!
WH
BONK
ARE YOU SAFE?!
SAFE?! FROM *WHAT*?!
FROM WHAT?
BZZZ
THAT *BUG*!
BUG?!

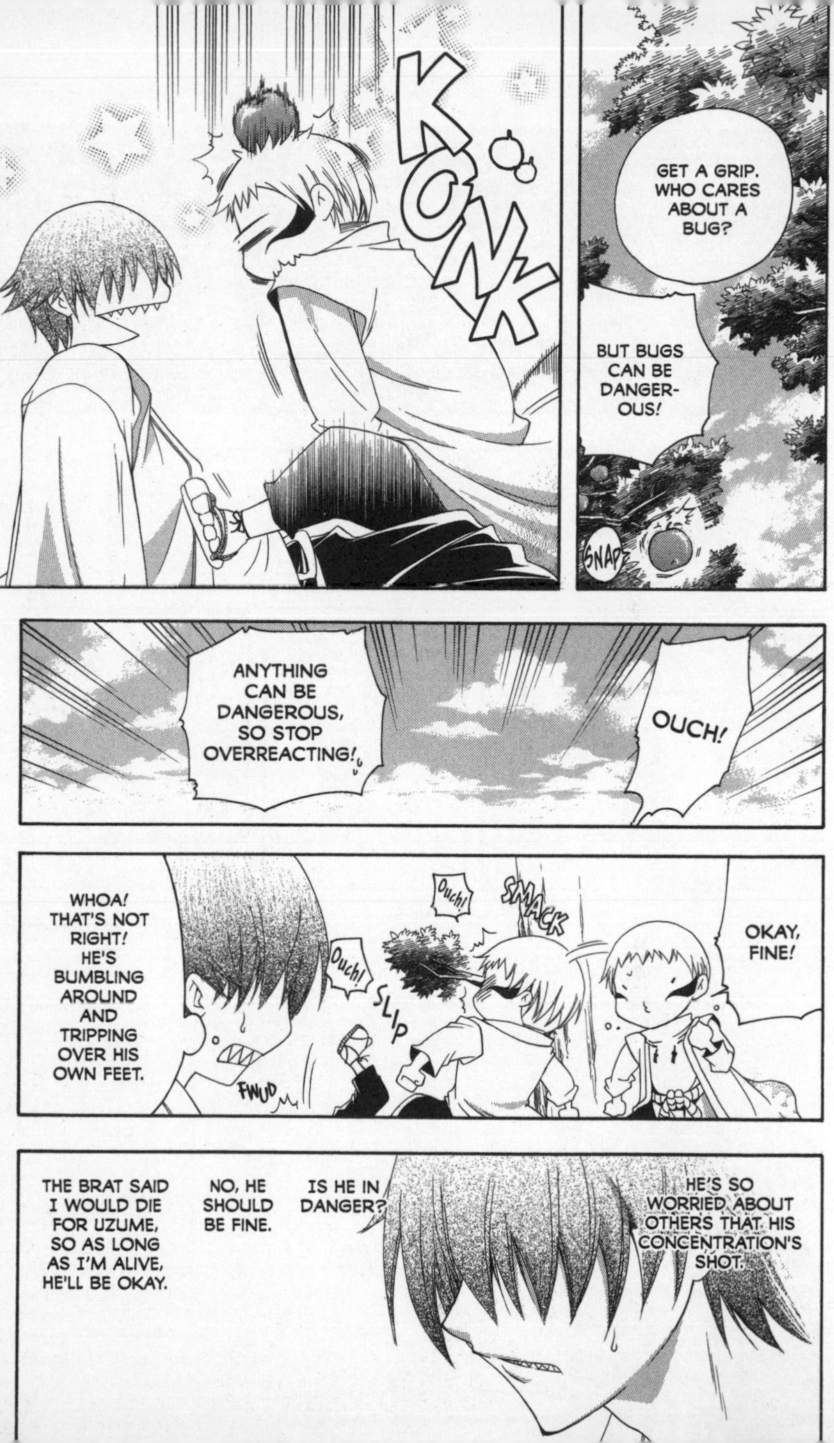
GET A GRIP. WHO CARES ABOUT A BUG?
BUT BUGS CAN BE DANGEROUS!
SNAP
KONK
OUCH!
ANYTHING CAN BE DANGEROUS, SO STOP OVERREACTING!
OKAY, FINE!
SMACK
Ouch!
Ouch!
SLIP
FWUD
WHOA! THAT'S NOT RIGHT! HE'S BUMBLING AROUND AND TRIPPING OVER HIS OWN FEET.
HE'S SO WORRIED ABOUT OTHERS THAT HIS CONCENTRATION'S SHOT.
IS HE IN DANGER?
NO, HE SHOULD BE FINE.
THE BRAT SAID I WOULD DIE FOR UZUME, SO AS LONG AS I'M ALIVE, HE'LL BE OKAY.

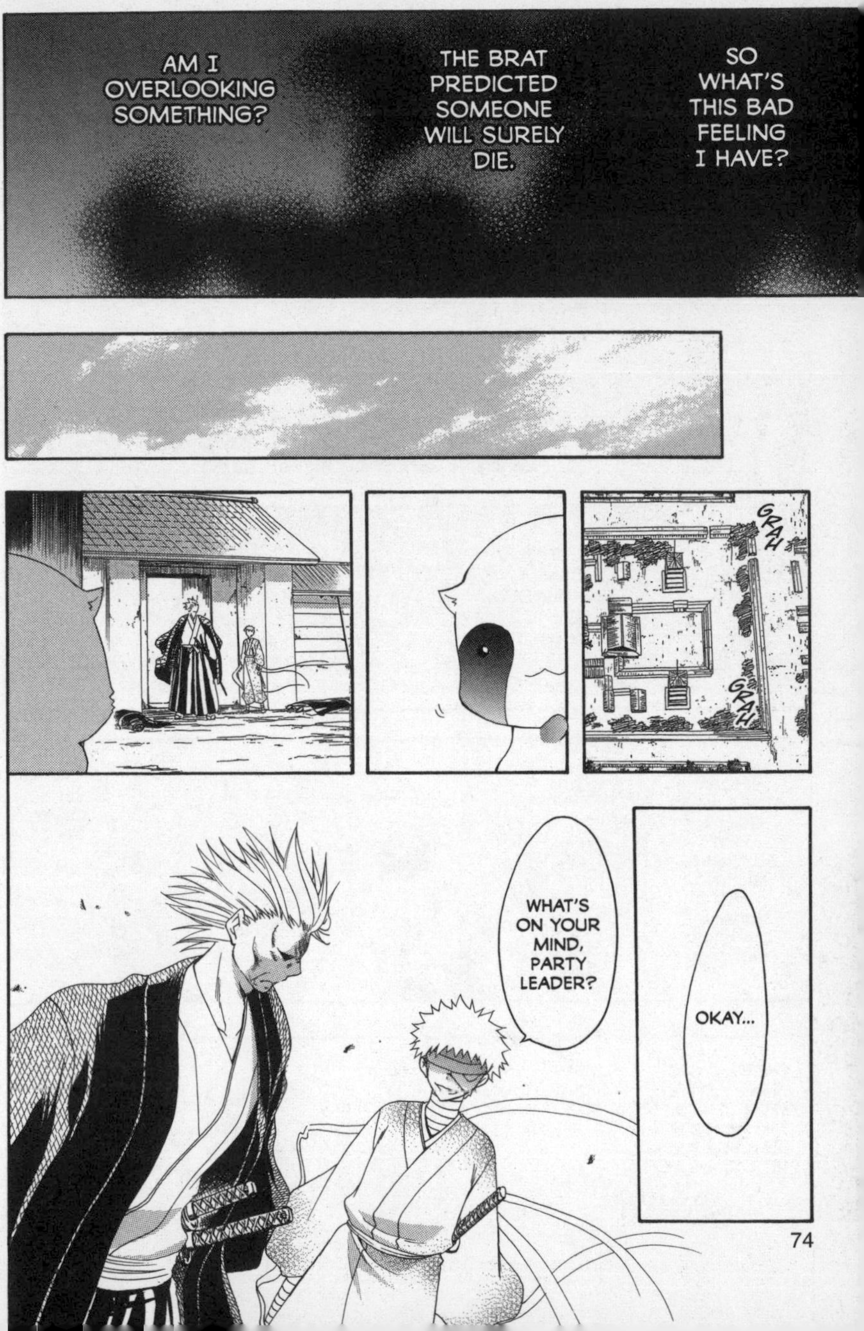
SO WHAT'S THIS BAD FEELING I HAVE?
THE BRAT PREDICTED SOMEONE WILL SURELY DIE.
AM I OVERLOOKING SOMETHING?
GRAH
GRAH
OKAY...
WHAT'S ON YOUR MIND, PARTY LEADER?

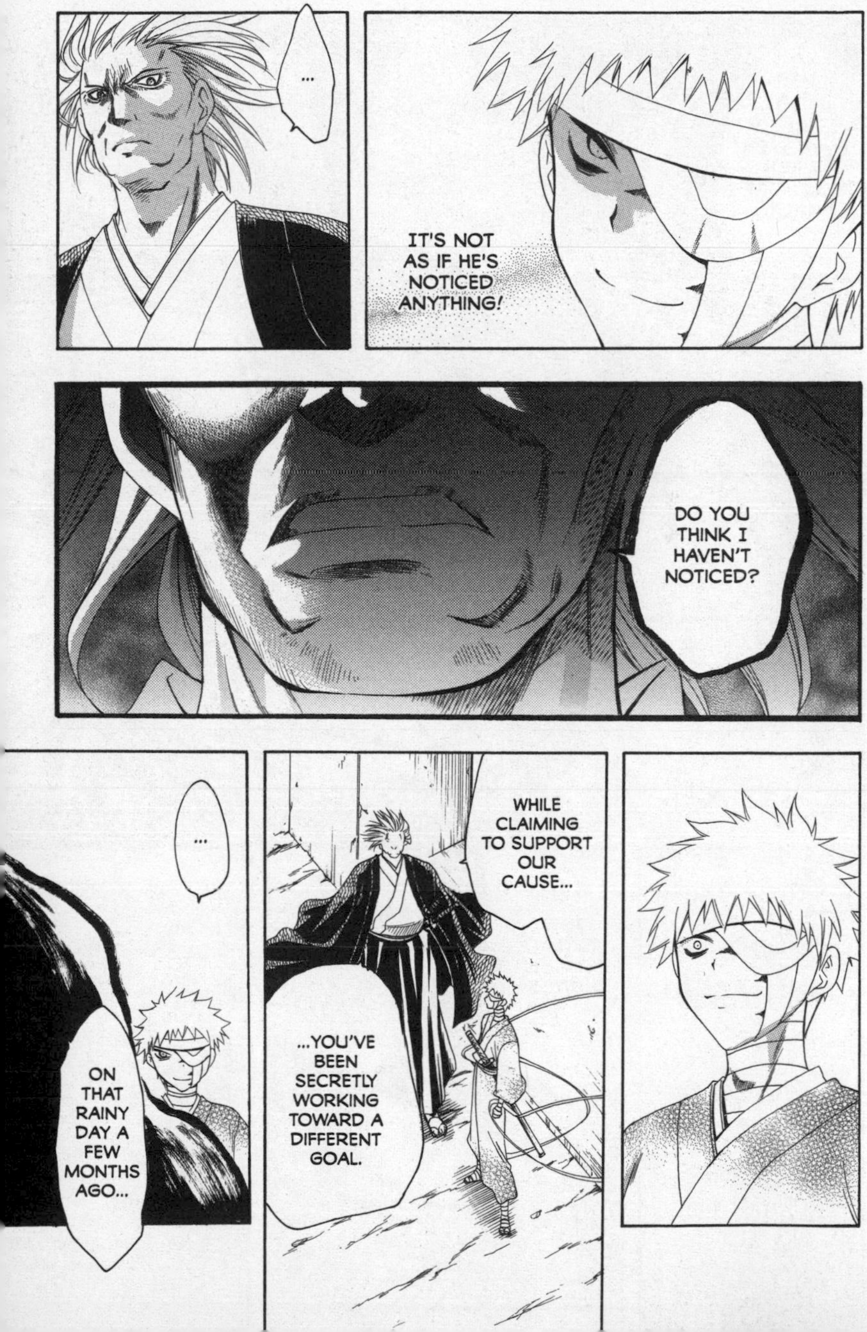
IT'S NOT AS IF HE'S NOTICED ANYTHING!
...
DO YOU THINK I HAVEN'T NOTICED?
WHILE CLAIMING TO SUPPORT OUR CAUSE...
...YOU'VE BEEN SECRETLY WORKING TOWARD A DIFFERENT GOAL.
...
ON THAT RAINY DAY A FEW MONTHS AGO...

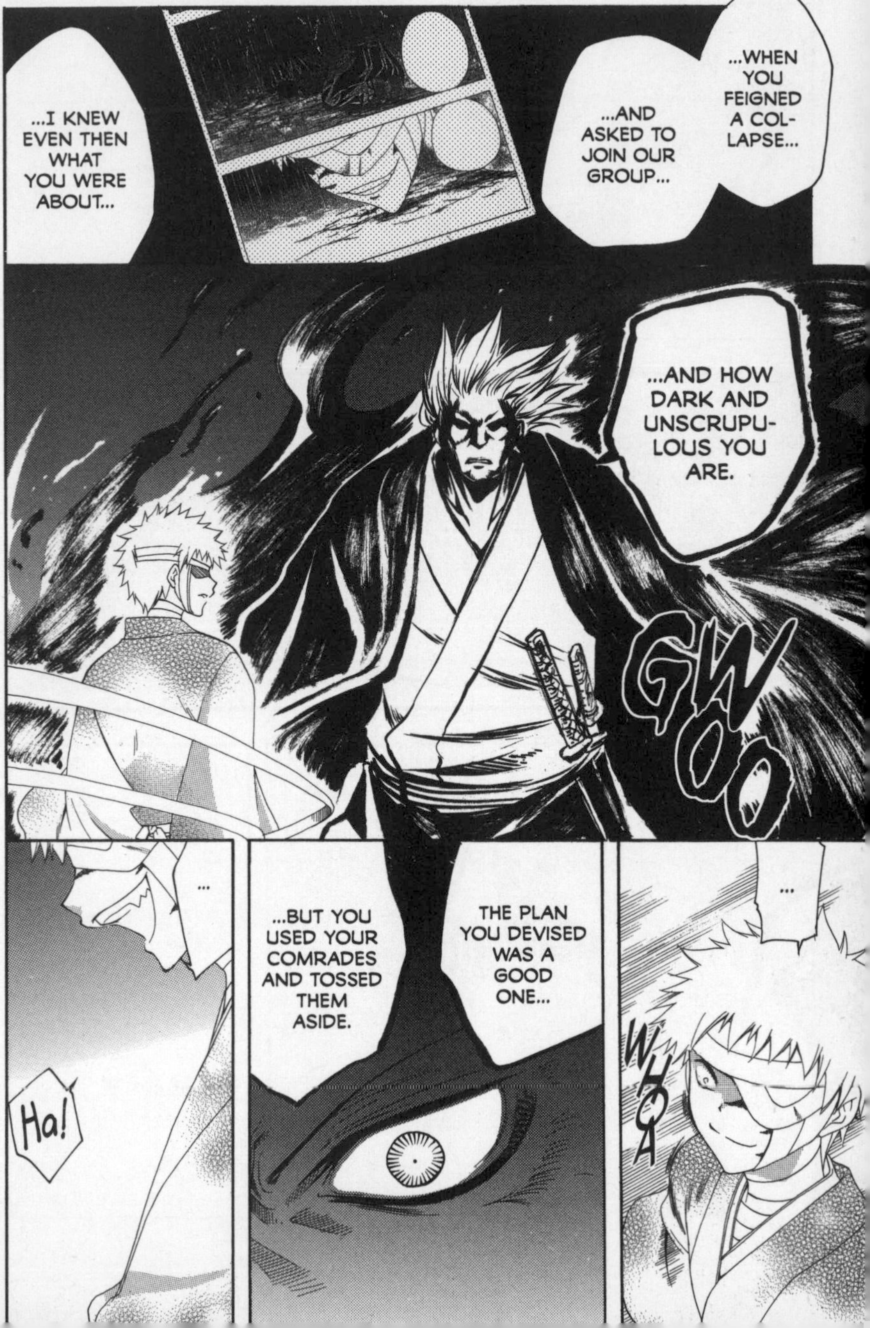
...WHEN YOU FEIGNED A COL-LAPSE...
...AND ASKED TO JOIN OUR GROUP...
...I KNEW EVEN THEN WHAT YOU WERE ABOUT...
...AND HOW DARK AND UNSCRUPU-LOUS YOU ARE.
GWOO
...
WHOA
THE PLAN YOU DEVISED WAS A GOOD ONE...
...BUT YOU USED YOUR COMRADES AND TOSSED THEM ASIDE.
...
Ha!

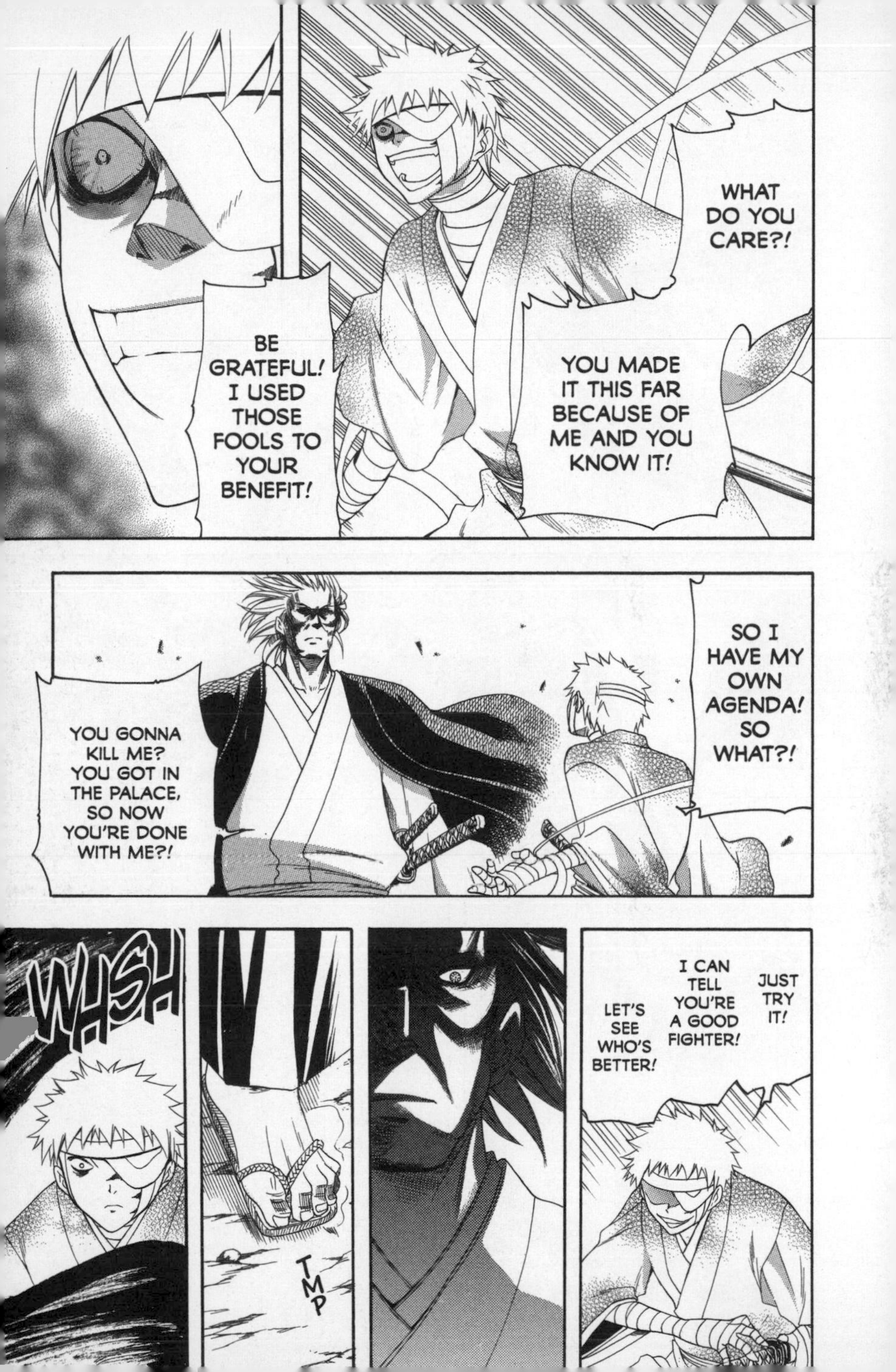
WHAT DO YOU CARE?!
YOU MADE IT THIS FAR BECAUSE OF ME AND YOU KNOW IT!
BE GRATEFUL! I USED THOSE FOOLS TO YOUR BENEFIT!
SO I HAVE MY OWN AGENDA! SO WHAT?!
YOU GONNA KILL ME? YOU GOT IN THE PALACE, SO NOW YOU'RE DONE WITH ME?!
JUST TRY IT!
I CAN TELL YOU'RE A GOOD FIGHTER!
LET'S SEE WHO'S BETTER!
TMP
WHSH

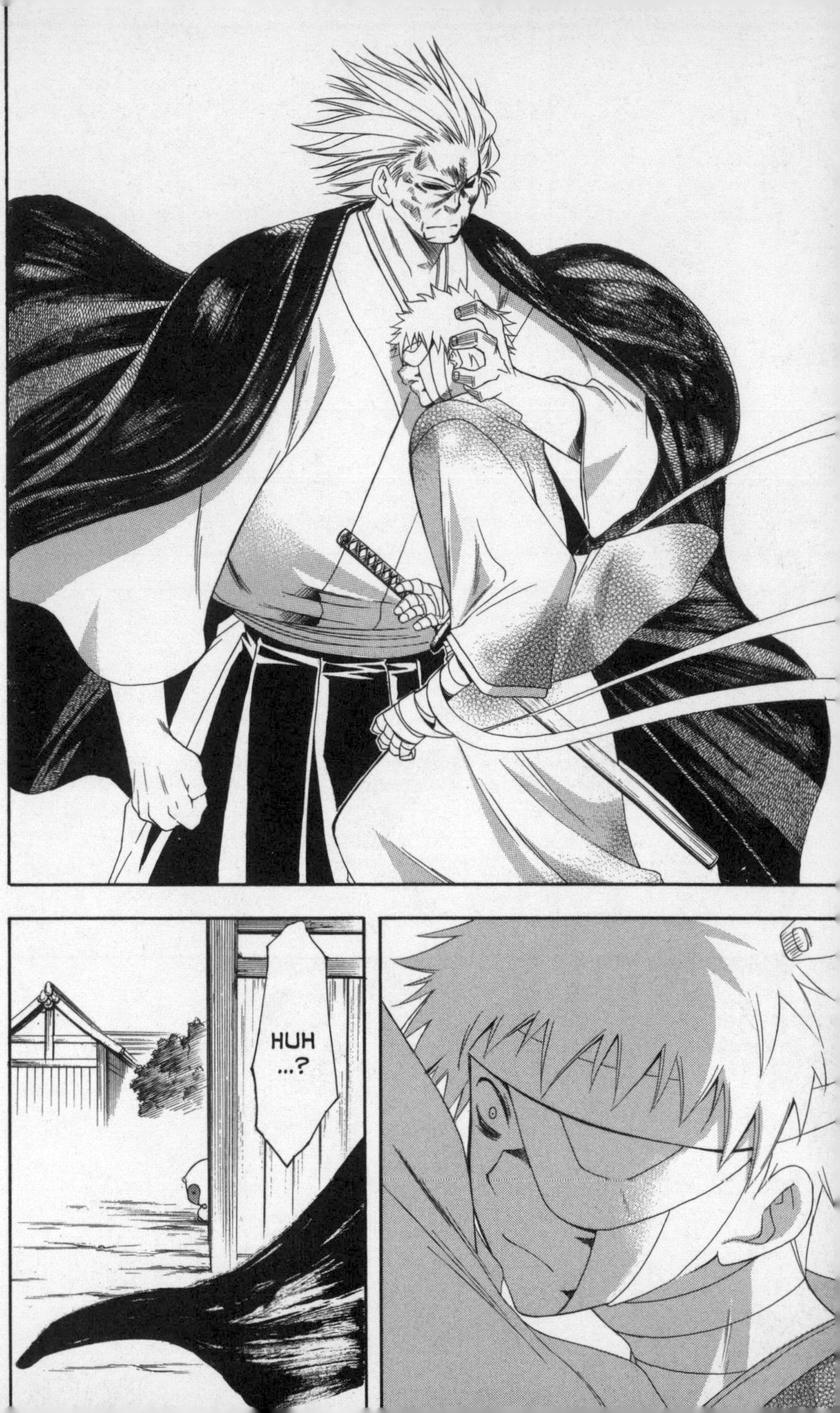
HUH ...?

Chapter 103 The Party Leader and Iriya

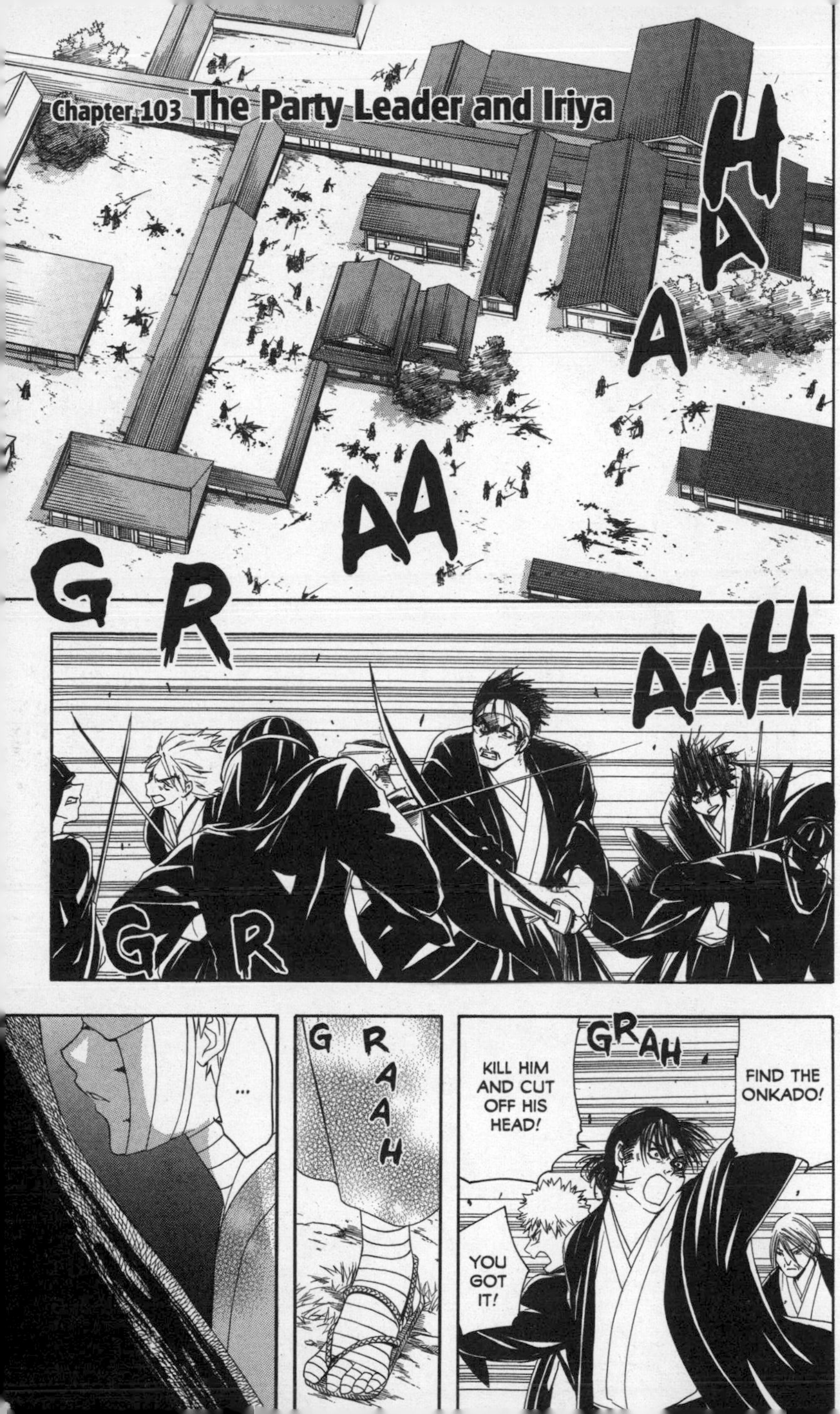
HAAA
AA
GR
AAH
GR
GRAH
FIND THE ONKADO!
KILL HIM AND CUT OFF HIS HEAD!
YOU GOT IT!
GRAAH
...

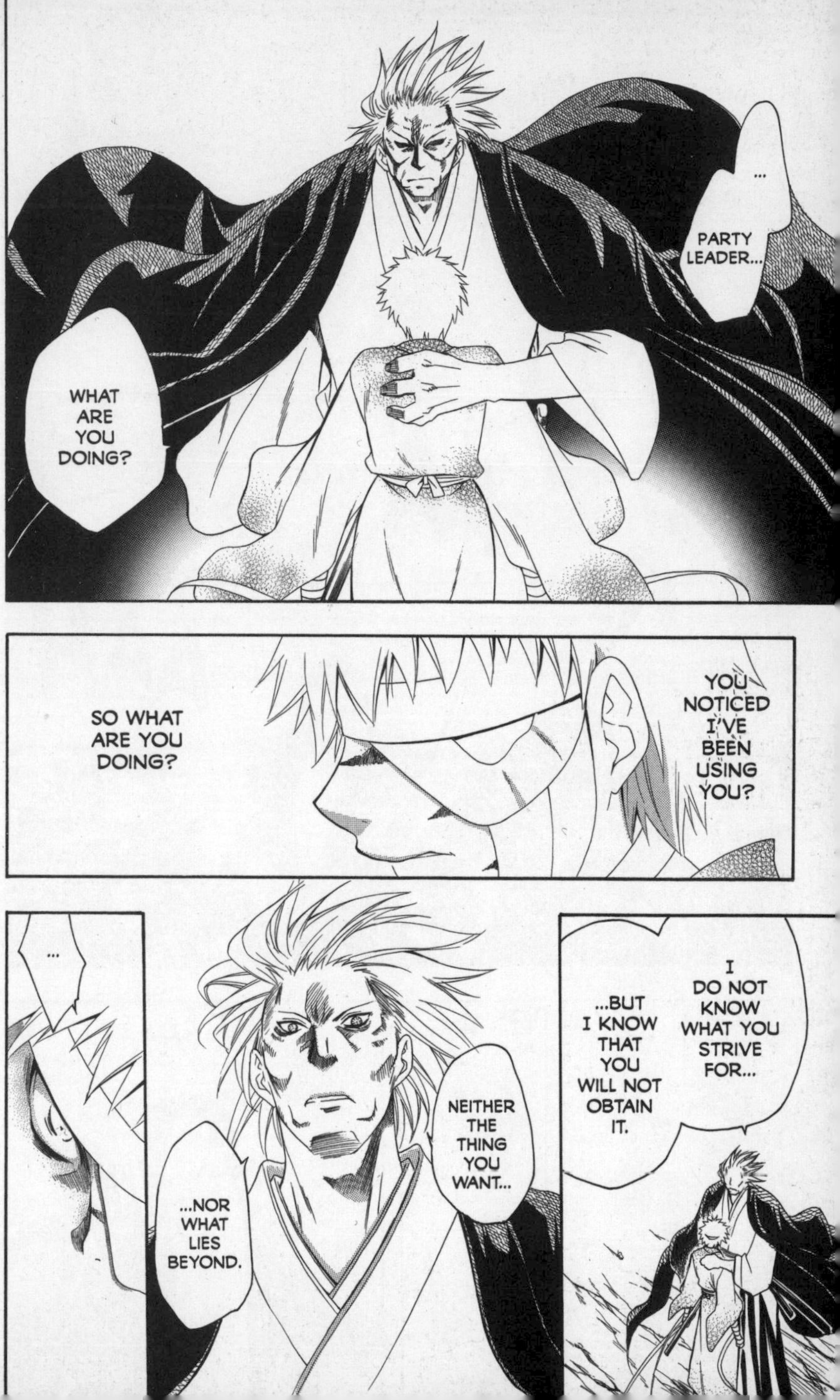
...
PARTY LEADER...
WHAT ARE YOU DOING?
YOU NOTICED I'VE BEEN USING YOU?
SO WHAT ARE YOU DOING?
I DO NOT KNOW WHAT YOU STRIVE FOR...
...BUT I KNOW THAT YOU WILL NOT OBTAIN IT.
NEITHER THE THING YOU WANT...
...NOR WHAT LIES BEYOND.
...

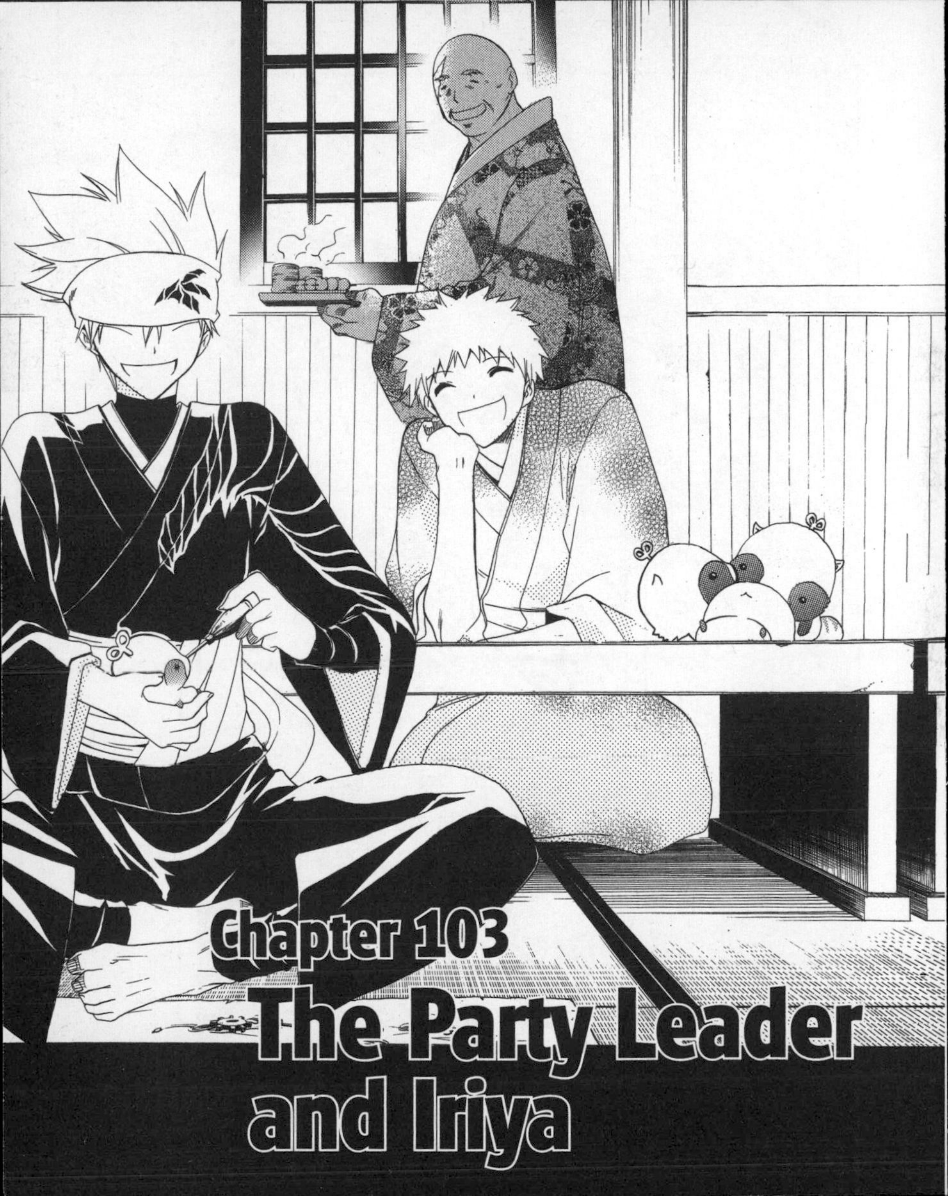
Chapter 103
The Party Leader and Iriya

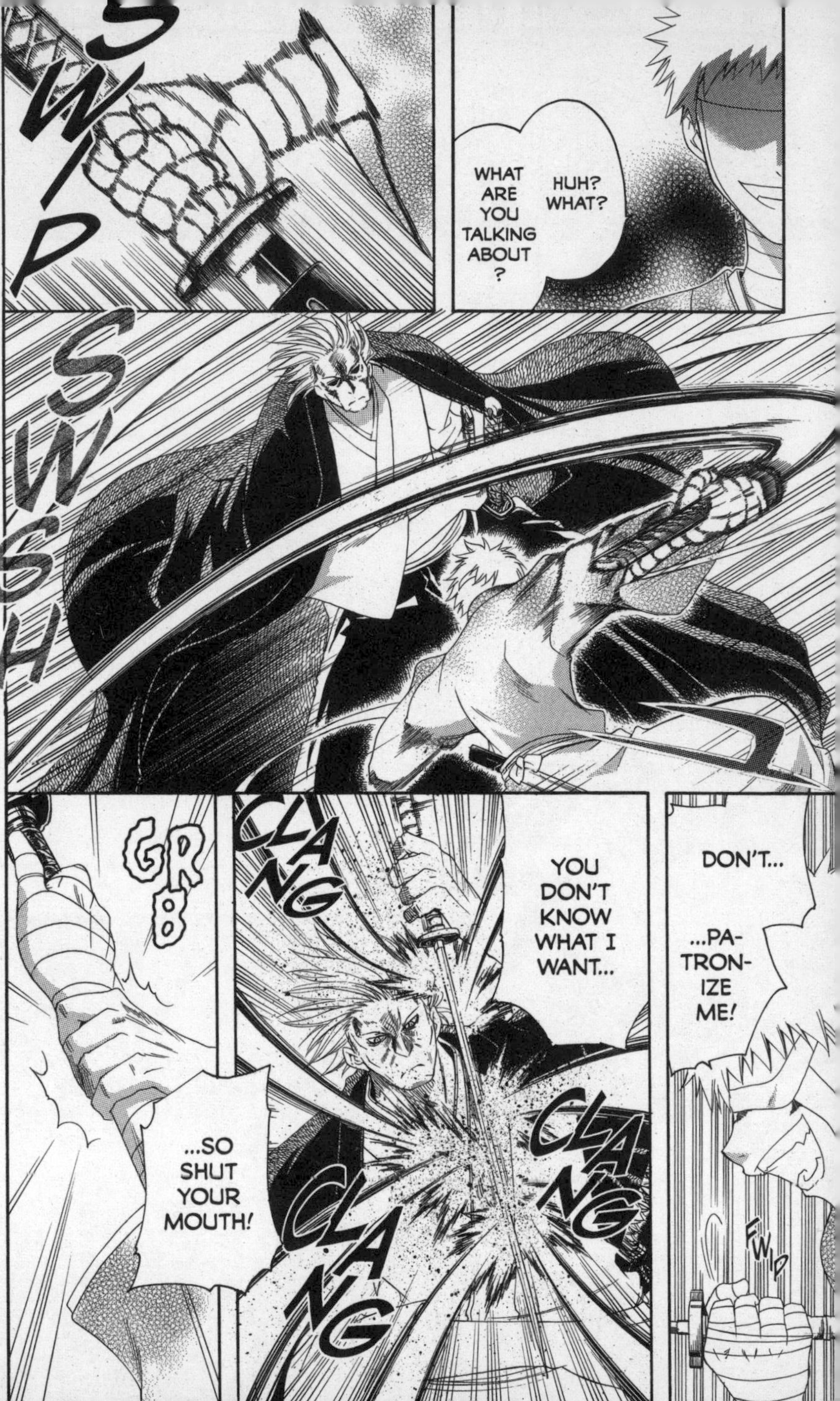
HUH? WHAT?
WHAT ARE YOU TALKING ABOUT?
SWIP
SWISH
DON'T...
...PA-TRON-IZE ME!
FWIP
YOU DON'T KNOW WHAT I WANT...
CLANG
CLANG
CLANG
GRB
...SO SHUT YOUR MOUTH!

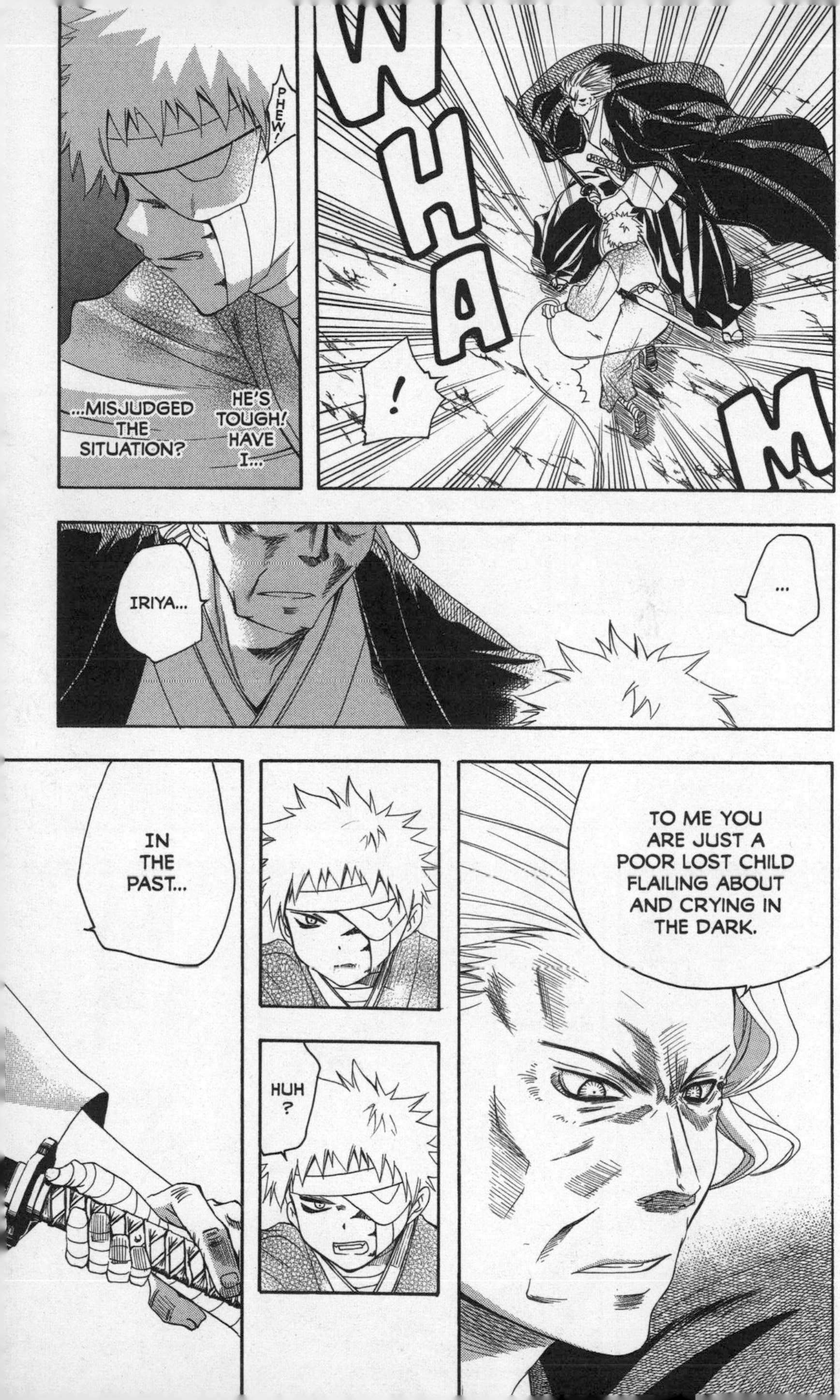

WHAM
!
PHEW!
HE'S TOUGH! HAVE I...
...MISJUDGED THE SITUATION?
...
IRIYA...
TO ME YOU ARE JUST A POOR LOST CHILD FLAILING ABOUT AND CRYING IN THE DARK.
HUH ?
IN THE PAST...

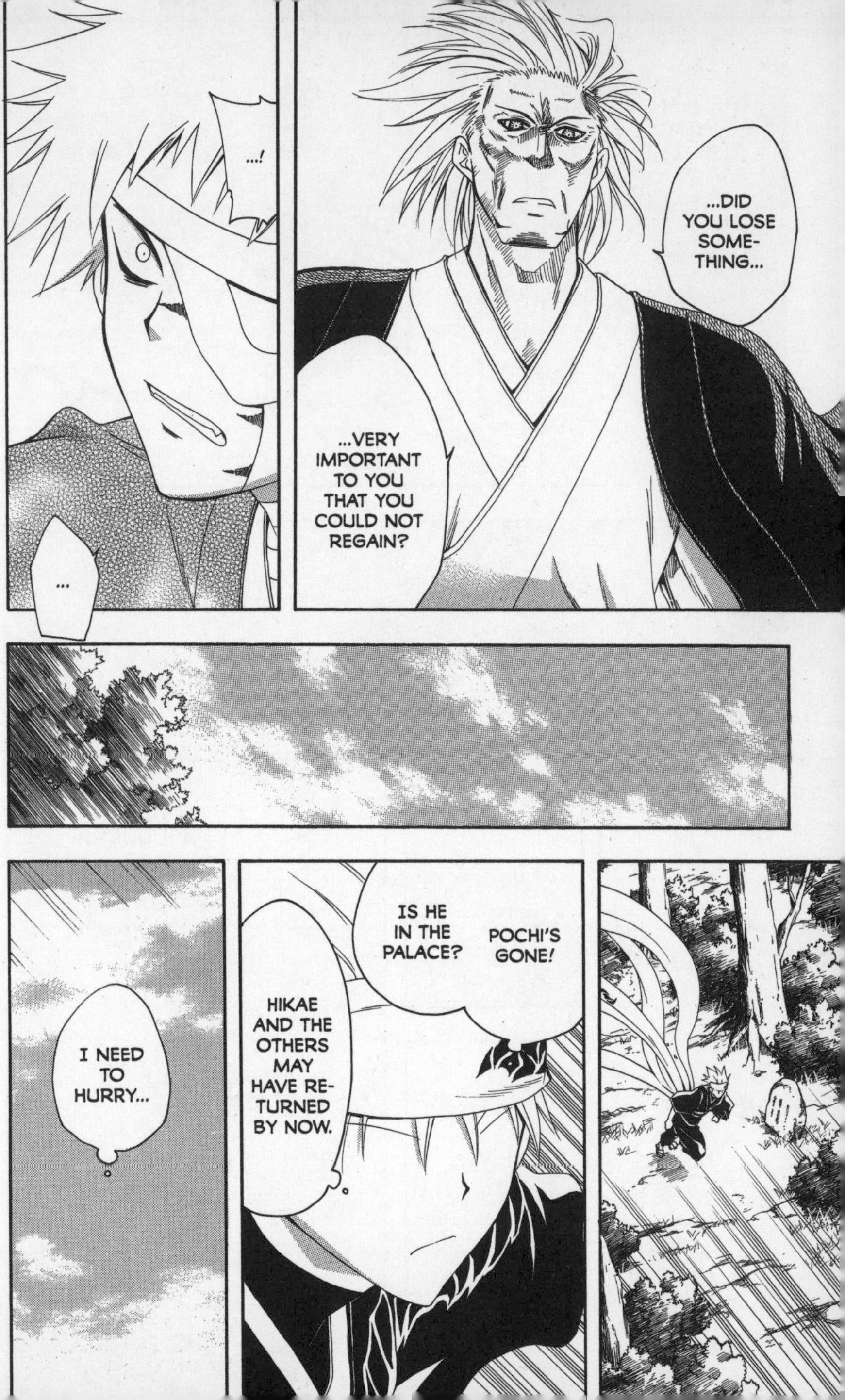
...DID YOU LOSE SOME-THING...
...VERY IMPORTANT TO YOU THAT YOU COULD NOT REGAIN?
...!
...
POCHI'S GONE!
IS HE IN THE PALACE?
HIKAE AND THE OTHERS MAY HAVE RE-TURNED BY NOW.
I NEED TO HURRY...

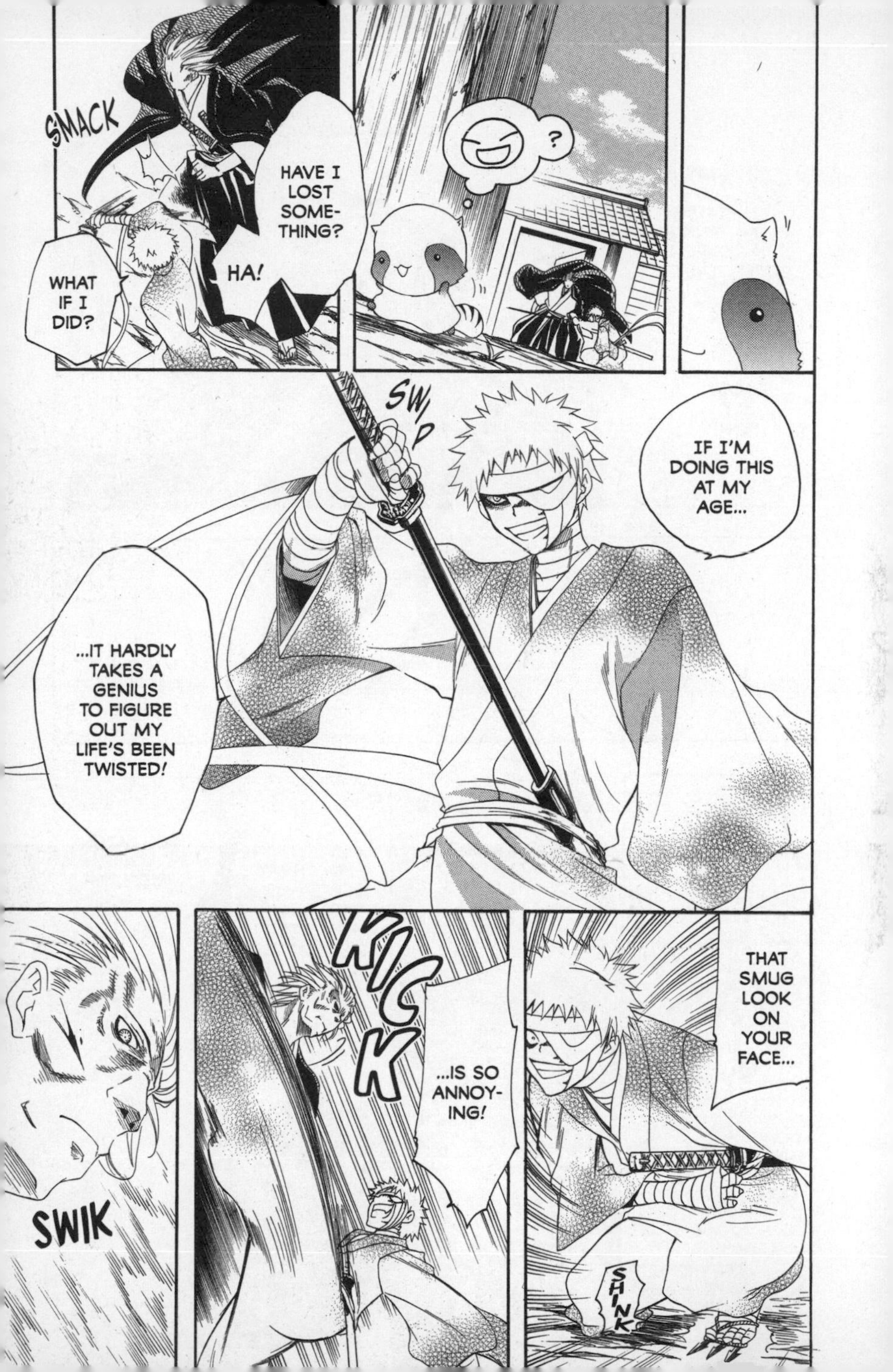
?
SMACK
HAVE I LOST SOMETHING?
HA!
WHAT IF I DID?
SWD
IF I'M DOING THIS AT MY AGE...
...IT HARDLY TAKES A GENIUS TO FIGURE OUT MY LIFE'S BEEN TWISTED!
THAT SMUG LOOK ON YOUR FACE...
SHINK
KICK
...IS SO ANNOYING!
SWIK

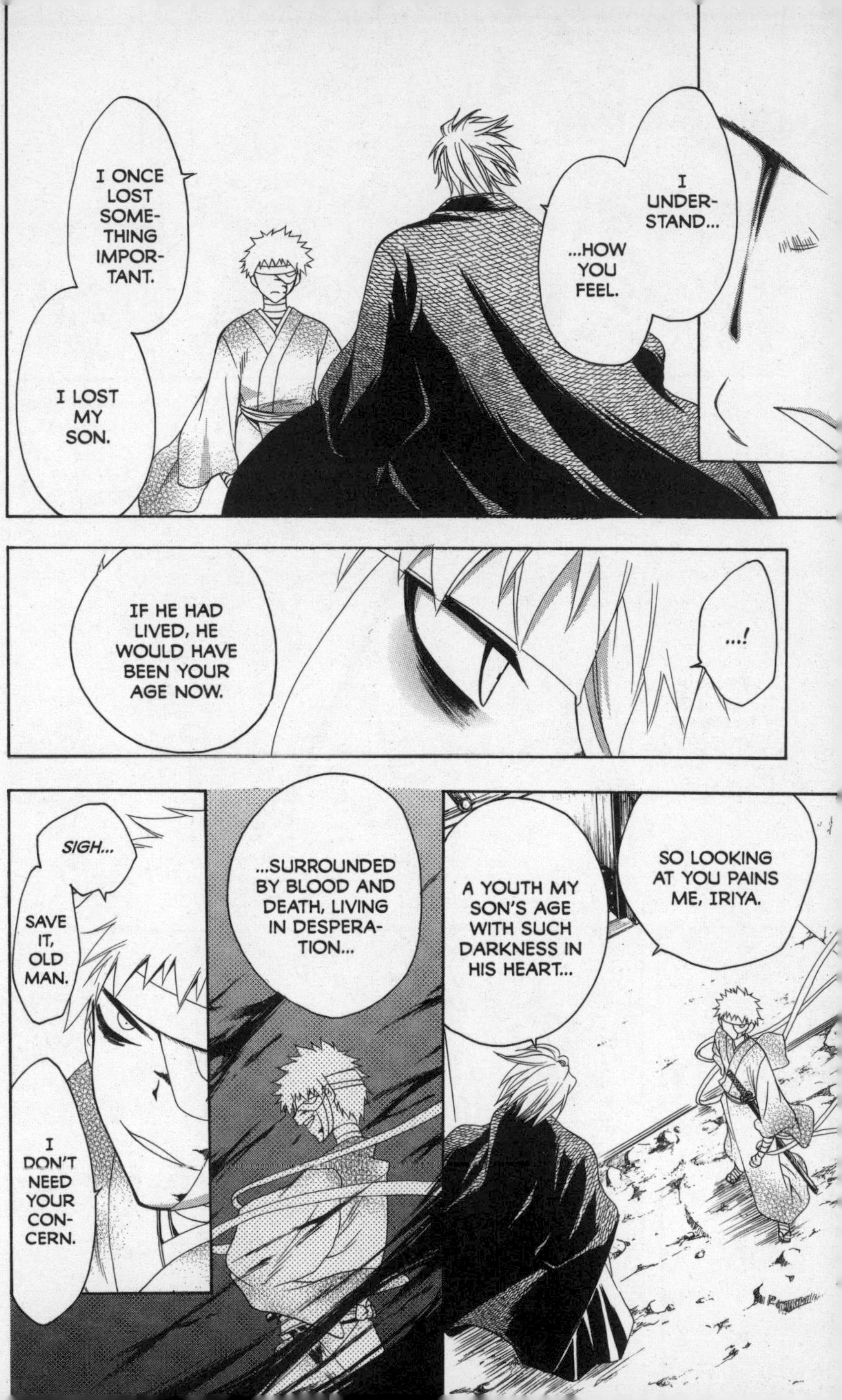
I UNDERSTAND...
...HOW YOU FEEL.
I ONCE LOST SOMETHING IMPORTANT.
I LOST MY SON.
...!
IF HE HAD LIVED, HE WOULD HAVE BEEN YOUR AGE NOW.
SO LOOKING AT YOU PAINS ME, IRIYA.
A YOUTH MY SON'S AGE WITH SUCH DARKNESS IN HIS HEART...
...SURROUNDED BY BLOOD AND DEATH, LIVING IN DESPERATION...
SIGH...
SAVE IT, OLD MAN.
I DON'T NEED YOUR CONCERN.

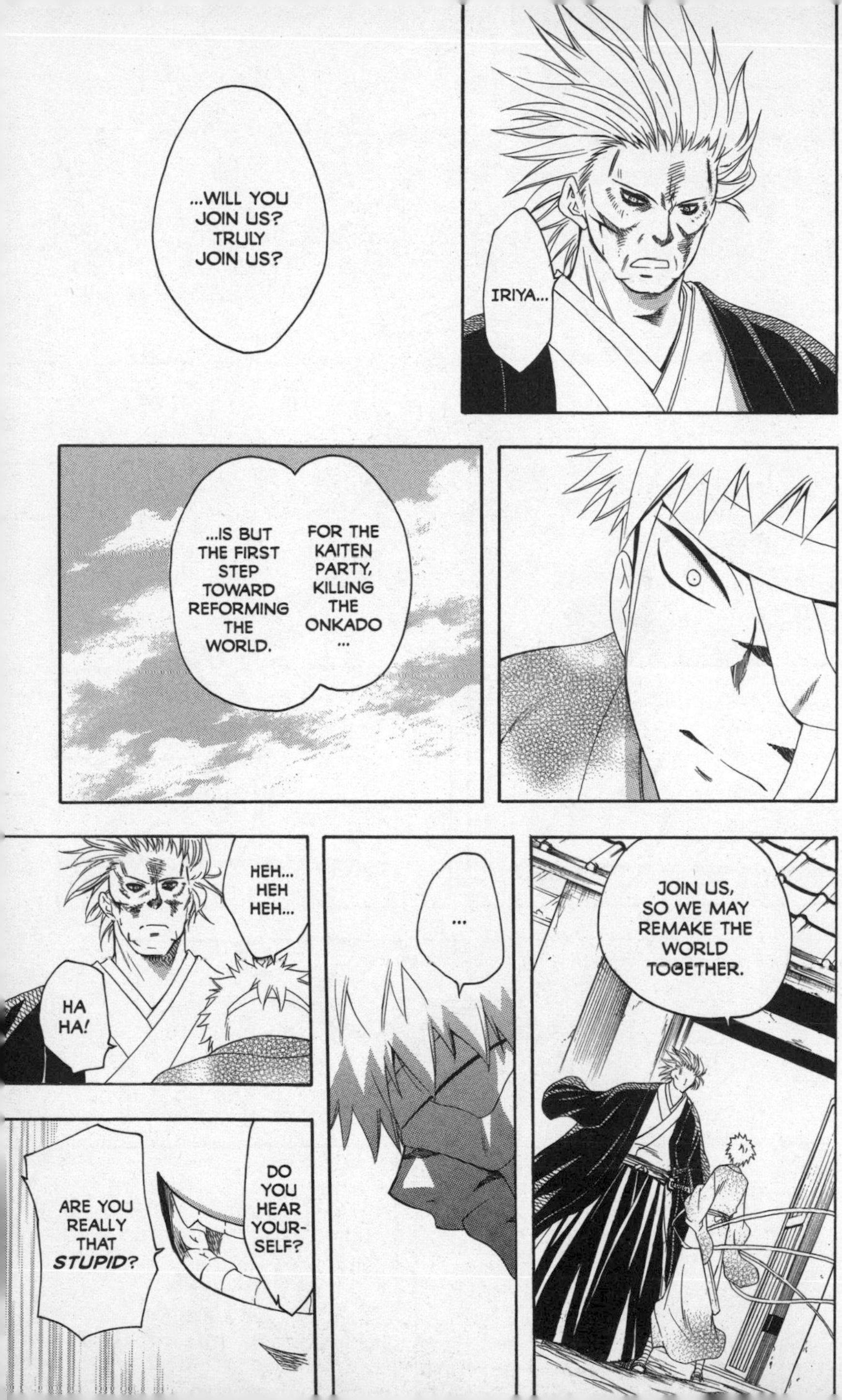
IRIYA...
...WILL YOU JOIN US? TRULY JOIN US?
FOR THE KAITEN PARTY, KILLING THE ONKADO ...
...IS BUT THE FIRST STEP TOWARD REFORMING THE WORLD.
JOIN US, SO WE MAY REMAKE THE WORLD TOGETHER.
...
HEH... HEH HEH...
HA HA!
DO YOU HEAR YOUR-SELF?
ARE YOU REALLY THAT *STUPID*?

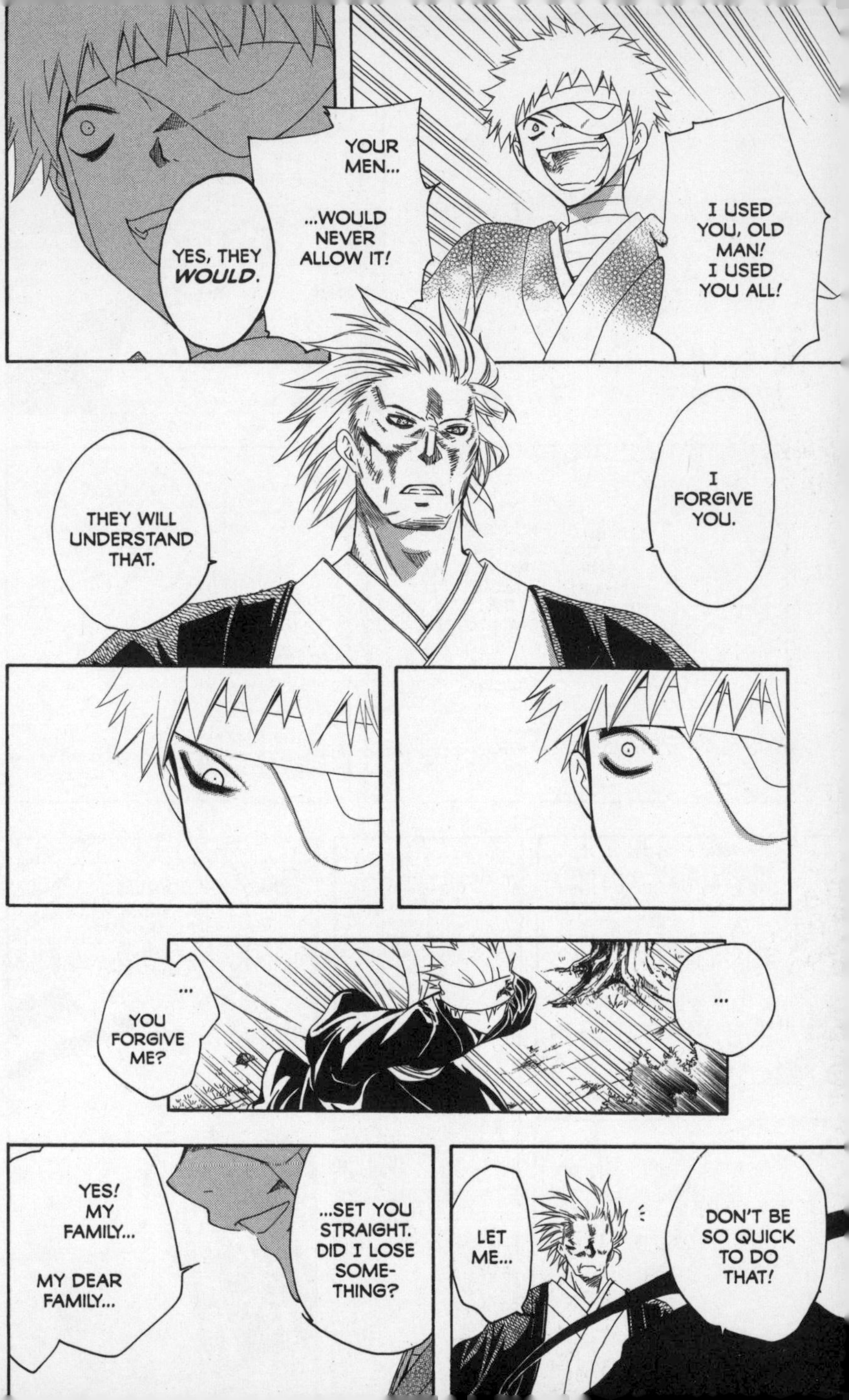
I USED YOU, OLD MAN! I USED YOU ALL!
YOUR MEN...
...WOULD NEVER ALLOW IT!
YES, THEY *WOULD*.
I FORGIVE YOU.
THEY WILL UNDERSTAND THAT.
...
...
YOU FORGIVE ME?
DON'T BE SO QUICK TO DO THAT!
LET ME...
...SET YOU STRAIGHT. DID I LOSE SOME-THING?
YES! MY FAMILY...
MY DEAR FAMILY...

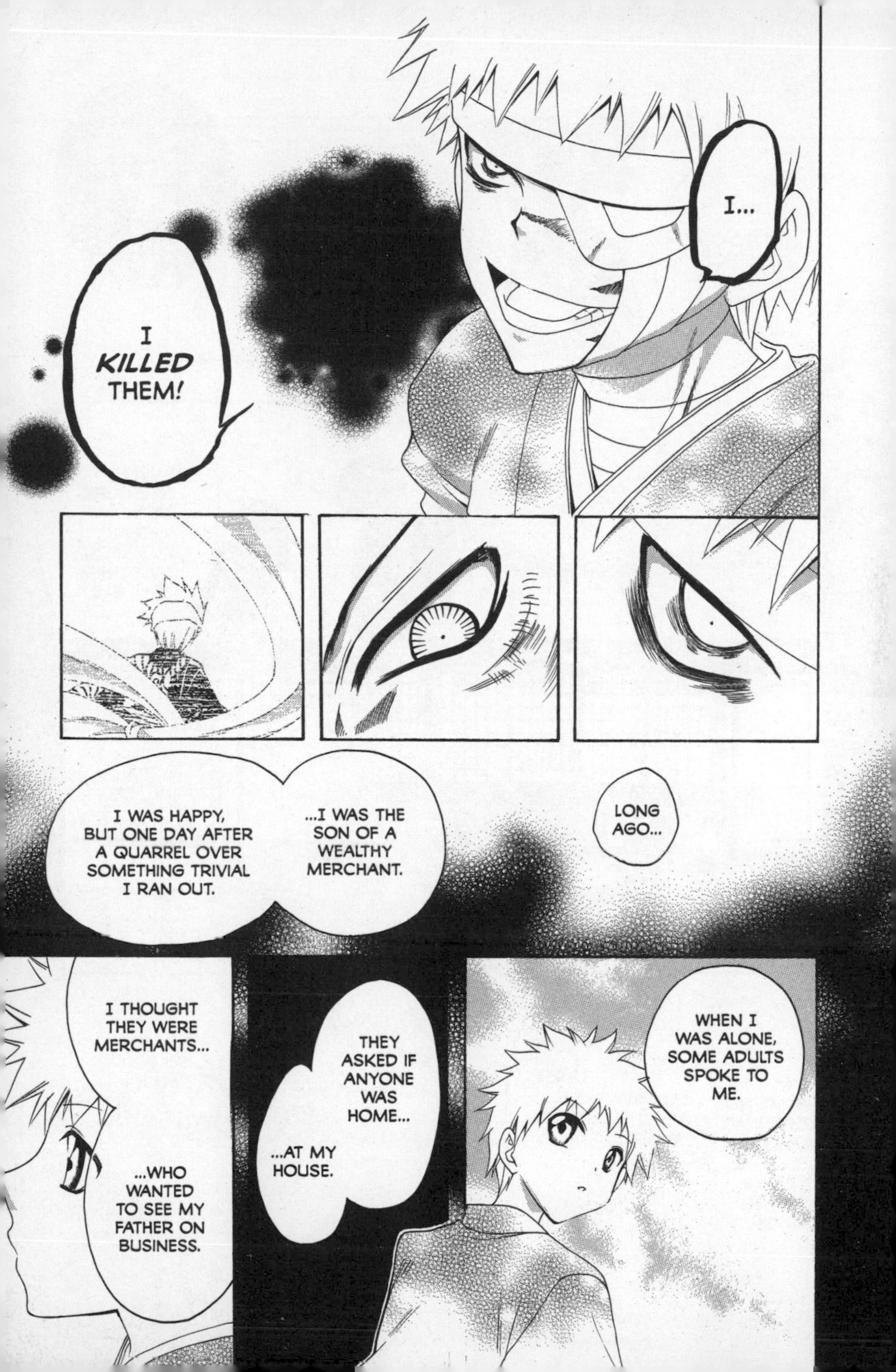
I...
I *KILLED* THEM!
LONG AGO...
...I WAS THE SON OF A WEALTHY MERCHANT.
I WAS HAPPY, BUT ONE DAY AFTER A QUARREL OVER SOMETHING TRIVIAL I RAN OUT.
WHEN I WAS ALONE, SOME ADULTS SPOKE TO ME.
THEY ASKED IF ANYONE WAS HOME...
...AT MY HOUSE.
I THOUGHT THEY WERE MERCHANTS...
...WHO WANTED TO SEE MY FATHER ON BUSINESS.

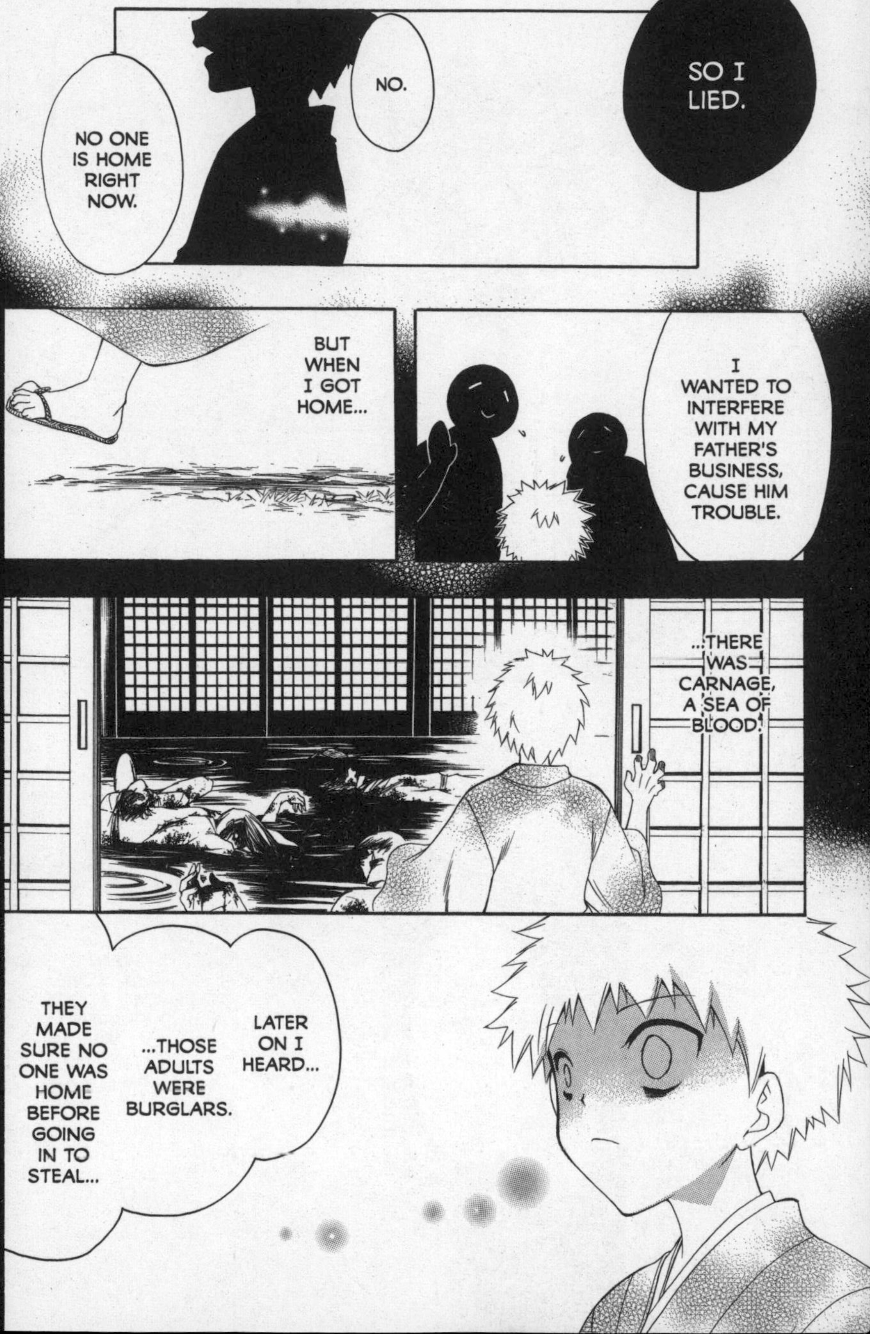
SO I LIED.
NO.
NO ONE IS HOME RIGHT NOW.
I WANTED TO INTERFERE WITH MY FATHER'S BUSINESS, CAUSE HIM TROUBLE.
BUT WHEN I GOT HOME...
...THERE WAS CARNAGE, A SEA OF BLOOD.
LATER ON I HEARD...
...THOSE ADULTS WERE BURGLARS.
THEY MADE SURE NO ONE WAS HOME BEFORE GOING IN TO STEAL...

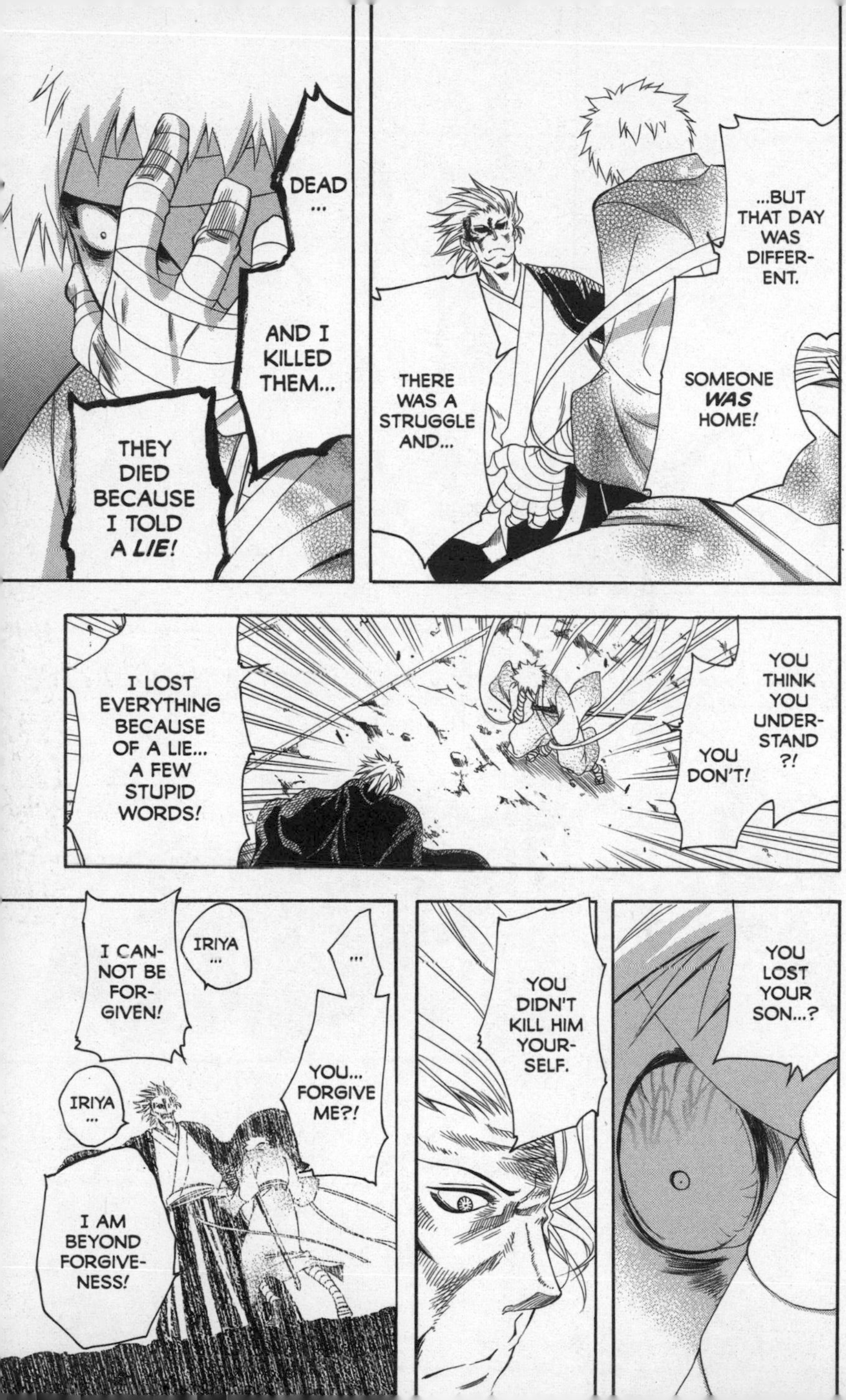
...BUT THAT DAY WAS DIFFERENT.
SOMEONE *WAS* HOME!
THERE WAS A STRUGGLE AND...
DEAD ...
AND I KILLED THEM...
THEY DIED BECAUSE I TOLD A *LIE*!
YOU THINK YOU UNDERSTAND ?!
YOU DON'T!
I LOST EVERYTHING BECAUSE OF A LIE... A FEW STUPID WORDS!
YOU LOST YOUR SON...?
YOU DIDN'T KILL HIM YOURSELF.
...
IRIYA ...
I CANNOT BE FORGIVEN!
YOU... FORGIVE ME?!
IRIYA ...
I AM BEYOND FORGIVENESS!

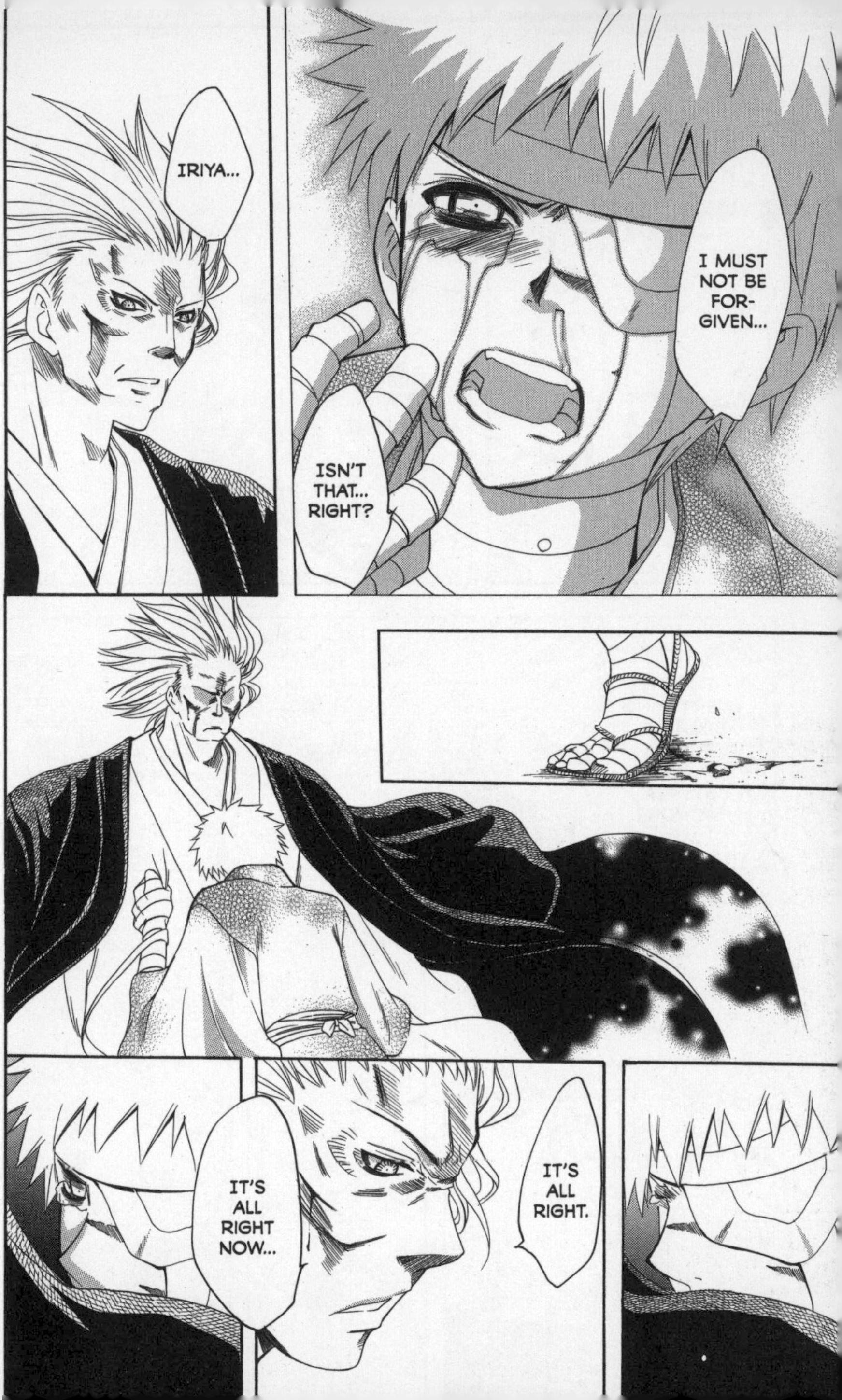
I MUST NOT BE FOR-GIVEN...
ISN'T THAT... RIGHT?
IRIYA...
IT'S ALL RIGHT.
IT'S ALL RIGHT NOW...

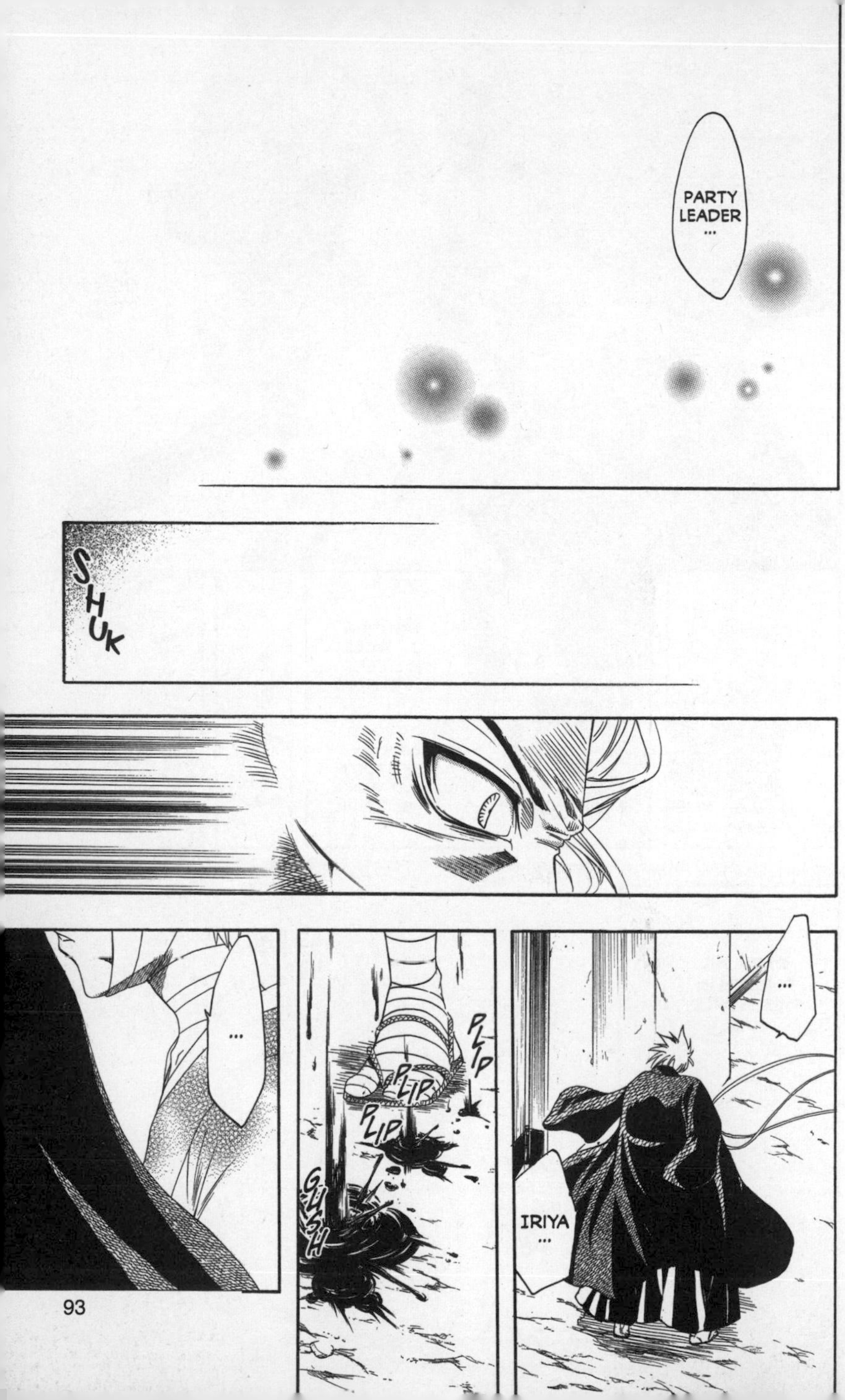
PARTY LEADER ...
SHUK
...
IRIYA ...
PLIP
PLIP
PLIP
GUSH
...

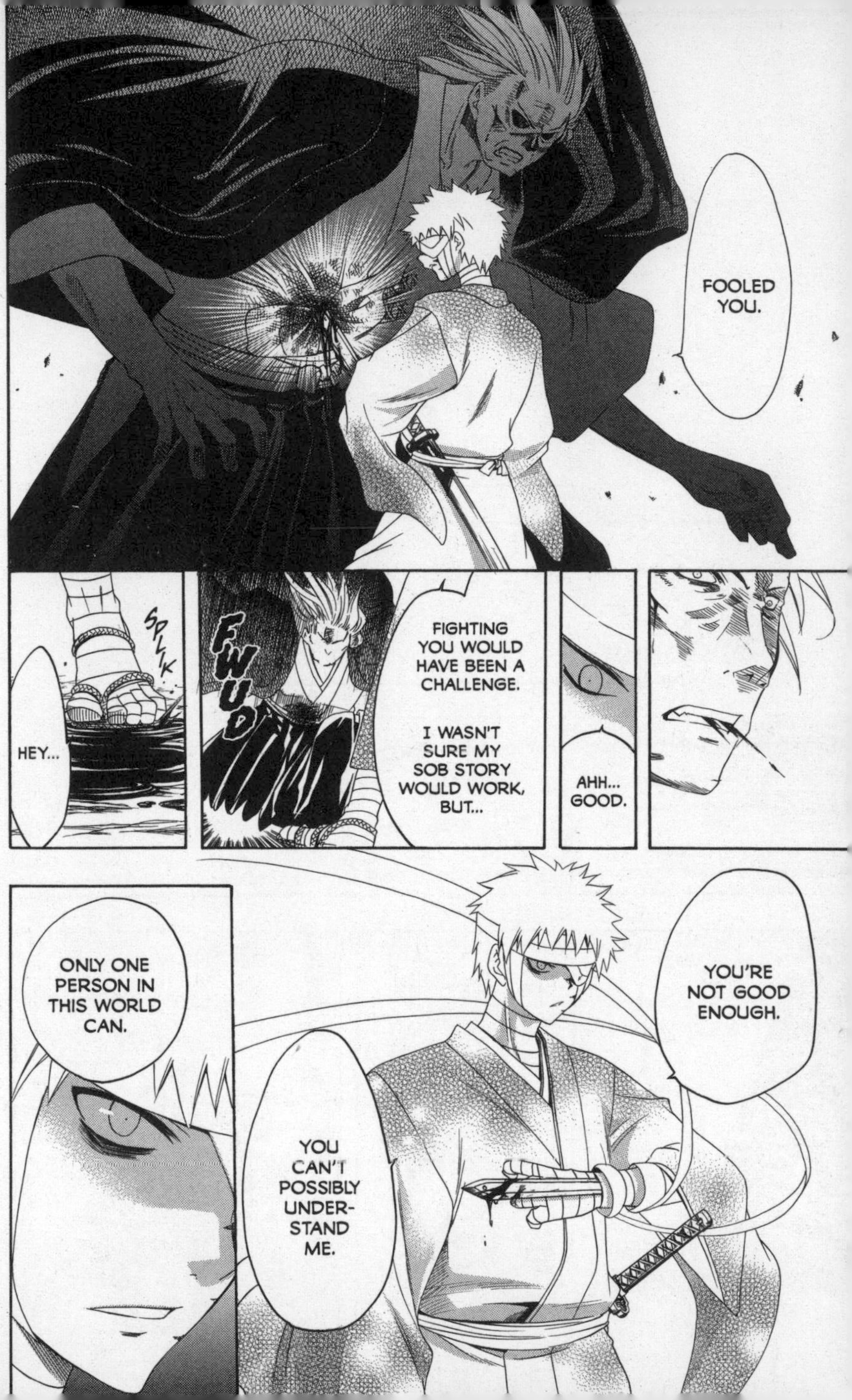
FOOLED YOU.
AHH... GOOD.
FIGHTING YOU WOULD HAVE BEEN A CHALLENGE.
I WASN'T SURE MY SOB STORY WOULD WORK, BUT...
FWUD
SPLIK
HEY...
YOU'RE NOT GOOD ENOUGH.
YOU CAN'T POSSIBLY UNDERSTAND ME.
ONLY ONE PERSON IN THIS WORLD CAN.

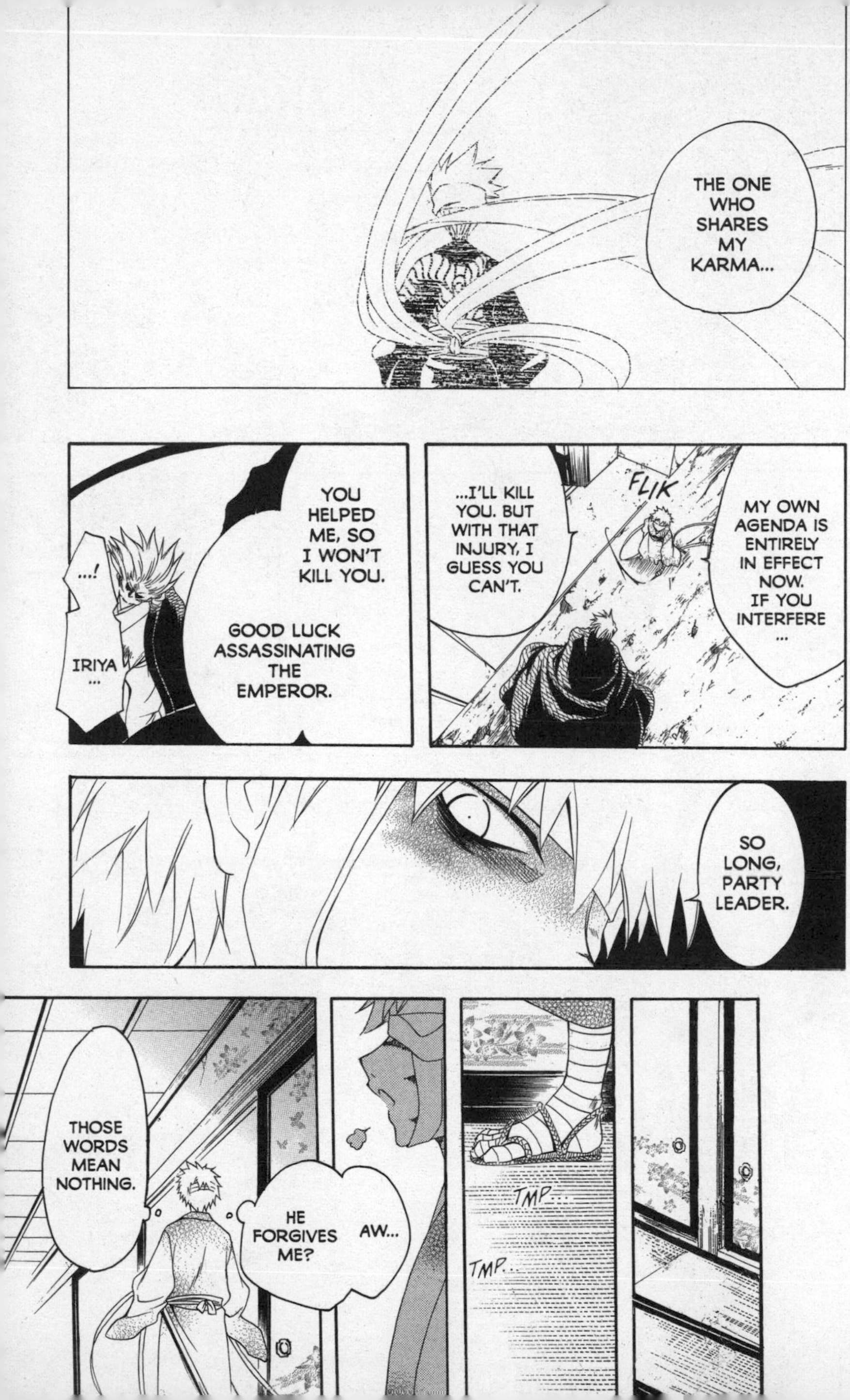
THE ONE WHO SHARES MY KARMA...
MY OWN AGENDA IS ENTIRELY IN EFFECT NOW. IF YOU INTERFERE ...
FLIK
...I'LL KILL YOU. BUT WITH THAT INJURY, I GUESS YOU CAN'T.
YOU HELPED ME, SO I WON'T KILL YOU.
GOOD LUCK ASSASSINATING THE EMPEROR.
...!
IRIYA ...
SO LONG, PARTY LEADER.
TMP...
TMP...
AW...
HE FORGIVES ME?
THOSE WORDS MEAN NOTHING.

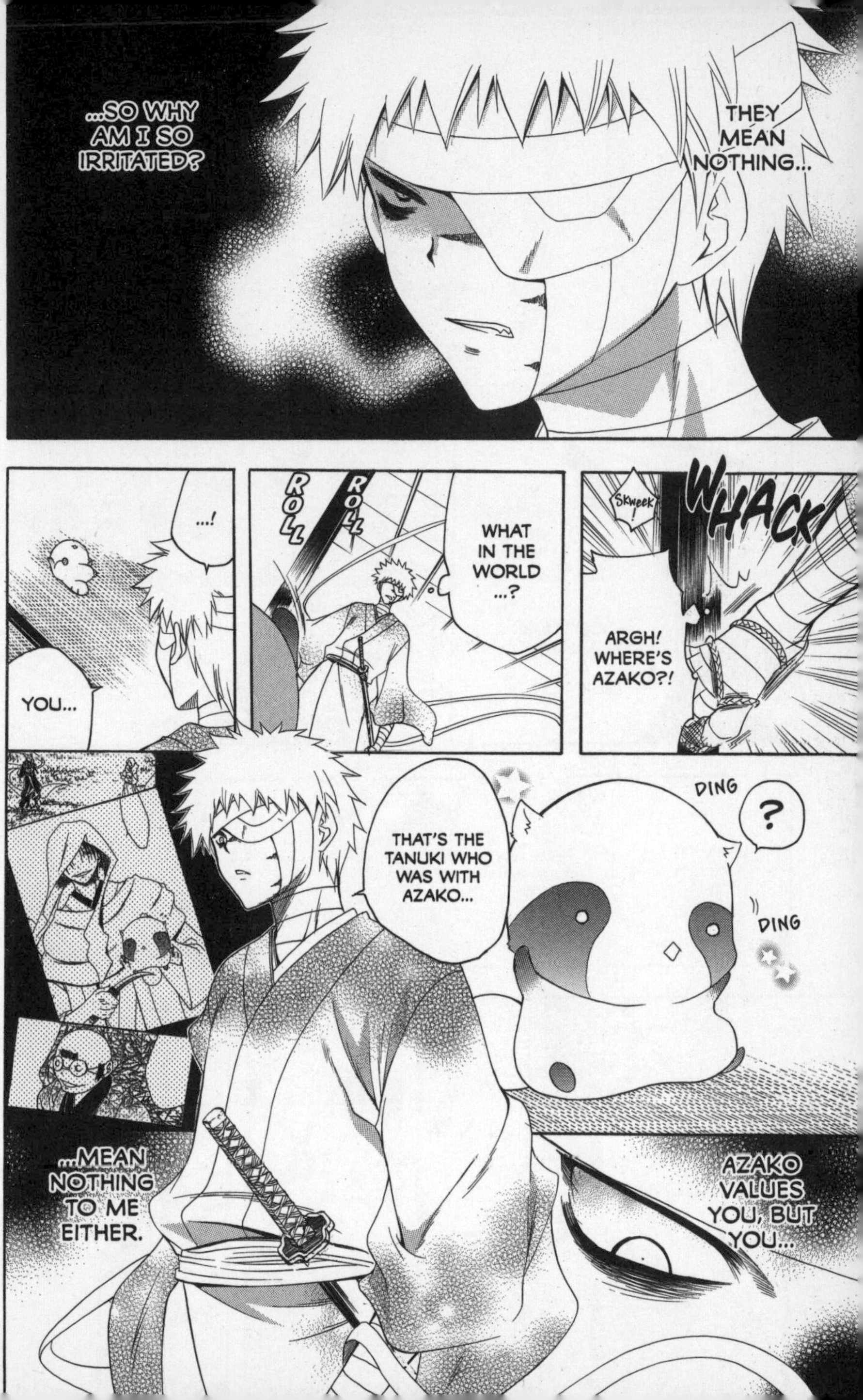
THEY MEAN NOTHING...
...SO WHY AM I SO IRRITATED?
SKWEEK!
WHACK!
ARGH! WHERE'S AZAKO?!
ROLL
ROLL
WHAT IN THE WORLD ...?
...!
YOU...
DING
?
DING
THAT'S THE TANUKI WHO WAS WITH AZAKO...
AZAKO VALUES YOU, BUT YOU...
...MEAN NOTHING TO ME EITHER.

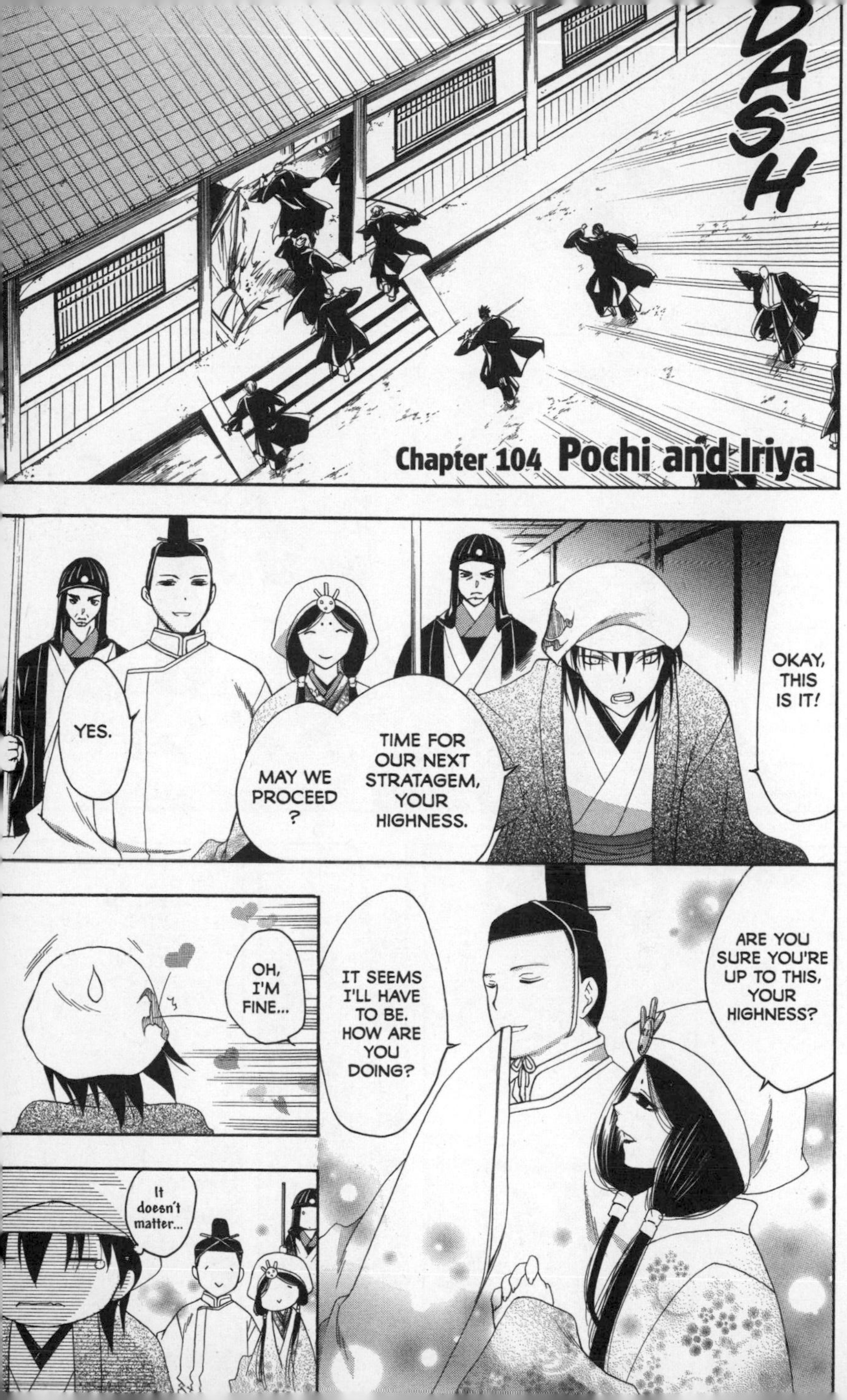
DASH
Chapter 104 Pochi and Iriya
OKAY, THIS IS IT!
TIME FOR OUR NEXT STRATAGEM, YOUR HIGHNESS.
MAY WE PROCEED?
YES.
ARE YOU SURE YOU'RE UP TO THIS, YOUR HIGHNESS?
IT SEEMS I'LL HAVE TO BE. HOW ARE YOU DOING?
OH, I'M FINE...
It doesn't matter...

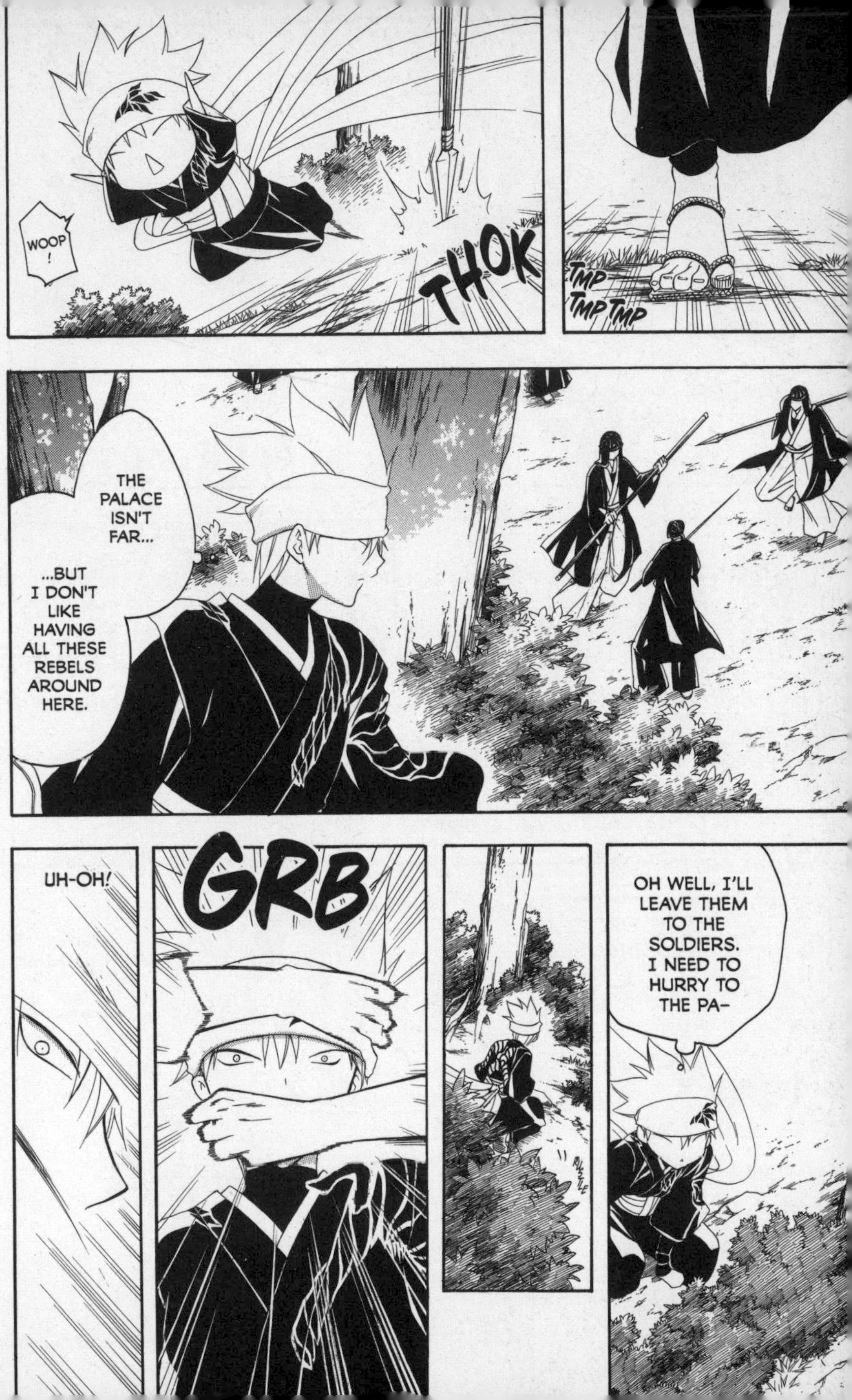
TMP
TMP TMP TMP
WOOP!
THOK
THE PALACE ISN'T FAR...
...BUT I DON'T LIKE HAVING ALL THESE REBELS AROUND HERE.
OH WELL, I'LL LEAVE THEM TO THE SOLDIERS. I NEED TO HURRY TO THE PA–
GRB
UH-OH!

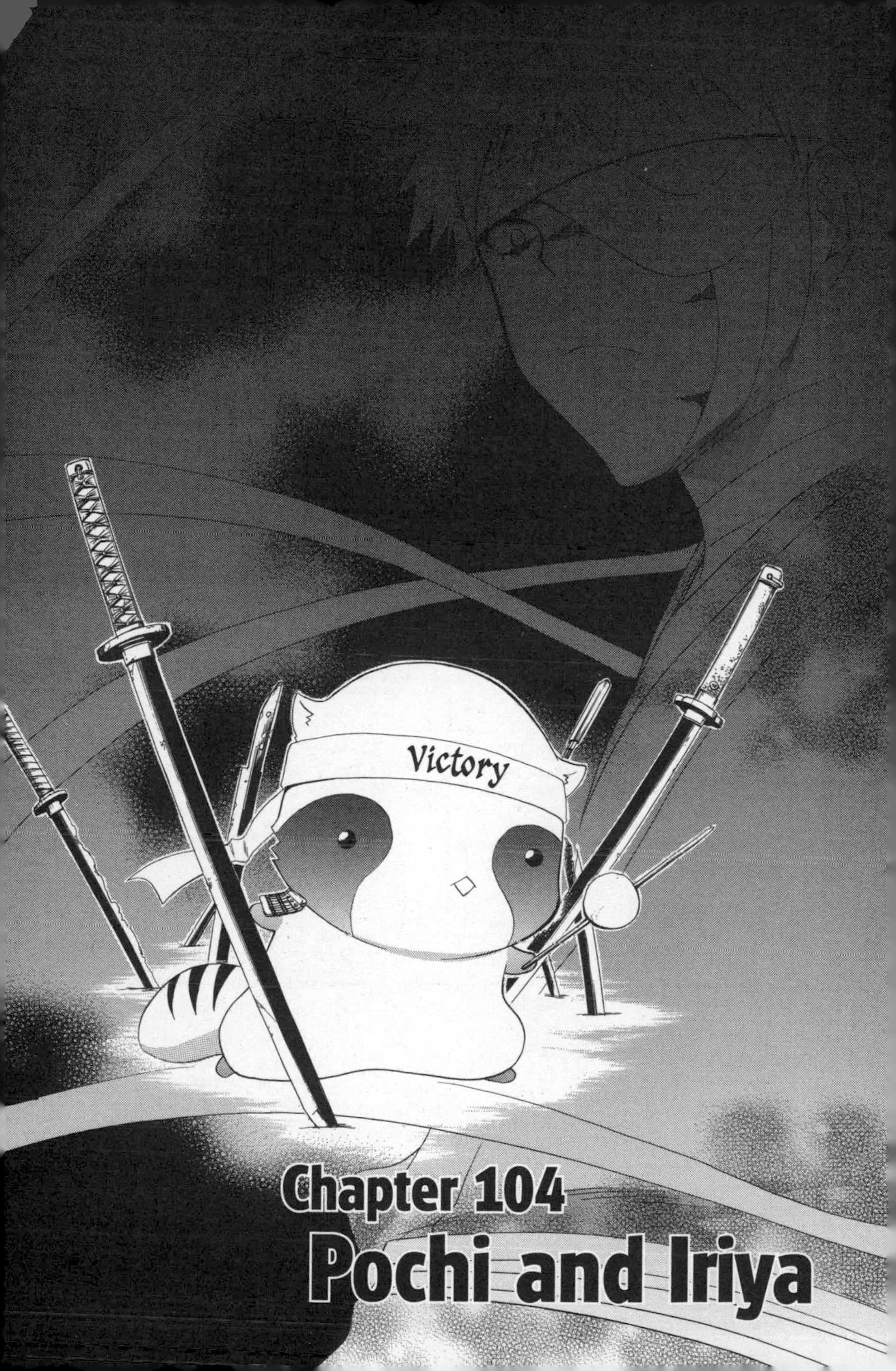
Victory

Chapter 104
Pochi and Iriya

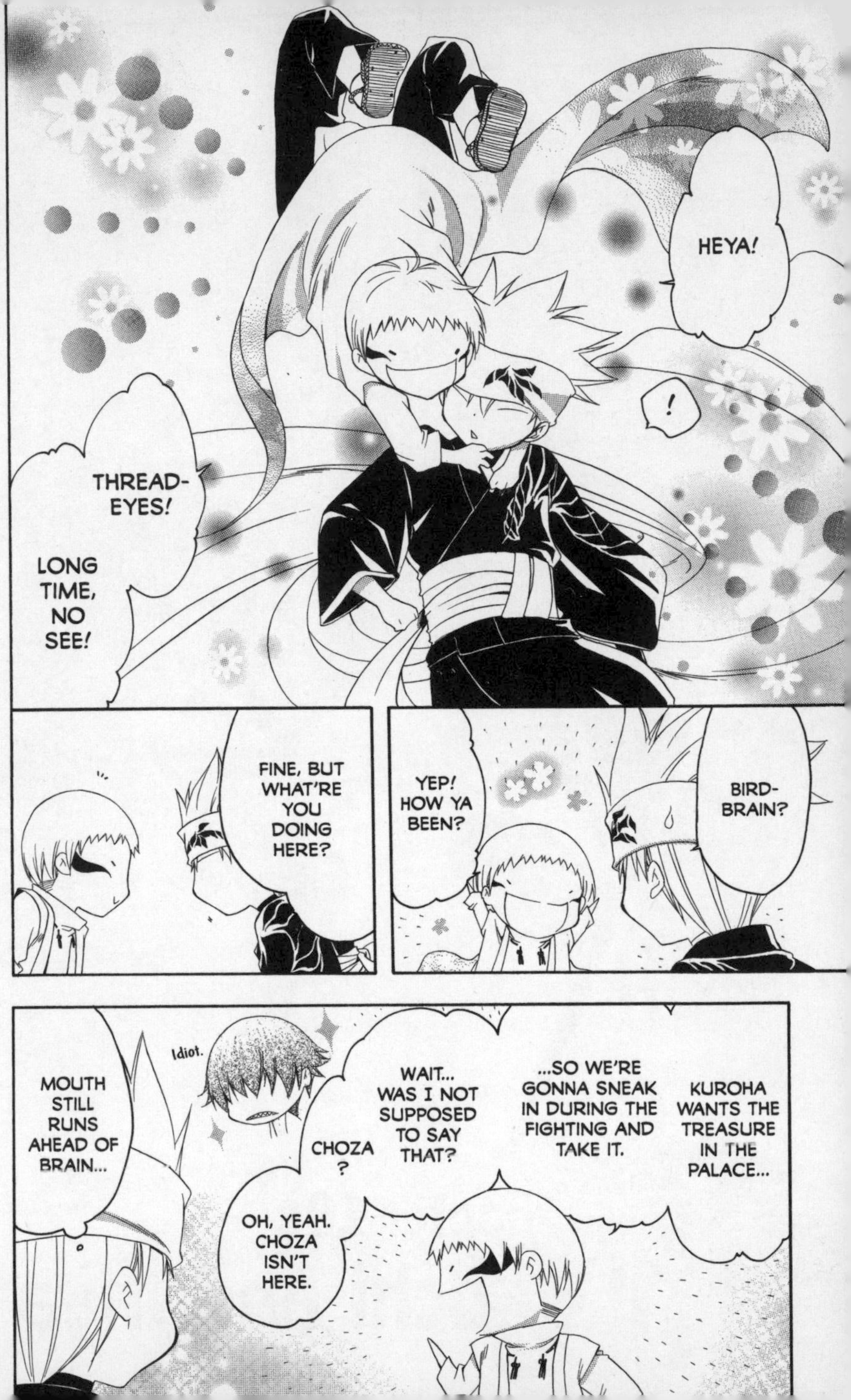
HEYA!
!
THREAD-EYES!
LONG TIME, NO SEE!
BIRD-BRAIN?
YEP! HOW YA BEEN?
FINE, BUT WHAT'RE YOU DOING HERE?
KUROHA WANTS THE TREASURE IN THE PALACE...
...SO WE'RE GONNA SNEAK IN DURING THE FIGHTING AND TAKE IT.
WAIT... WAS I NOT SUPPOSED TO SAY THAT?
CHOZA?
OH, YEAH. CHOZA ISN'T HERE.
Idiot.
MOUTH STILL RUNS AHEAD OF BRAIN...

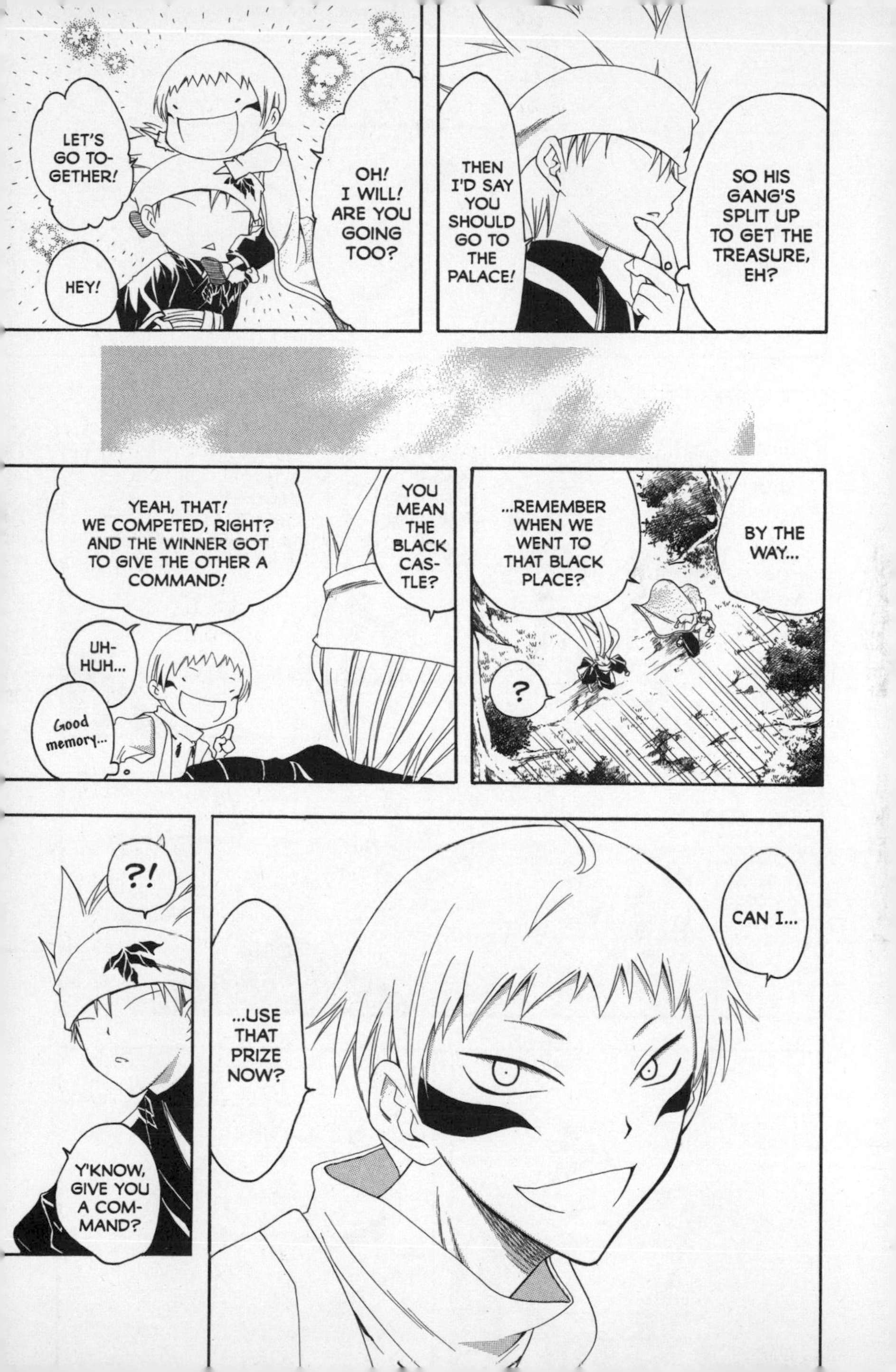
SO HIS GANG'S SPLIT UP TO GET THE TREASURE, EH?
THEN I'D SAY YOU SHOULD GO TO THE PALACE!
OH! I WILL! ARE YOU GOING TOO?
LET'S GO TO-GETHER!
HEY!
BY THE WAY...
...REMEMBER WHEN WE WENT TO THAT BLACK PLACE?
?
YOU MEAN THE BLACK CAS-TLE?
YEAH, THAT! WE COMPETED, RIGHT? AND THE WINNER GOT TO GIVE THE OTHER A COMMAND!
UH-HUH...
Good memory...
CAN I...
...USE THAT PRIZE NOW?
?!
Y'KNOW, GIVE YOU A COM-MAND?

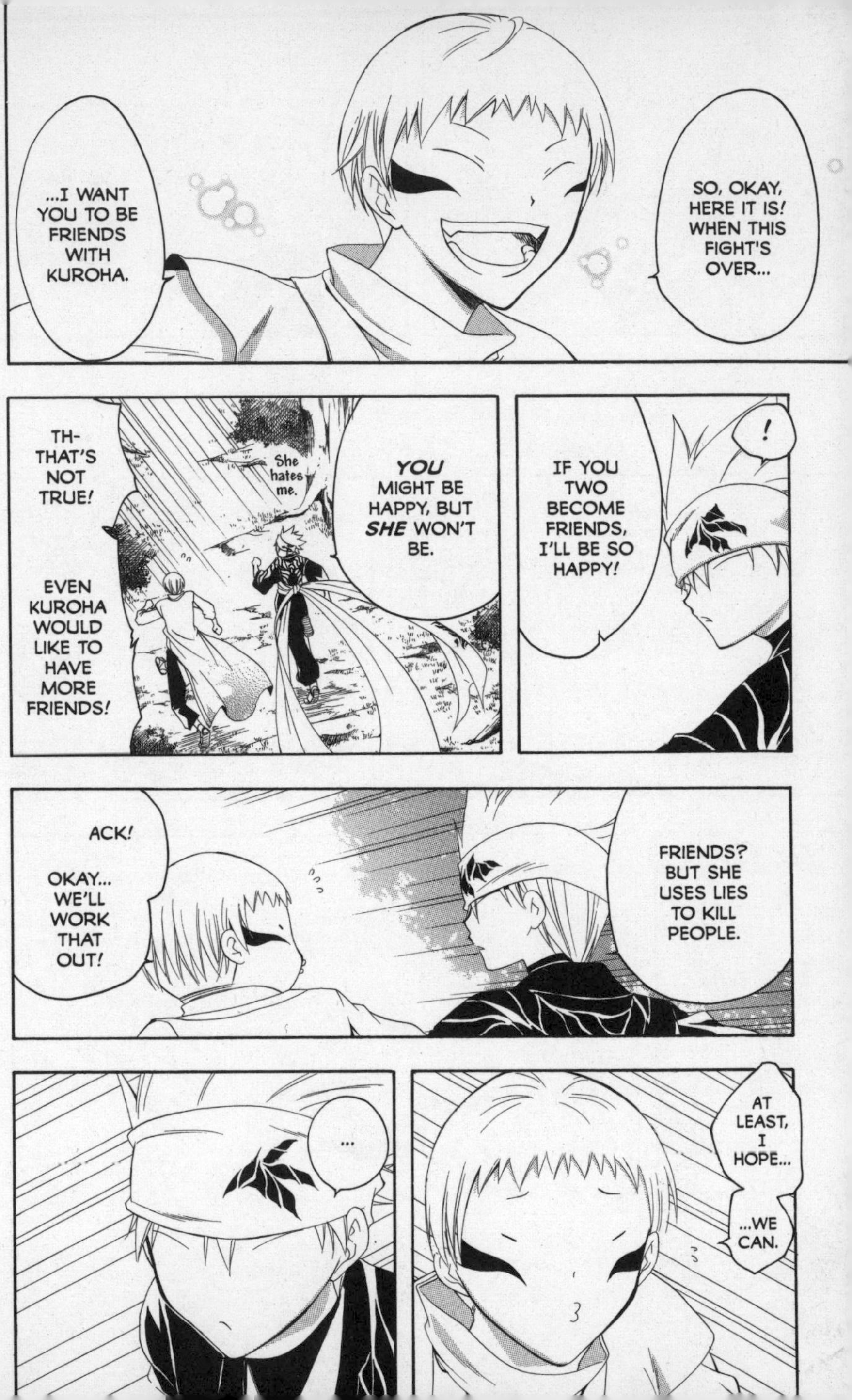
SO, OKAY, HERE IT IS! WHEN THIS FIGHT'S OVER...
...I WANT YOU TO BE FRIENDS WITH KUROHA.
!
IF YOU TWO BECOME FRIENDS, I'LL BE SO HAPPY!
YOU MIGHT BE HAPPY, BUT SHE WON'T BE.
She hates me.
TH-THAT'S NOT TRUE!
EVEN KUROHA WOULD LIKE TO HAVE MORE FRIENDS!
FRIENDS? BUT SHE USES LIES TO KILL PEOPLE.
ACK!
OKAY... WE'LL WORK THAT OUT!
AT LEAST, I HOPE...
...WE CAN.
...

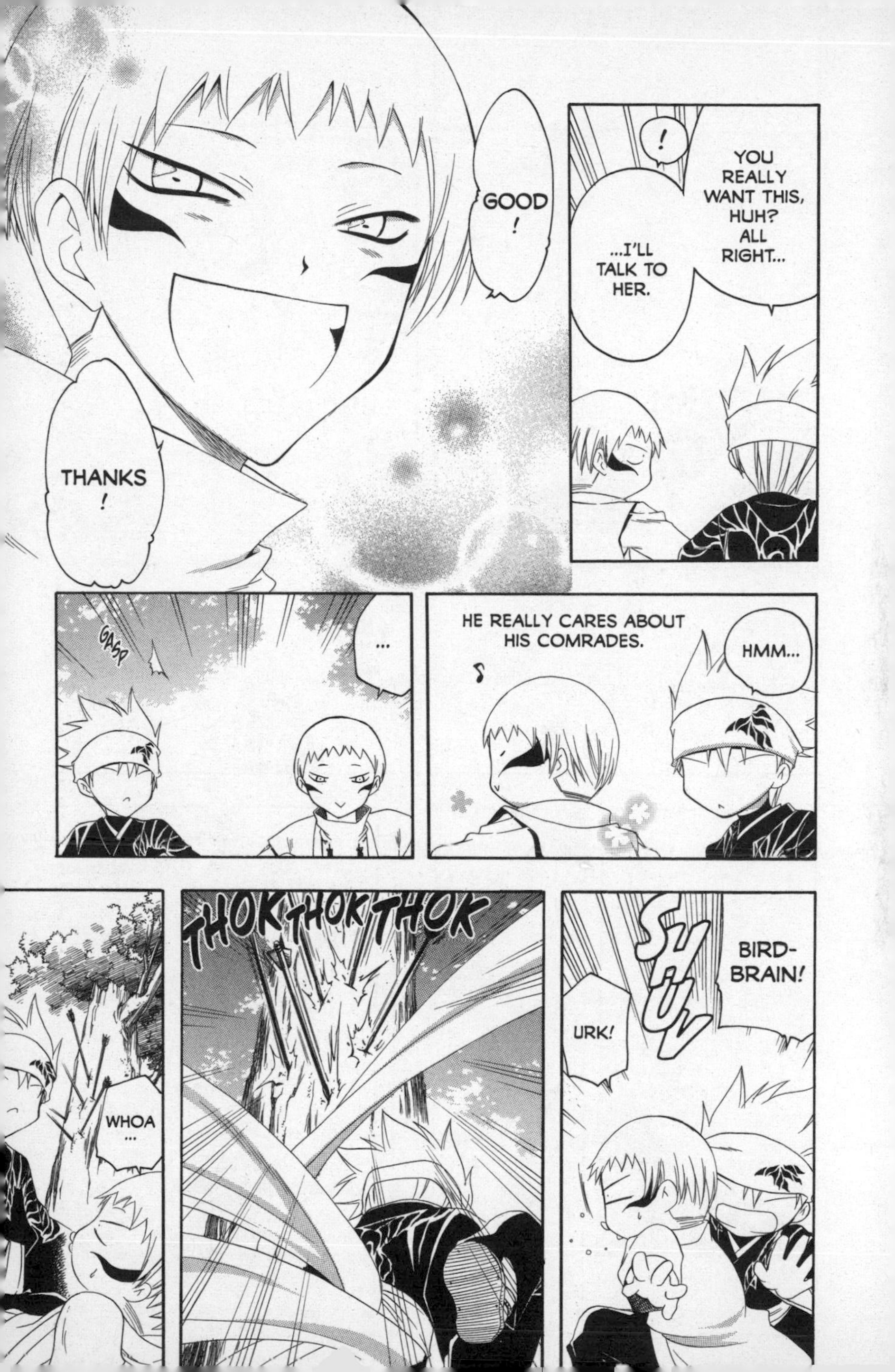
!
YOU REALLY WANT THIS, HUH? ALL RIGHT...
...I'LL TALK TO HER.
GOOD!
THANKS!
HMM...
HE REALLY CARES ABOUT HIS COMRADES.
...
GASP
BIRD-BRAIN!
SHUW
URK!
THOK THOK THOK
WHOA...

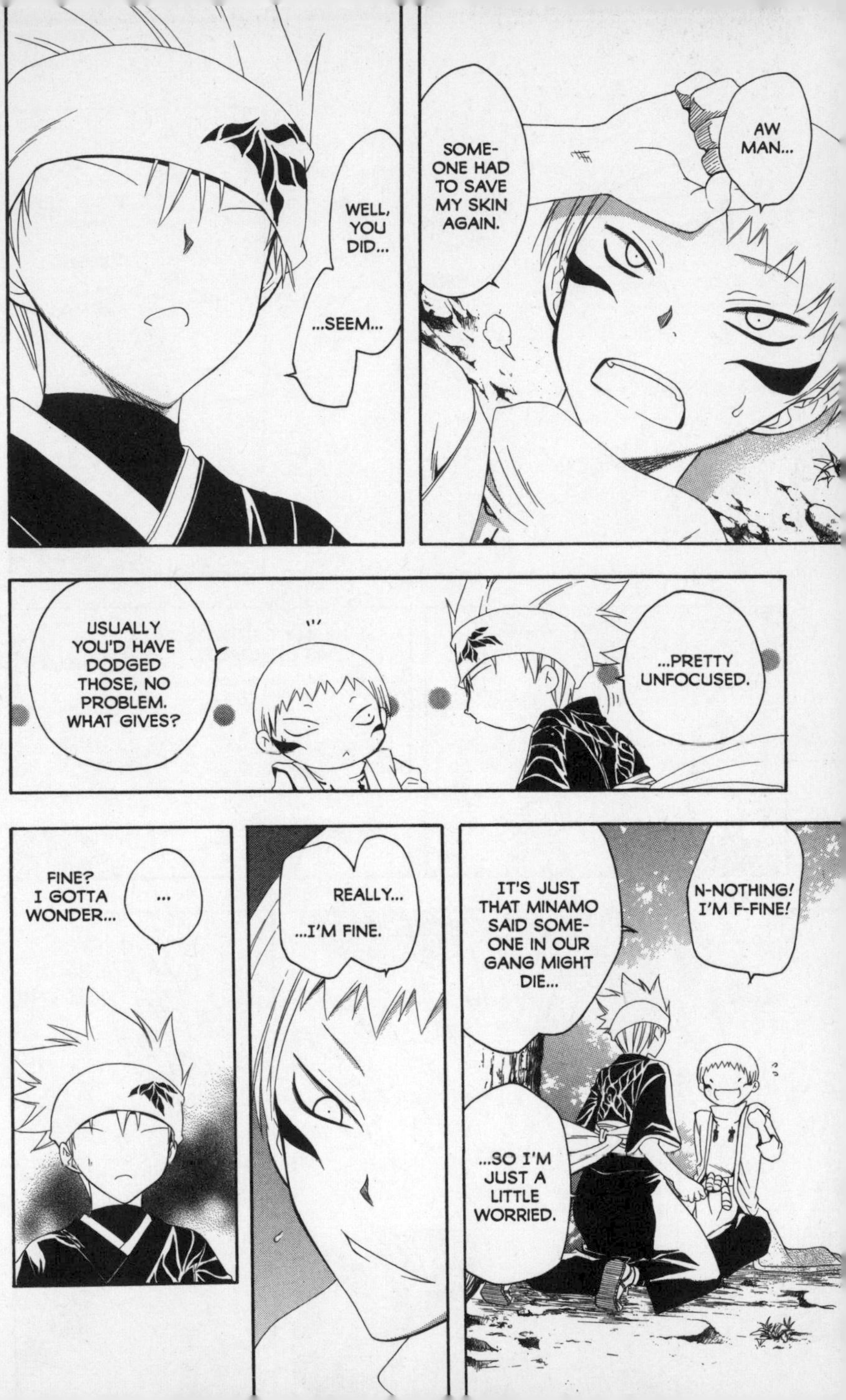
AW MAN...
SOME-ONE HAD TO SAVE MY SKIN AGAIN.
WELL, YOU DID...
...SEEM...
...PRETTY UNFOCUSED.
USUALLY YOU'D HAVE DODGED THOSE, NO PROBLEM. WHAT GIVES?
N-NOTHING! I'M F-FINE!
IT'S JUST THAT MINAMO SAID SOME-ONE IN OUR GANG MIGHT DIE...
...SO I'M JUST A LITTLE WORRIED.
REALLY... ...I'M FINE.
...
FINE? I GOTTA WONDER...

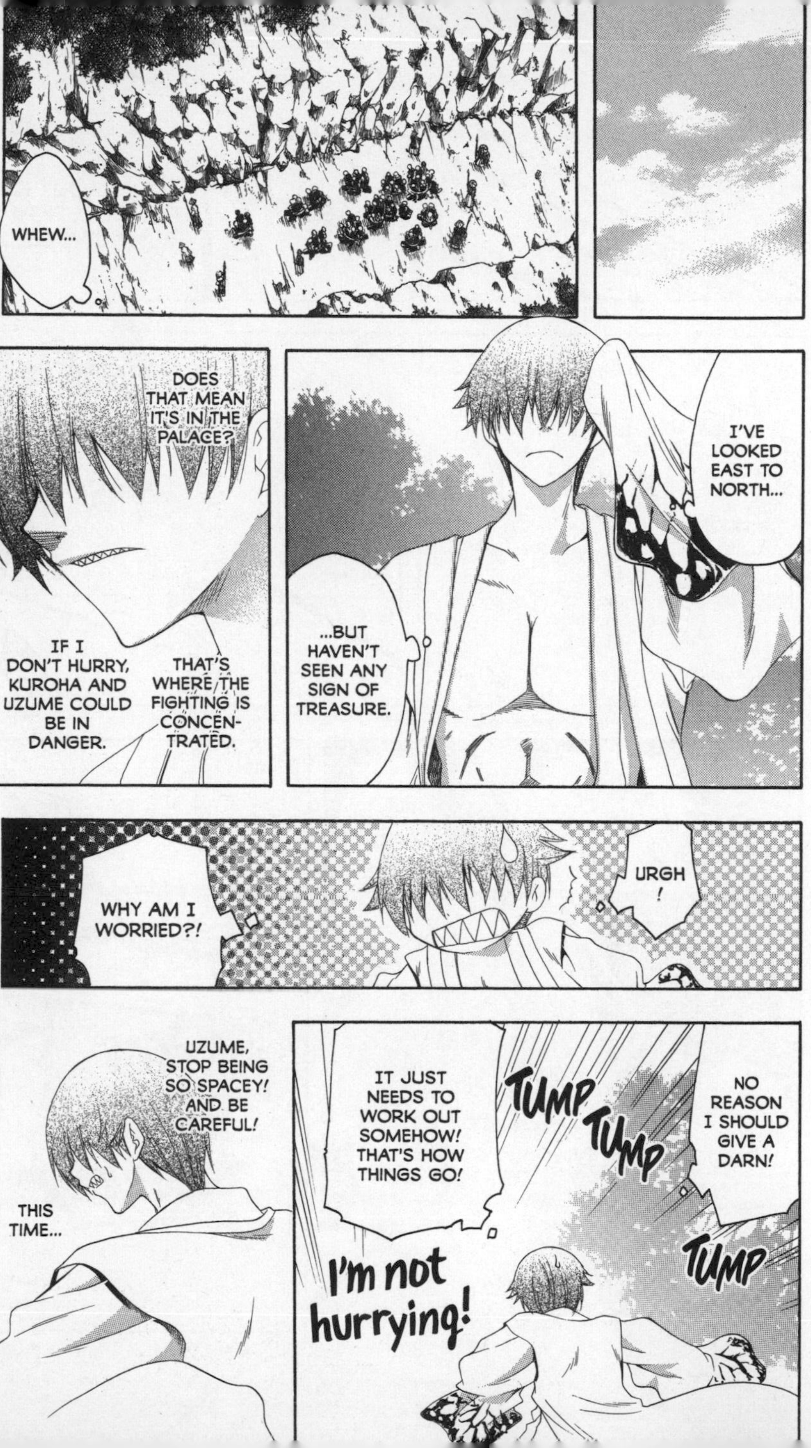
WHEW...
I'VE LOOKED EAST TO NORTH...
...BUT HAVEN'T SEEN ANY SIGN OF TREASURE.
DOES THAT MEAN IT'S IN THE PALACE?
THAT'S WHERE THE FIGHTING IS CONCEN-TRATED.
IF I DON'T HURRY, KUROHA AND UZUME COULD BE IN DANGER.
URGH!
WHY AM I WORRIED?!
NO REASON I SHOULD GIVE A DARN!
TUMP
TUMP
IT JUST NEEDS TO WORK OUT SOMEHOW! THAT'S HOW THINGS GO!
TUMP
I'm not hurrying!
UZUME, STOP BEING SO SPACEY! AND BE CAREFUL!
THIS TIME...

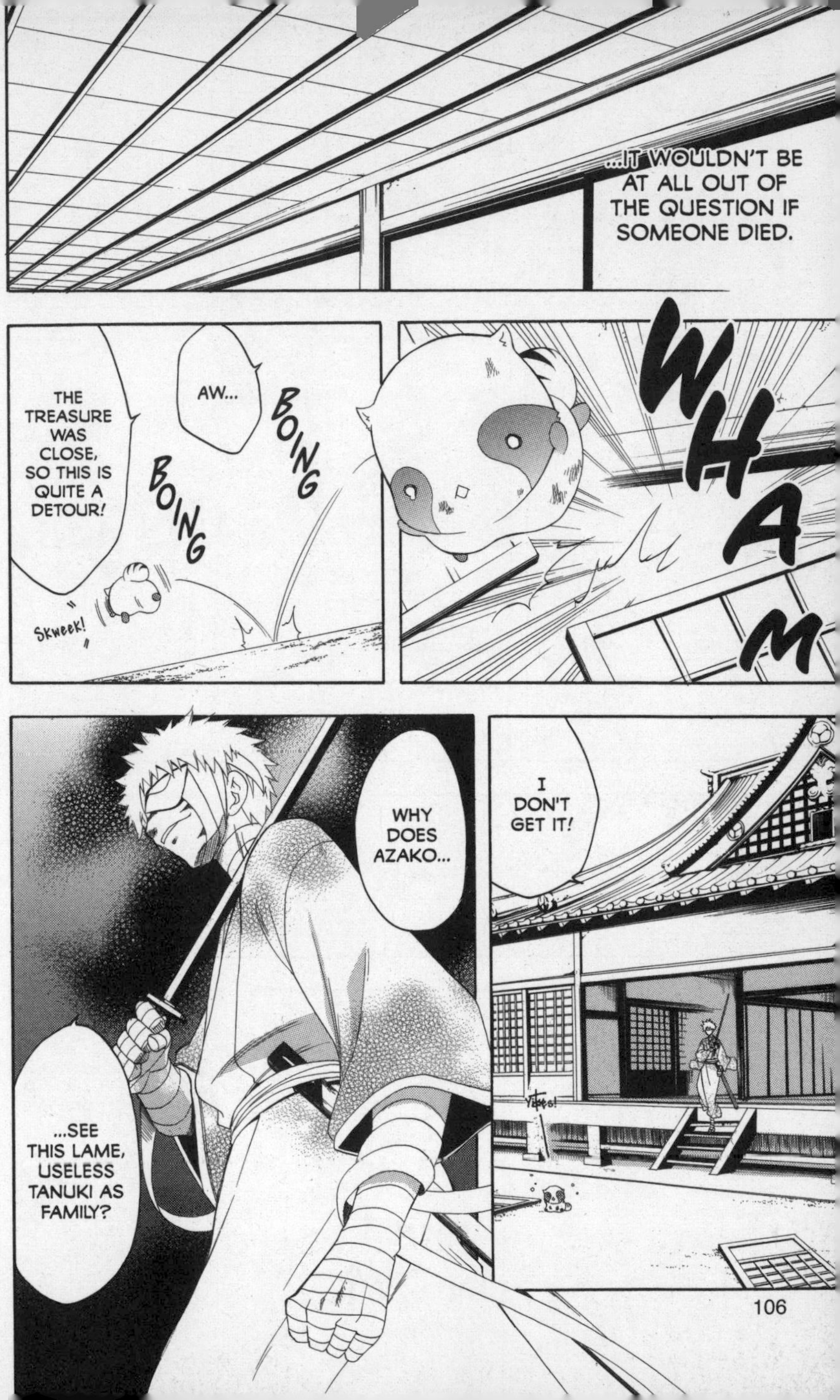
...IT WOULDN'T BE AT ALL OUT OF THE QUESTION IF SOMEONE DIED.
WHAM
AW...
BOING
THE TREASURE WAS CLOSE, SO THIS IS QUITE A DETOUR!
BOING
Skweek!
I DON'T GET IT!
WHY DOES AZAKO...
...SEE THIS LAME, USELESS TANUKI AS FAMILY?

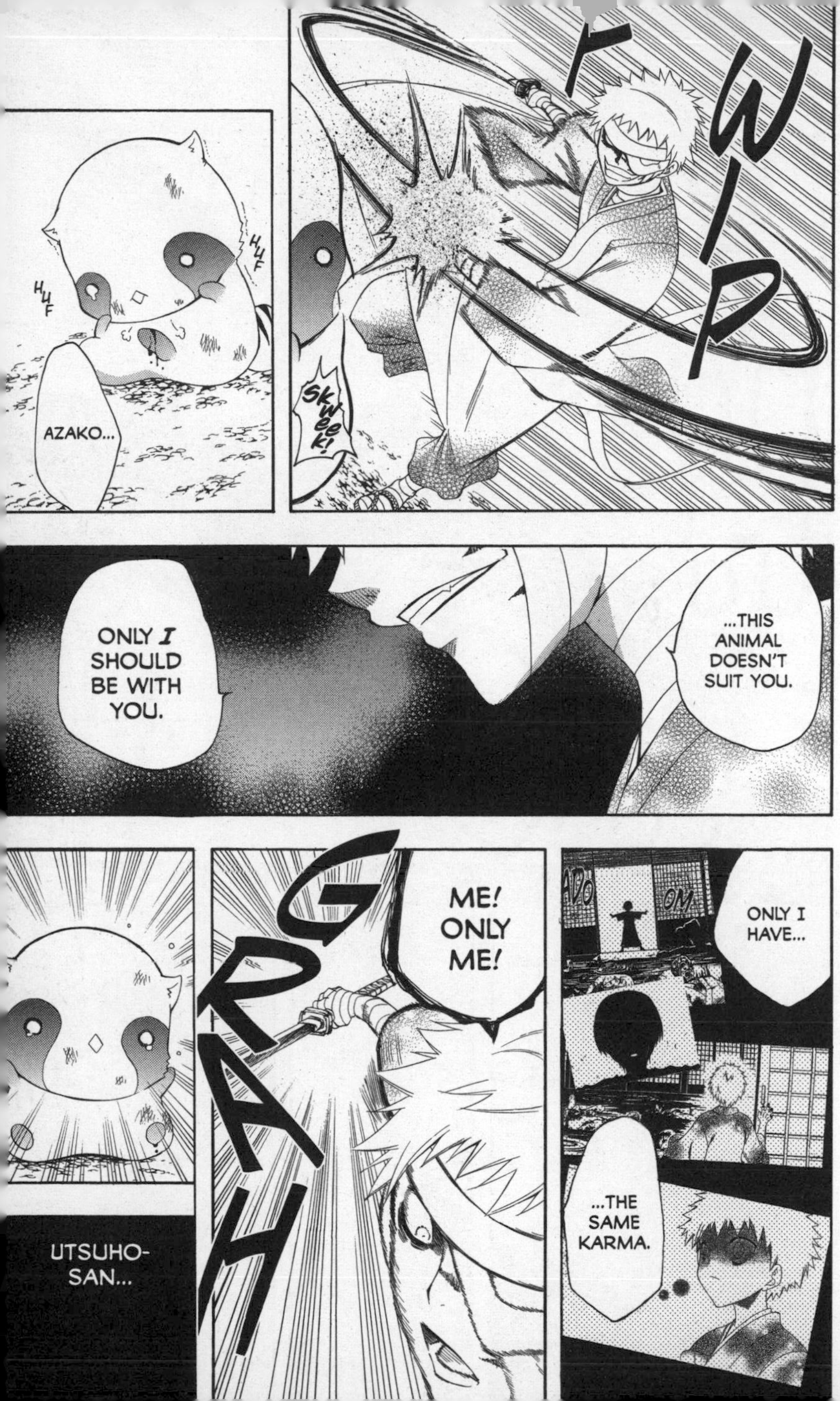
WIP
Skweek!
HUF
HUF
AZAKO...
...THIS ANIMAL DOESN'T SUIT YOU.
ONLY I SHOULD BE WITH YOU.
ONLY I HAVE...
...THE SAME KARMA.
ME! ONLY ME!
GRAH
UTSUHO-SAN...

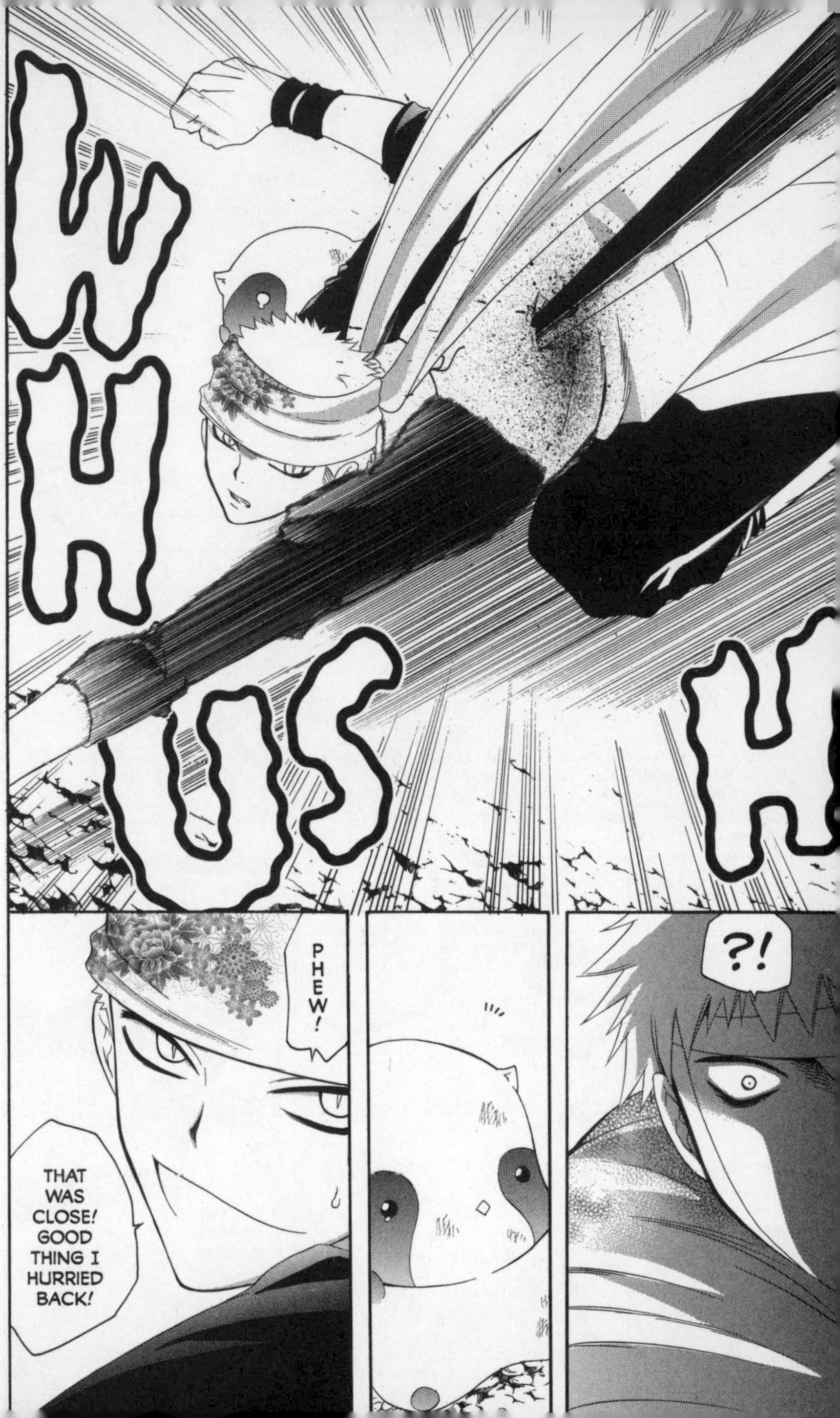
WHOOSH
?!
PHEW!
THAT WAS CLOSE! GOOD THING I HURRIED BACK!

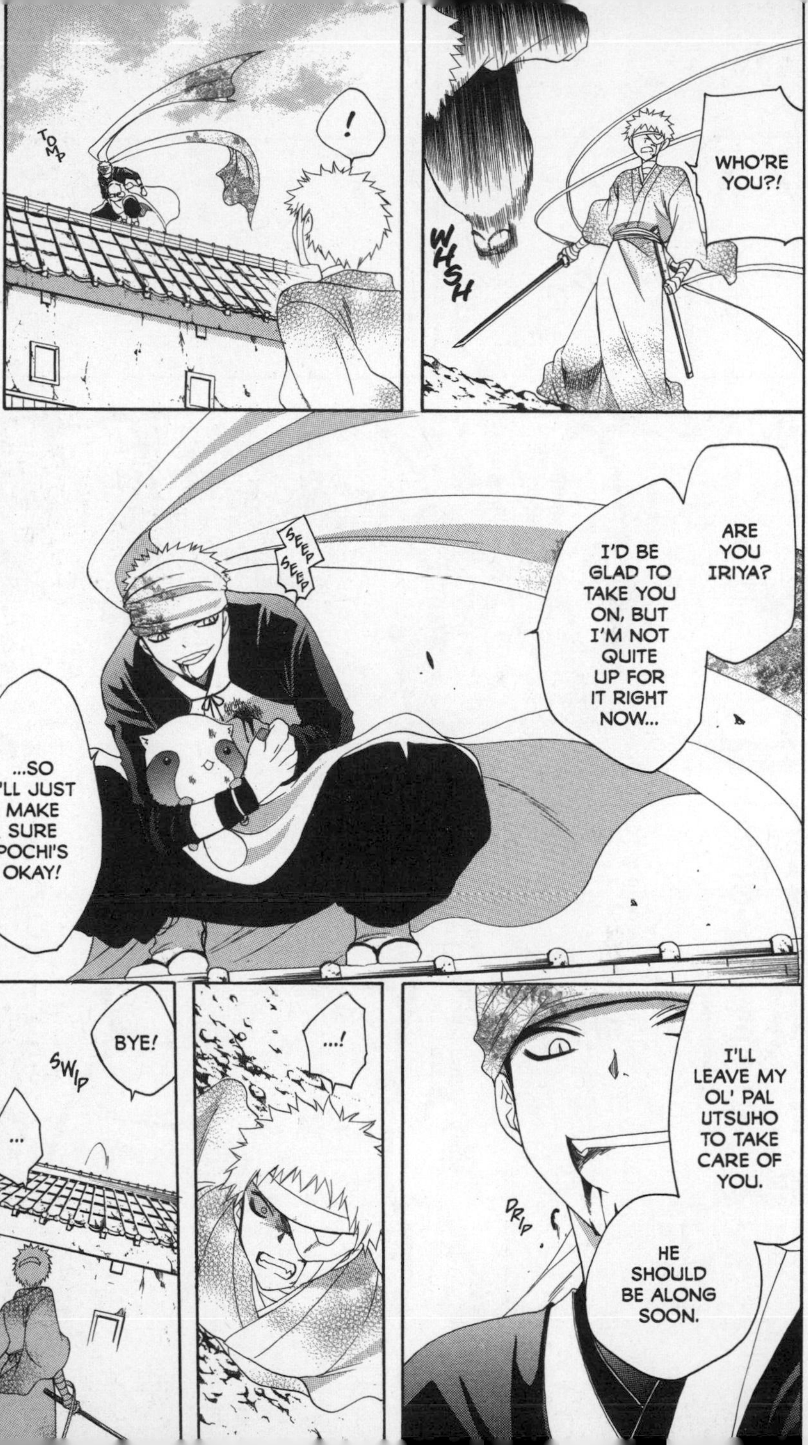
WHSH
WHO'RE YOU?!
!
TOMP
ARE YOU IRIYA?
I'D BE GLAD TO TAKE YOU ON, BUT I'M NOT QUITE UP FOR IT RIGHT NOW...
SEEP SEEP
...SO I'LL JUST MAKE SURE POCHI'S OKAY!
I'LL LEAVE MY OL' PAL UTSUHO TO TAKE CARE OF YOU.
HE SHOULD BE ALONG SOON.
DRIP
...!
BYE!
SWIP
...

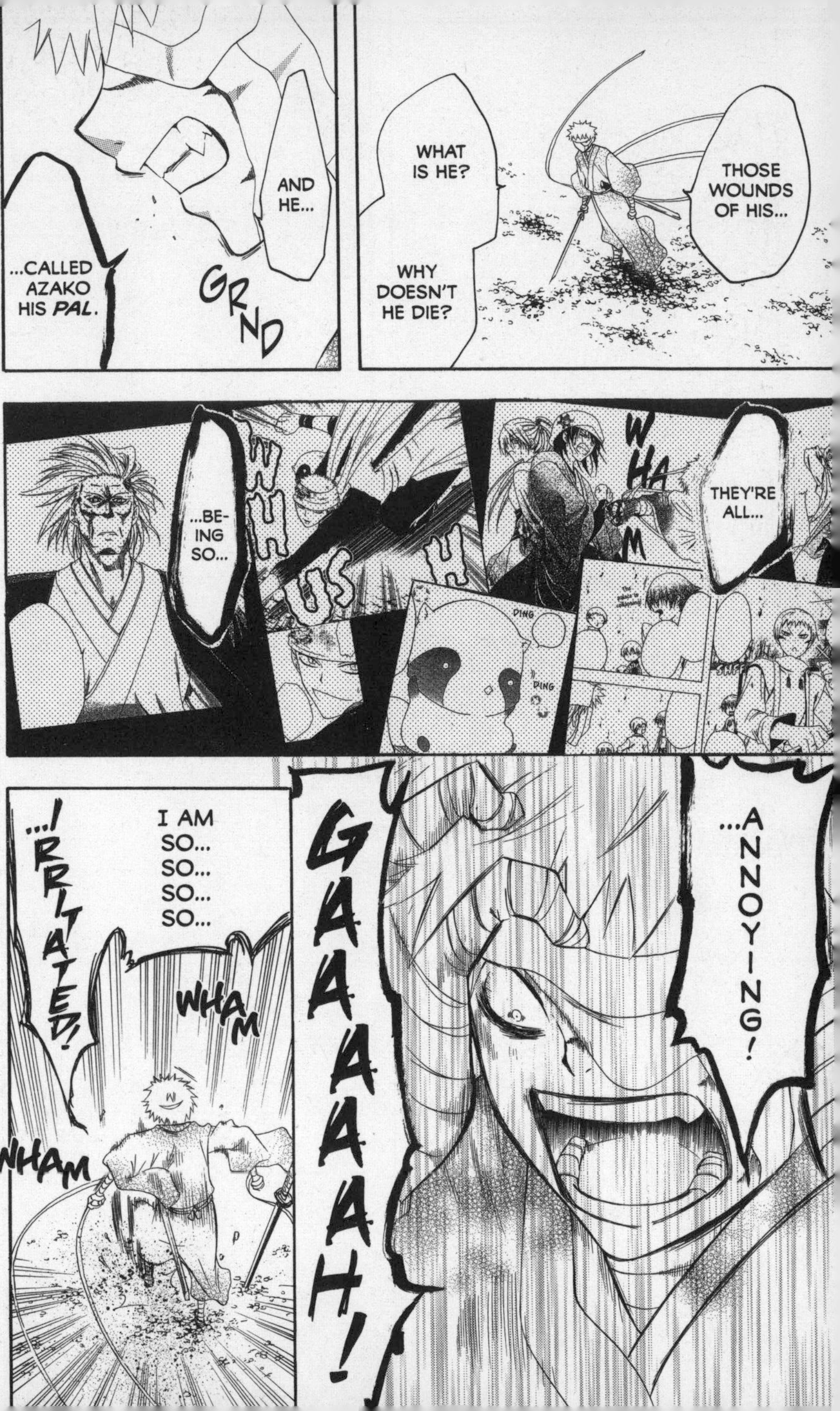
THOSE WOUNDS OF HIS...
WHAT IS HE?
WHY DOESN'T HE DIE?
AND HE...
...CALLED AZAKO HIS *PAL*.
GRND
THEY'RE ALL...
WHAM
DING
DING
...BE-ING SO...
...ANNOYING!
GAAAAAH!
I AM SO... SO... SO... SO...
...IRRITATED!
WHAM
WHAM

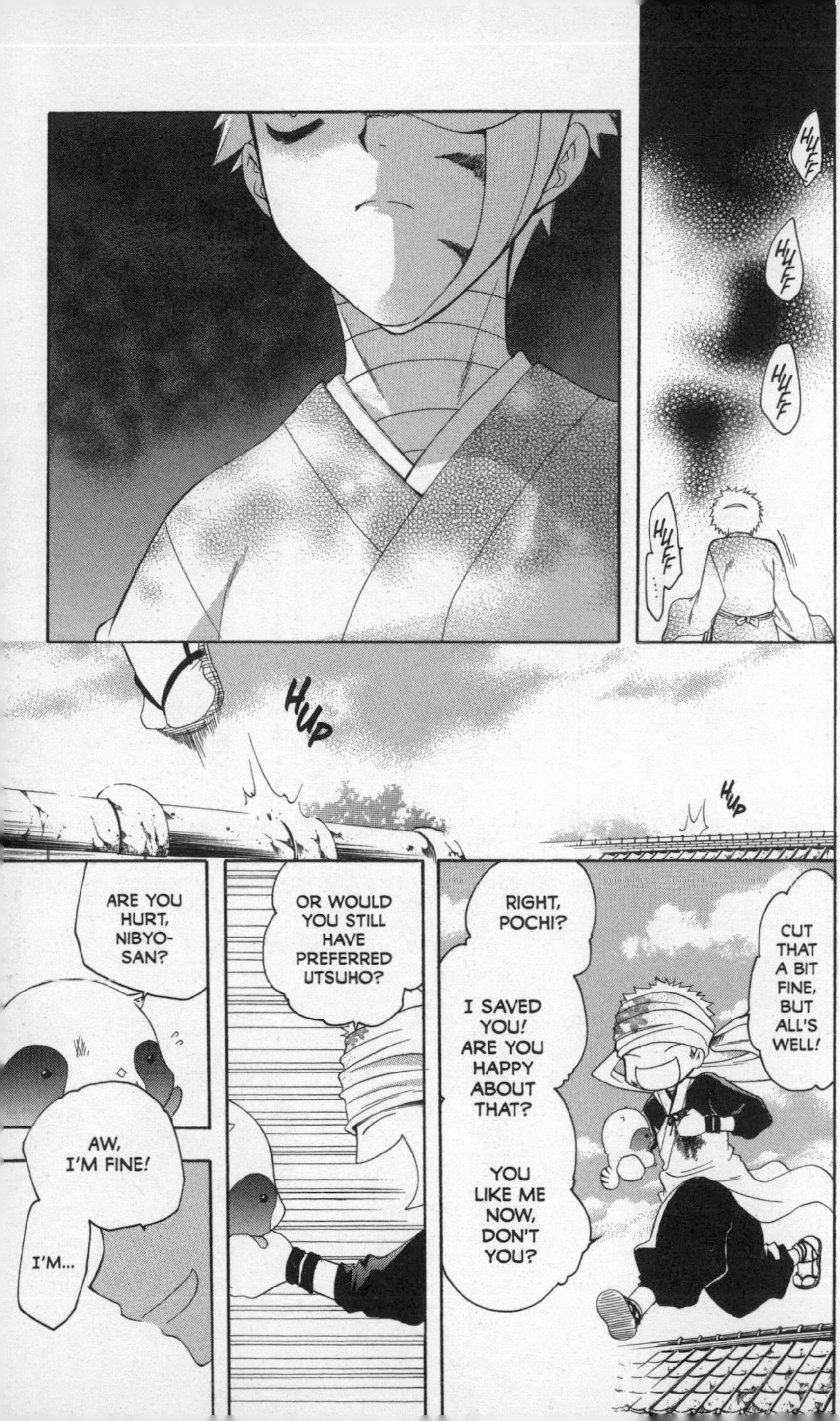
HUFF
HUFF
HUFF
HUFF
HUP
HUP
CUT THAT A BIT FINE, BUT ALL'S WELL!
RIGHT, POCHI?
I SAVED YOU! ARE YOU HAPPY ABOUT THAT?
YOU LIKE ME NOW, DON'T YOU?
OR WOULD YOU STILL HAVE PREFERRED UTSUHO?
ARE YOU HURT, NIBYO-SAN?
AW, I'M FINE!
I'M...

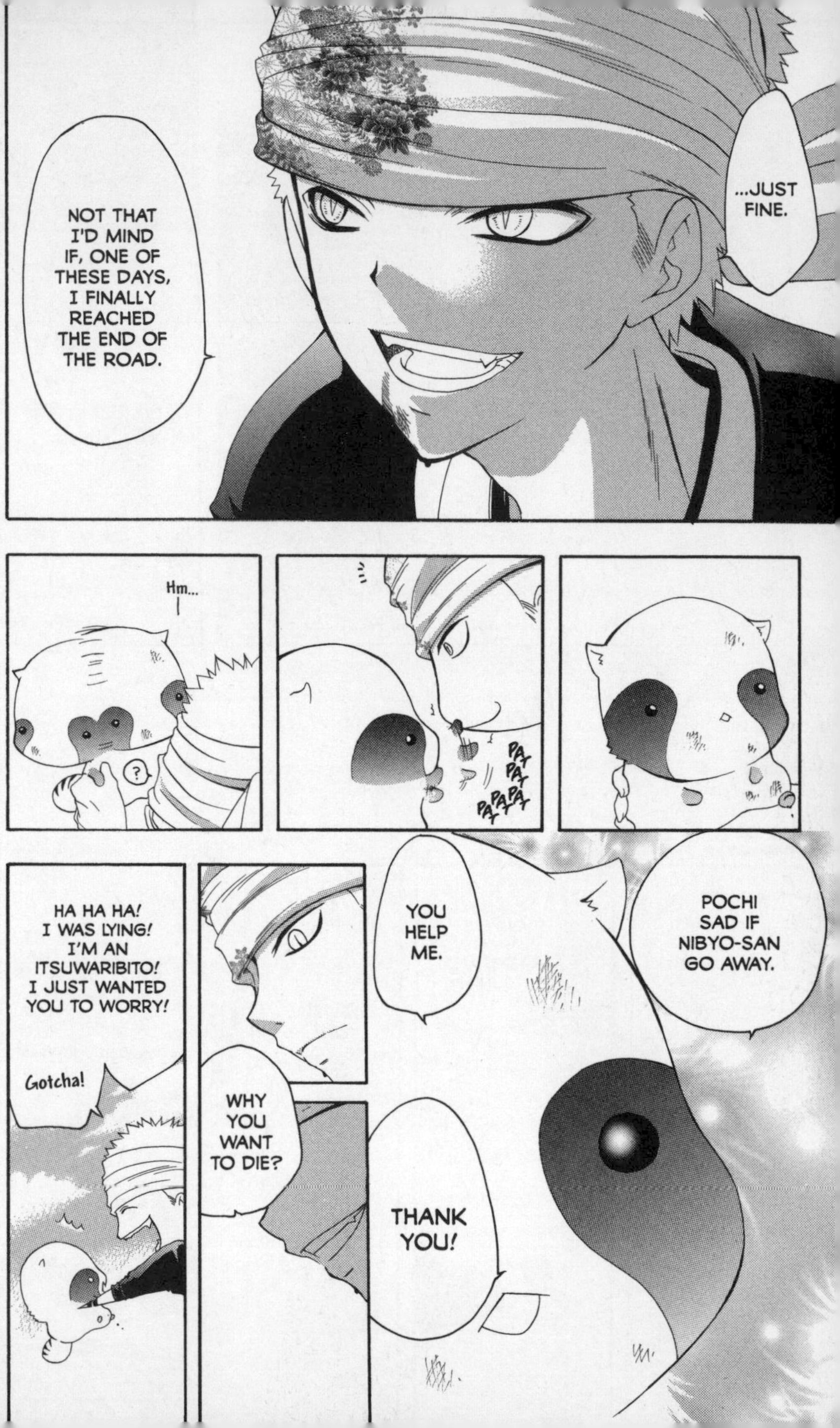
...JUST FINE.
NOT THAT I'D MIND IF, ONE OF THESE DAYS, I FINALLY REACHED THE END OF THE ROAD.
PAT PAT PAT PAT PAT PAT
Hm...
?
POCHI SAD IF NIBYO-SAN GO AWAY.
YOU HELP ME.
THANK YOU!
WHY YOU WANT TO DIE?
HA HA HA! I WAS LYING! I'M AN ITSUWARIBITO! I JUST WANTED YOU TO WORRY!
Gotcha!

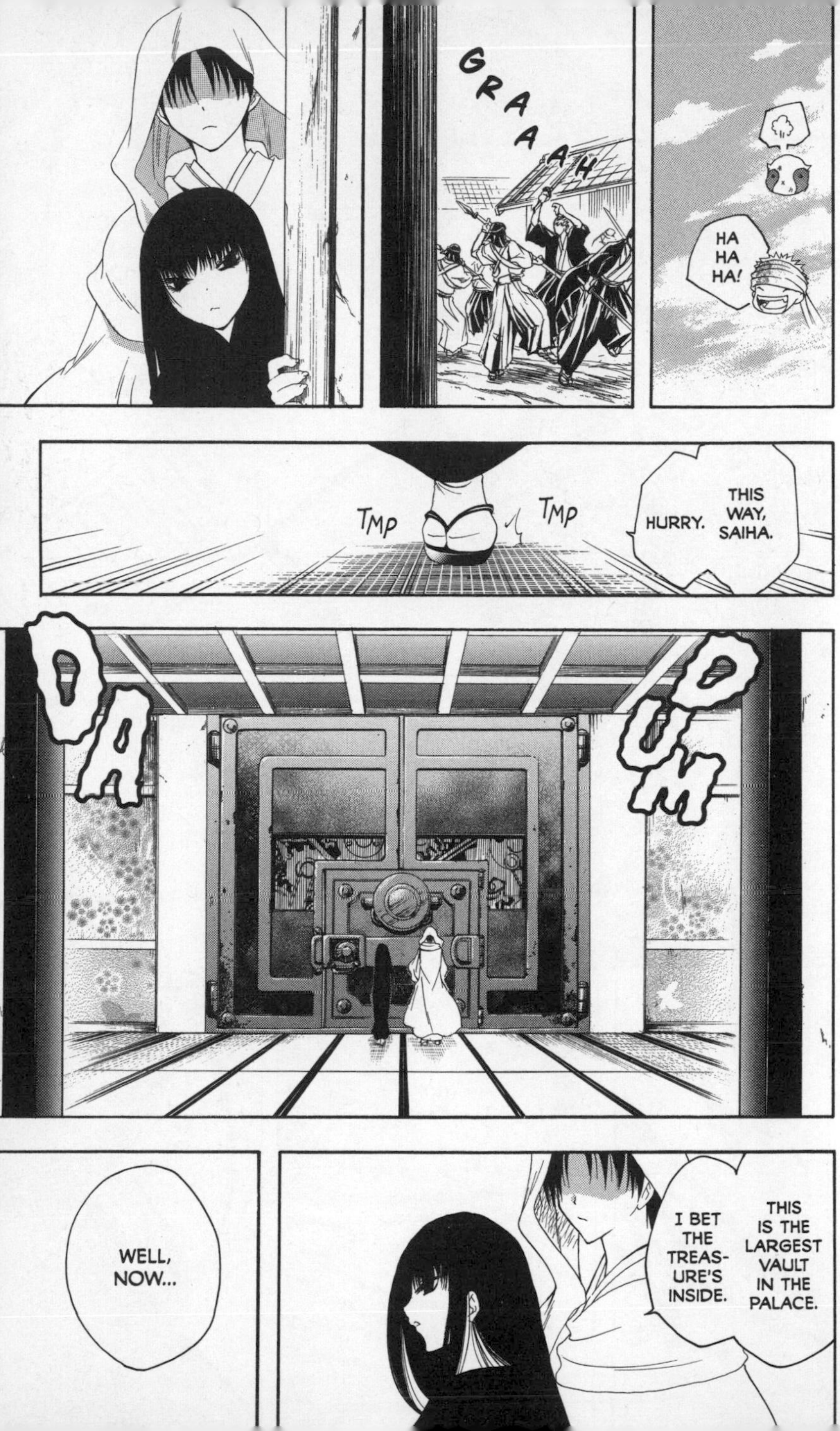
HA HA HA!
GRAAAAH
THIS WAY, SAIHA.
HURRY.
TMP
TMP
DUM
DA
THIS IS THE LARGEST VAULT IN THE PALACE.
I BET THE TREASURE'S INSIDE.
WELL, NOW...

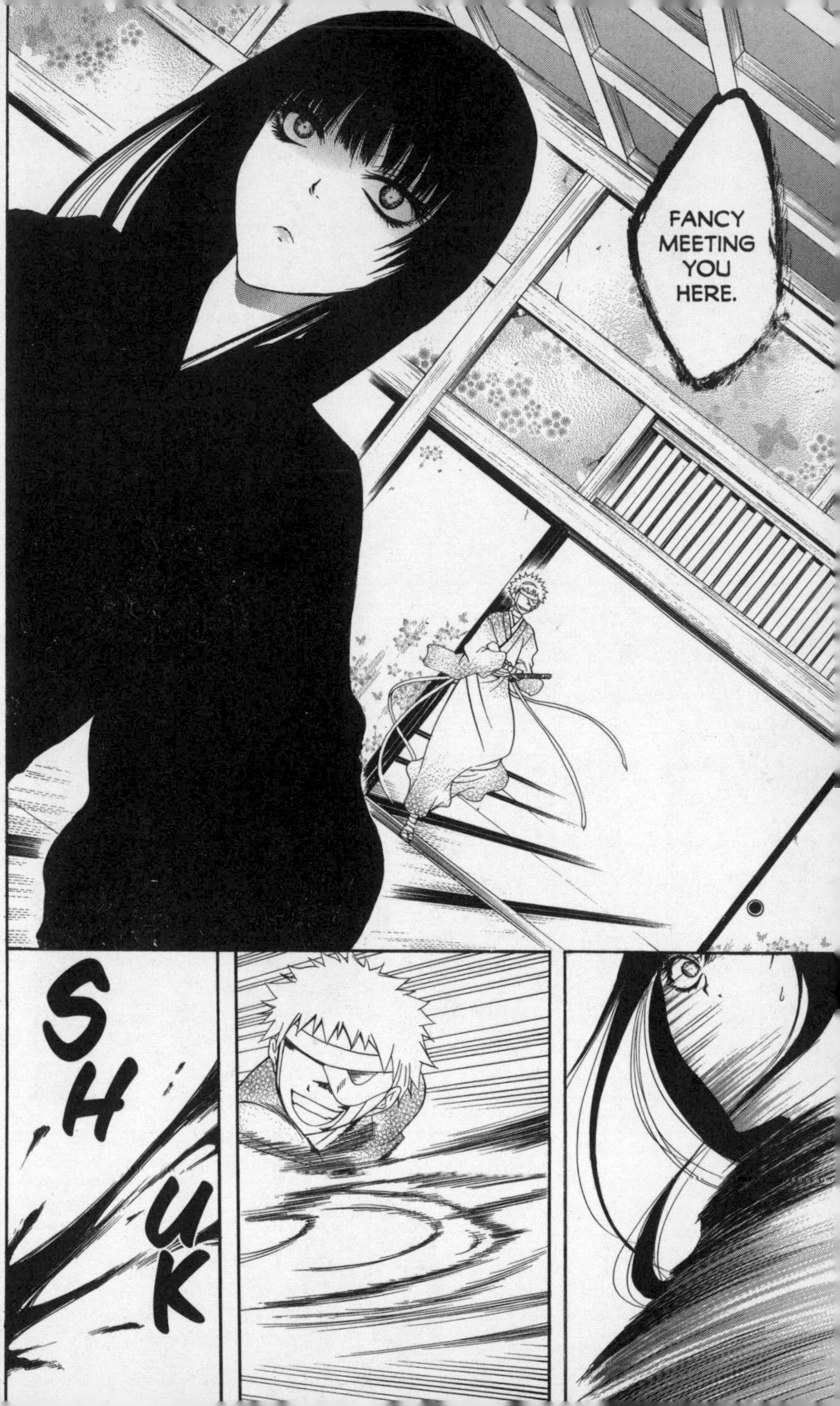
FANCY MEETING YOU HERE.
SHUK

Chapter 105 Happiness

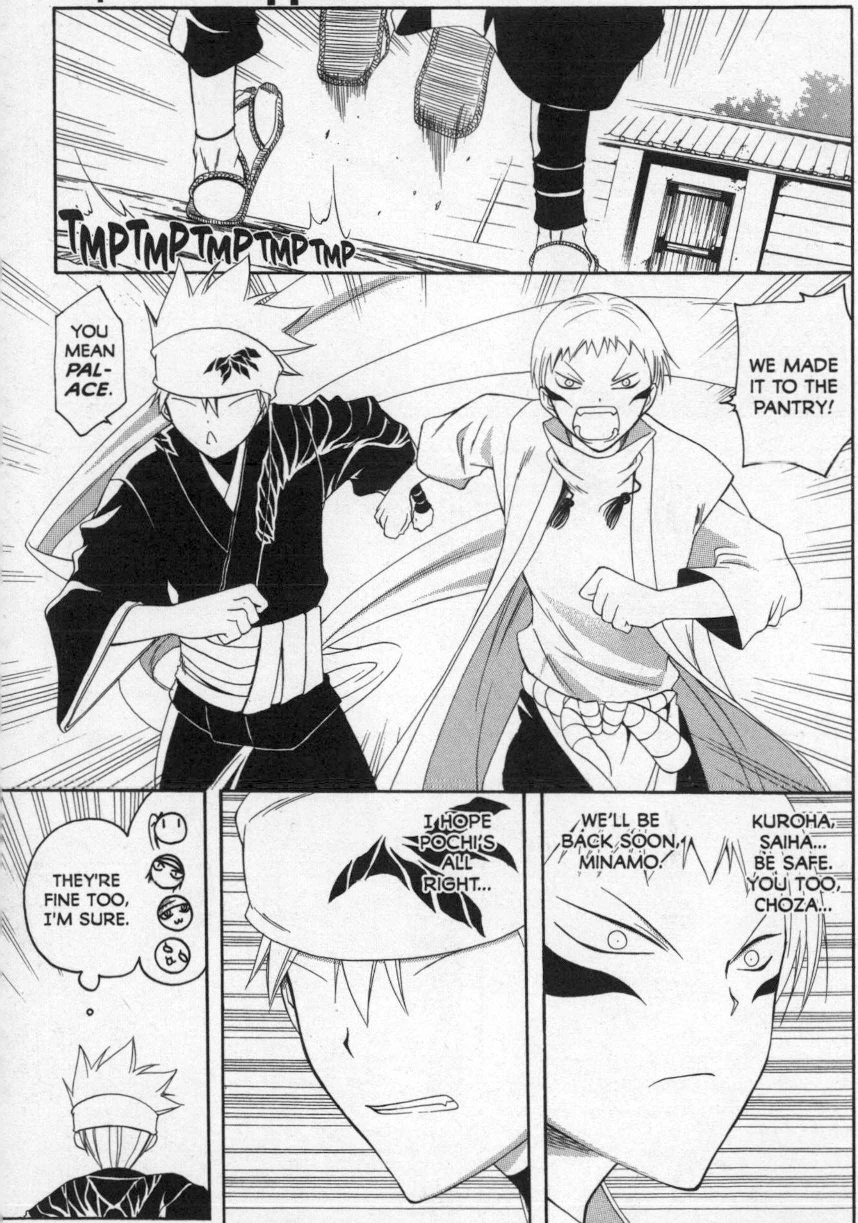
TMPTMPTMPTMPTMP
WE MADE IT TO THE PANTRY!
YOU MEAN PALACE.
KUROHA, SAIHA... BE SAFE. YOU TOO, CHOZA...
WE'LL BE BACK SOON, MINAMO!
I HOPE POCHI'S ALL RIGHT...
THEY'RE FINE TOO, I'M SURE.

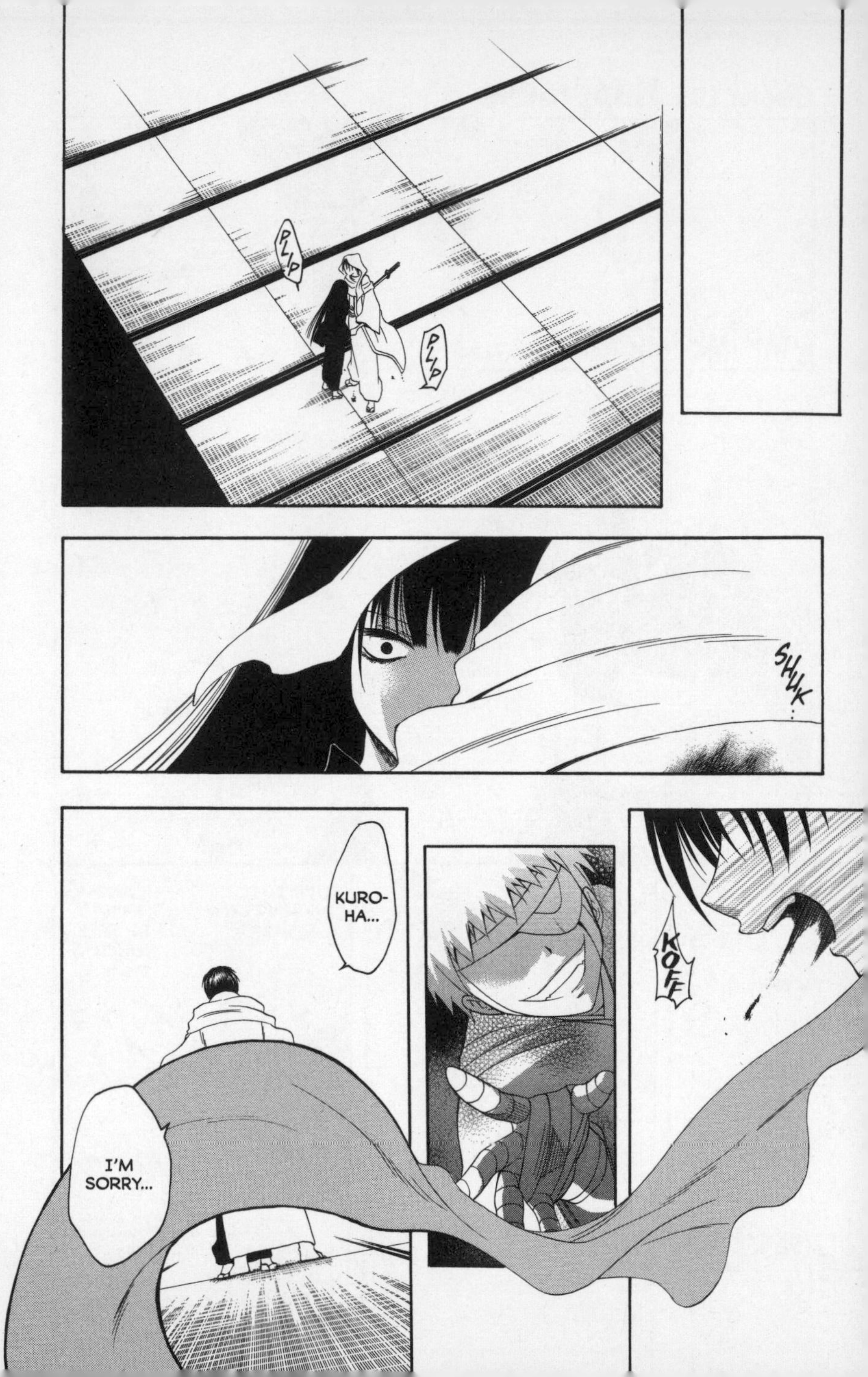
PLIP
PLIP
SHUK
KOFF
KURO-HA...
I'M SORRY...

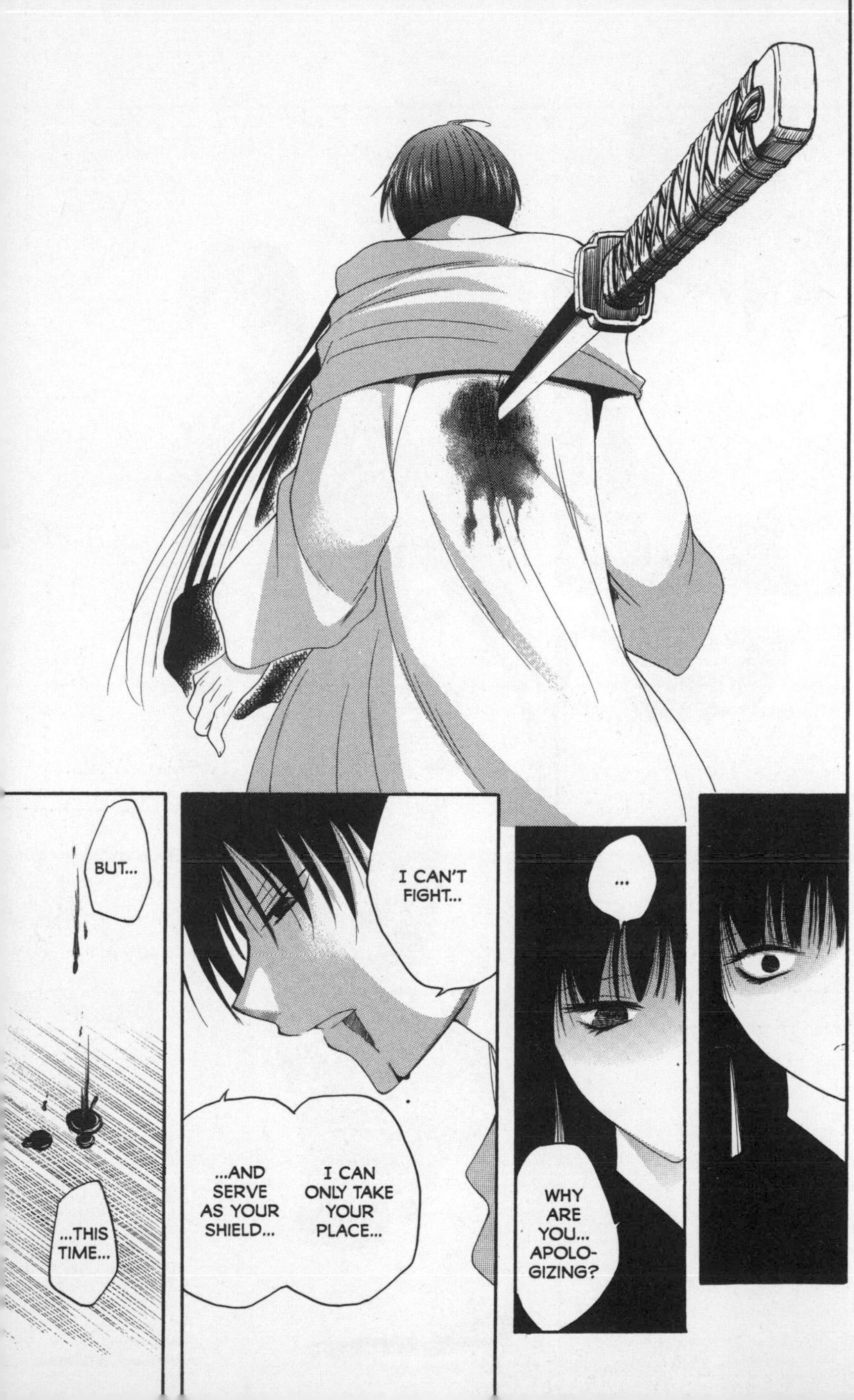
...
WHY ARE YOU... APOLOGIZING?
I CAN'T FIGHT...
I CAN ONLY TAKE YOUR PLACE...
...AND SERVE AS YOUR SHIELD...
BUT...
...THIS TIME...

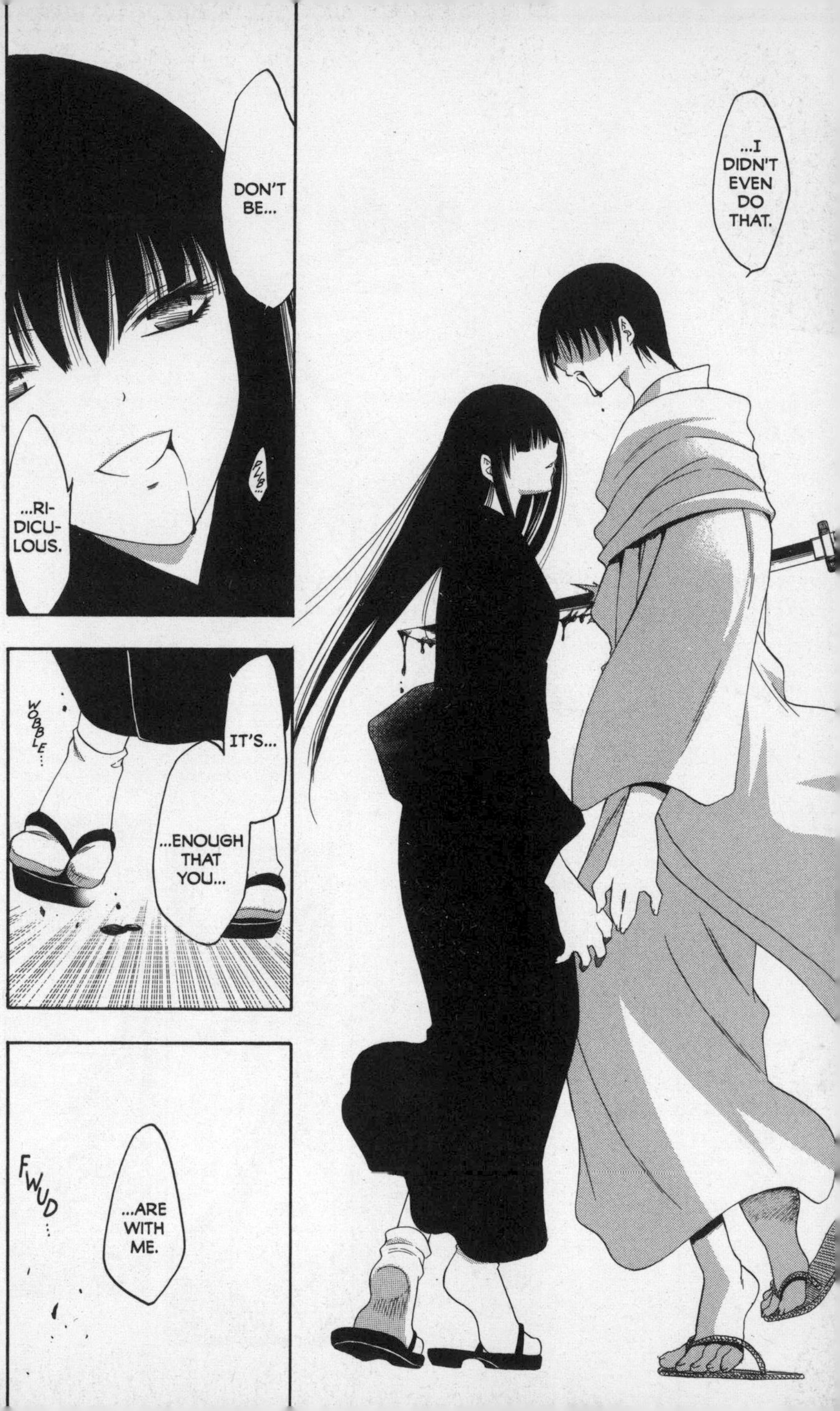
...I DIDN'T EVEN DO THAT.
DON'T BE...
PLIB...
...RI-DICU-LOUS.
IT'S...
WOBBLE...
...ENOUGH THAT YOU...
FWUD...
...ARE WITH ME.

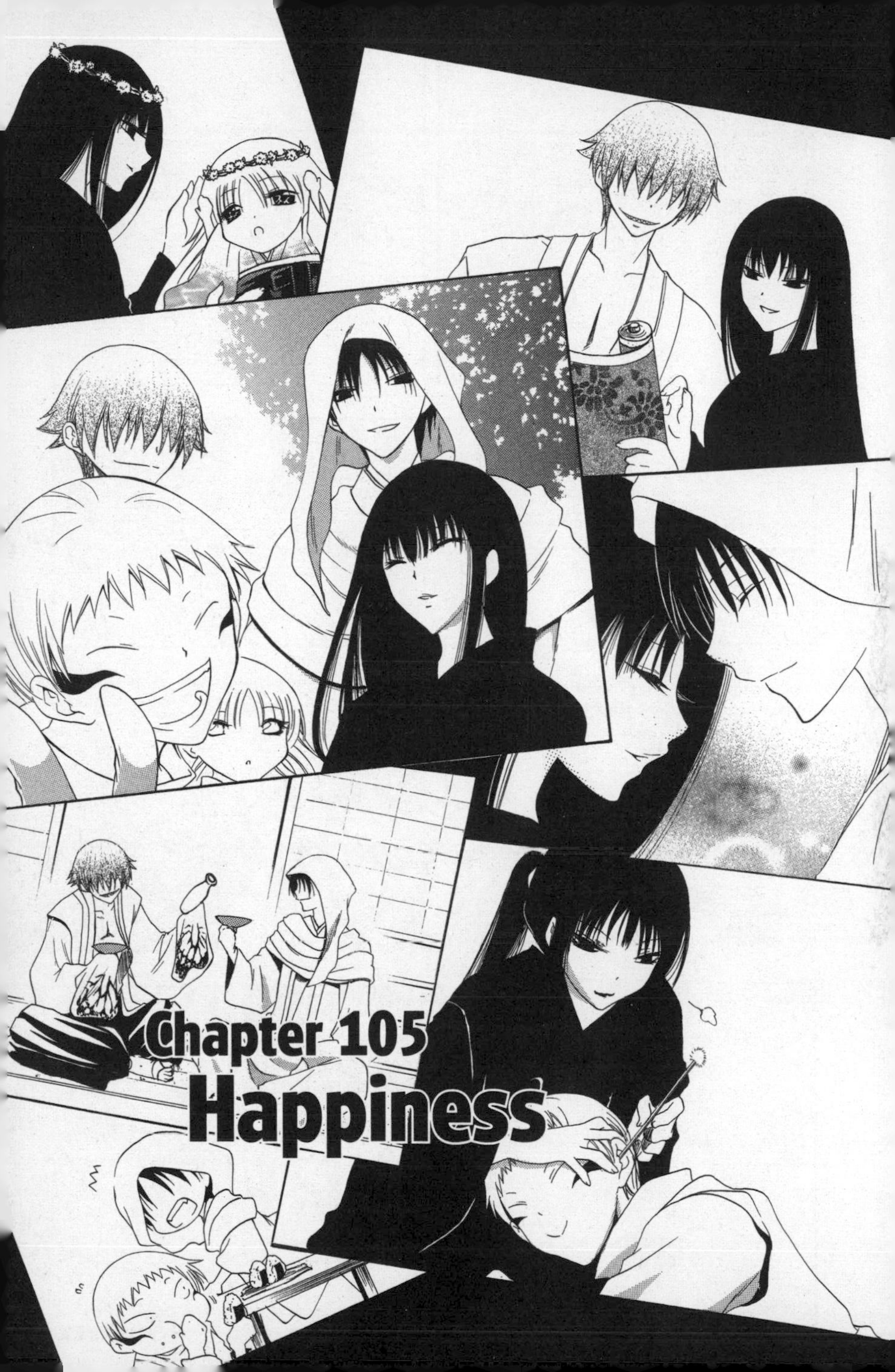
Chapter 105
Happiness

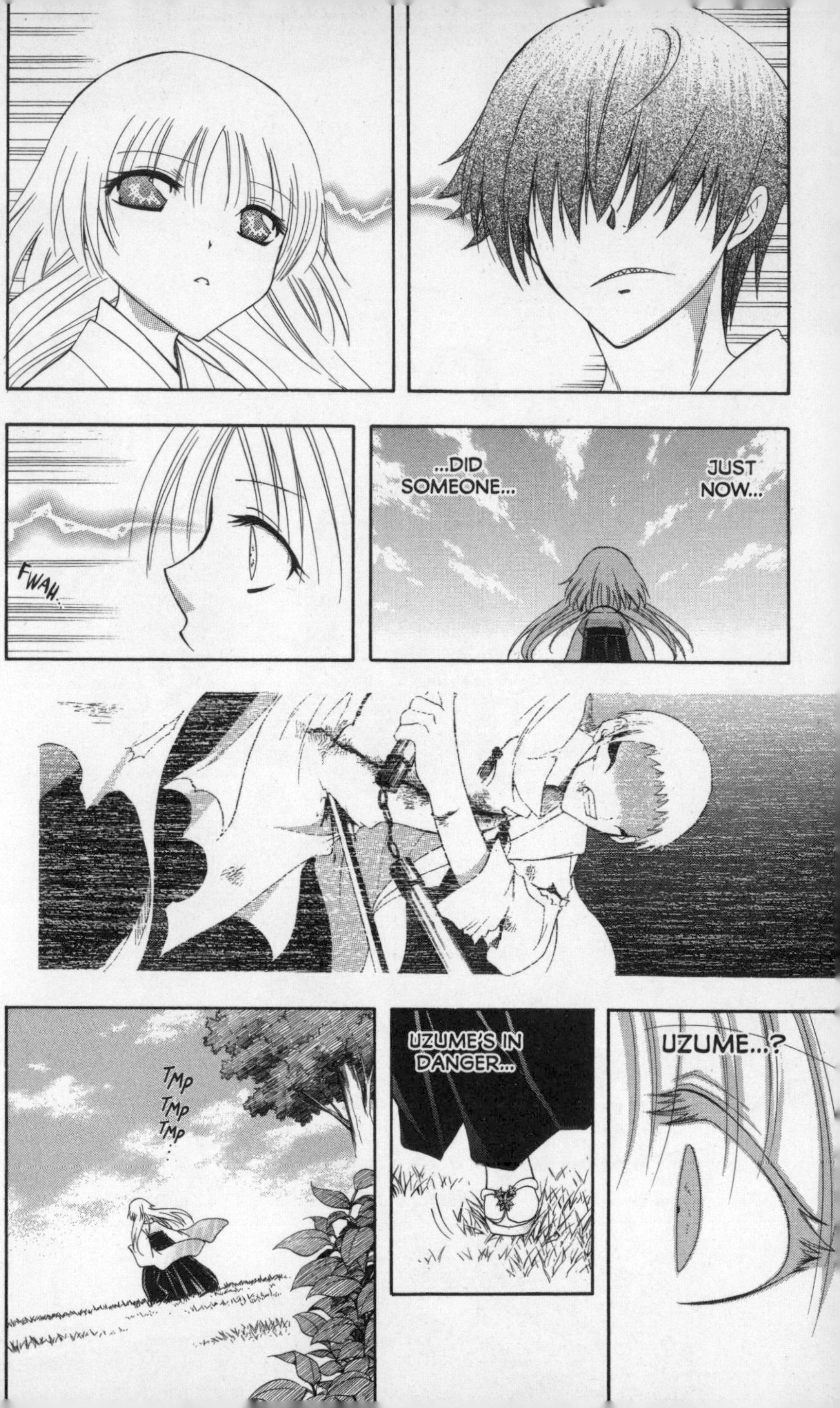
JUST NOW...
...DID SOMEONE...
FWAH..
UZUME...?
UZUME'S IN DANGER...
TMP TMP TMP...

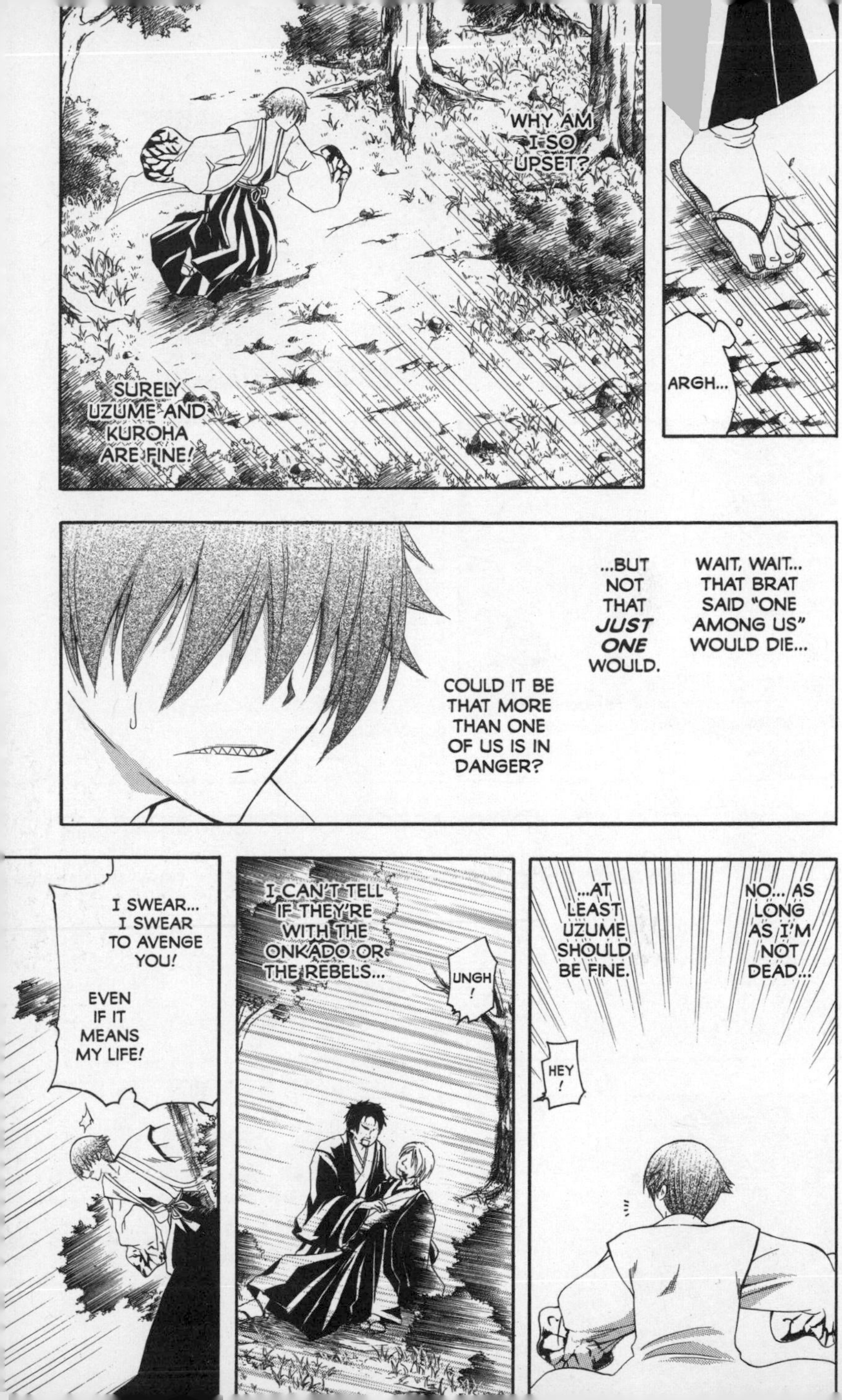
ARGH...
WHY AM I SO UPSET?
SURELY UZUME AND KUROHA ARE FINE!
WAIT, WAIT... THAT BRAT SAID "ONE AMONG US" WOULD DIE...
...BUT NOT THAT *JUST ONE* WOULD.
COULD IT BE THAT MORE THAN ONE OF US IS IN DANGER?
NO... AS LONG AS I'M NOT DEAD...
...AT LEAST UZUME SHOULD BE FINE.
HEY!
UNGH!
I CAN'T TELL IF THEY'RE WITH THE ONKADO OR THE REBELS...
I SWEAR... I SWEAR TO AVENGE YOU!
EVEN IF IT MEANS MY LIFE!

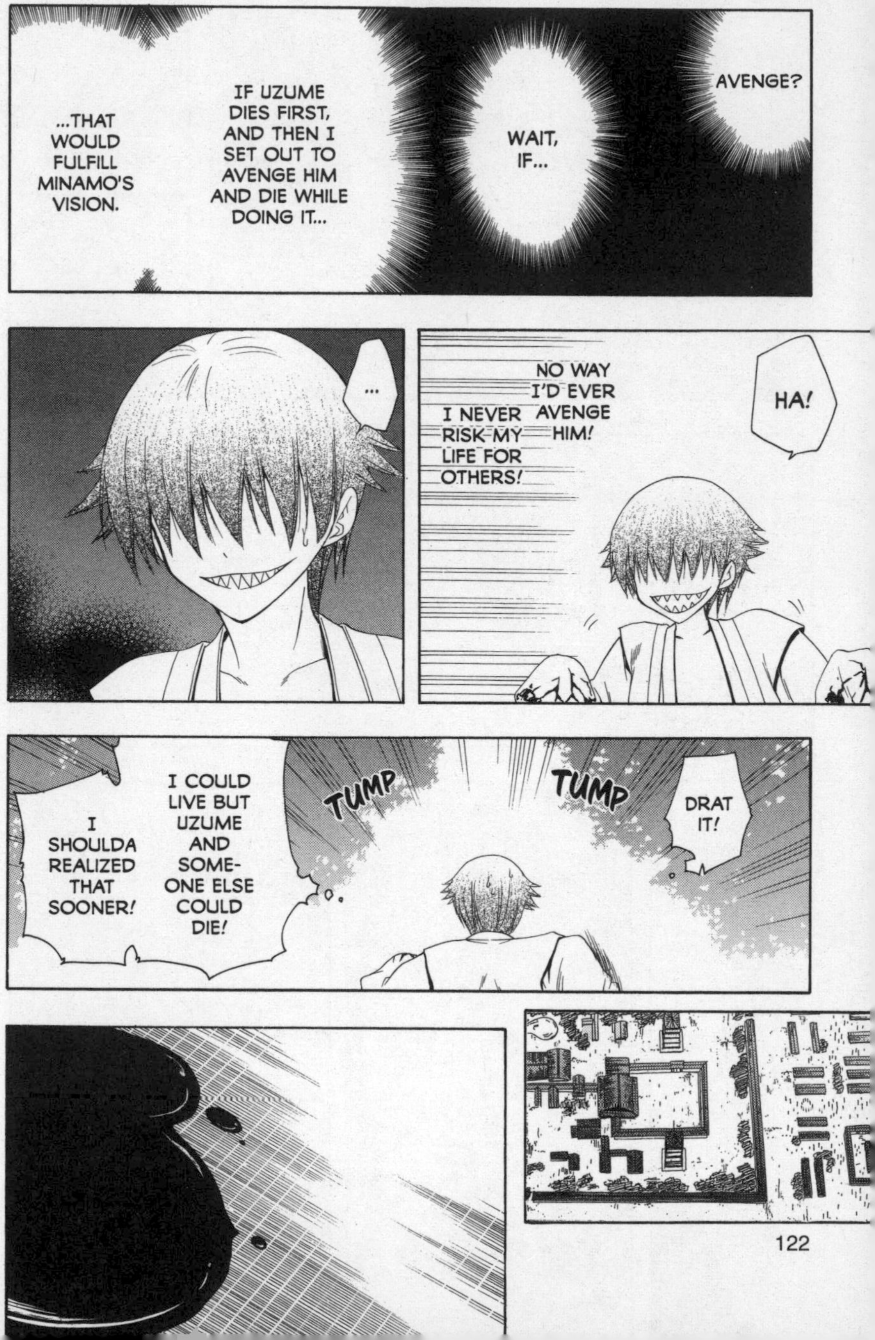
AVENGE?
WAIT, IF...
IF UZUME DIES FIRST, AND THEN I SET OUT TO AVENGE HIM AND DIE WHILE DOING IT...
...THAT WOULD FULFILL MINAMO'S VISION.
HA!
NO WAY I'D EVER AVENGE HIM!
I NEVER RISK MY LIFE FOR OTHERS!
...
DRAT IT!
TUMP
TUMP
I COULD LIVE BUT UZUME AND SOME-ONE ELSE COULD DIE!
I SHOULDA REALIZED THAT SOONER!

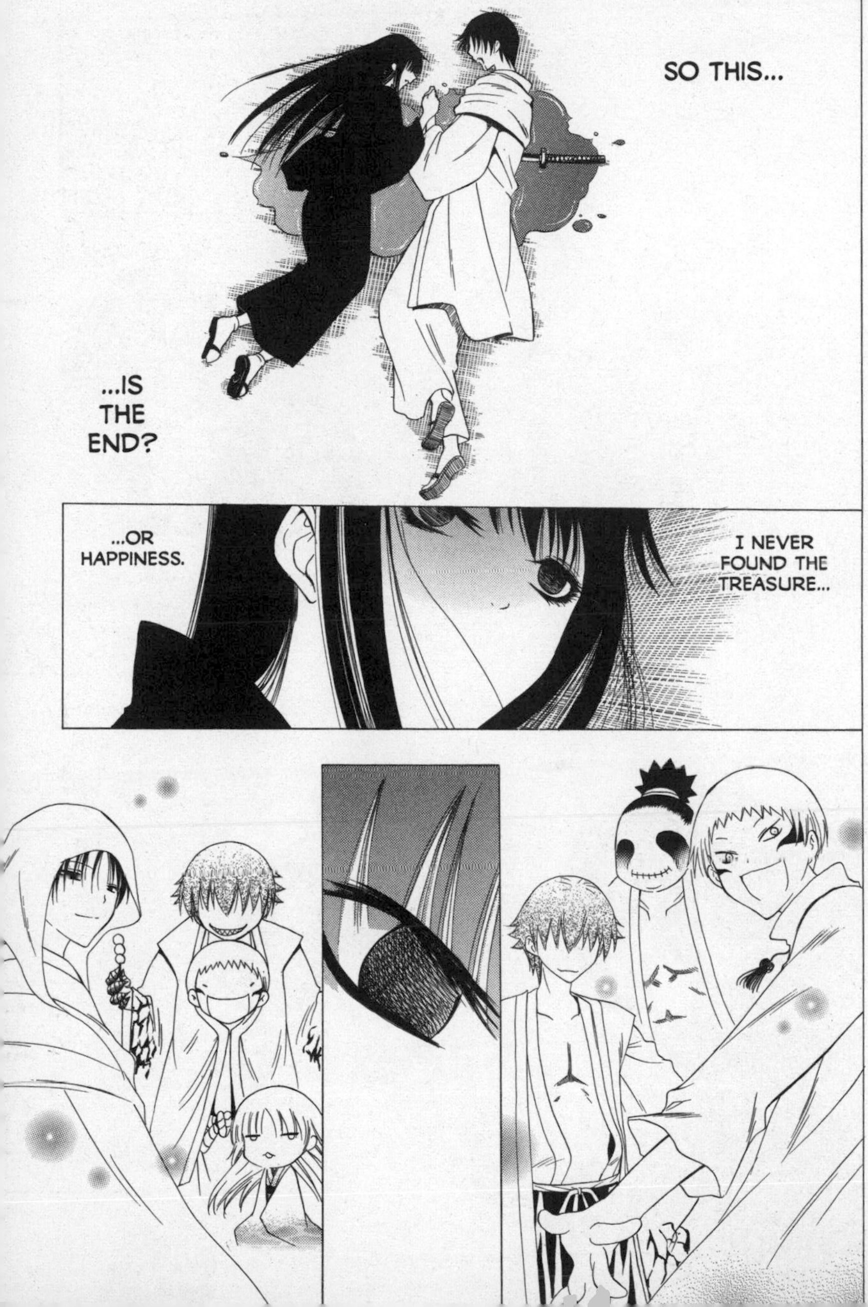
SO THIS...
...IS THE END?
I NEVER FOUND THE TREASURE...
...OR HAPPINESS.

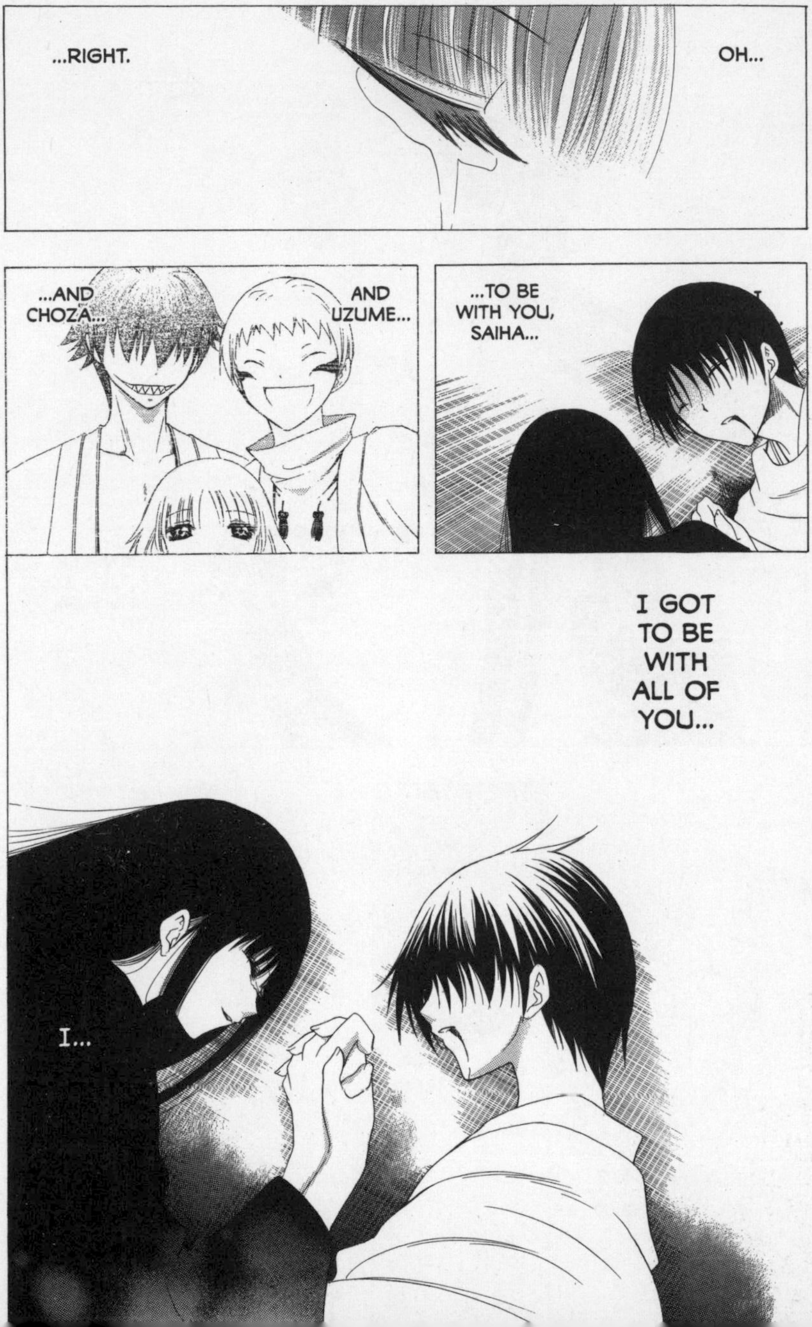
OH...
...RIGHT.
I...
...TO BE WITH YOU, SAIHA...
AND UZUME...
...AND CHOZA...
I GOT TO BE WITH ALL OF YOU...
I...

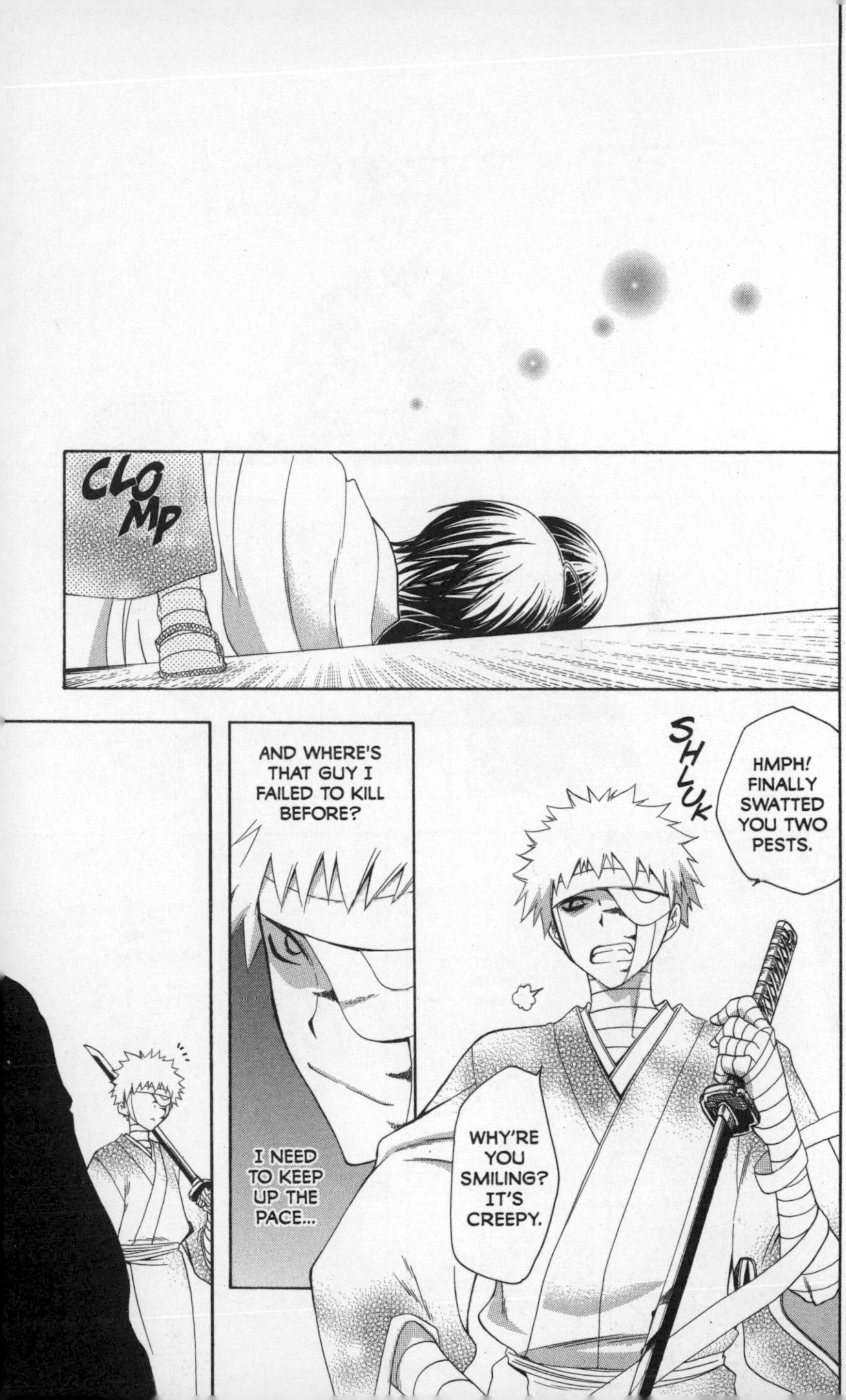
CLOMP
SHLUK
HMPH! FINALLY SWATTED YOU TWO PESTS.
WHY'RE YOU SMILING? IT'S CREEPY.
AND WHERE'S THAT GUY I FAILED TO KILL BEFORE?
I NEED TO KEEP UP THE PACE...

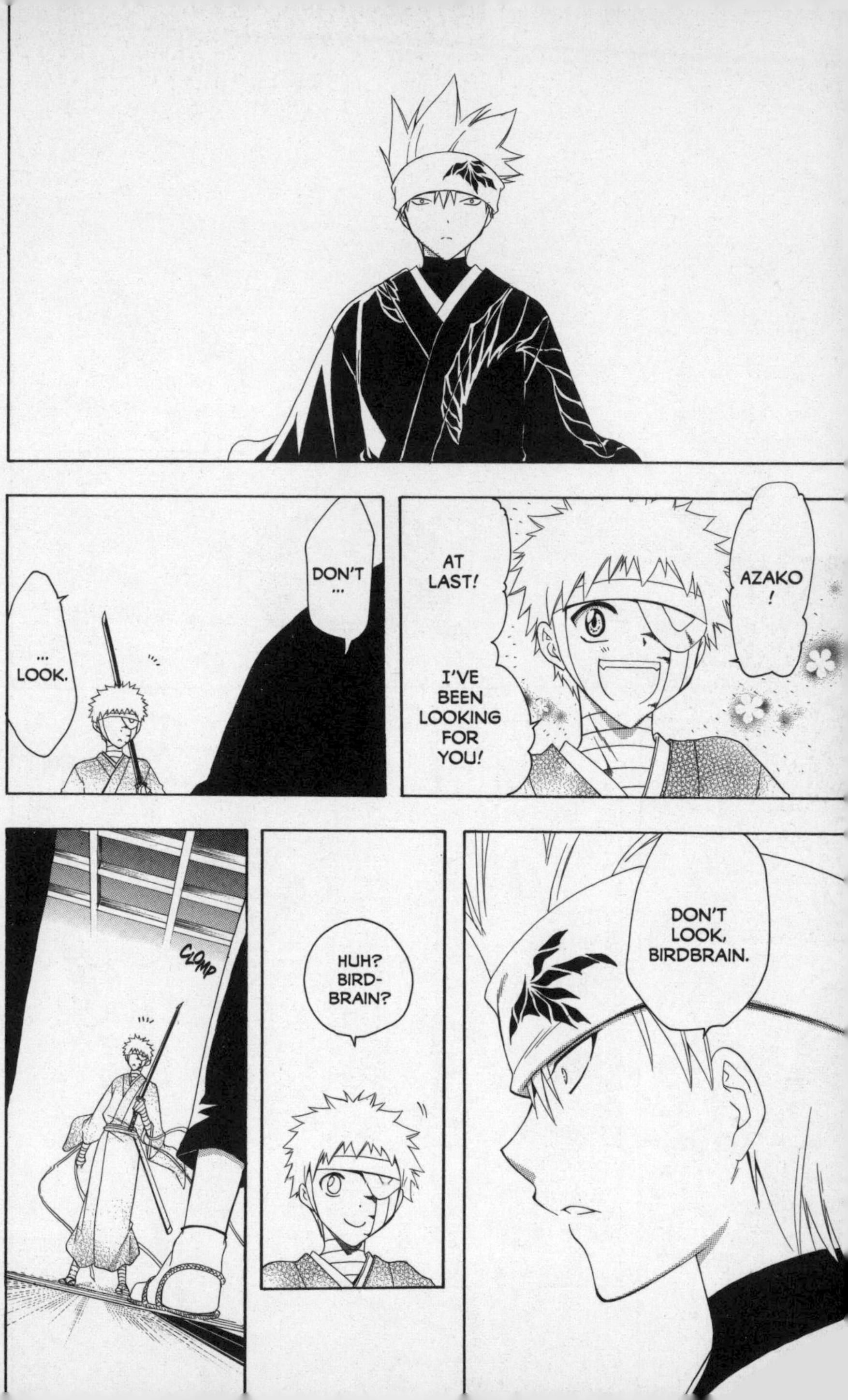
AZAKO!
AT LAST!
I'VE BEEN LOOKING FOR YOU!
DON'T ...
... LOOK.
DON'T LOOK, BIRDBRAIN.
HUH? BIRD-BRAIN?
CLOMP

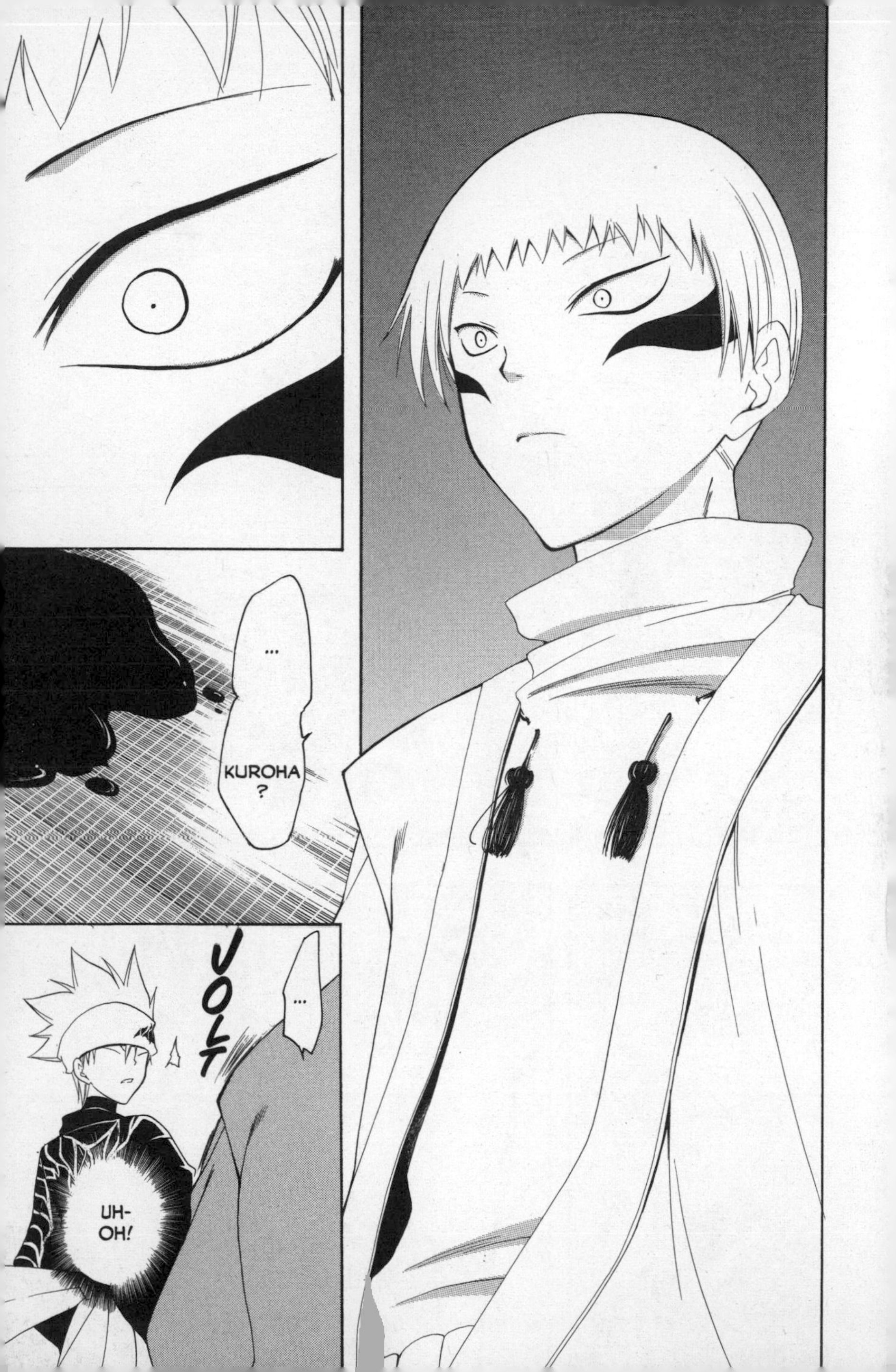
...
KUROHA?
...
JOLT
UH-OH!

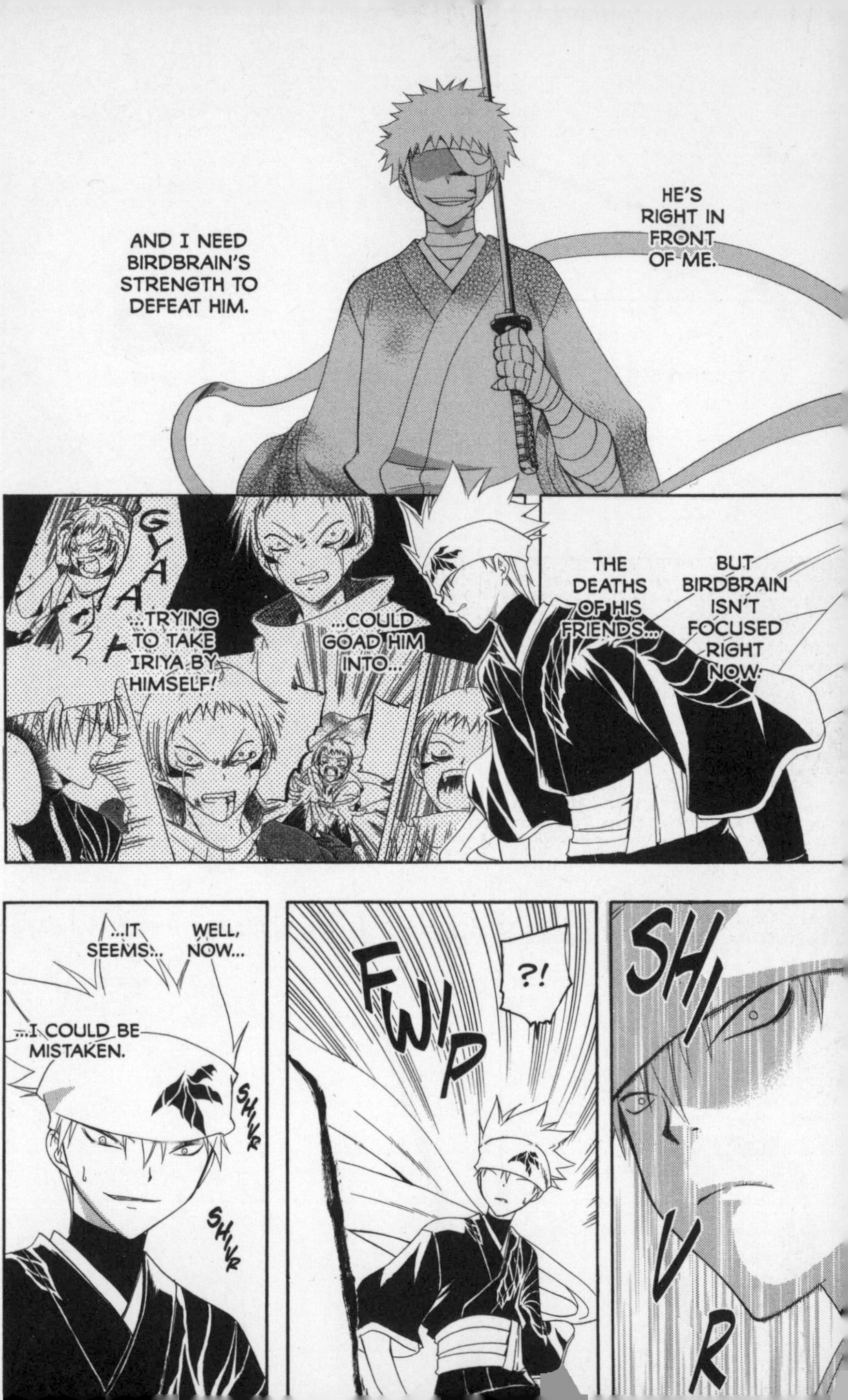
HE'S RIGHT IN FRONT OF ME.
AND I NEED BIRDBRAIN'S STRENGTH TO DEFEAT HIM.
BUT BIRDBRAIN ISN'T FOCUSED RIGHT NOW.
THE DEATHS OF HIS FRIENDS...
...COULD GOAD HIM INTO...
...TRYING TO TAKE IRIYA BY HIMSELF!
GYAA
SHIVVR
?!
FWIP
WELL, NOW...
...IT SEEMS...
...I COULD BE MISTAKEN.
SHIVR
SHIVR

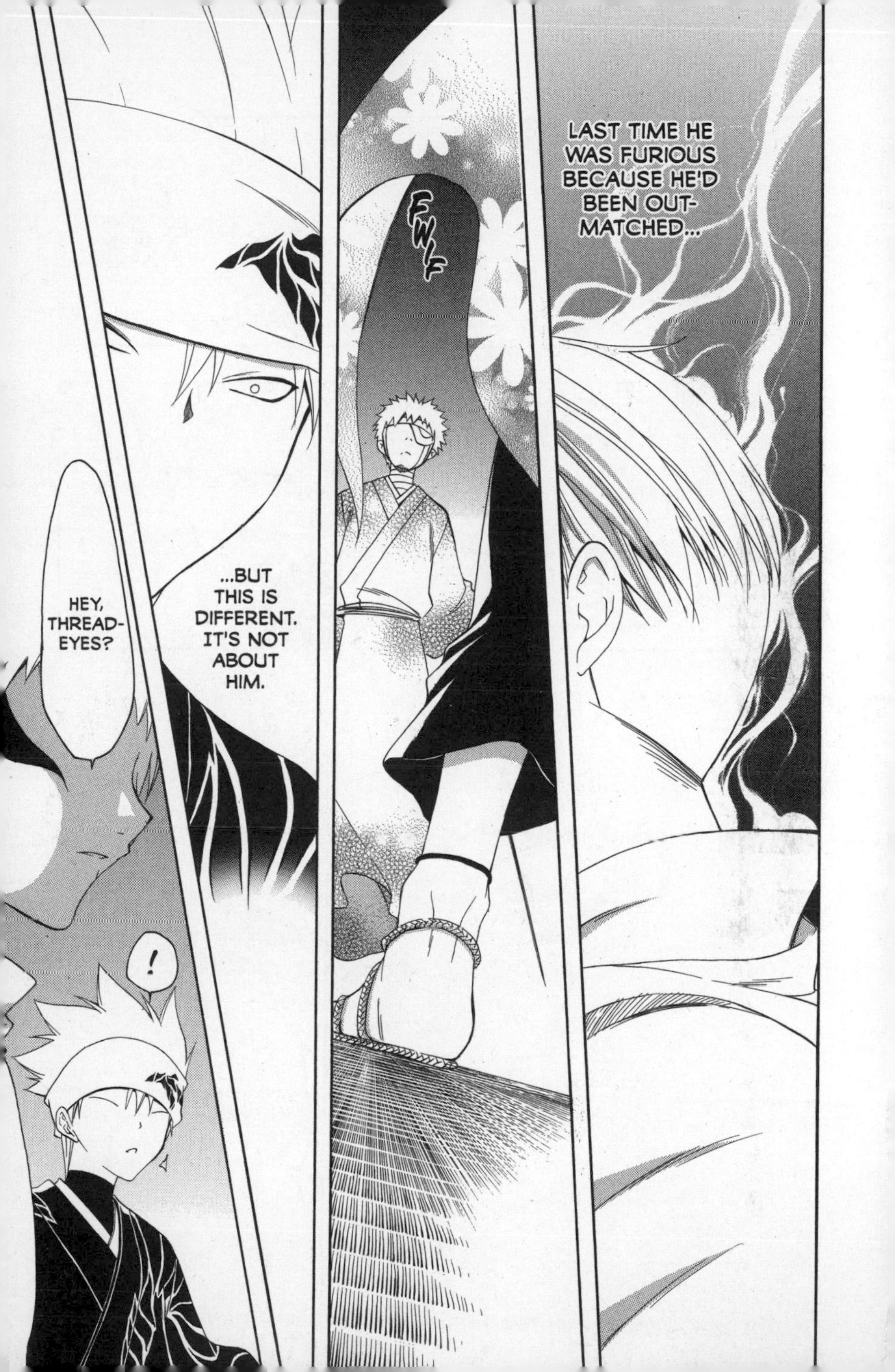

LAST TIME HE WAS FURIOUS BECAUSE HE'D BEEN OUT-MATCHED...
FWIF
...BUT THIS IS DIFFERENT. IT'S NOT ABOUT HIM.
HEY, THREAD-EYES?
!

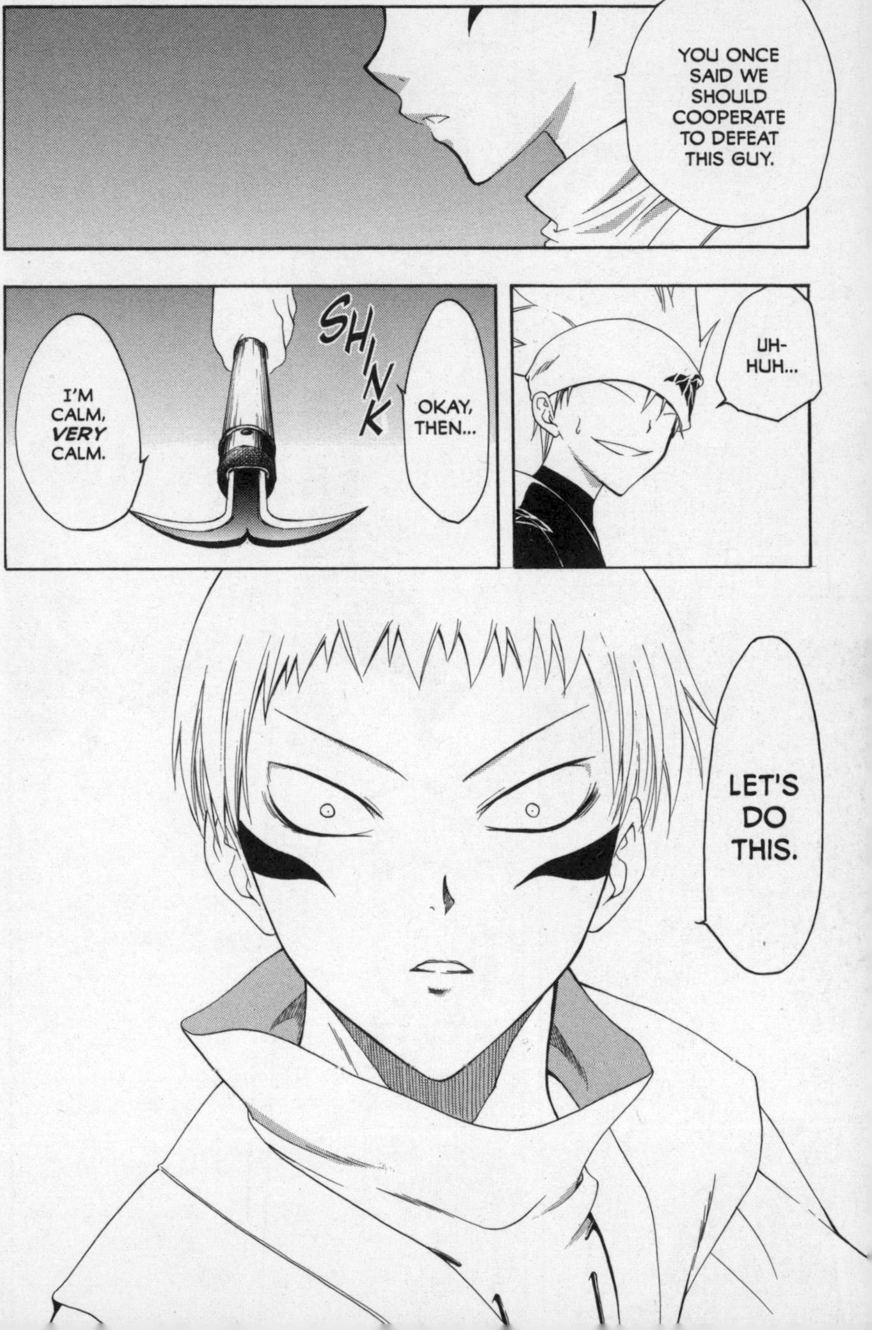
YOU ONCE SAID WE SHOULD COOPERATE TO DEFEAT THIS GUY.
UH-HUH...
OKAY, THEN...
SHINK
I'M CALM, *VERY* CALM.
LET'S DO THIS.

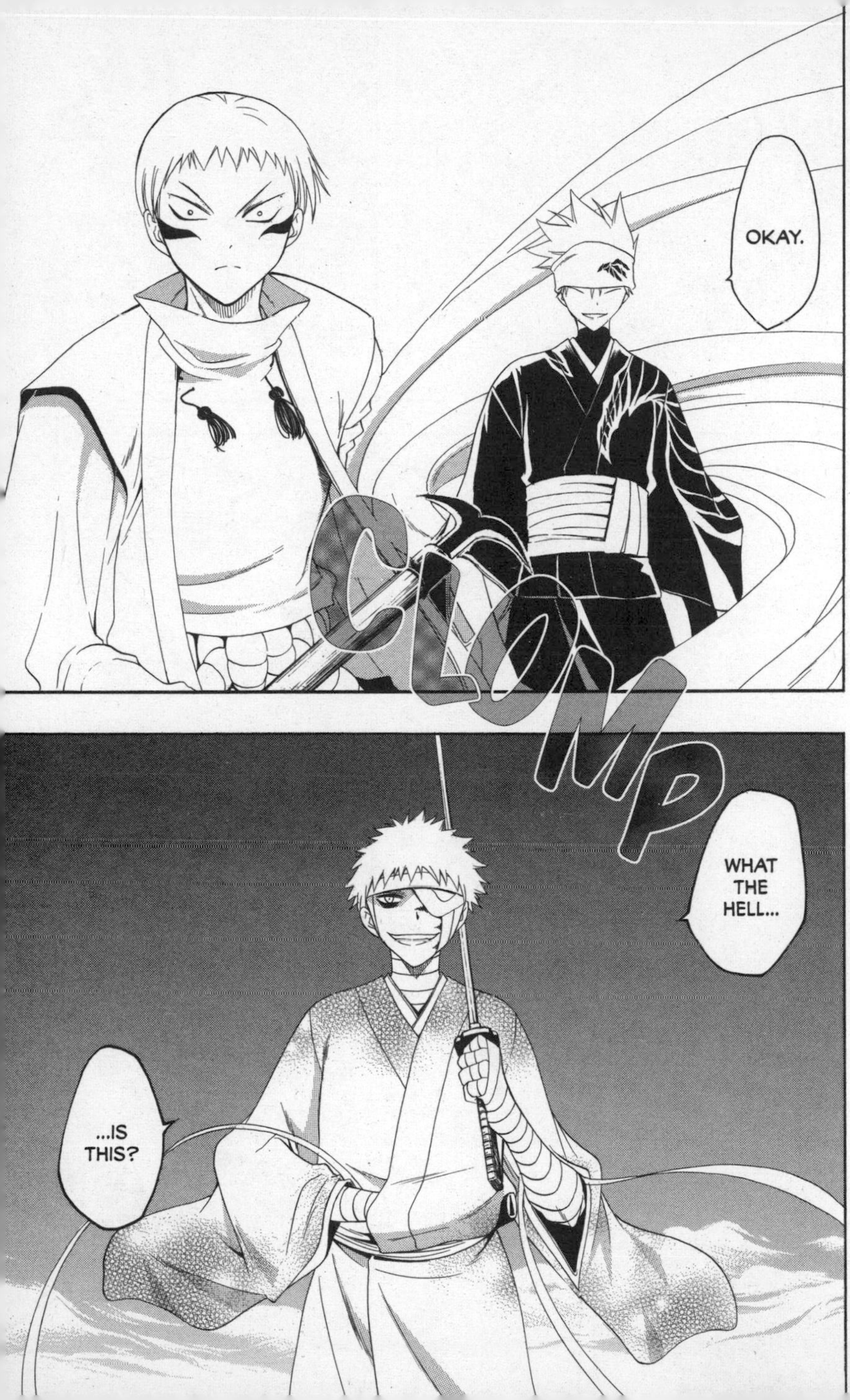
OKAY.
CLOMP
WHAT THE HELL...
...IS THIS?

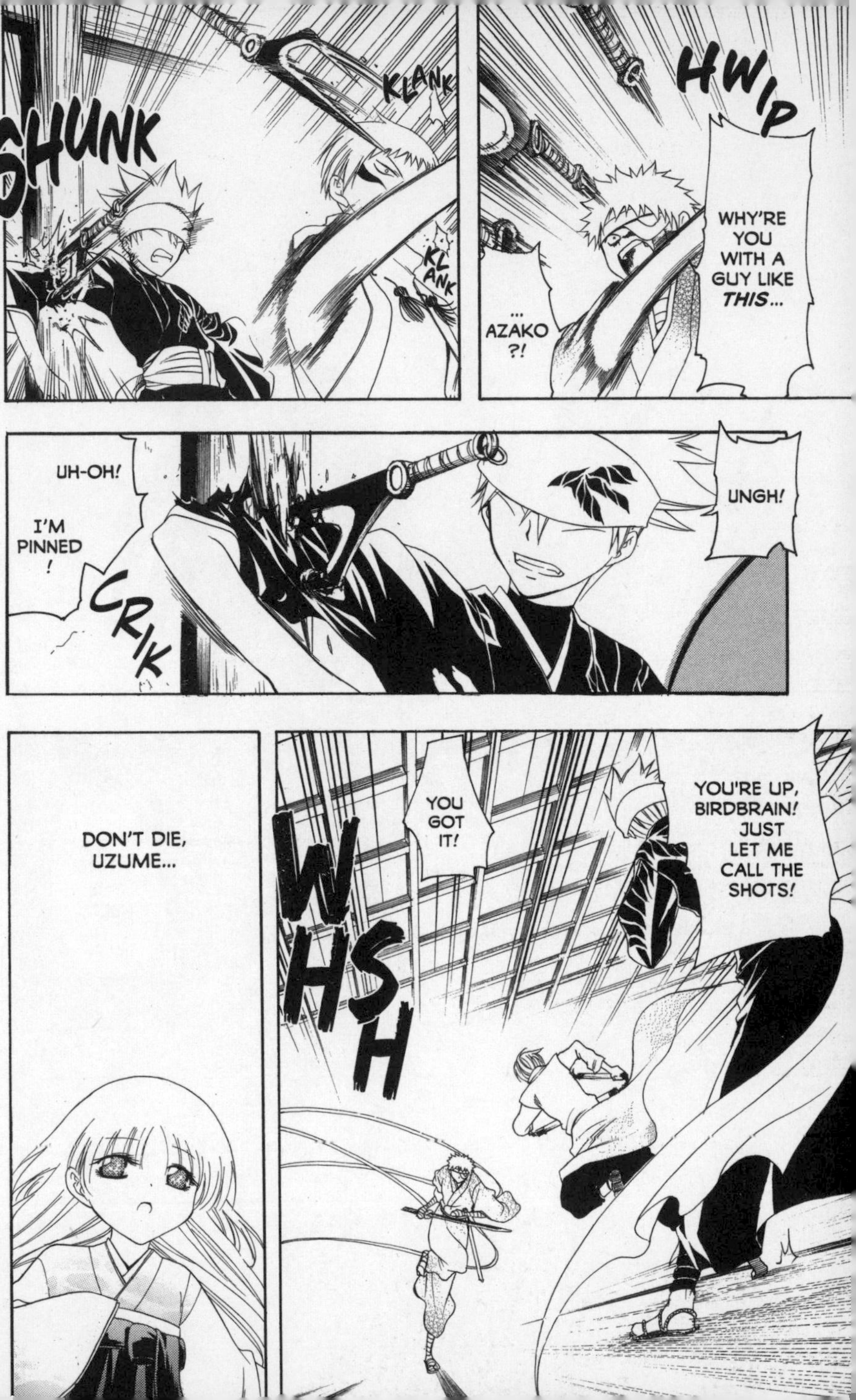
HWIP
WHY'RE YOU WITH A GUY LIKE *THIS*...
... AZAKO ?!
KLANK
SHUNK
KLANK
UNGH!
UH-OH!
I'M PINNED!
CRIK
YOU'RE UP, BIRDBRAIN! JUST LET ME CALL THE SHOTS!
YOU GOT IT!
WHSH
DON'T DIE, UZUME...

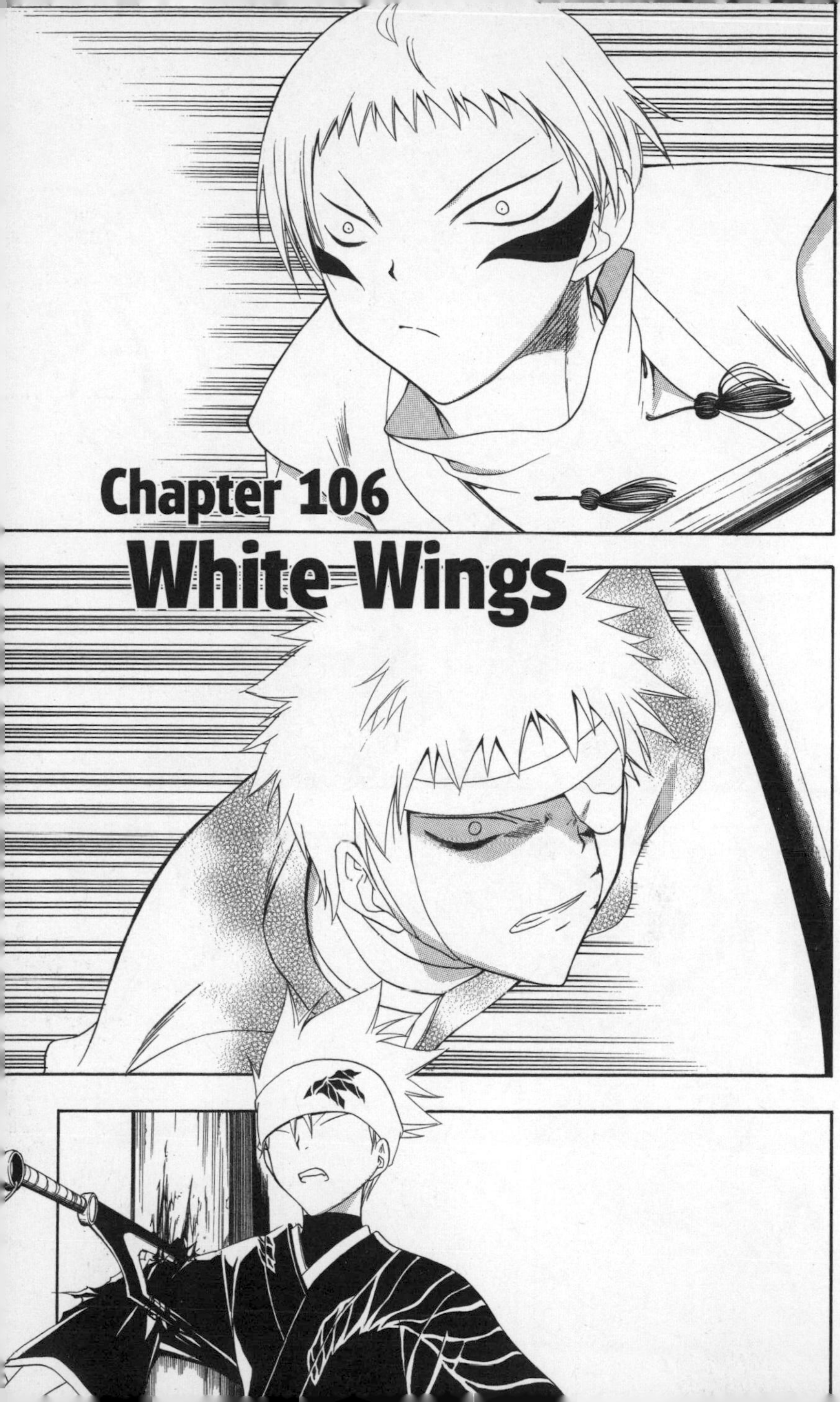
Chapter 106
White Wings

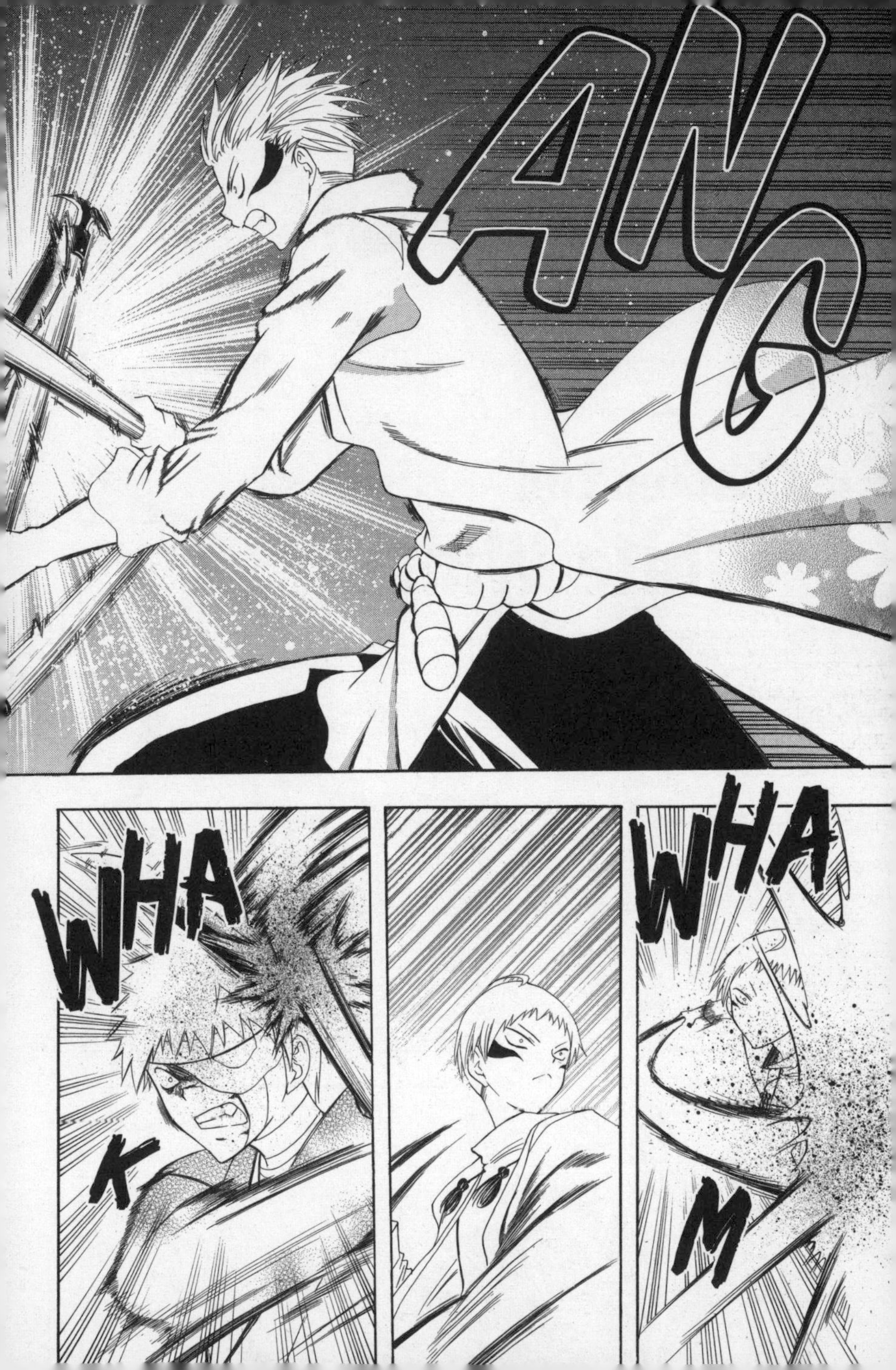
ANG
WHA
M
WHA
K

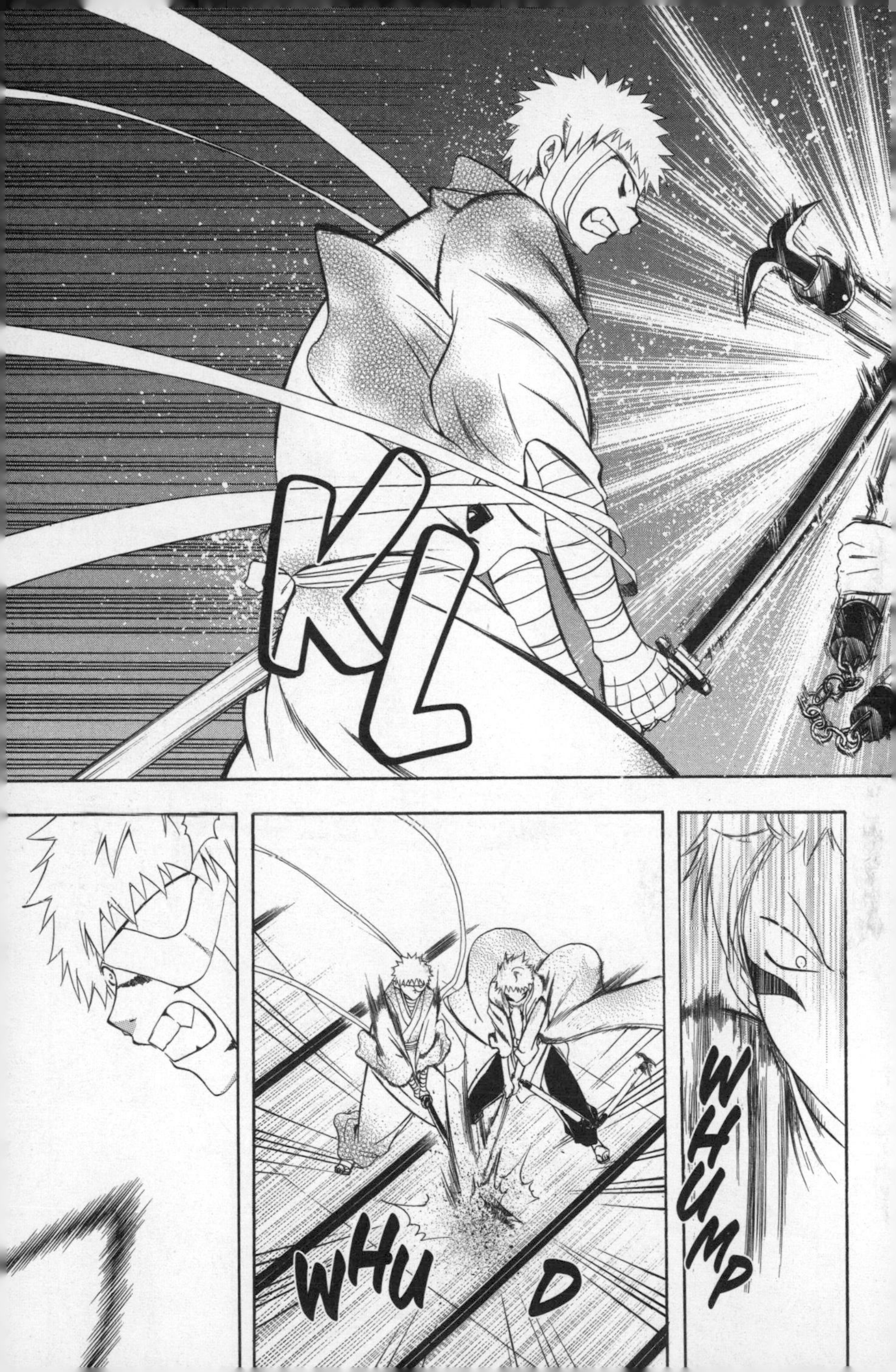
KL
WHUMP
WHU D

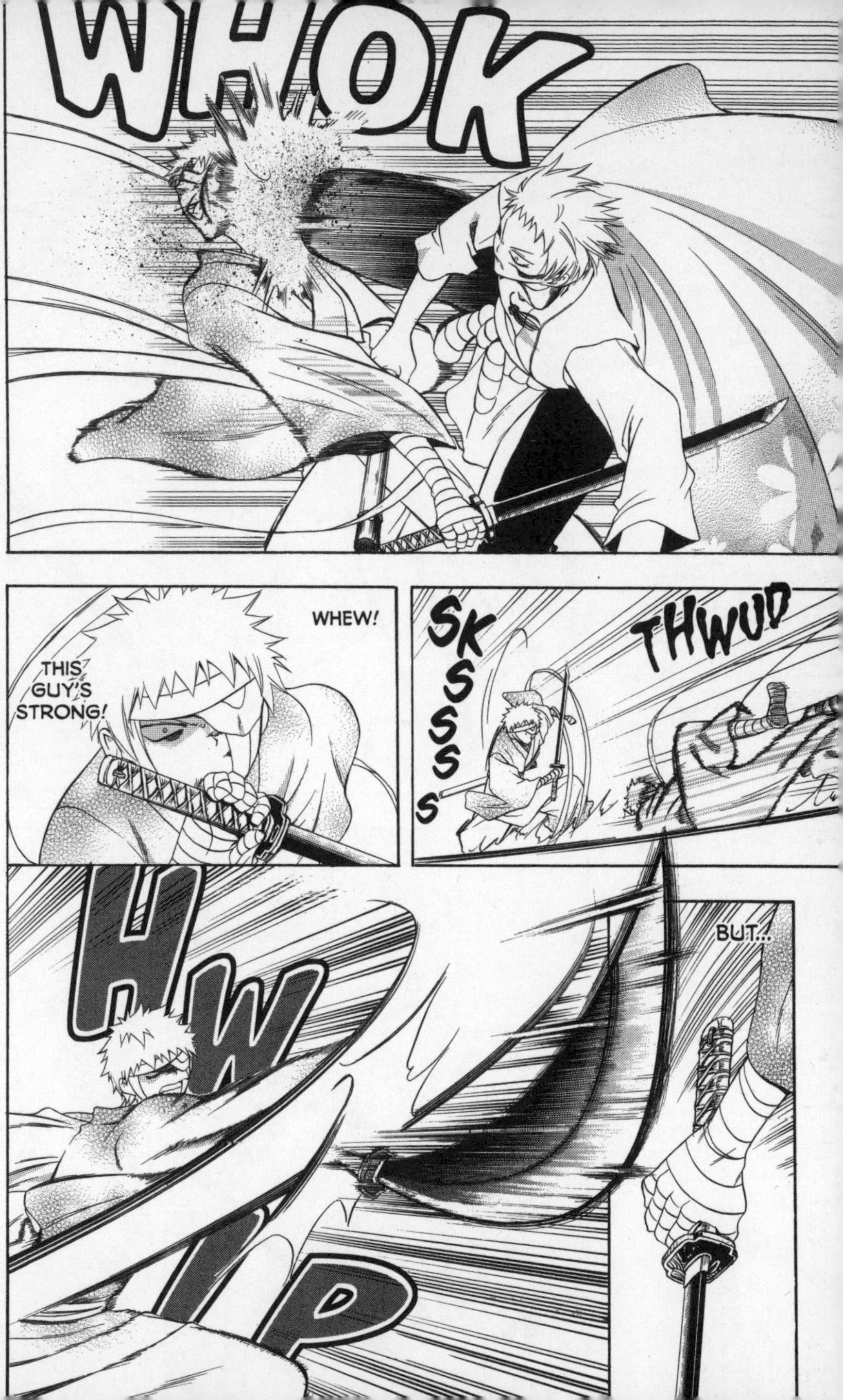
WHOK
THWUD
SKSSSSS
WHEW!
THIS GUY'S STRONG!
BUT...
HWIP

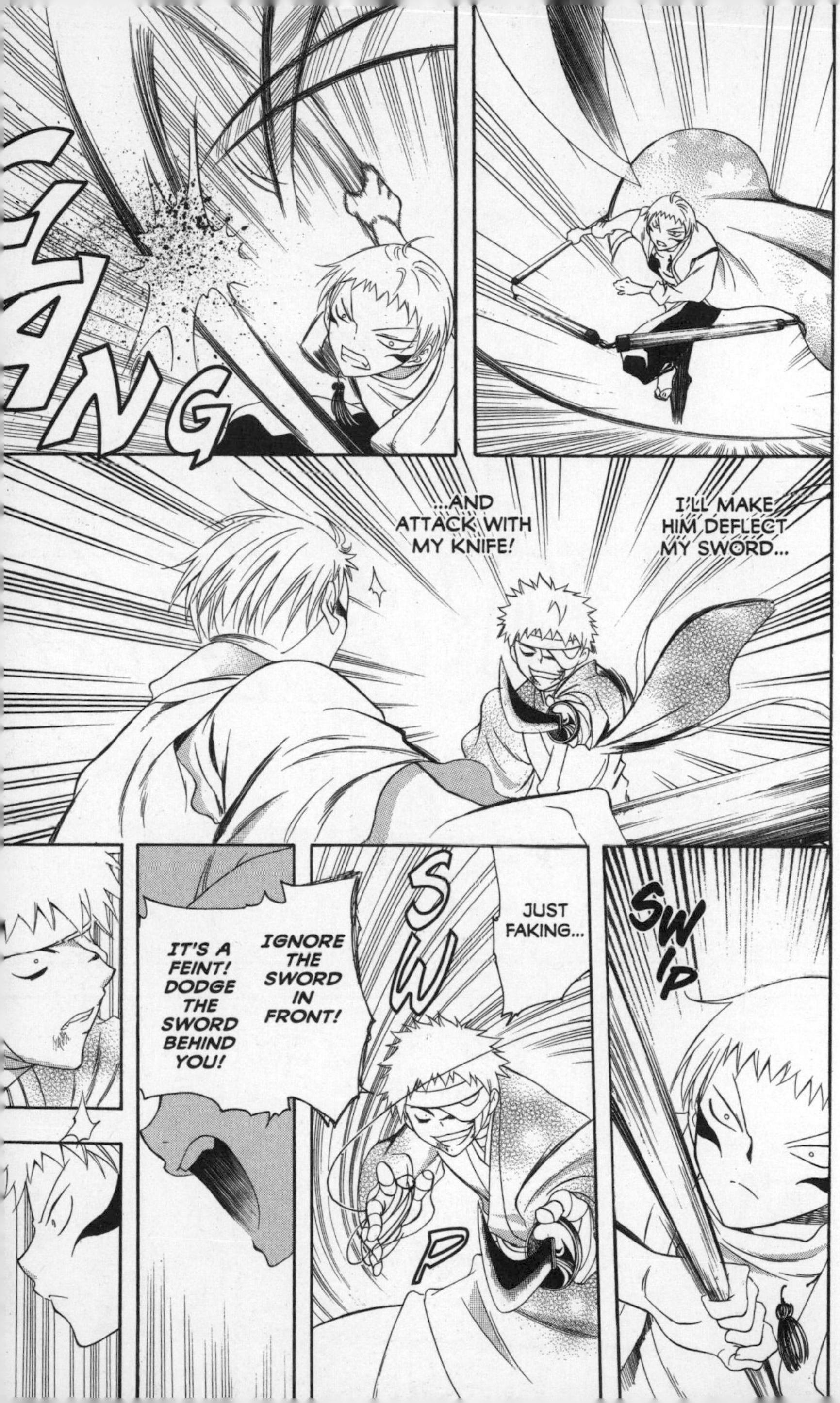
CLANG
I'LL MAKE HIM DEFLECT MY SWORD...
...AND ATTACK WITH MY KNIFE!
SWIP
JUST FAKING...
SWP
IGNORE THE SWORD IN FRONT!
IT'S A FEINT! DODGE THE SWORD BEHIND YOU!

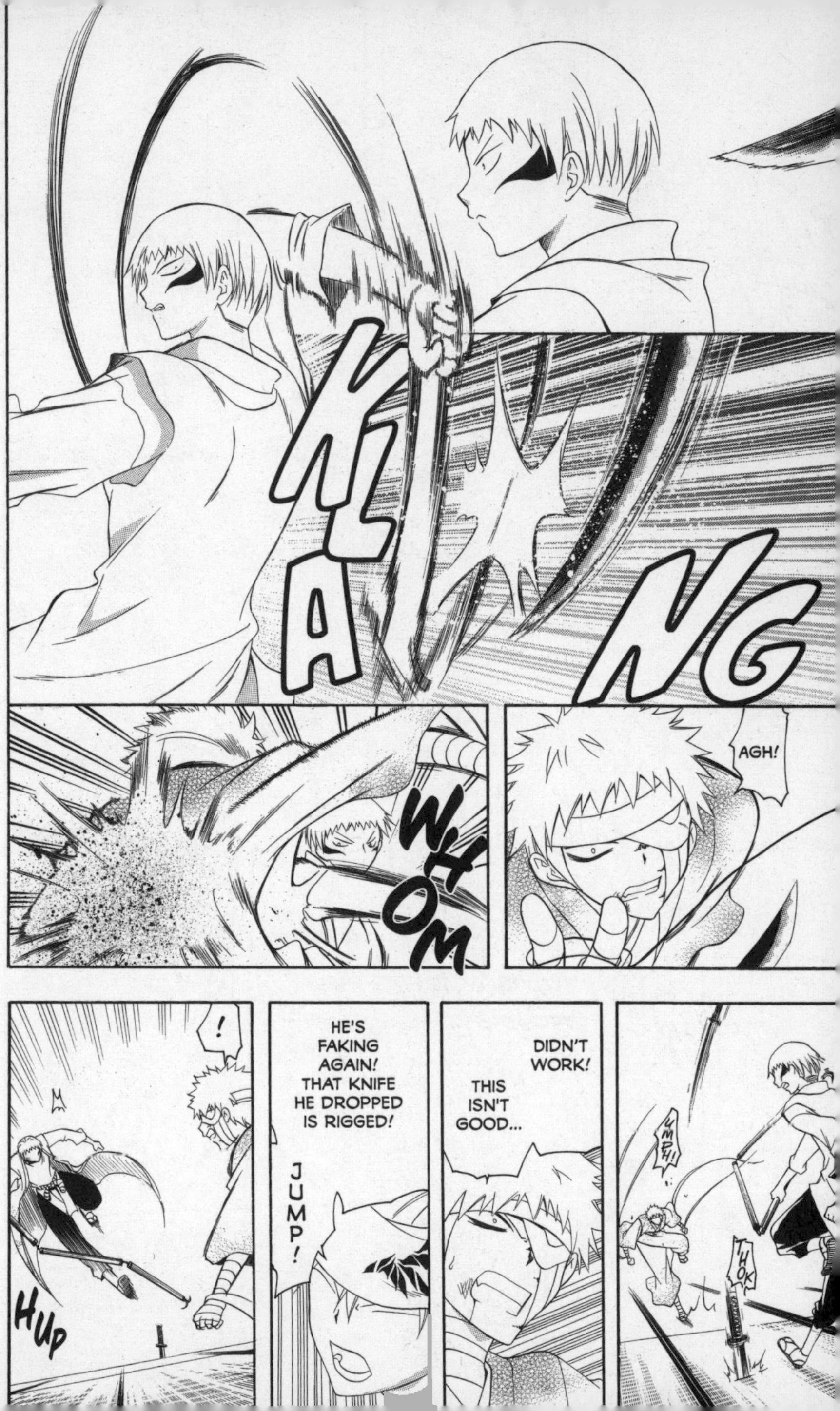
KLANG
AGH!
WHOOM
UMPH!
THOK
DIDN'T WORK!
THIS ISN'T GOOD...
HE'S FAKING AGAIN! THAT KNIFE HE DROPPED IS RIGGED!
JUMP!
!
HUP

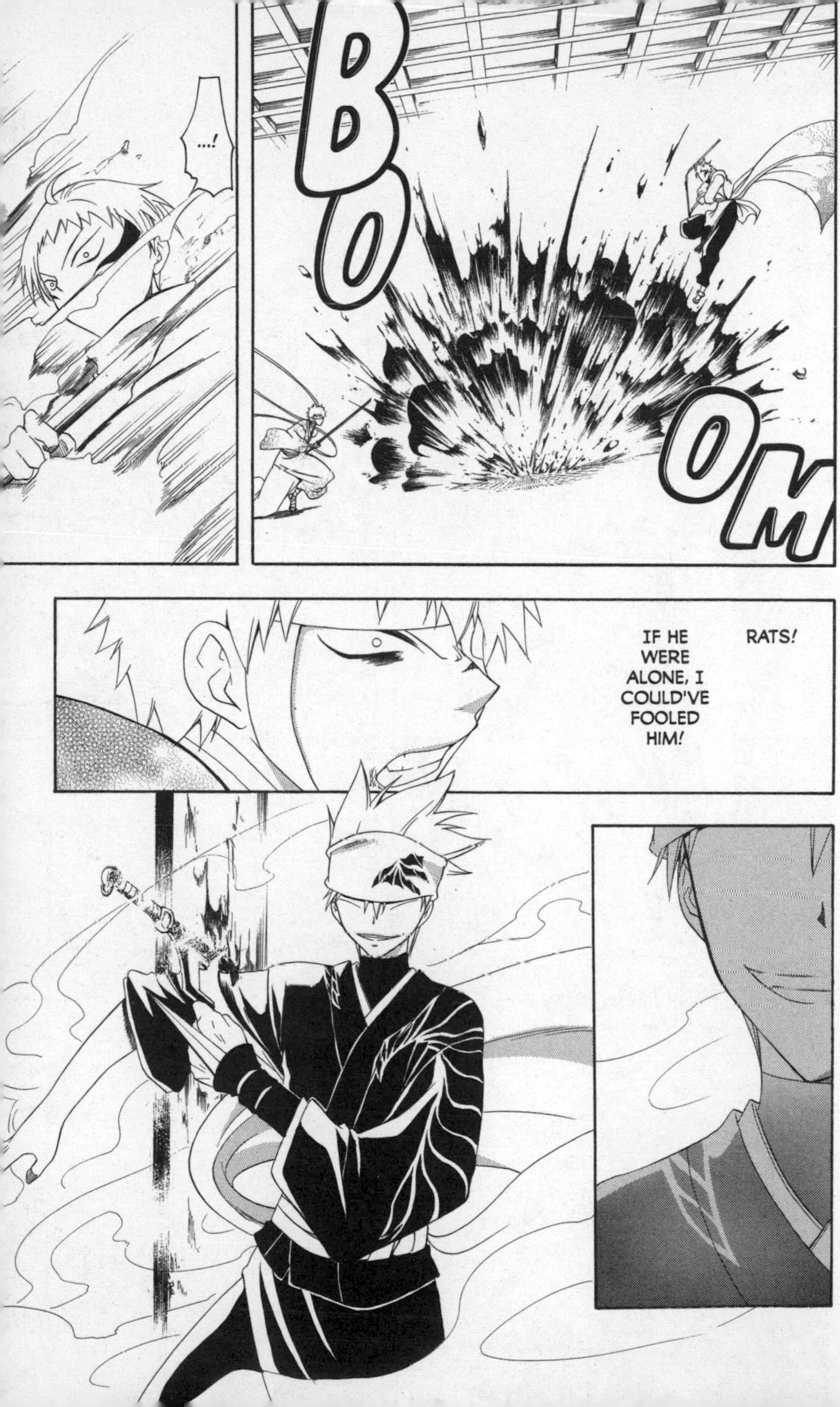
BOOOM
...!
RATS!
IF HE WERE ALONE, I COULD'VE FOOLED HIM!

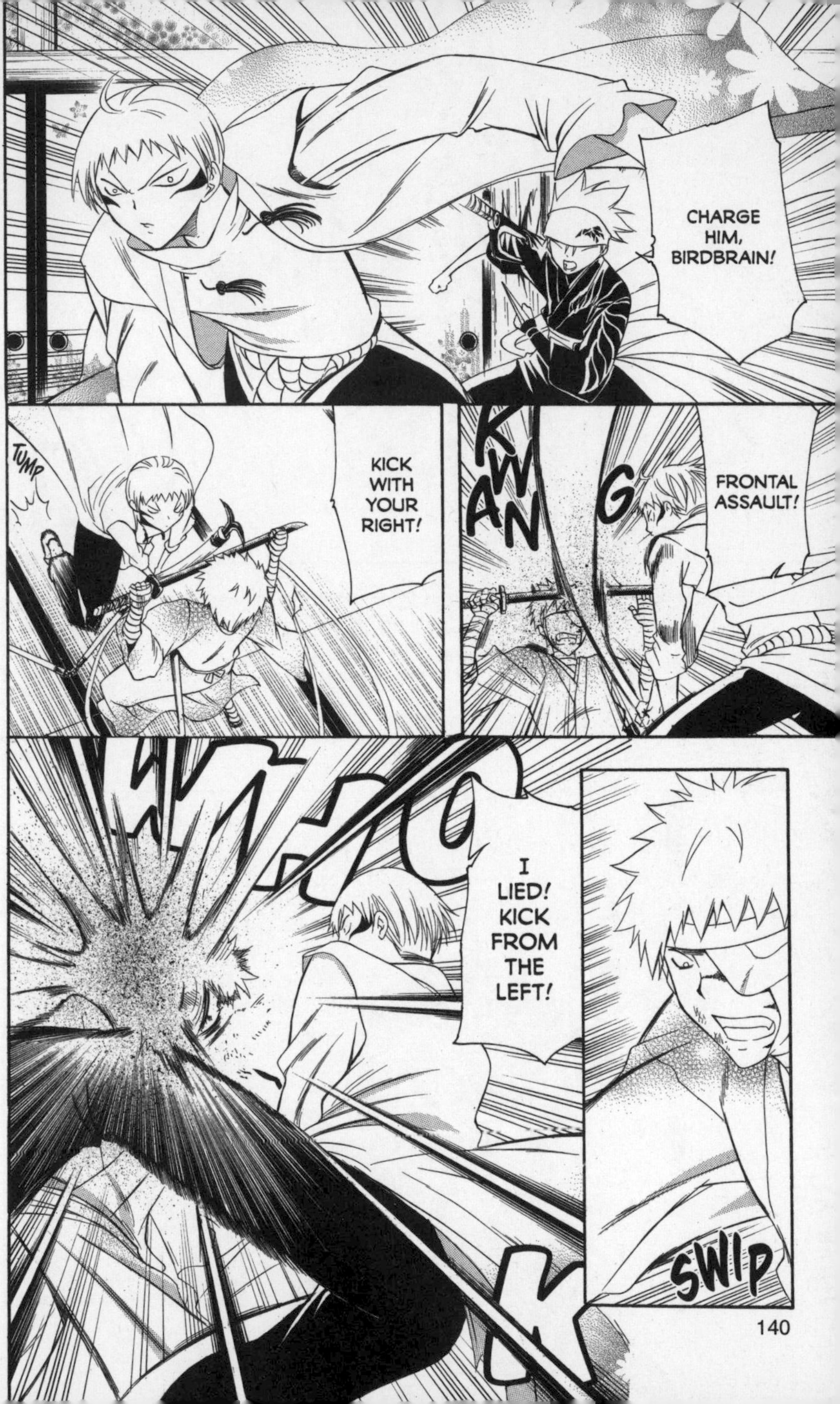
CHARGE HIM, BIRDBRAIN!
KWANG
FRONTAL ASSAULT!
KICK WITH YOUR RIGHT!
TUMP
I LIED! KICK FROM THE LEFT!
SWIP

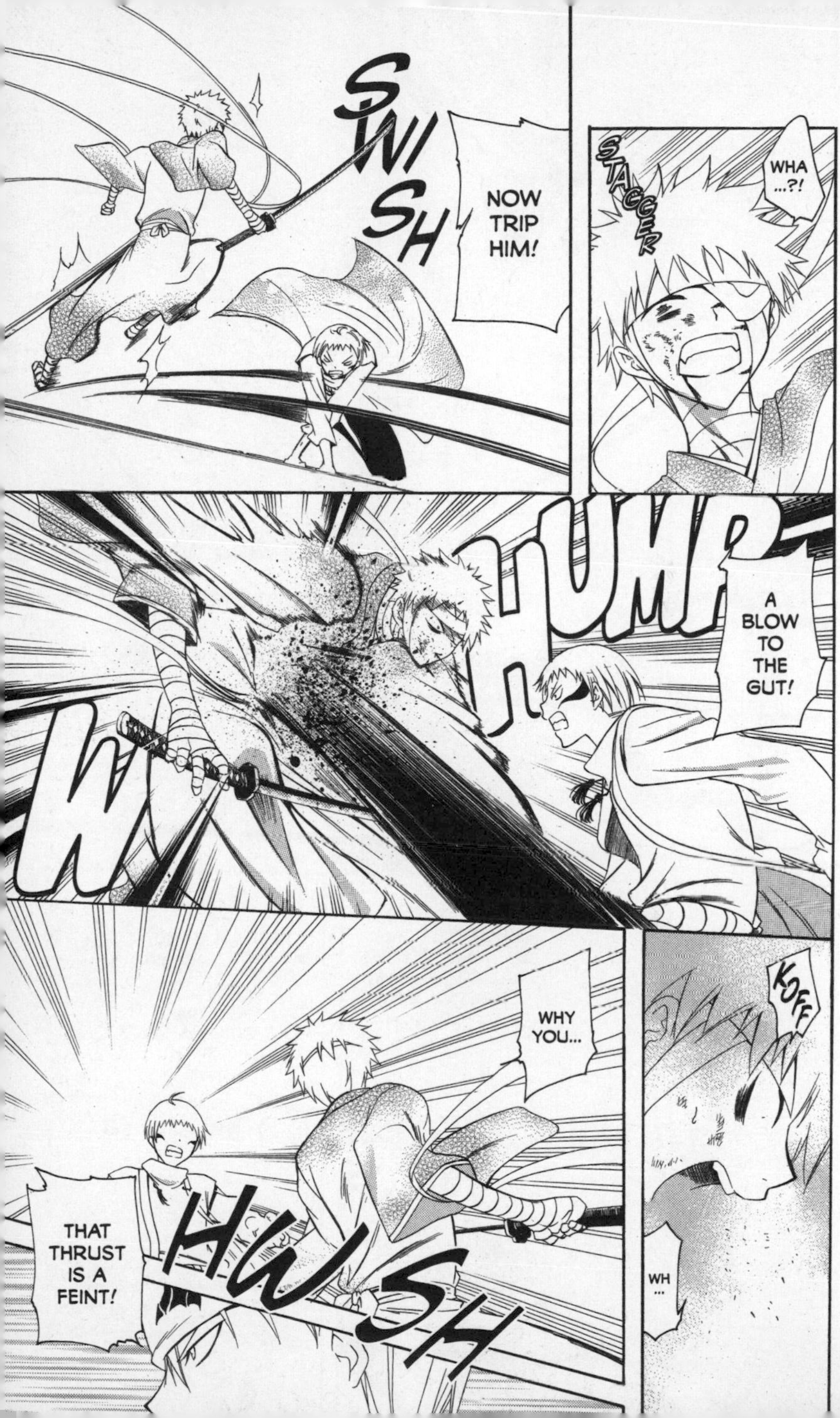
STAGGER
WHA ...?!
SWISH
NOW TRIP HIM!
A BLOW TO THE GUT!
WHUMP
KOFF
WH ...
WHY YOU...
THAT THRUST IS A FEINT!
HWSH

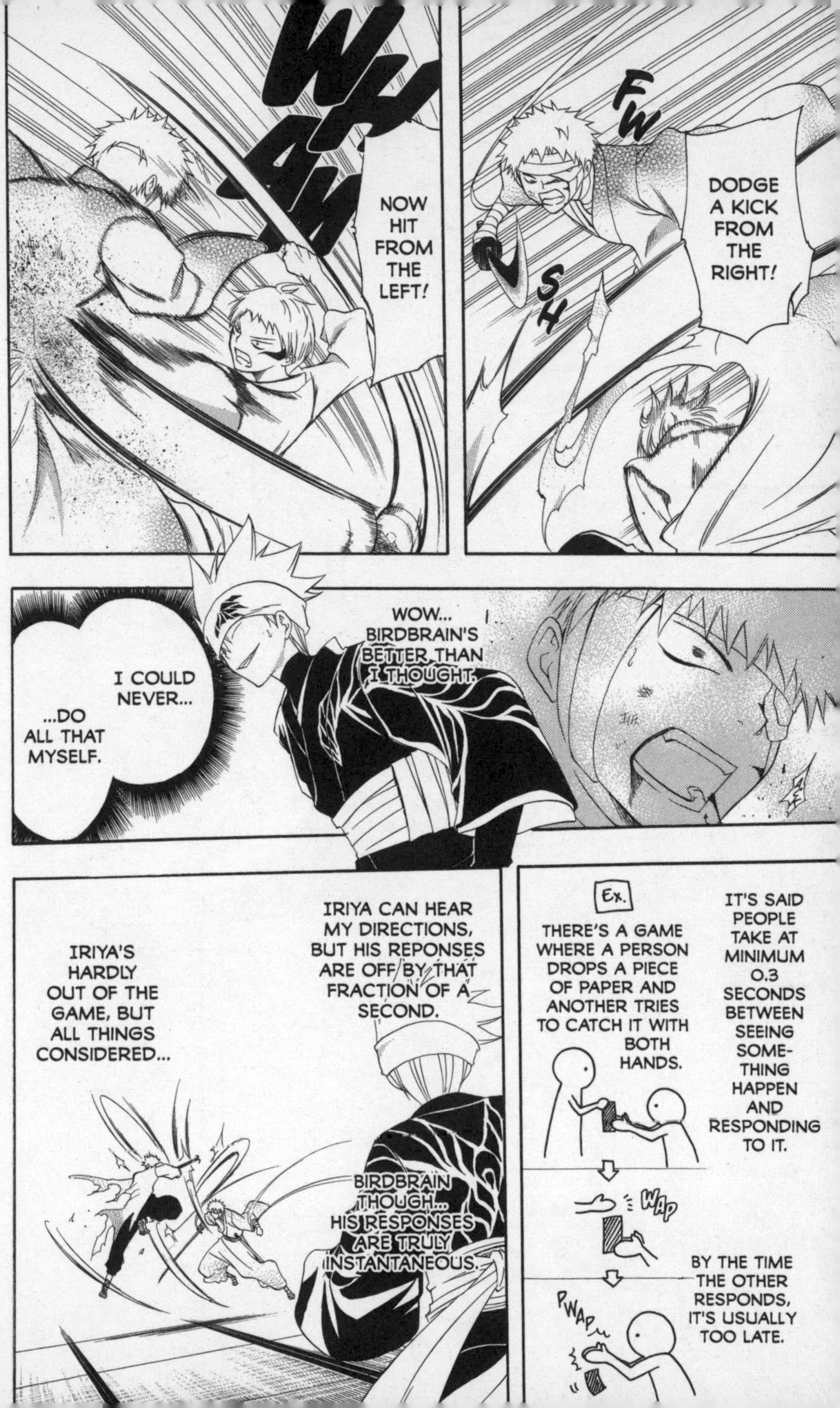
FW
SH
DODGE A KICK FROM THE RIGHT!
WHAM
NOW HIT FROM THE LEFT!
WOW... BIRDBRAIN'S BETTER THAN I THOUGHT.
I COULD NEVER...
...DO ALL THAT MYSELF.
IT'S SAID PEOPLE TAKE AT MINIMUM 0.3 SECONDS BETWEEN SEEING SOME-THING HAPPEN AND RESPONDING TO IT.
Ex.
THERE'S A GAME WHERE A PERSON DROPS A PIECE OF PAPER AND ANOTHER TRIES TO CATCH IT WITH BOTH HANDS.
WAP
BY THE TIME THE OTHER RESPONDS, IT'S USUALLY TOO LATE.
PWAP
IRIYA CAN HEAR MY DIRECTIONS, BUT HIS REPONSES ARE OFF BY THAT FRACTION OF A SECOND.
IRIYA'S HARDLY OUT OF THE GAME, BUT ALL THINGS CONSIDERED...
BIRDBRAIN THOUGH... HIS RESPONSES ARE TRULY INSTANTANEOUS.

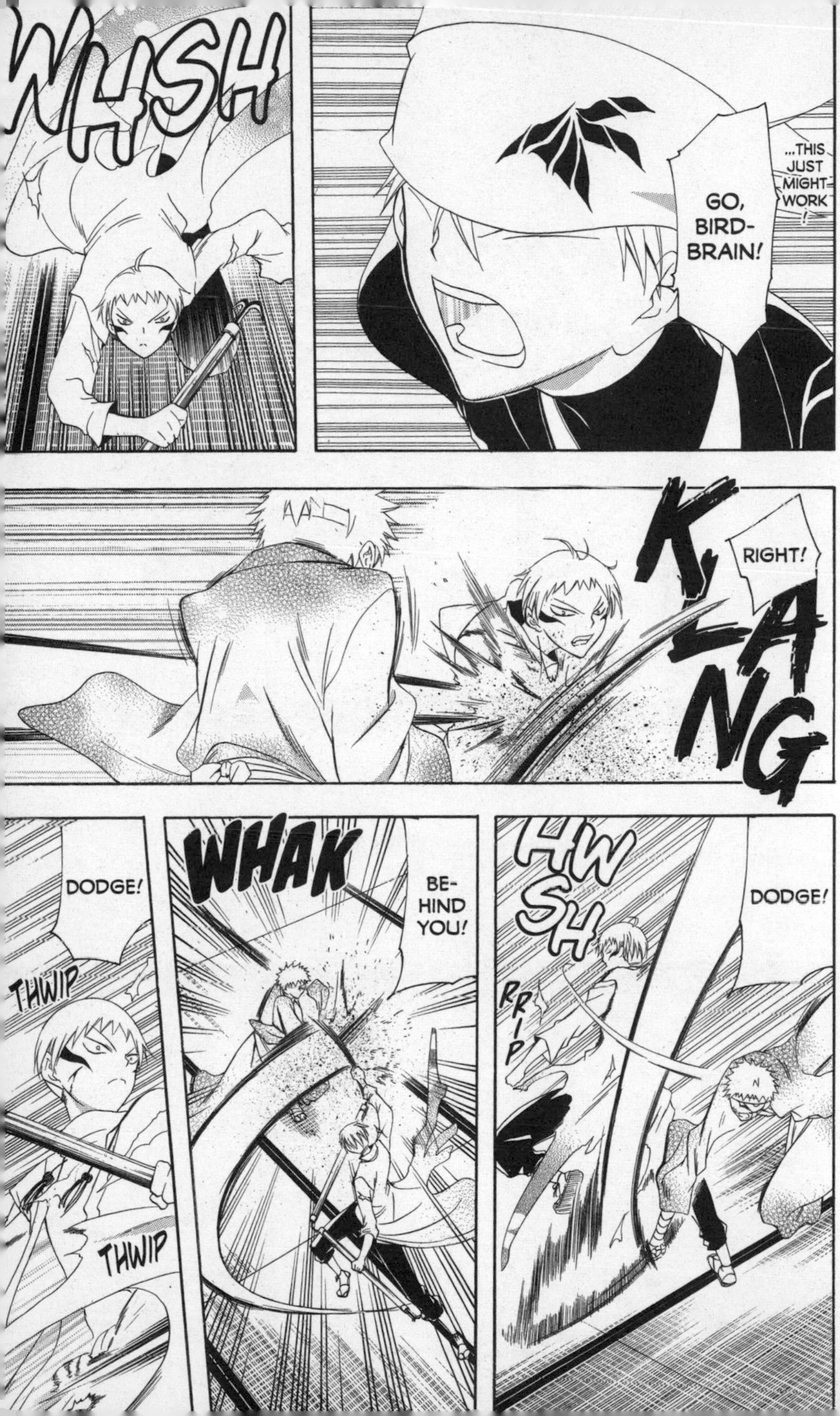
...THIS JUST MIGHT WORK!
GO, BIRD-BRAIN!
WHSH
RIGHT!
KLANG
DODGE!
HWSH
RRIP
BE-HIND YOU!
WHAK
DODGE!
THWIP
THWIP

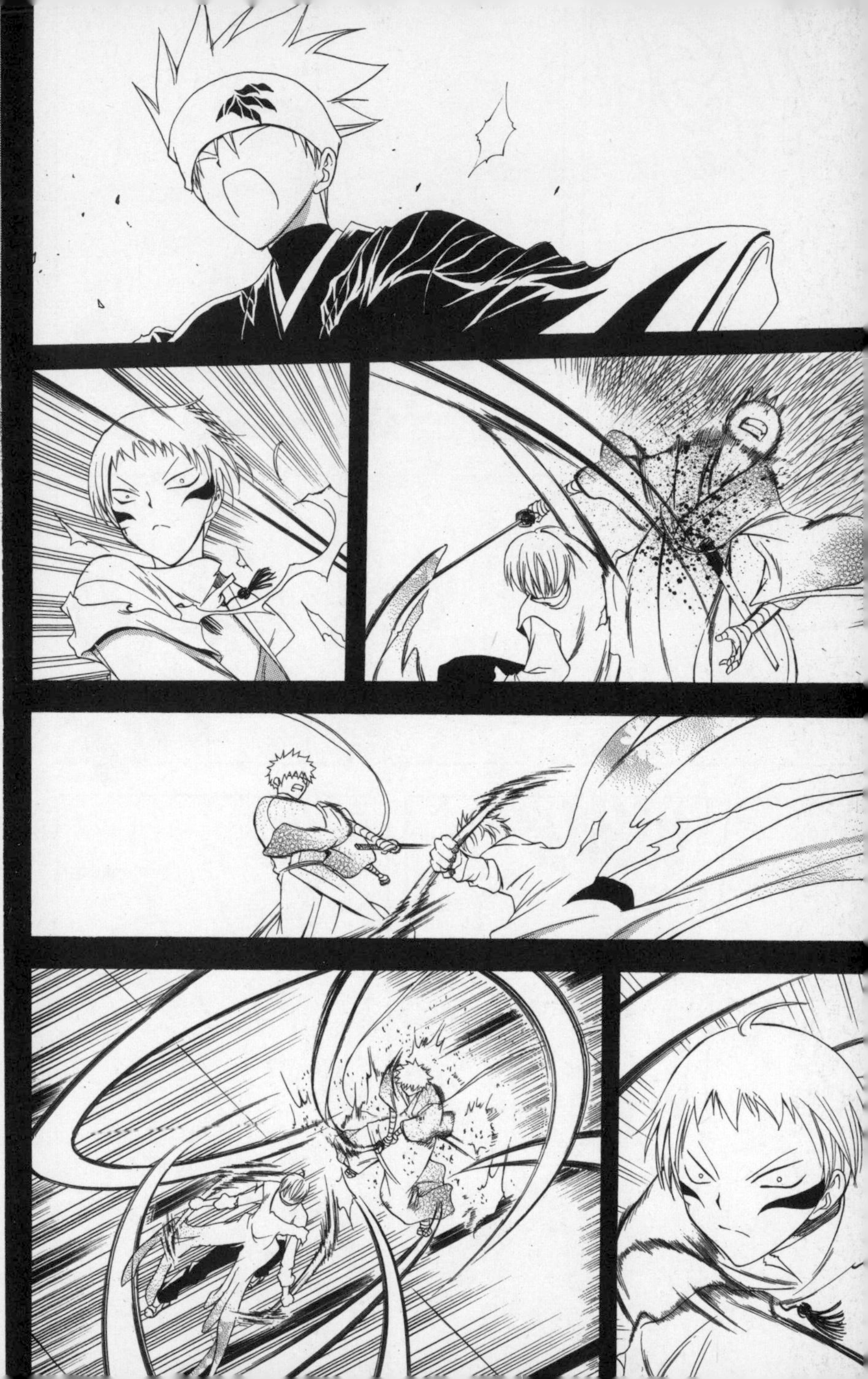

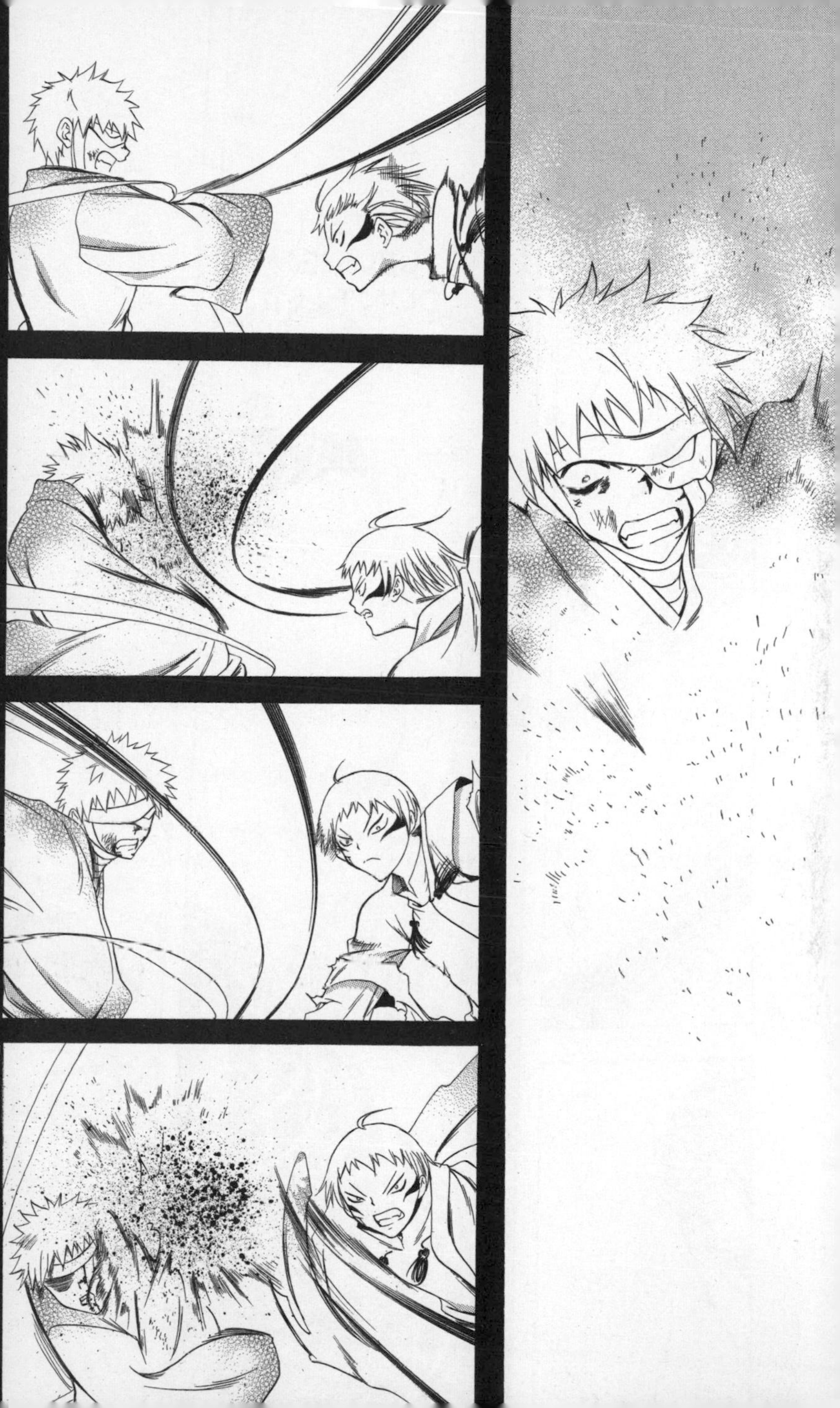

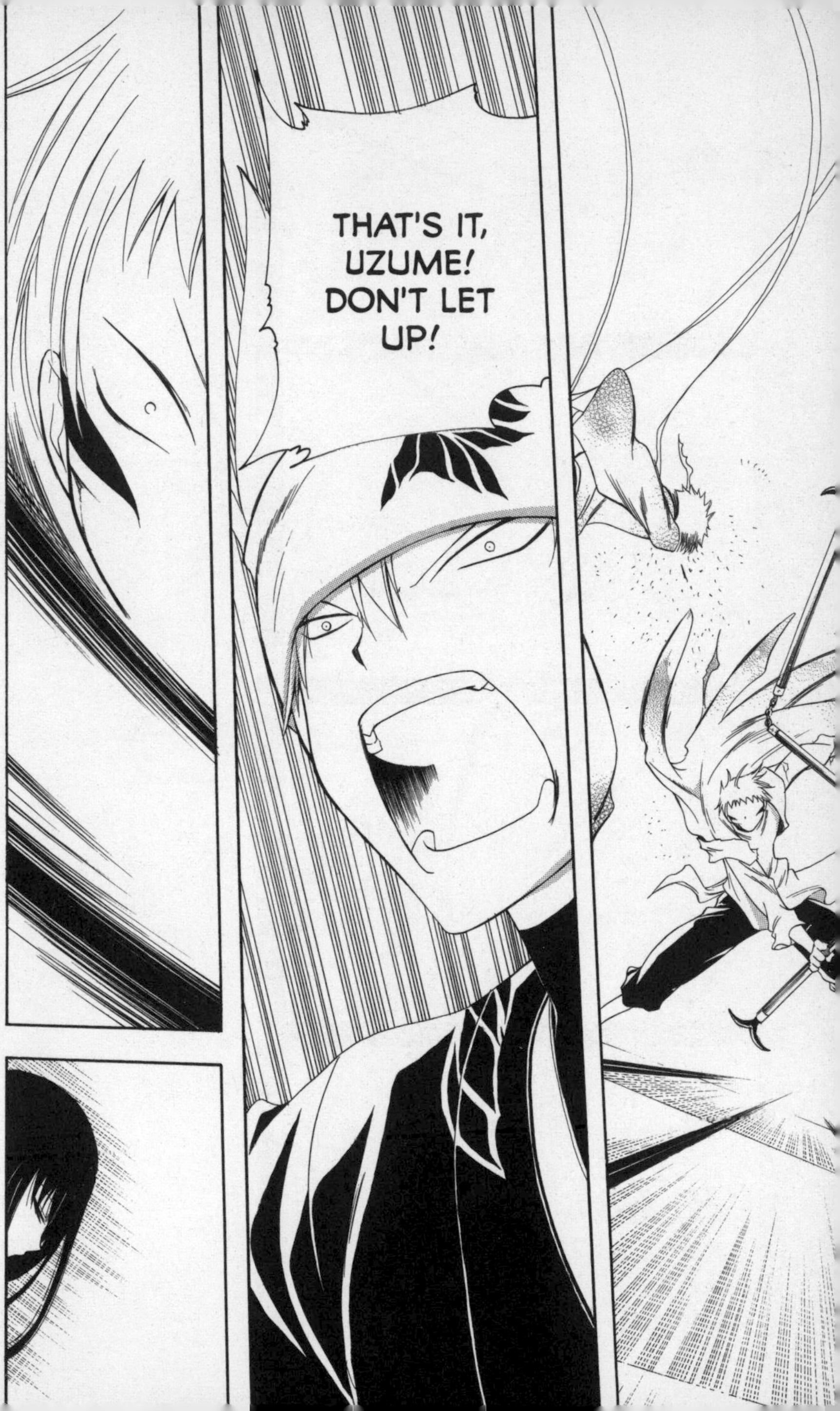
THAT'S IT, UZUME! DON'T LET UP!

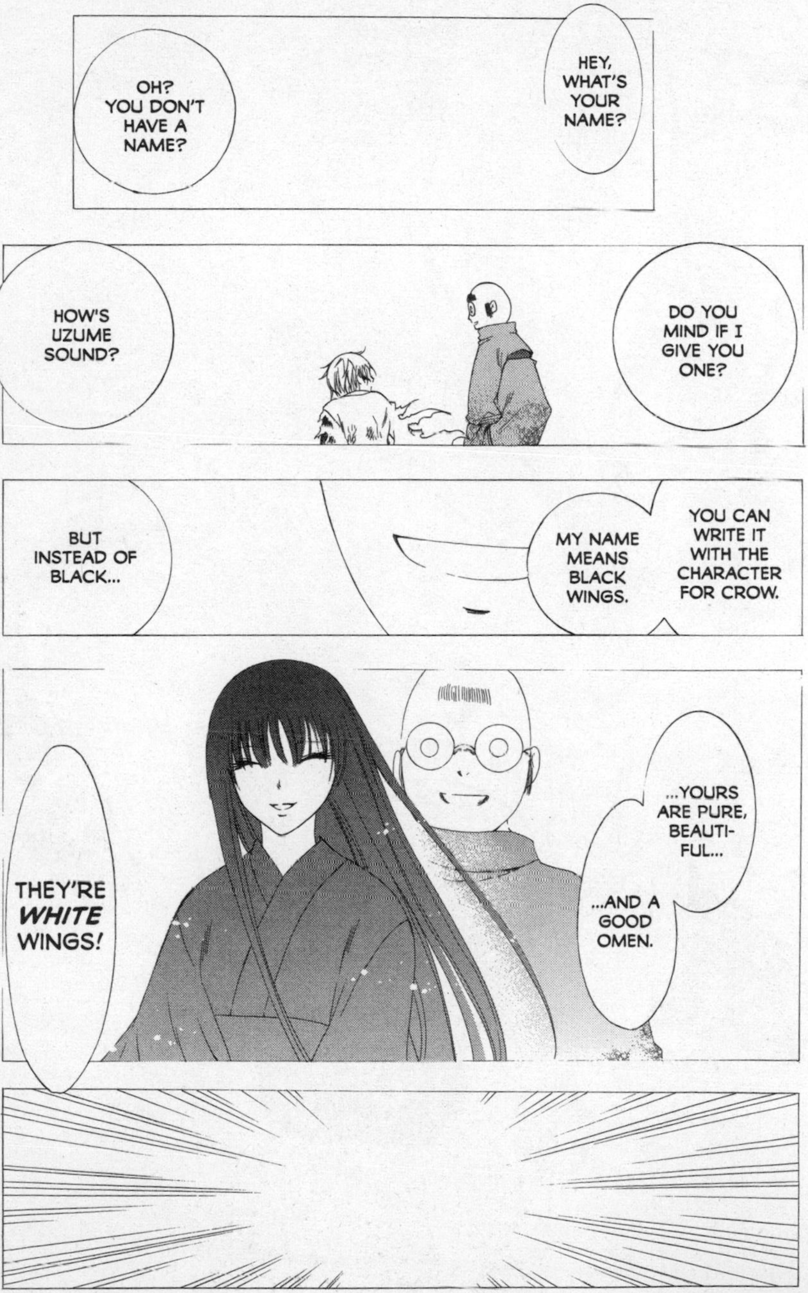
HEY, WHAT'S YOUR NAME?
OH? YOU DON'T HAVE A NAME?
DO YOU MIND IF I GIVE YOU ONE?
HOW'S UZUME SOUND?
YOU CAN WRITE IT WITH THE CHARACTER FOR CROW.
MY NAME MEANS BLACK WINGS.
BUT INSTEAD OF BLACK...
...YOURS ARE PURE, BEAUTIFUL...
...AND A GOOD OMEN.
THEY'RE *WHITE* WINGS!

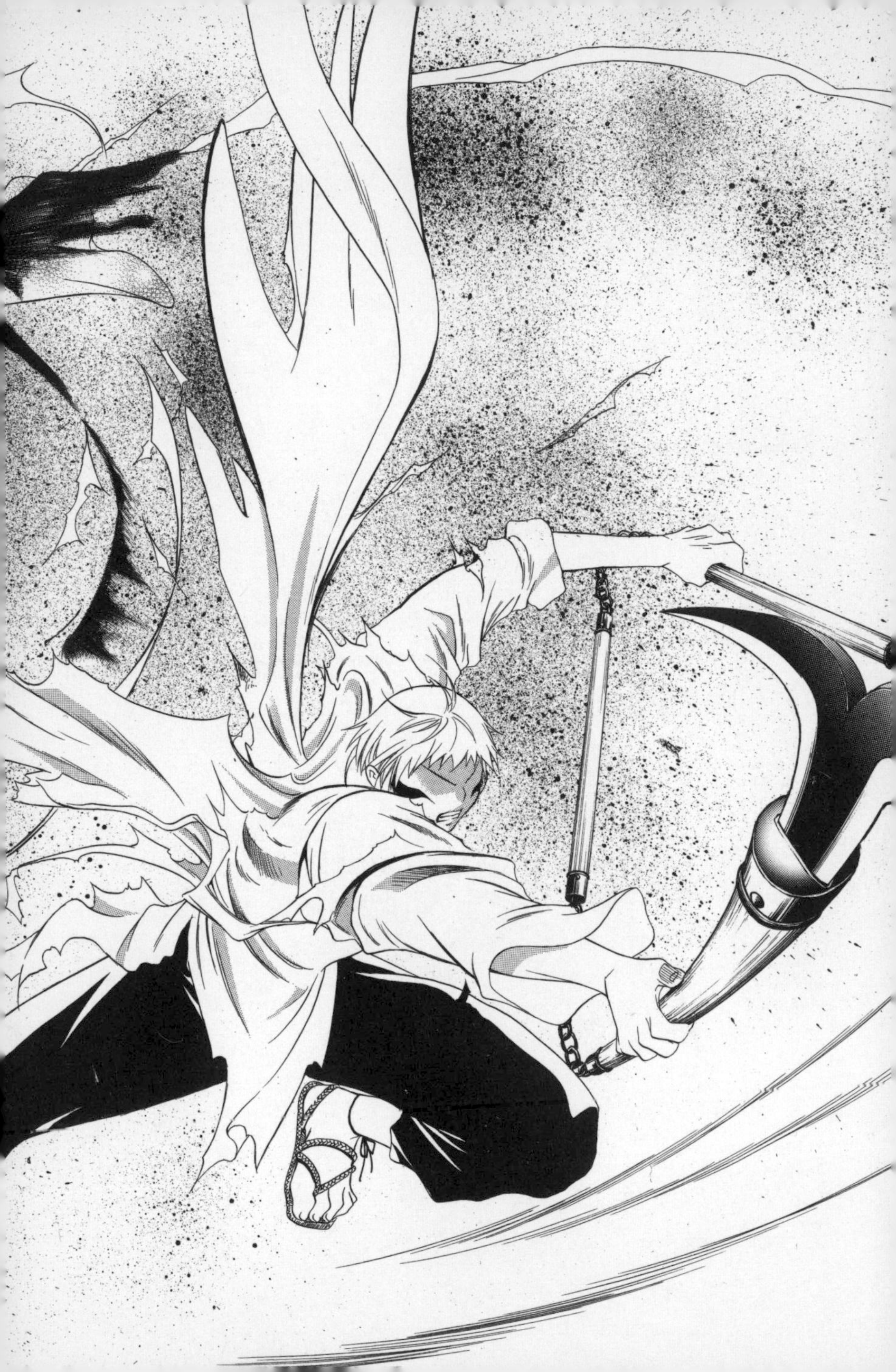

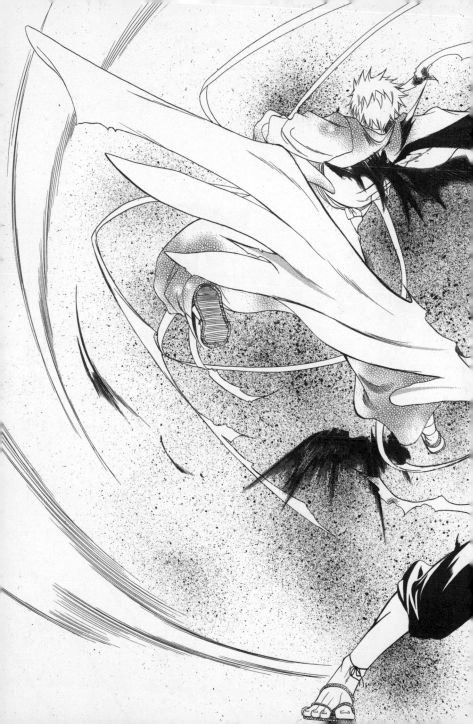

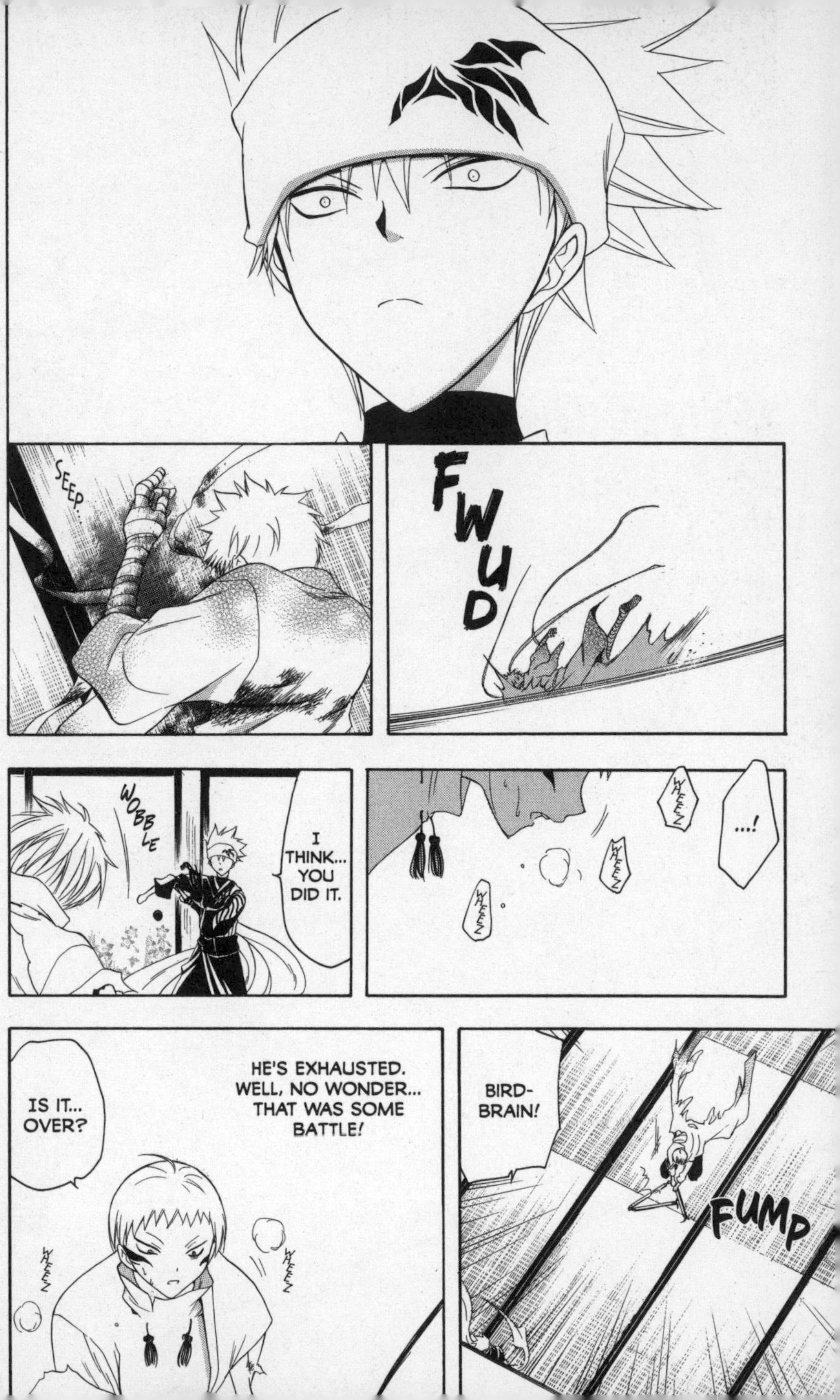
FWUD
SEEP...
...!
WHEEZ
WHEEZ
WHEEZ
I THINK... YOU DID IT.
WOBBLE
BIRD-BRAIN!
FUMP
HE'S EXHAUSTED. WELL, NO WONDER... THAT WAS SOME BATTLE!
IS IT... OVER?
WHEEZ
WHEEZ

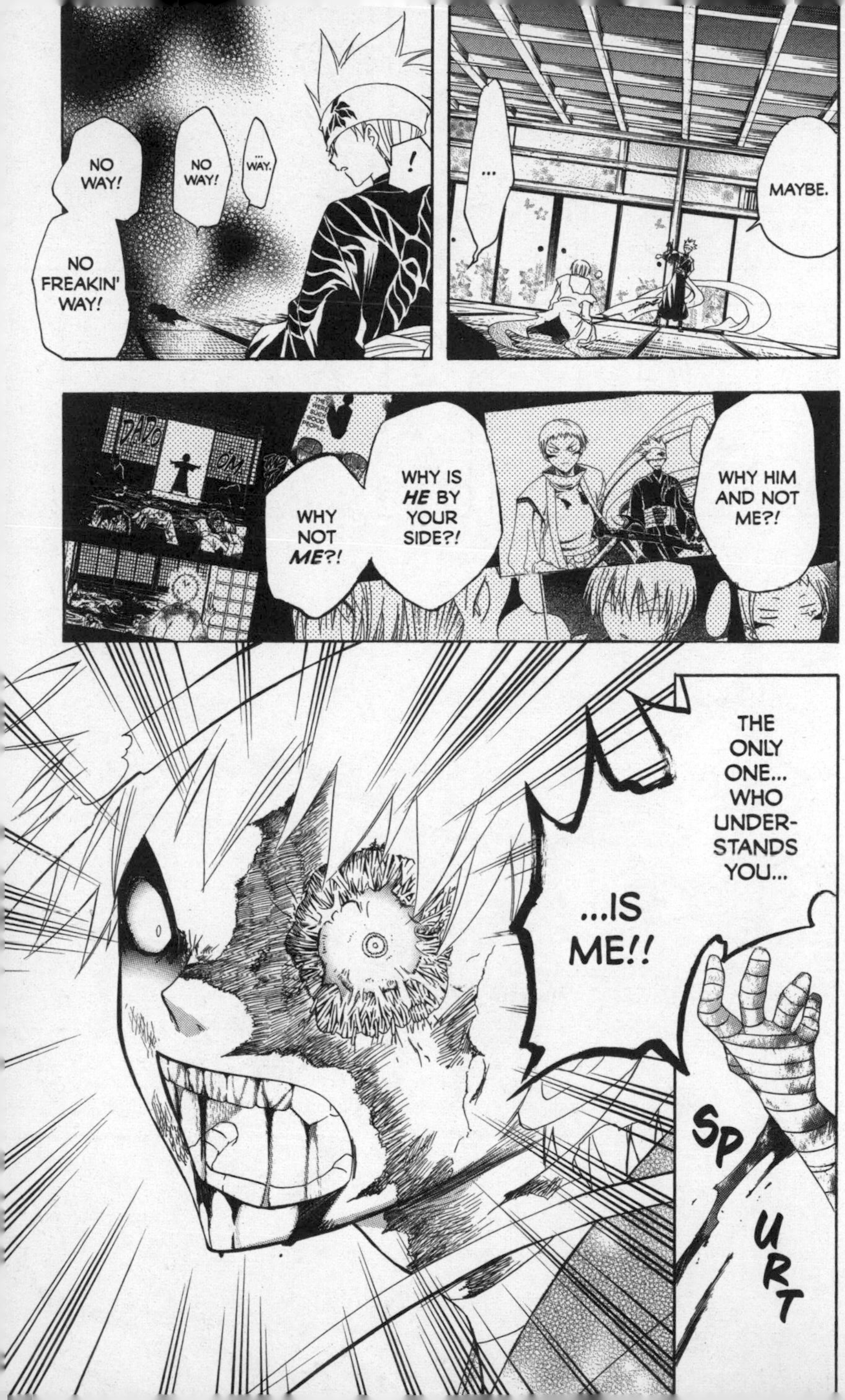
MAYBE.
...
!
...WAY.
NO WAY!
NO WAY!
NO FREAKIN' WAY!
WHY HIM AND NOT ME?!
WHY IS *HE* BY YOUR SIDE?!
WHY NOT *ME*?!
THE ONLY ONE... WHO UNDER-STANDS YOU...
...IS ME!!
SPURT

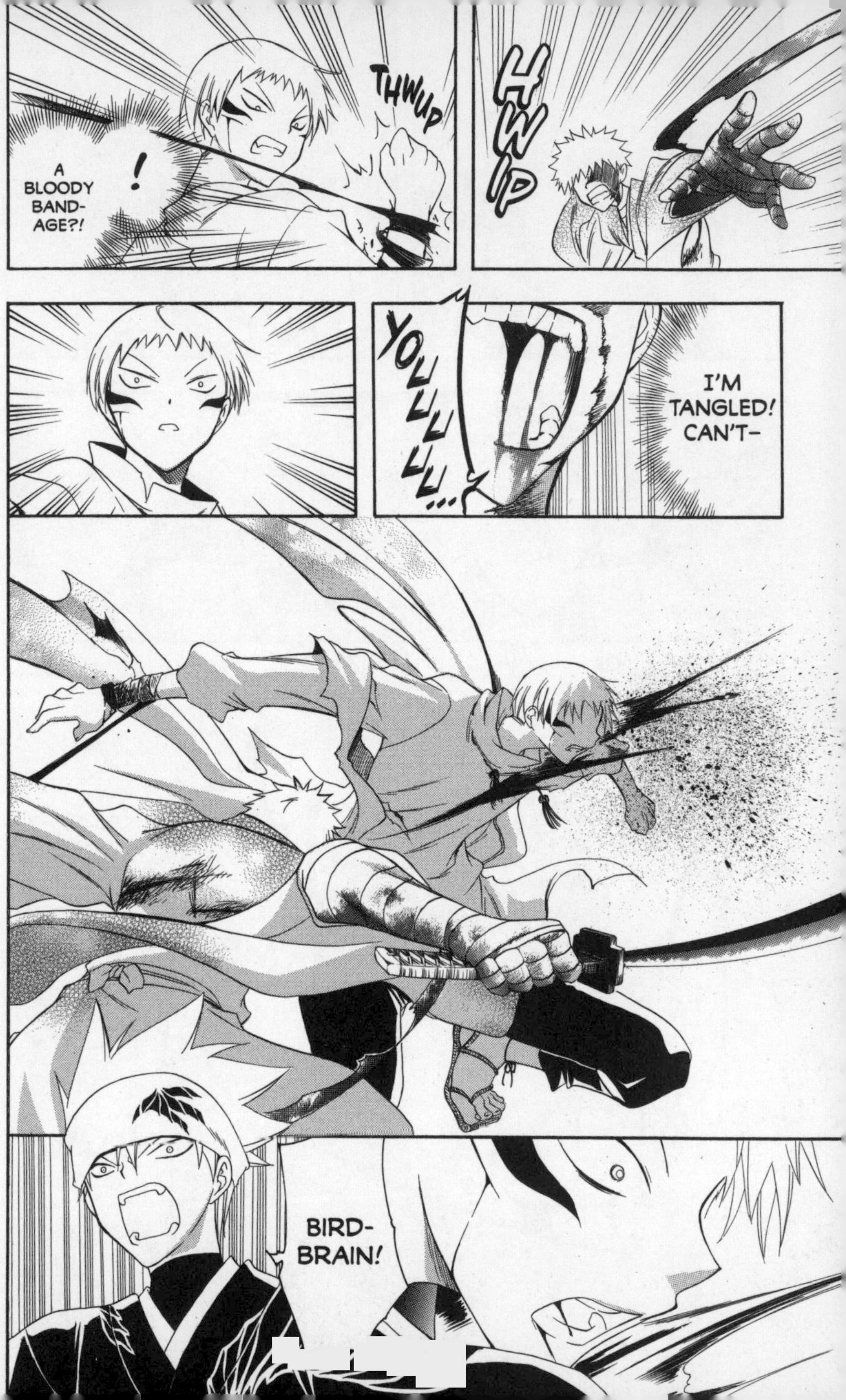
HWIP
THWUP
!
A BLOODY BAND-AGE?!
YOUUUUUUU...
I'M TANGLED! CAN'T-
BIRD-BRAIN!

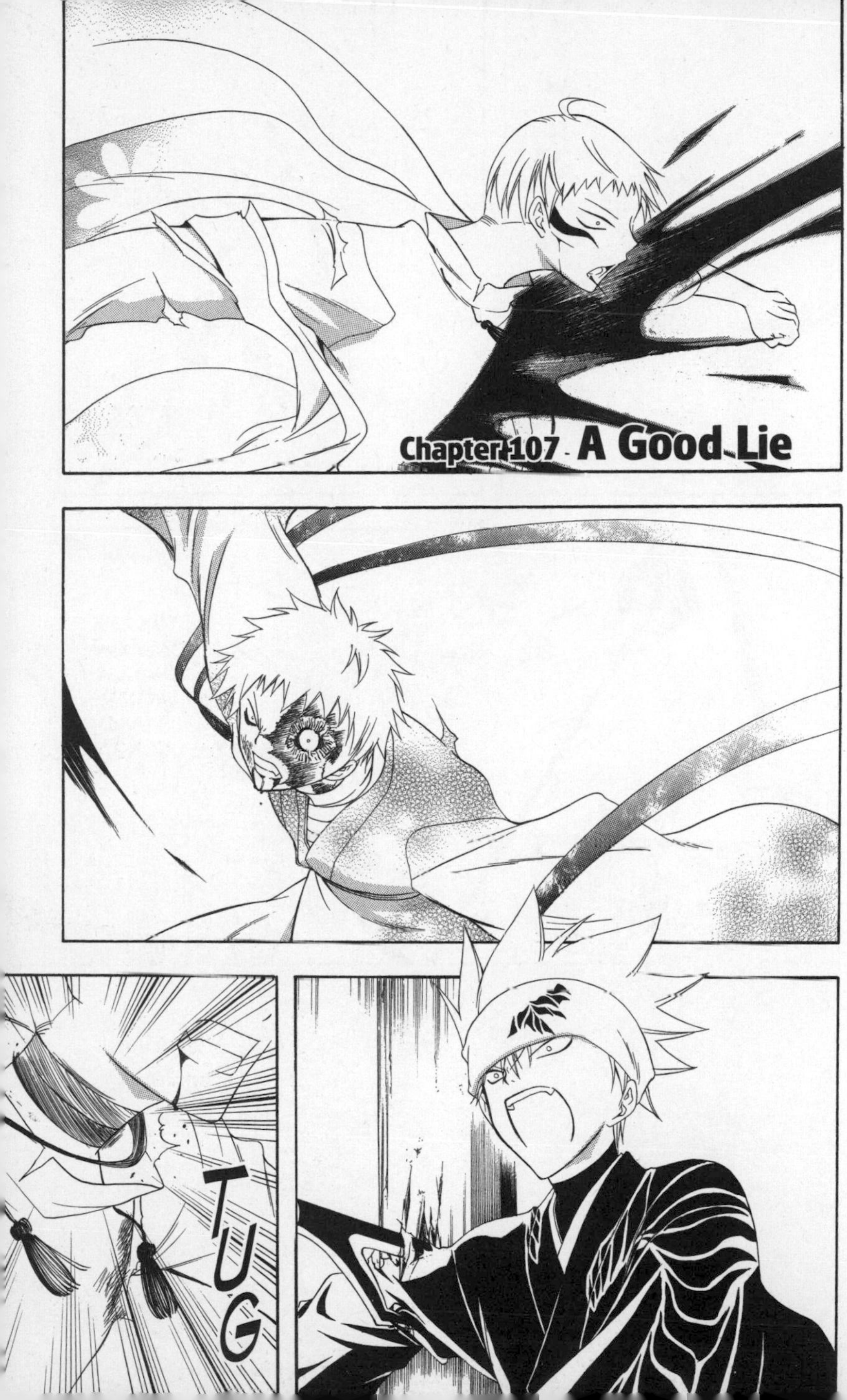
Chapter 107 - A Good Lie
TUG

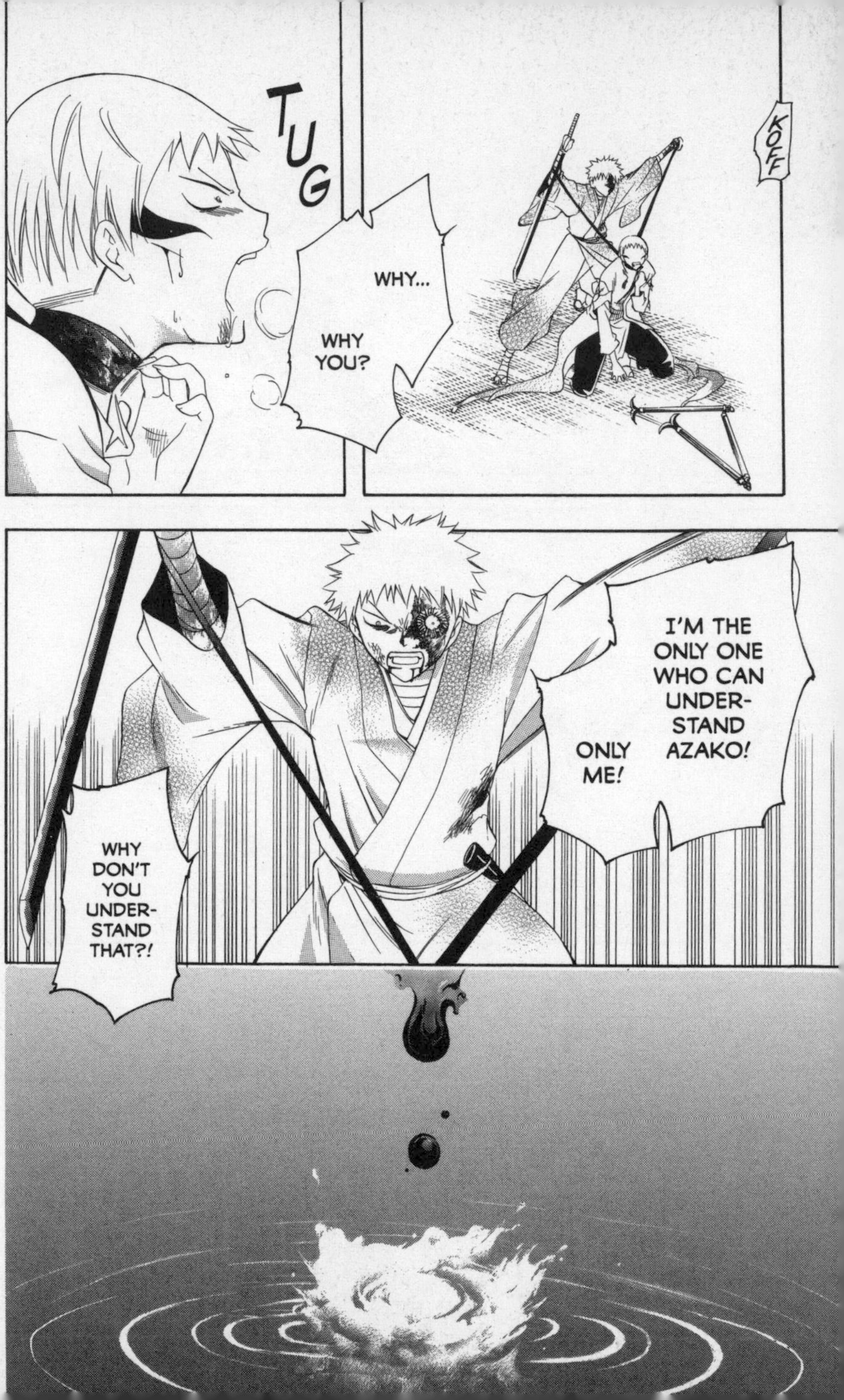
KOFF
WHY... WHY YOU?
TUG
I'M THE ONLY ONE WHO CAN UNDER-STAND AZAKO!
ONLY ME!
WHY DON'T YOU UNDER-STAND THAT?!

Chapter 107
A Good Lie

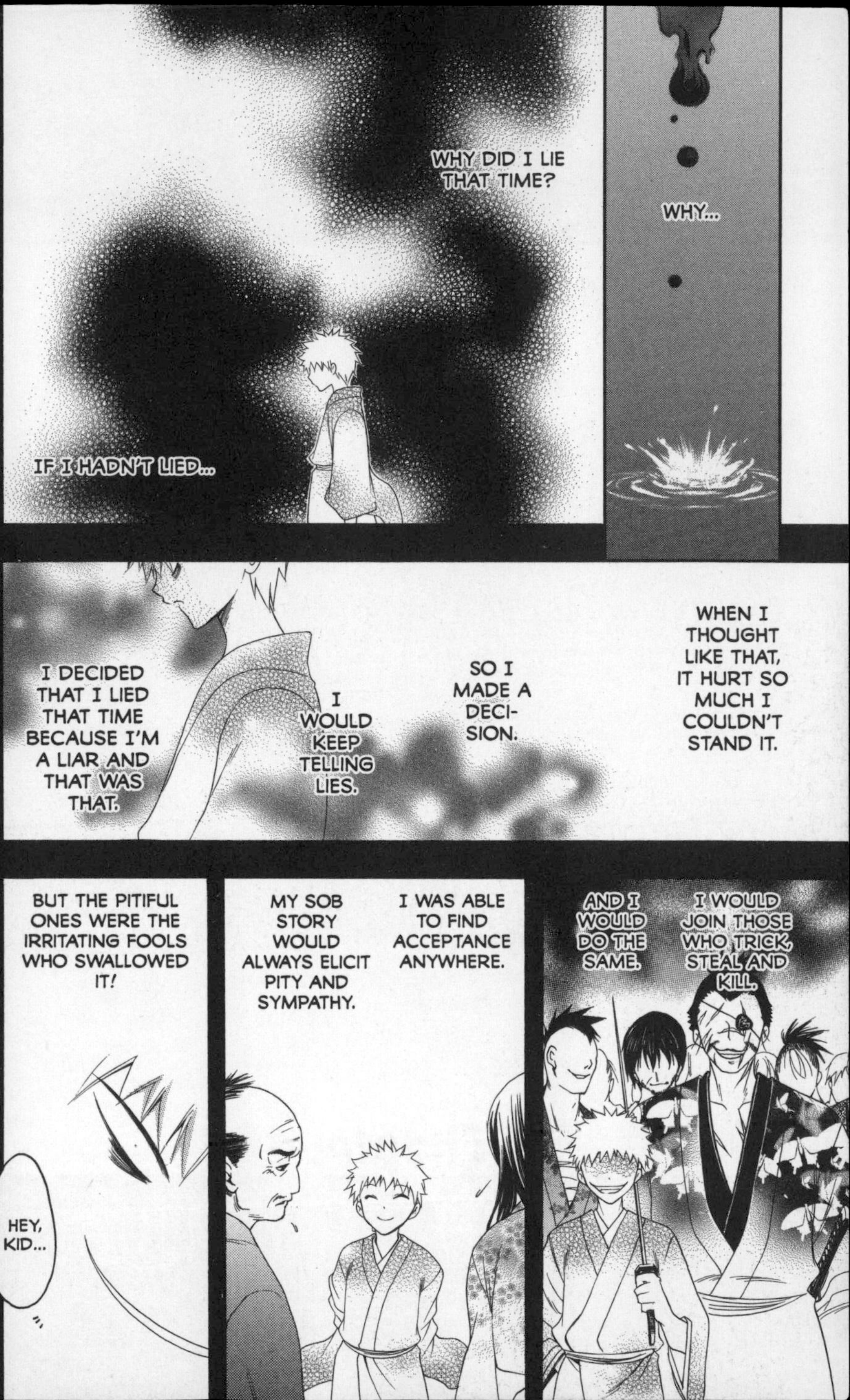
WHY...
WHY DID I LIE THAT TIME?
IF I HADN'T LIED...
WHEN I THOUGHT LIKE THAT, IT HURT SO MUCH I COULDN'T STAND IT.
SO I MADE A DECI- SION.
I WOULD KEEP TELLING LIES.
I DECIDED THAT I LIED THAT TIME BECAUSE I'M A LIAR AND THAT WAS THAT.
I WOULD JOIN THOSE WHO TRICK, STEAL AND KILL.
AND I WOULD DO THE SAME.
I WAS ABLE TO FIND ACCEPTANCE ANYWHERE.
MY SOB STORY WOULD ALWAYS ELICIT PITY AND SYMPATHY.
BUT THE PITIFUL ONES WERE THE IRRITATING FOOLS WHO SWALLOWED IT!
HEY, KID...

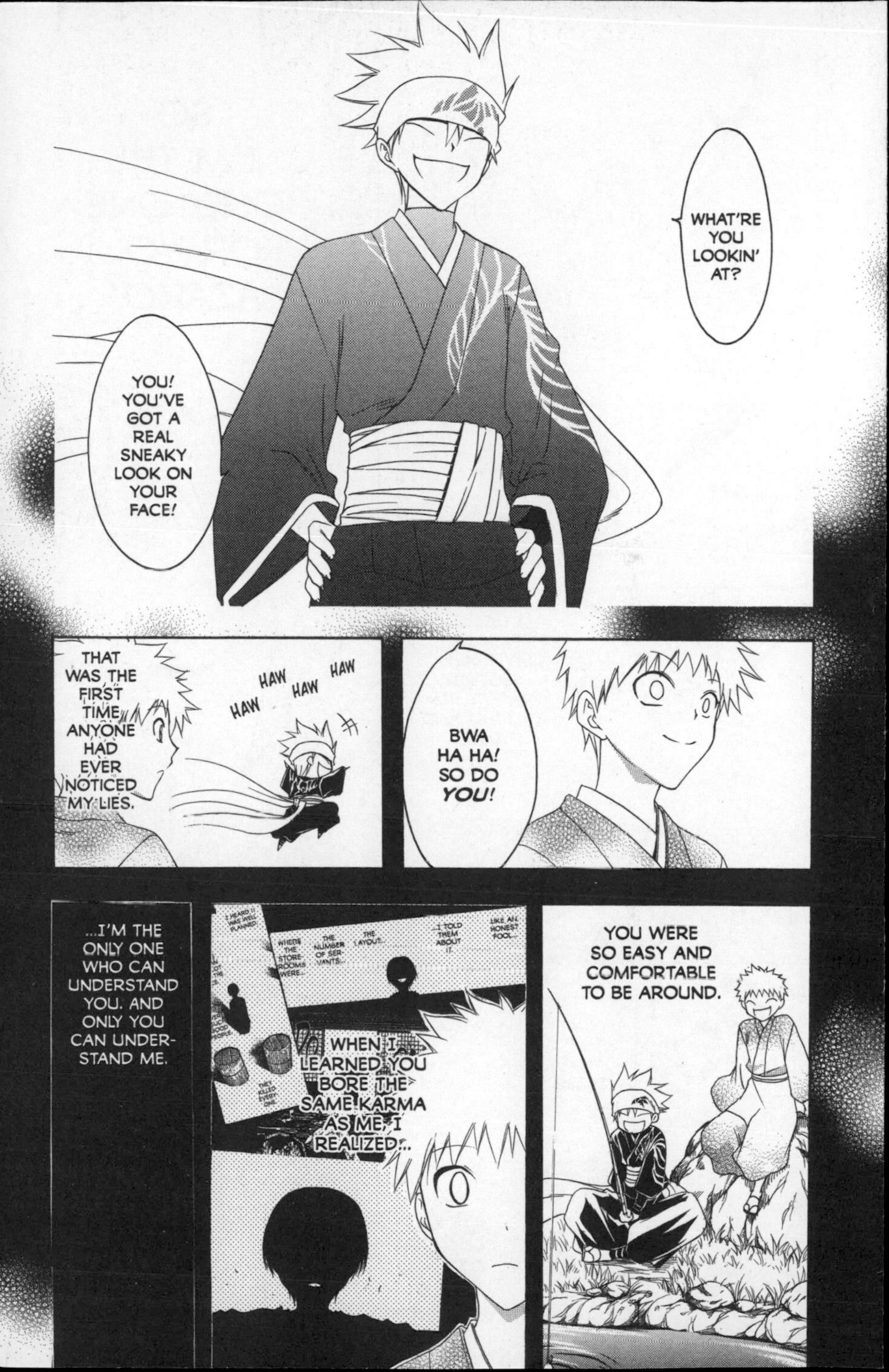
WHAT'RE YOU LOOKIN' AT?
YOU! YOU'VE GOT A REAL SNEAKY LOOK ON YOUR FACE!
BWA HA HA! SO DO *YOU*!
HAW HAW HAW HAW
THAT WAS THE FIRST TIME ANYONE HAD EVER NOTICED MY LIES.
YOU WERE SO EASY AND COMFORTABLE TO BE AROUND.
LIKE AN HONEST FOOL...
...I TOLD THEM ABOUT IT.
THE LAYOUT...
THE NUMBER OF SERVANTS...
WHERE THE STOREROOMS WERE...
I HEARD IT WAS WELL PLANNED.
THEY KILLED EVERYONE.
WHEN I LEARNED YOU BORE THE SAME KARMA AS ME, I REALIZED...
...I'M THE ONLY ONE WHO CAN UNDERSTAND YOU. AND ONLY YOU CAN UNDERSTAND ME.

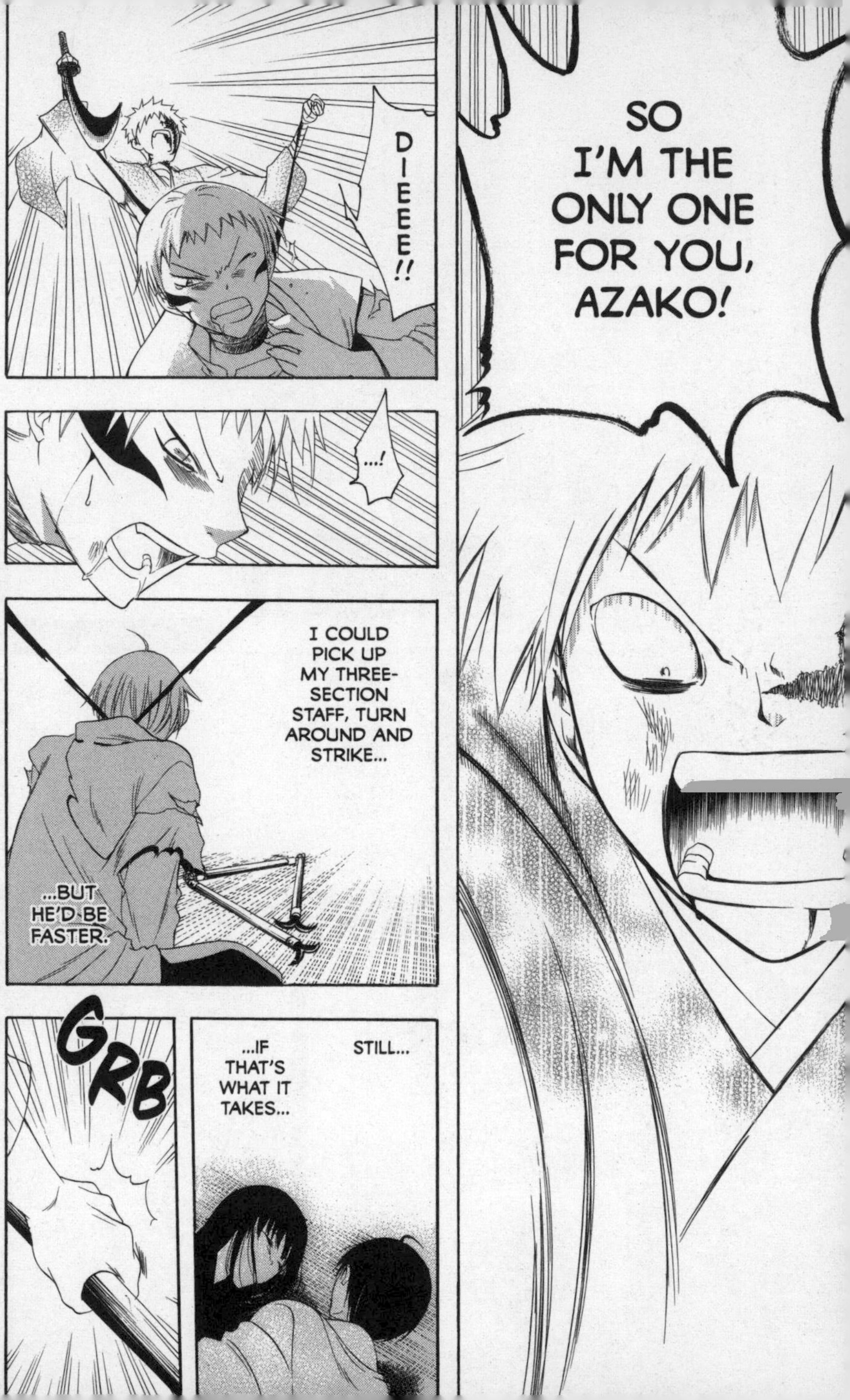
SO I'M THE ONLY ONE FOR YOU, AZAKO!
DIEEEE!!
...!
I COULD PICK UP MY THREE-SECTION STAFF, TURN AROUND AND STRIKE...
...BUT HE'D BE FASTER.
STILL...
...IF THAT'S WHAT IT TAKES...
GRB

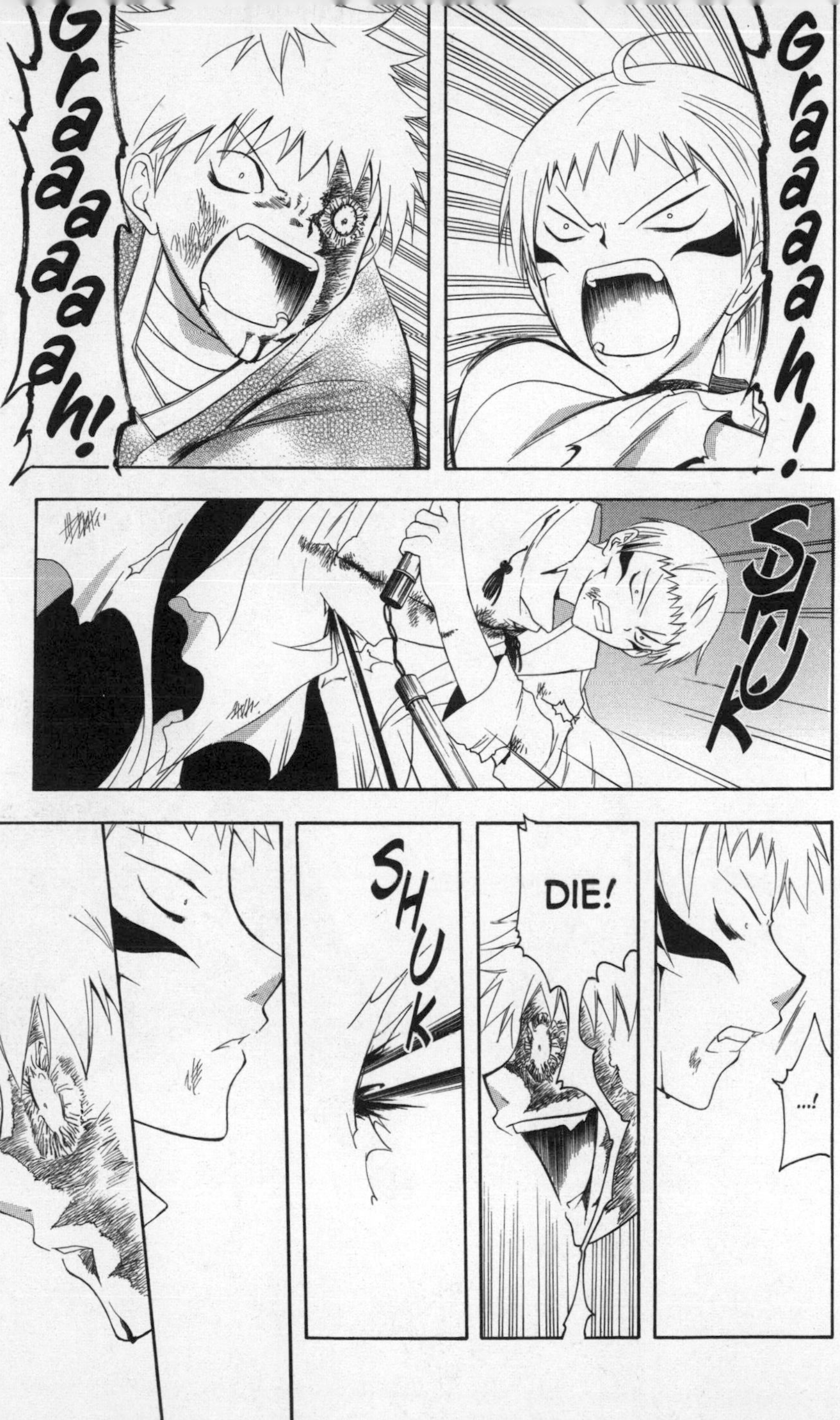
Graaaah!
Graaaaaaah!
SHUK
...!
DIE!
SHUK

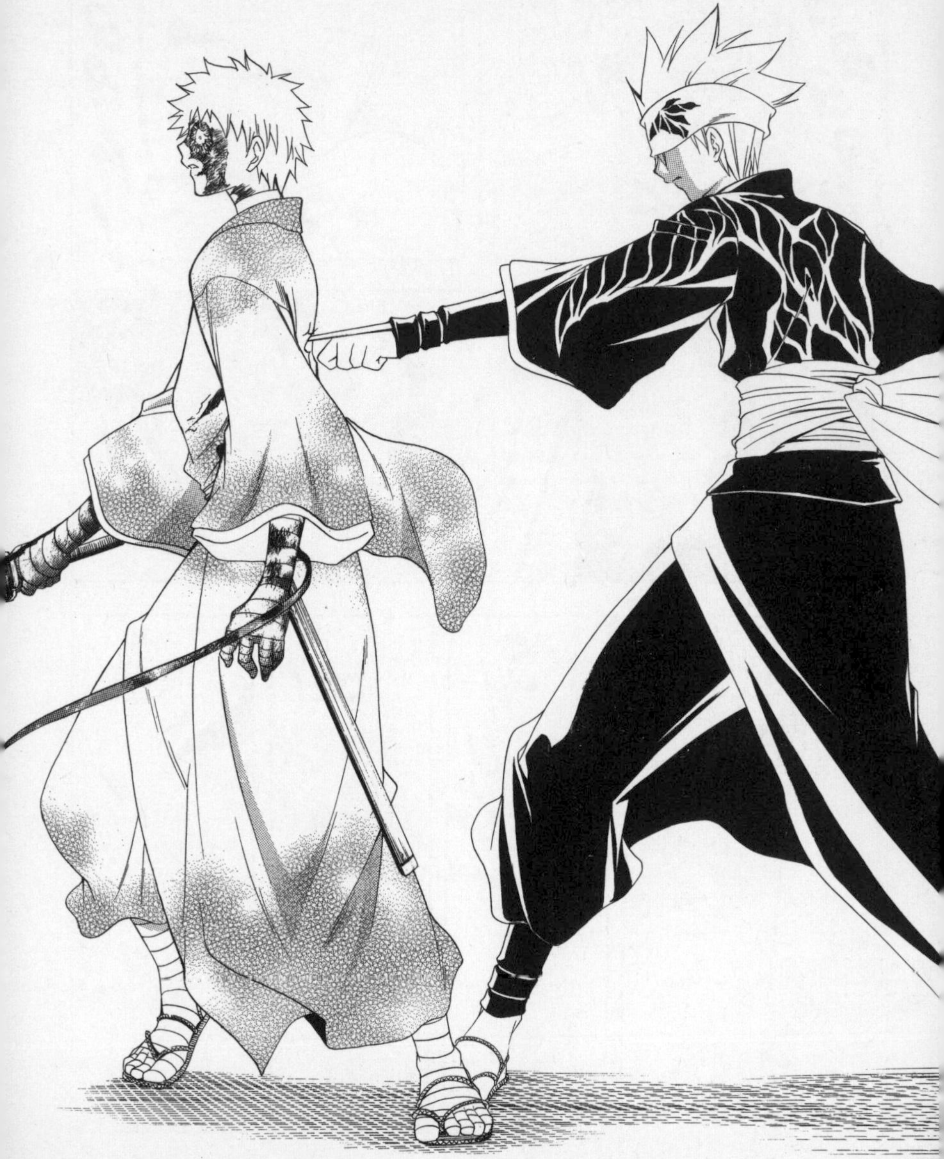

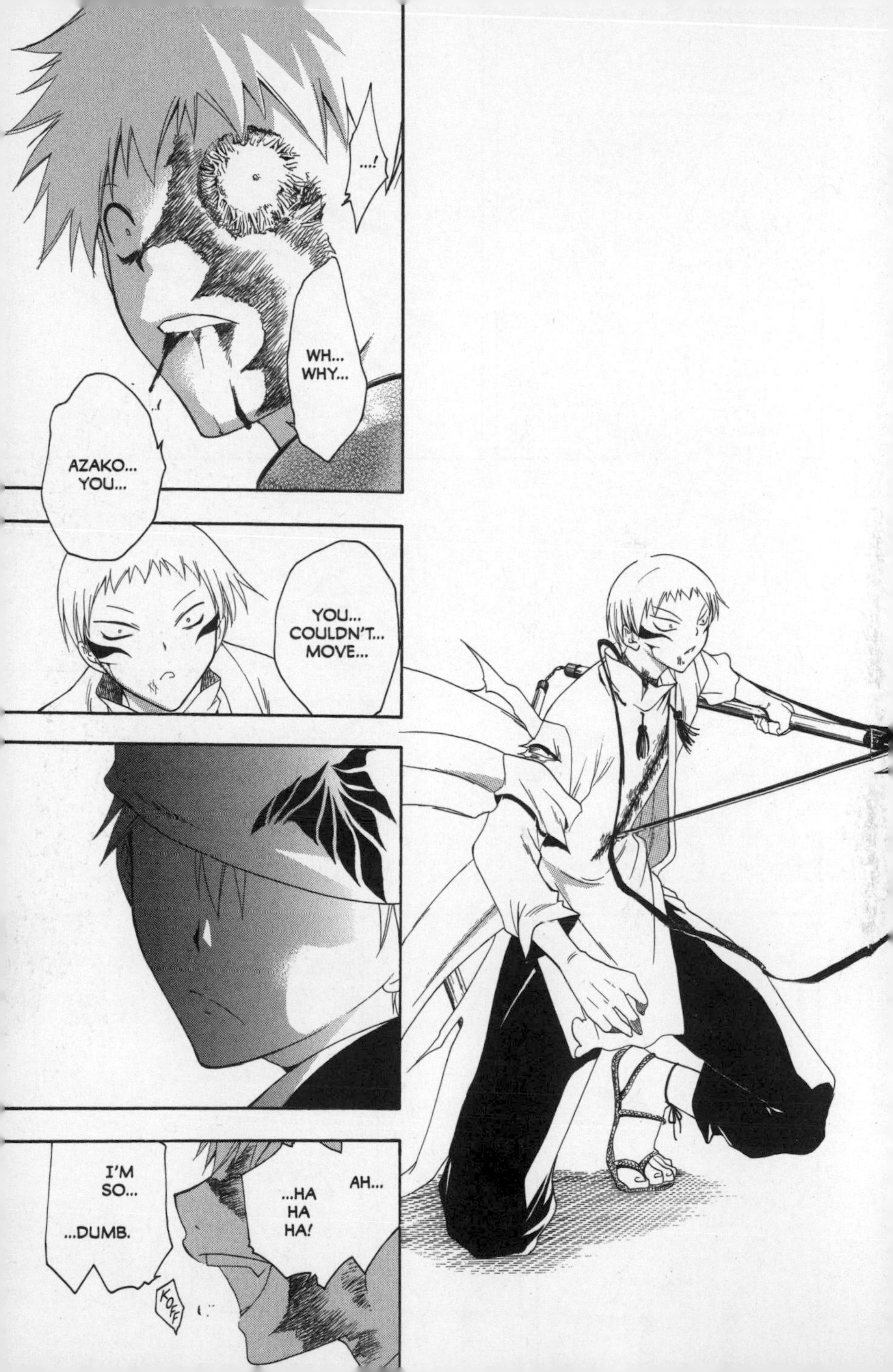
...!
WH... WHY...
AZAKO... YOU...
YOU... COULDN'T... MOVE...
AH...
...HA HA HA!
I'M SO... ...DUMB.
KOFF

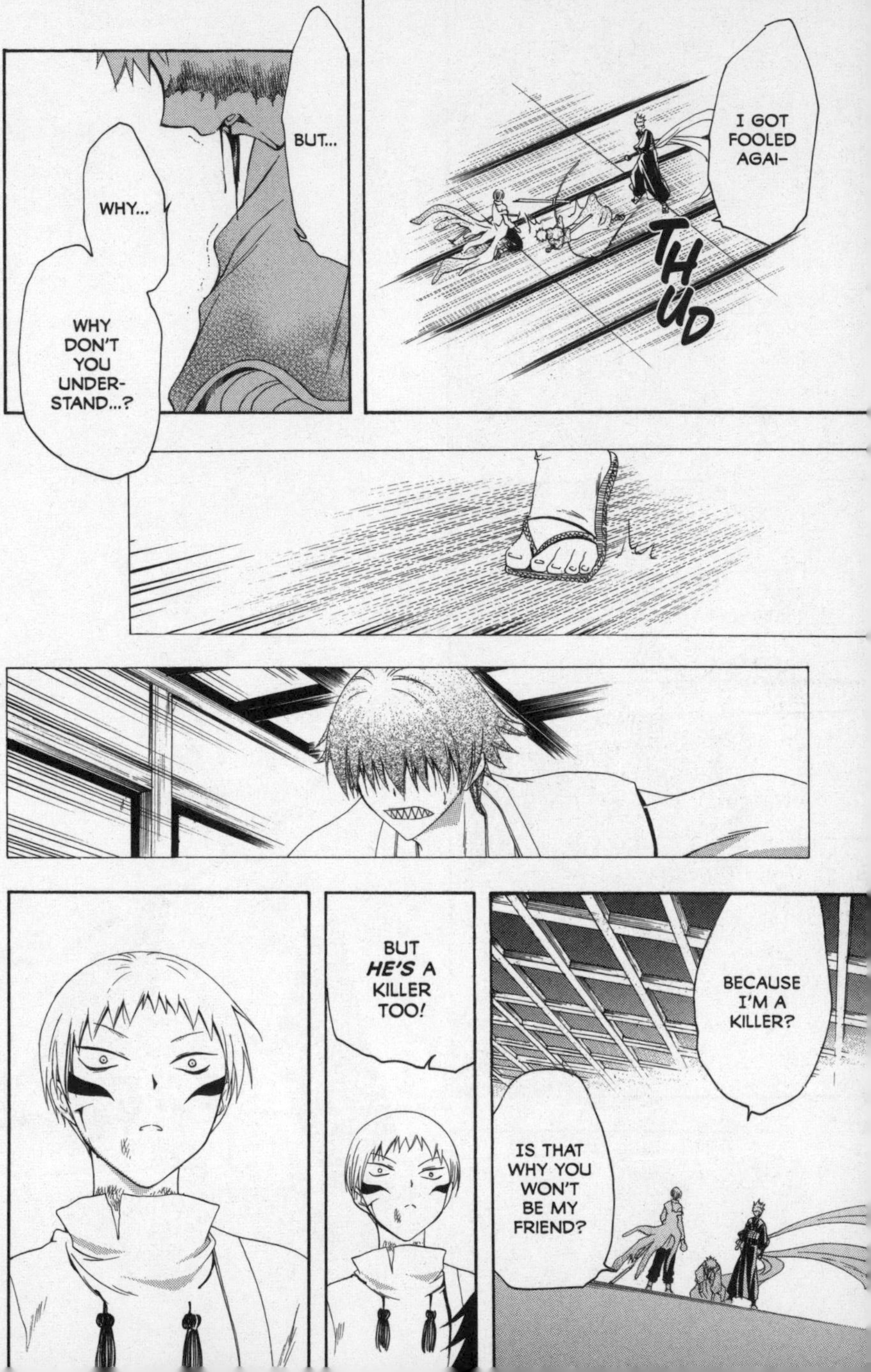
I GOT FOOLED AGAI-
THUD
BUT...
WHY...
WHY DON'T YOU UNDER-STAND...?
BECAUSE I'M A KILLER?
IS THAT WHY YOU WON'T BE MY FRIEND?
BUT *HE'S* A KILLER TOO!

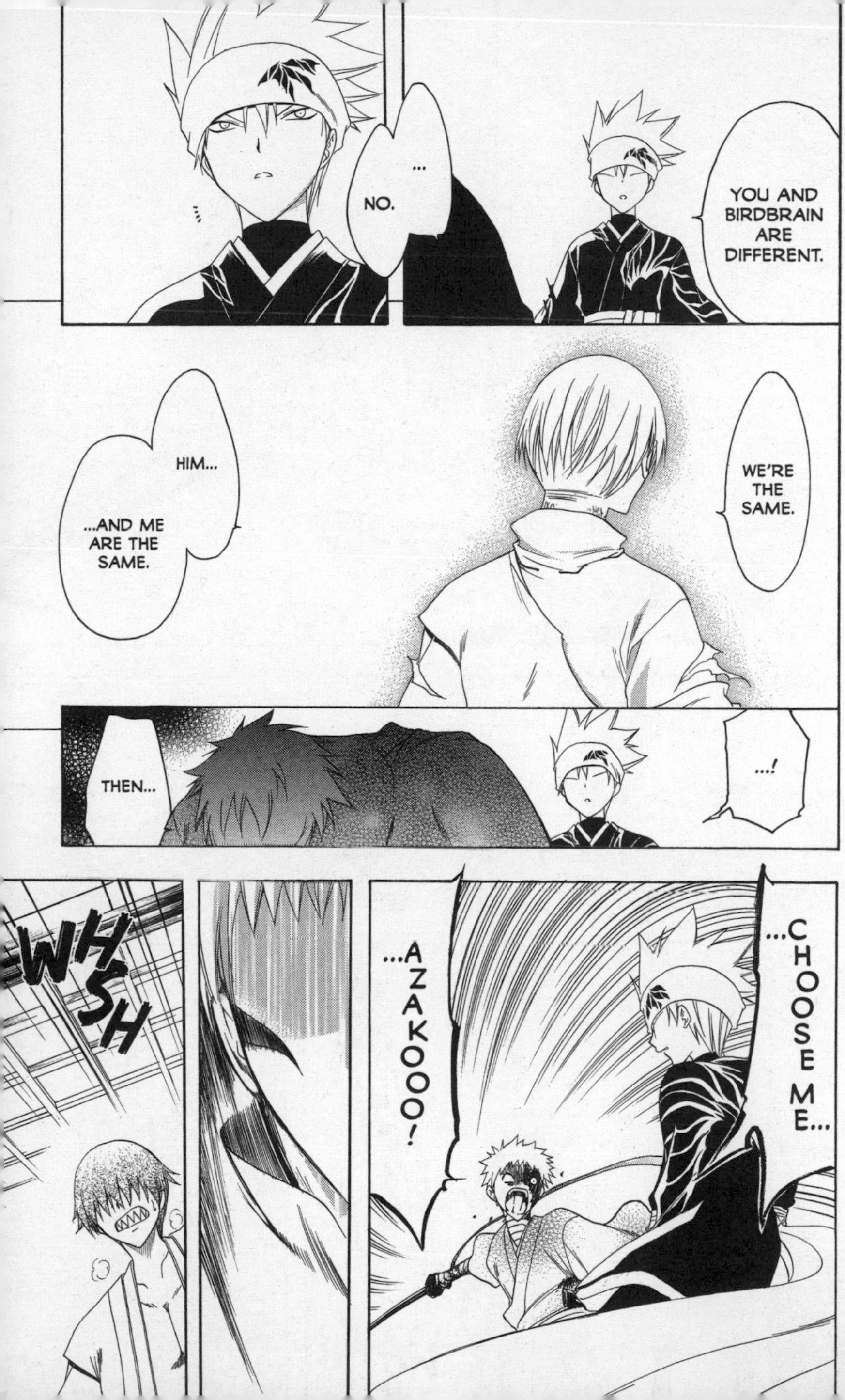
YOU AND BIRDBRAIN ARE DIFFERENT.
...
NO.
WE'RE THE SAME.
HIM...
...AND ME ARE THE SAME.
...!
THEN...
...CHOOSE ME...
...AZAKOOO!
WHSH

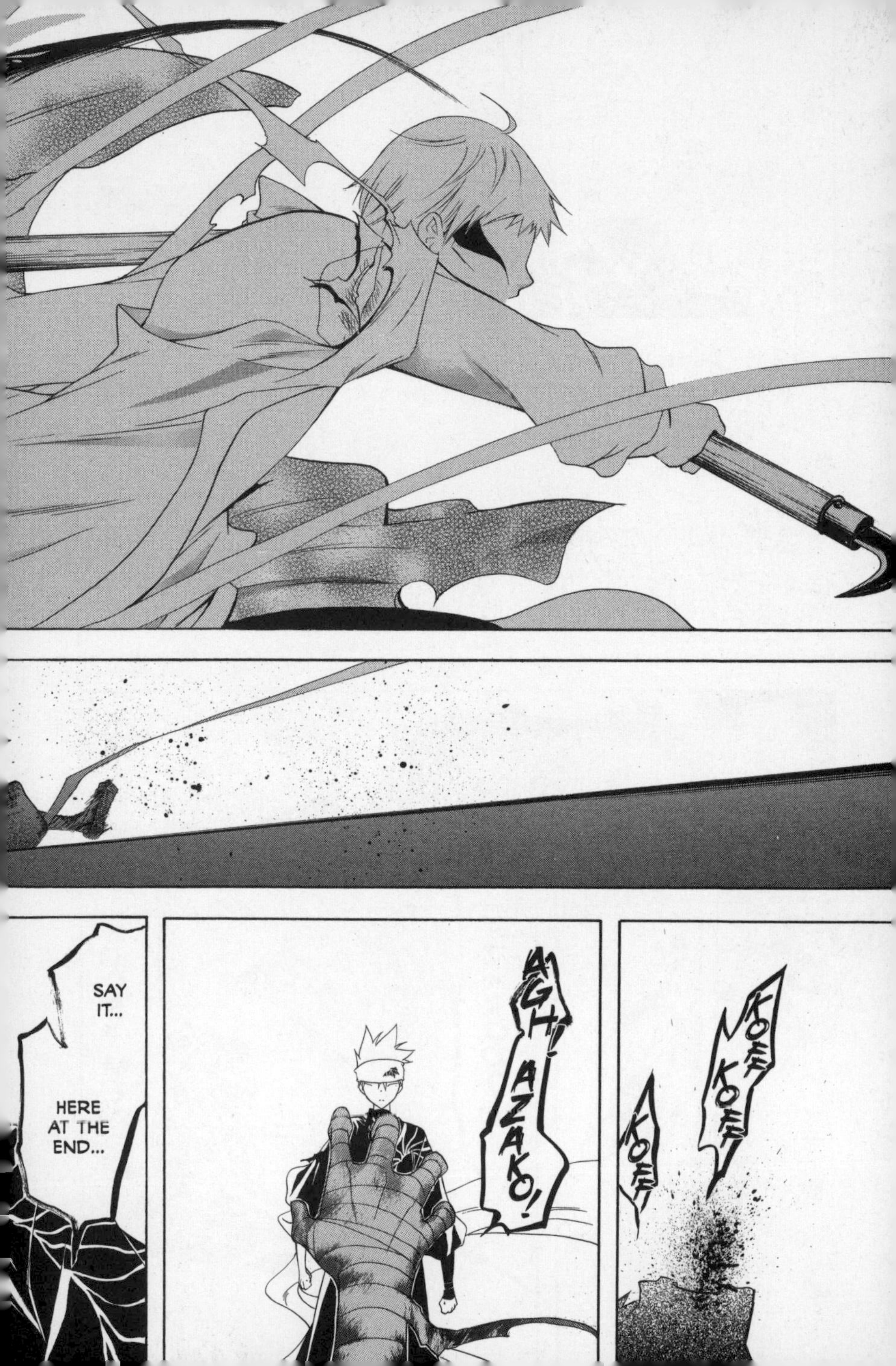
KOFF KOFF
KOFF
AGH! AZAKO!
SAY IT...
HERE AT THE END...

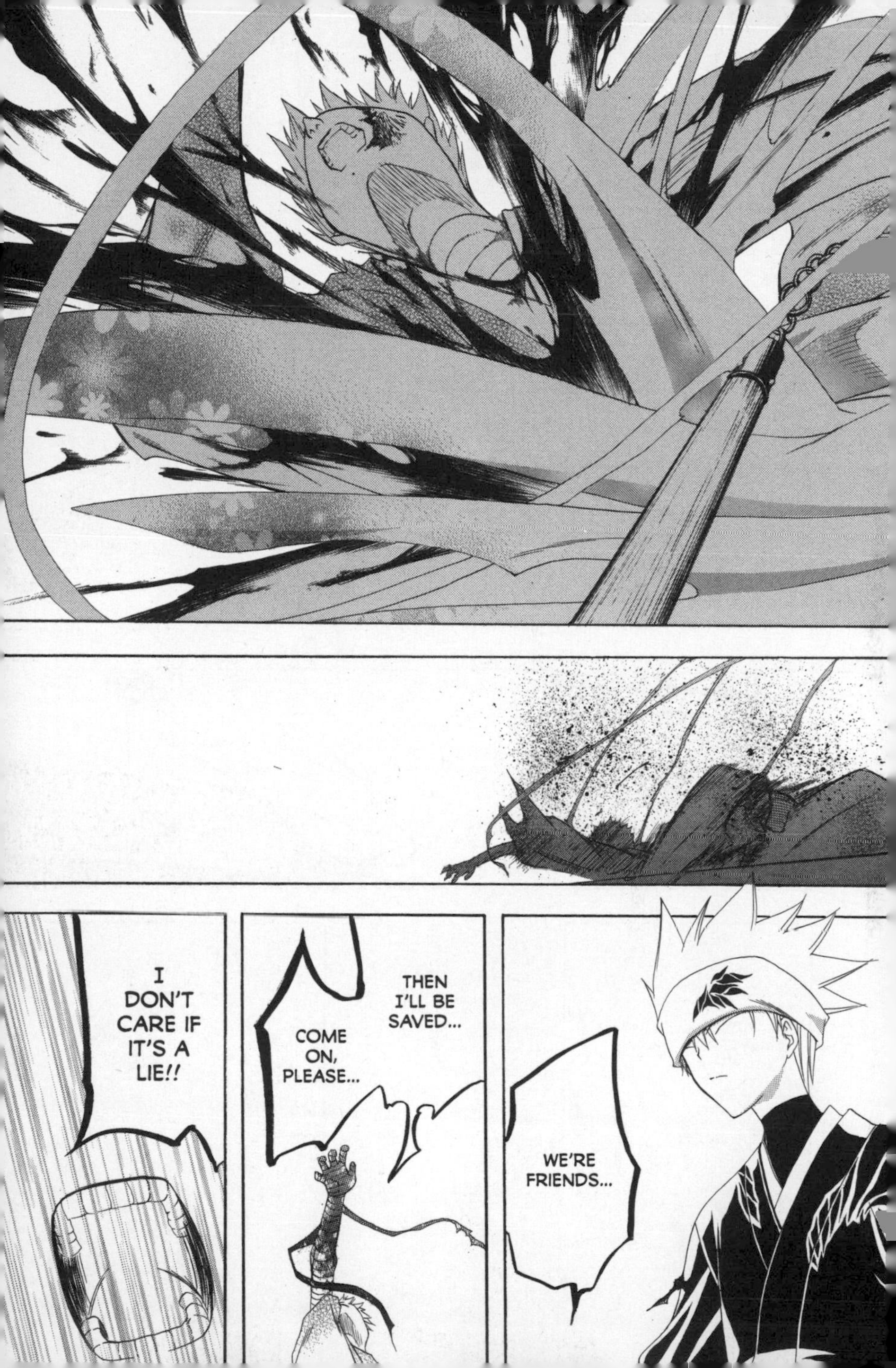
WE'RE FRIENDS...
THEN I'LL BE SAVED...
COME ON, PLEASE...
I DON'T CARE IF IT'S A LIE!!

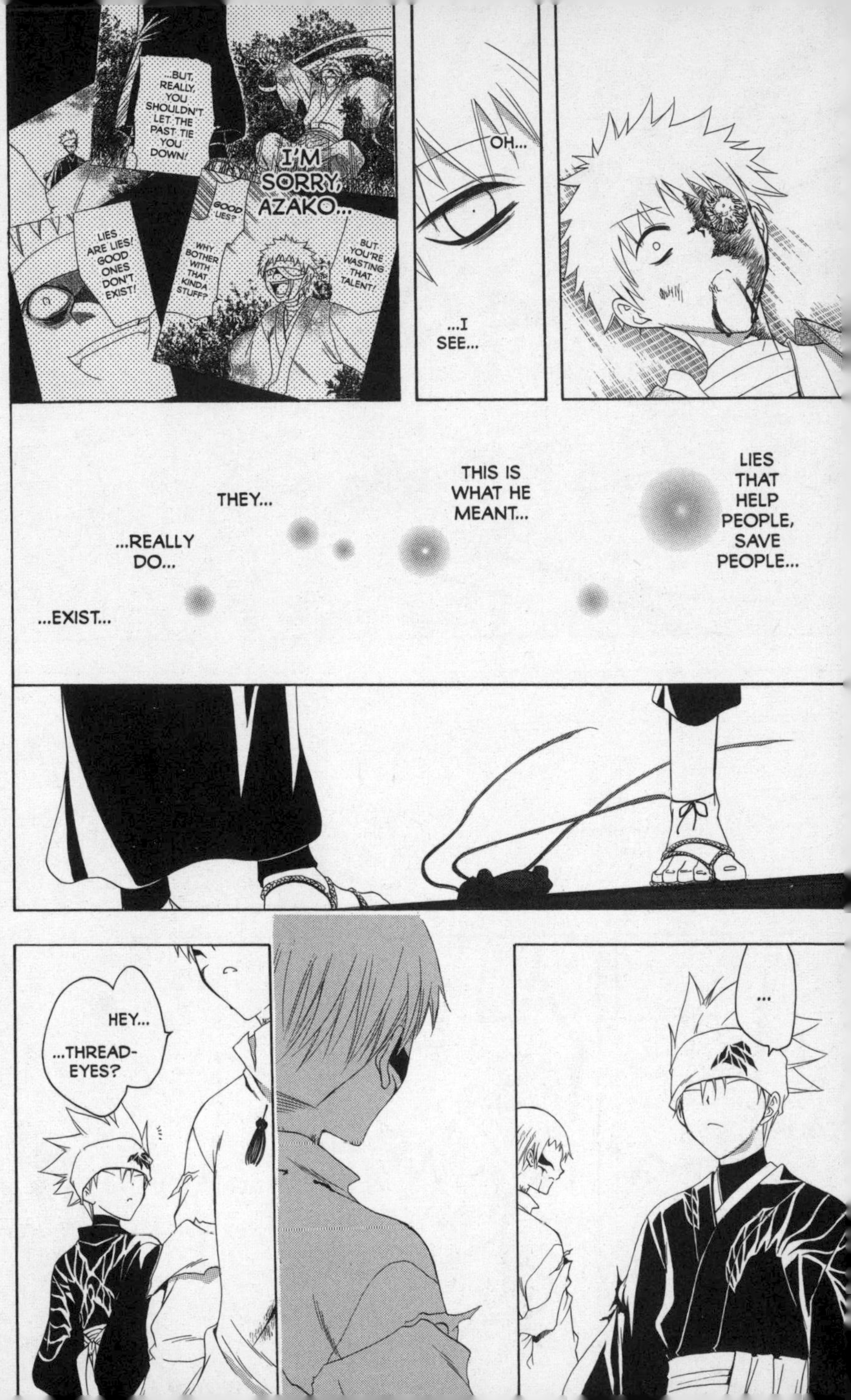
OH...
...I SEE...
...BUT, REALLY, YOU SHOULDN'T LET THE PAST TIE YOU DOWN!
I'M SORRY, AZAKO...
BUT YOU'RE WASTING THAT TALENT!
GOOD LIES?
WHY BOTHER WITH THAT KINDA STUFF?
LIES ARE LIES! GOOD ONES DON'T EXIST!
LIES THAT HELP PEOPLE, SAVE PEOPLE...
THIS IS WHAT HE MEANT...
THEY...
...REALLY DO...
...EXIST...
...
HEY...
...THREAD-EYES?

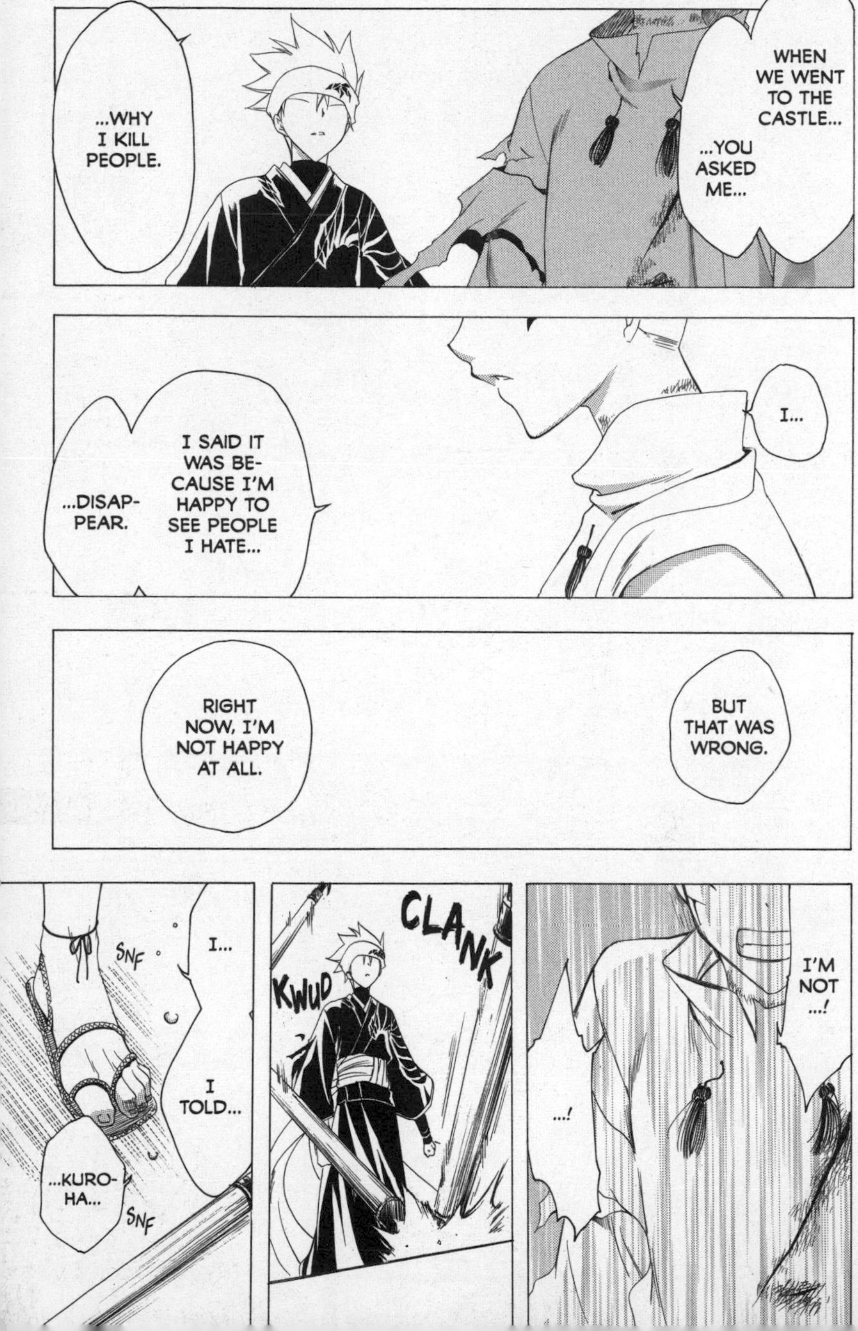
WHEN WE WENT TO THE CASTLE...
...YOU ASKED ME...
...WHY I KILL PEOPLE.
I...
I SAID IT WAS BE-CAUSE I'M HAPPY TO SEE PEOPLE I HATE...
...DISAP-PEAR.
BUT THAT WAS WRONG.
RIGHT NOW, I'M NOT HAPPY AT ALL.
I'M NOT ...!
...!
CLANK
KWUD
I...
SNF
I TOLD...
...KURO-HA...
SNF

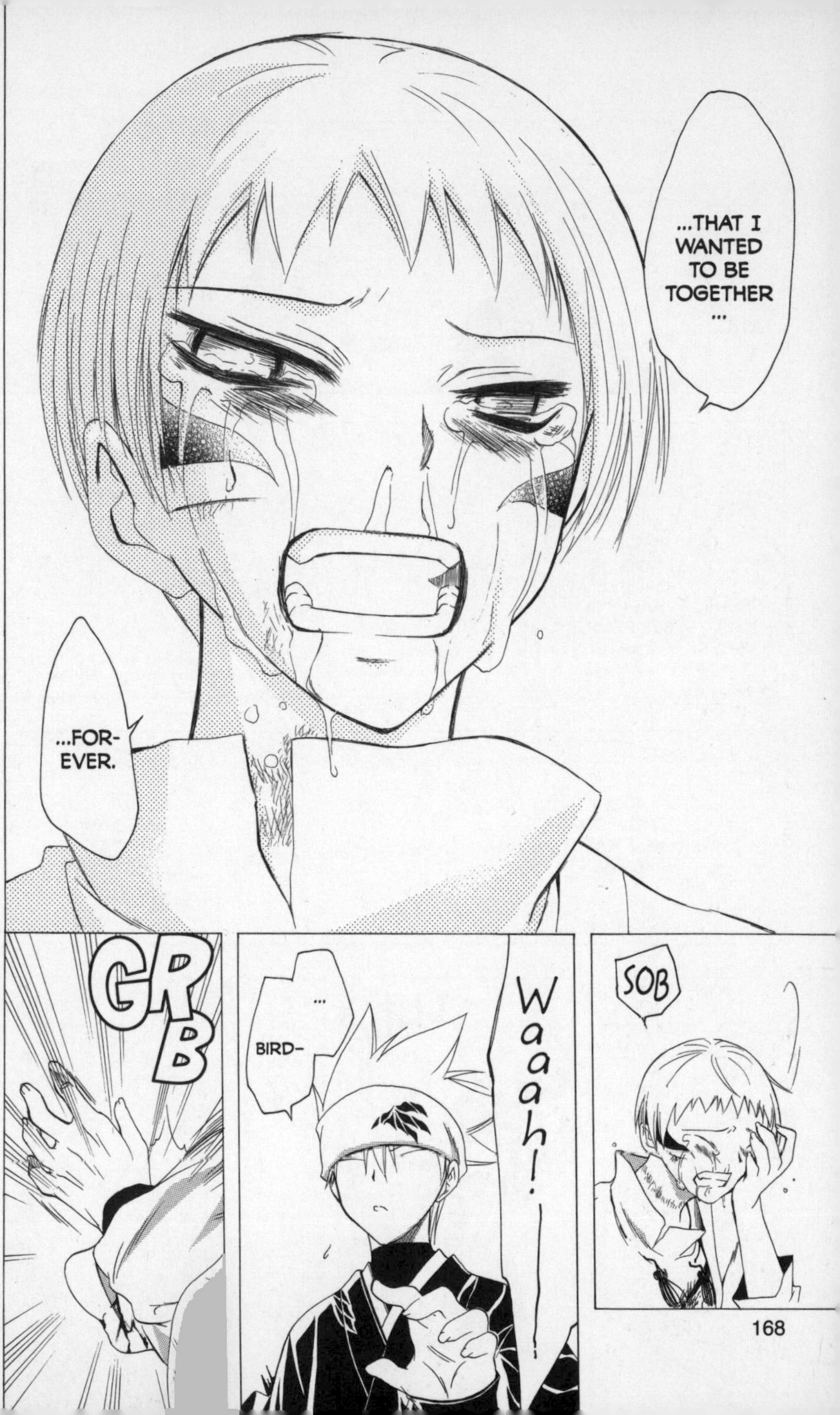
...THAT I WANTED TO BE TOGETHER ...
...FOR-EVER.
SOB
Waaah!
... BIRD-
GRB

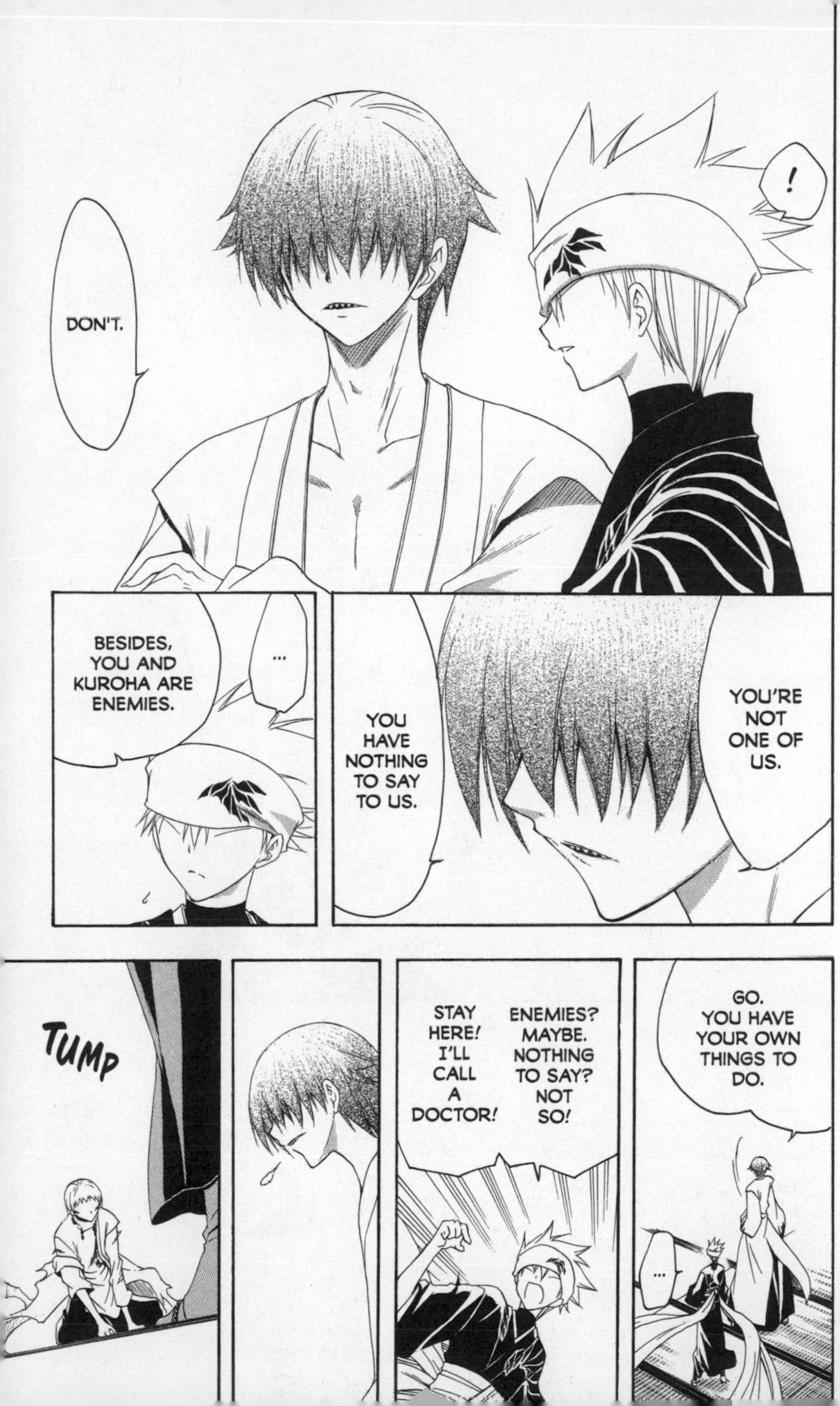
!
DON'T.
YOU'RE NOT ONE OF US.
YOU HAVE NOTHING TO SAY TO US.
...
BESIDES, YOU AND KUROHA ARE ENEMIES.
GO. YOU HAVE YOUR OWN THINGS TO DO.
...
ENEMIES? MAYBE. NOTHING TO SAY? NOT SO!
STAY HERE! I'LL CALL A DOCTOR!
TUMP

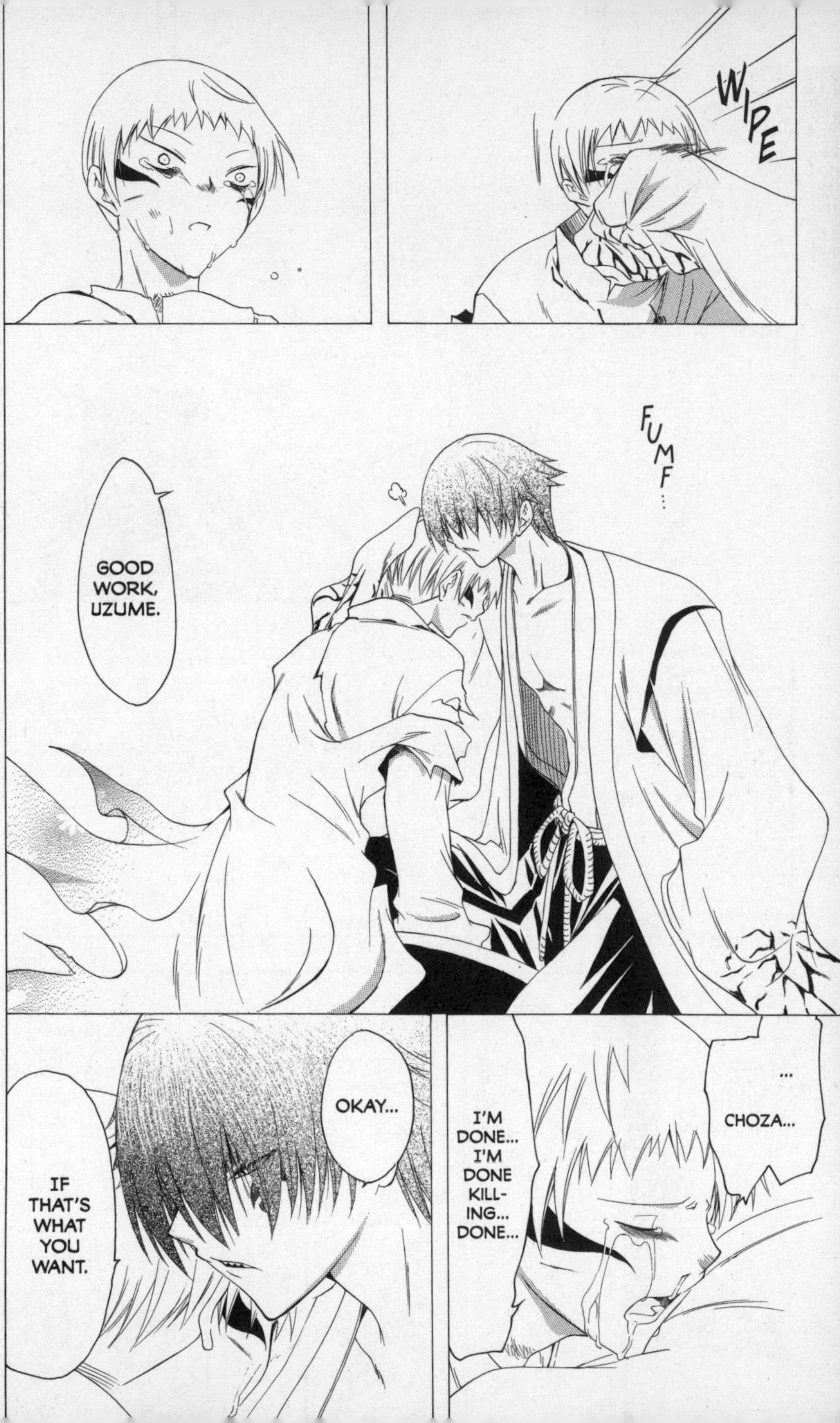
WIPE
FUMF...
GOOD WORK, UZUME.
...
CHOZA...
I'M DONE... I'M DONE KILL-ING... DONE...
OKAY...
IF THAT'S WHAT YOU WANT.

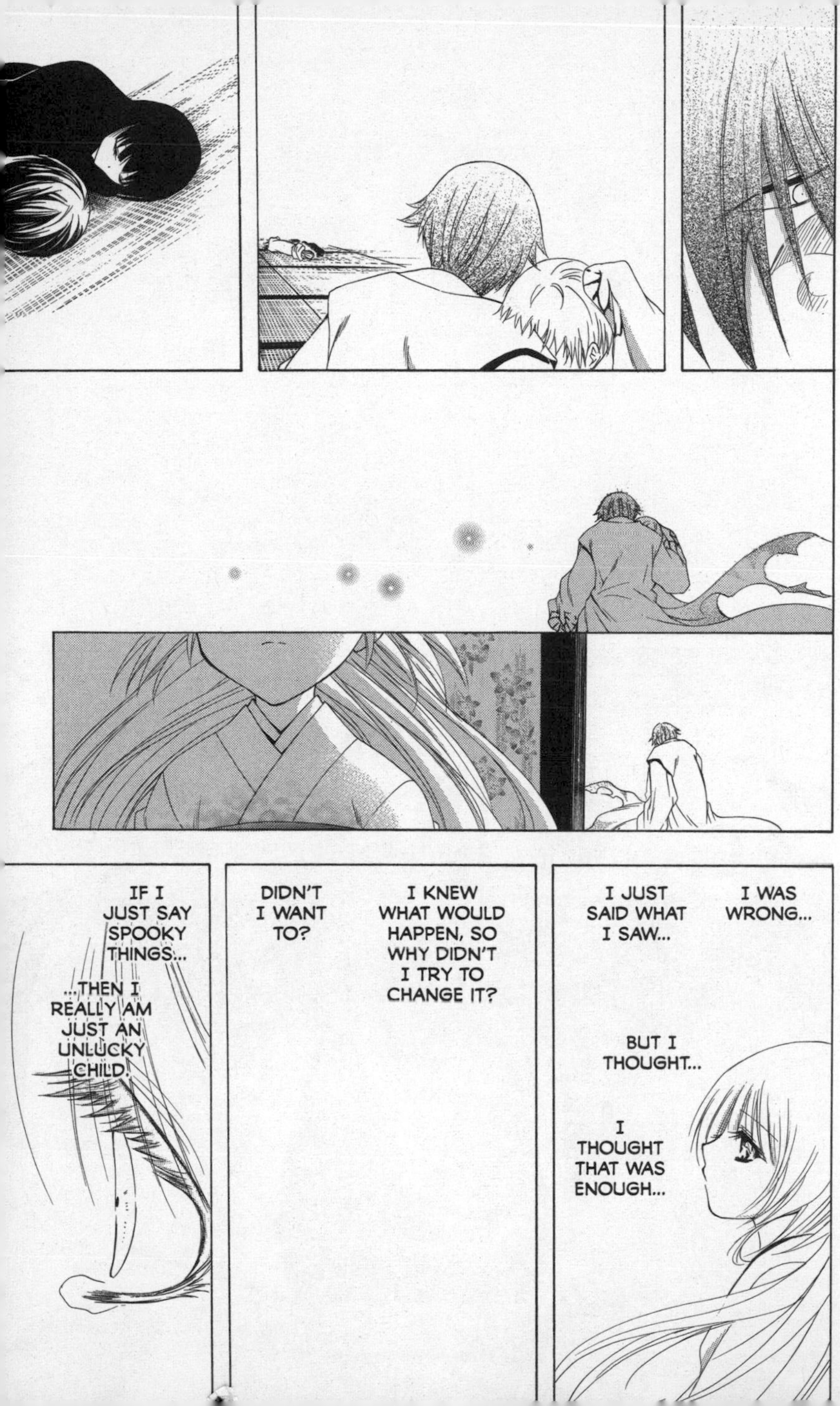
I WAS WRONG...
I JUST SAID WHAT I SAW...
BUT I THOUGHT...
I THOUGHT THAT WAS ENOUGH...
I KNEW WHAT WOULD HAPPEN, SO WHY DIDN'T I TRY TO CHANGE IT?
DIDN'T I WANT TO?
IF I JUST SAY SPOOKY THINGS...
...THEN I REALLY AM JUST AN UNLUCKY CHILD.

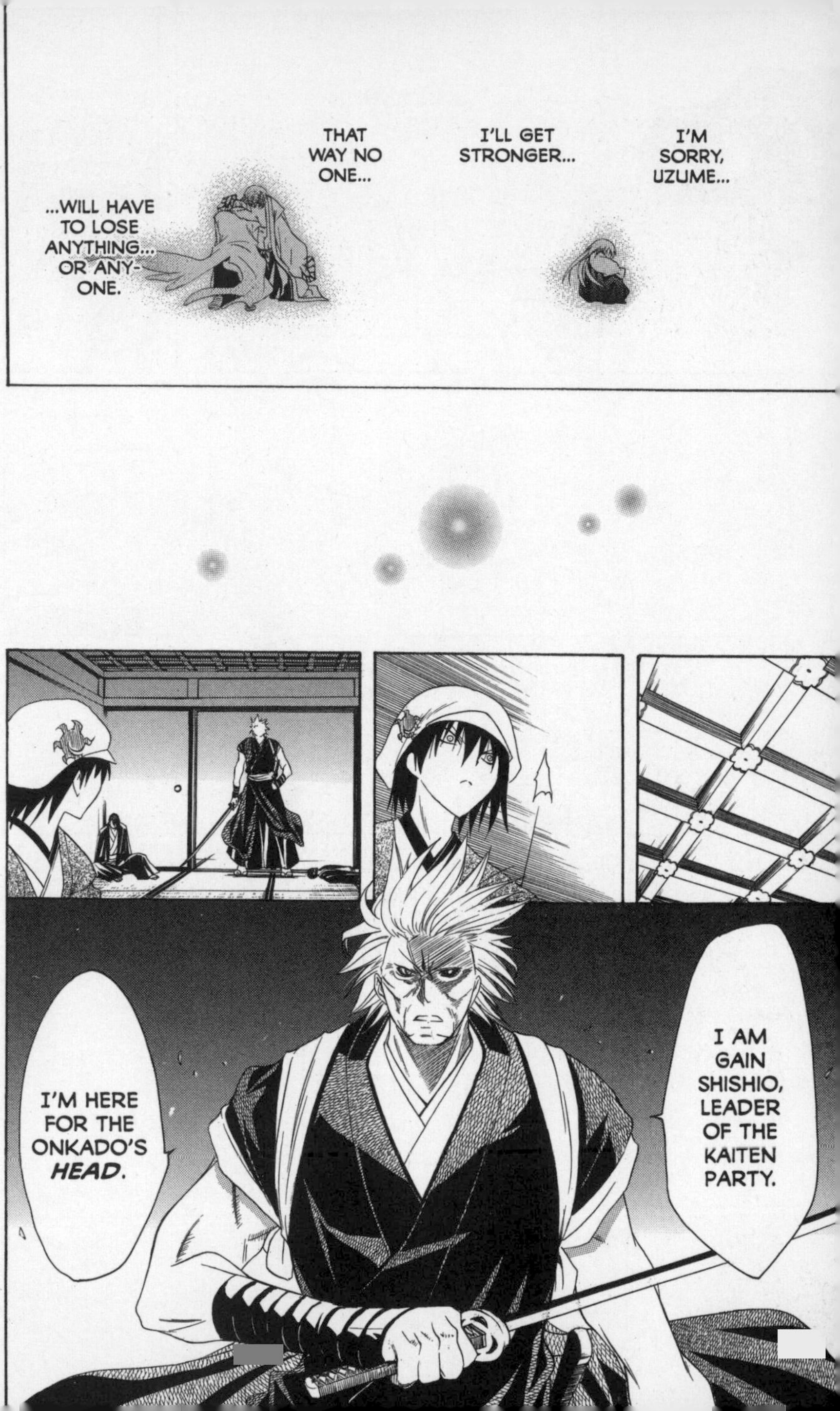
I'M SORRY, UZUME...
I'LL GET STRONGER...
THAT WAY NO ONE...
...WILL HAVE TO LOSE ANYTHING... OR ANY-ONE.
I AM GAIN SHISHIO, LEADER OF THE KAITEN PARTY.
I'M HERE FOR THE ONKADO'S *HEAD*.

*THIS BONUS MANGA APPEARED IMMEDIATELY PRIOR TO CHAPTER 100 AS CHAPTER 99.

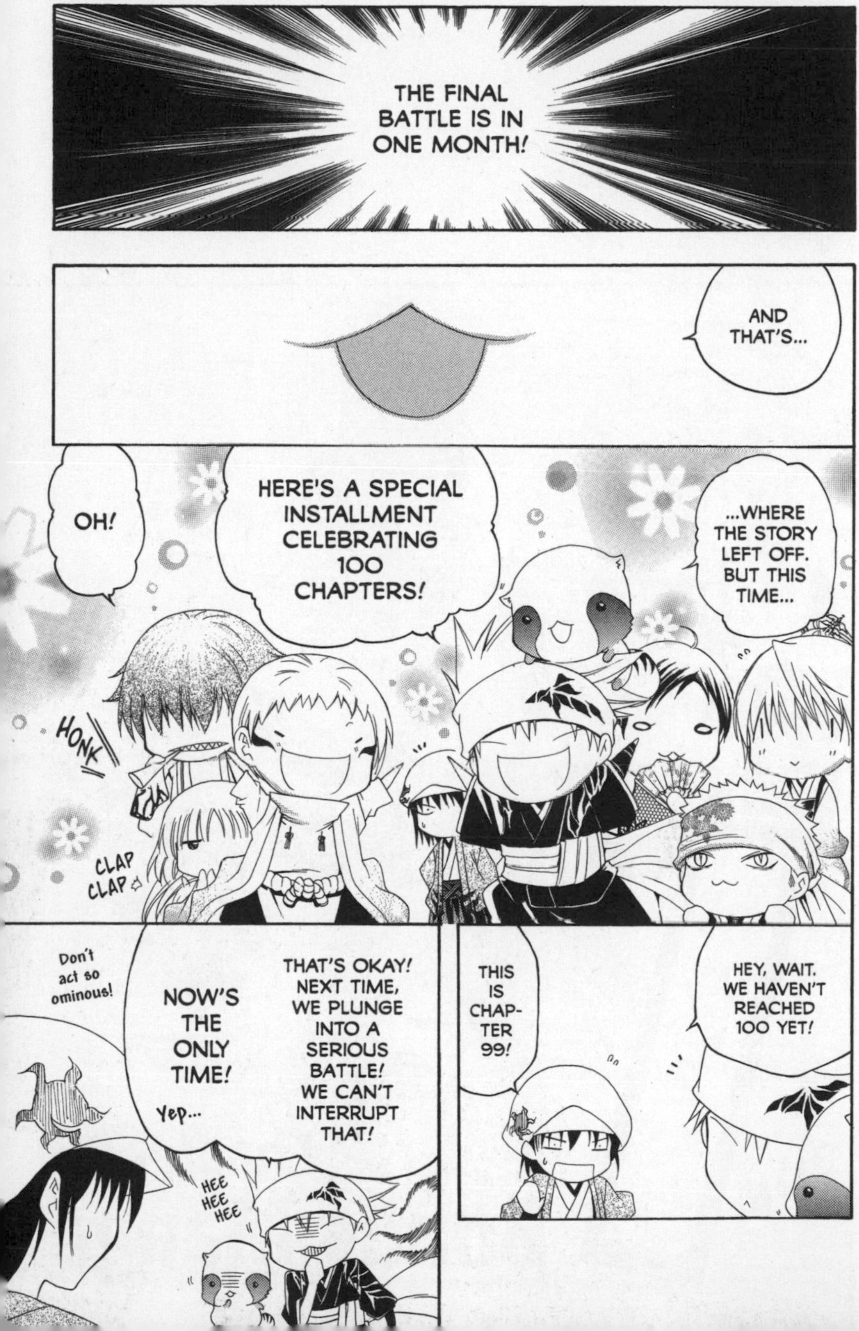
THE FINAL BATTLE IS IN ONE MONTH!
AND THAT'S...
...WHERE THE STORY LEFT OFF. BUT THIS TIME...
HERE'S A SPECIAL INSTALLMENT CELEBRATING 100 CHAPTERS!
OH!
HONK
CLAP CLAP
HEY, WAIT. WE HAVEN'T REACHED 100 YET!
THIS IS CHAPTER 99!
THAT'S OKAY! NEXT TIME, WE PLUNGE INTO A SERIOUS BATTLE! WE CAN'T INTERRUPT THAT!
NOW'S THE ONLY TIME!
Yep...
Don't act so ominous!
HEE HEE HEE

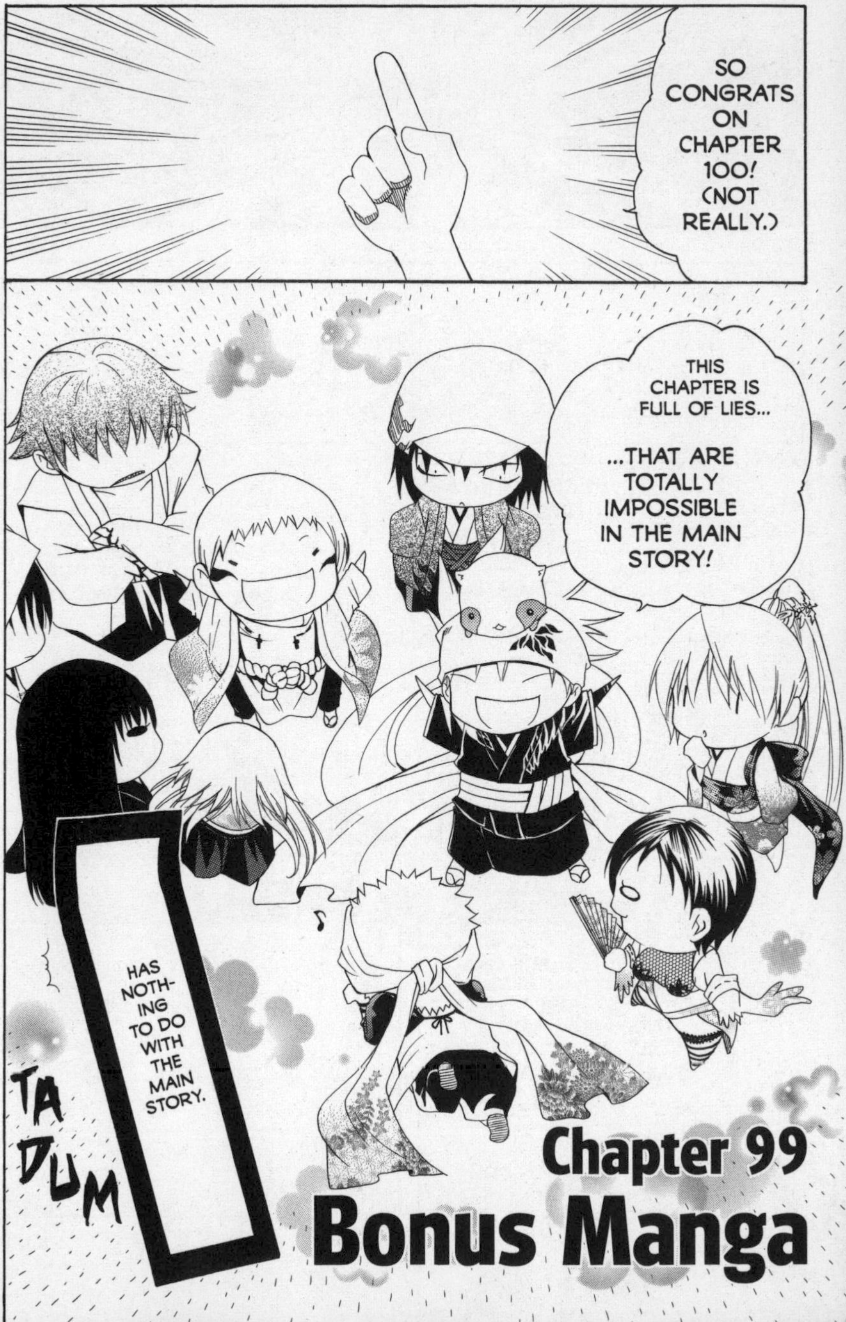
SO CONGRATS ON CHAPTER 100! (NOT REALLY.)
THIS CHAPTER IS FULL OF LIES...
...THAT ARE TOTALLY IMPOSSIBLE IN THE MAIN STORY!
Chapter 99
Bonus Manga
HAS NOTH-ING TO DO WITH THE MAIN STORY.
TA DUM

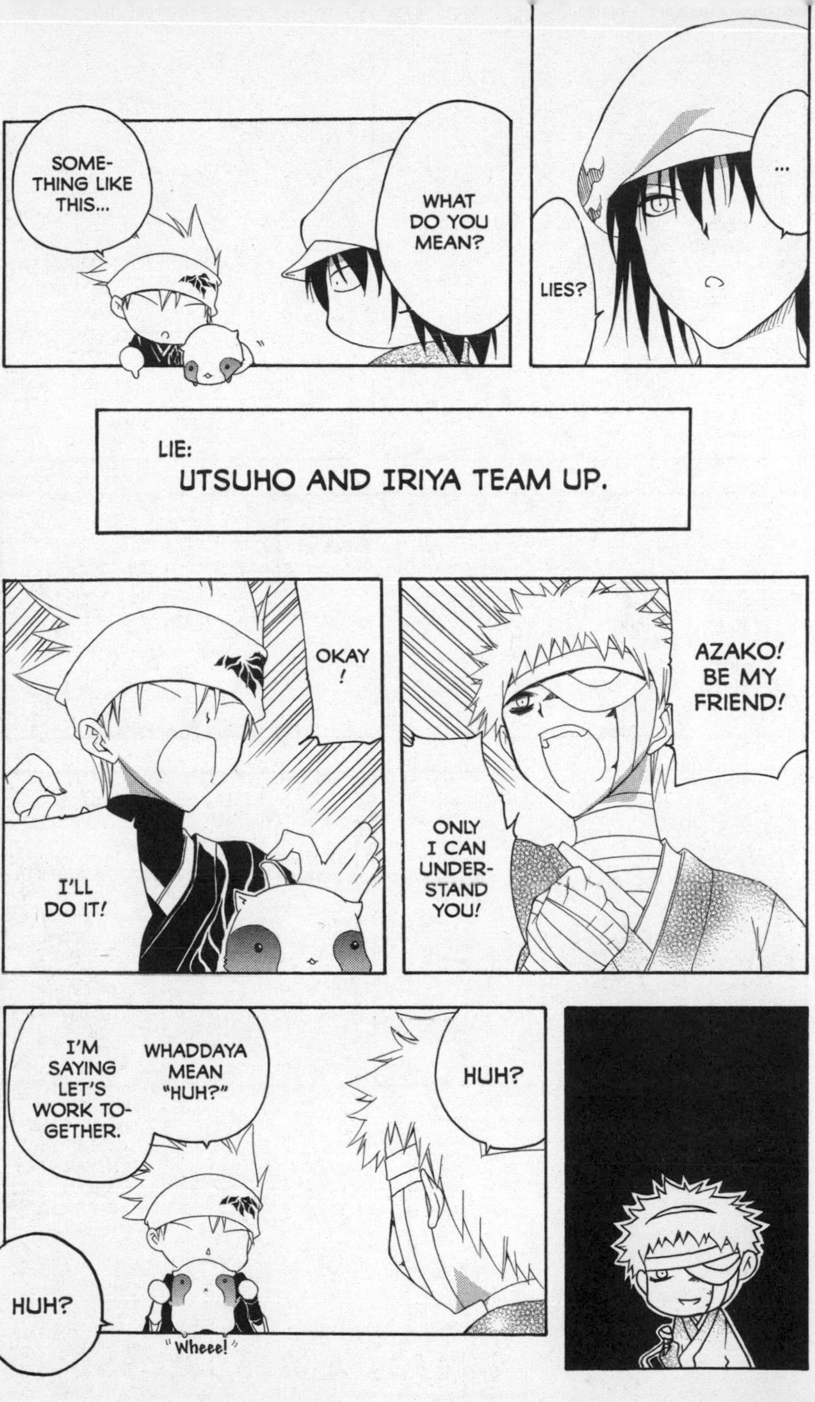
...
LIES?
WHAT DO YOU MEAN?
SOME-THING LIKE THIS...
LIE:
UTSUHO AND IRIYA TEAM UP.
AZAKO! BE MY FRIEND!
ONLY I CAN UNDER-STAND YOU!
OKAY!
I'LL DO IT!
HUH?
WHADDAYA MEAN "HUH?"
I'M SAYING LET'S WORK TO-GETHER.
HUH?
"Wheee!"

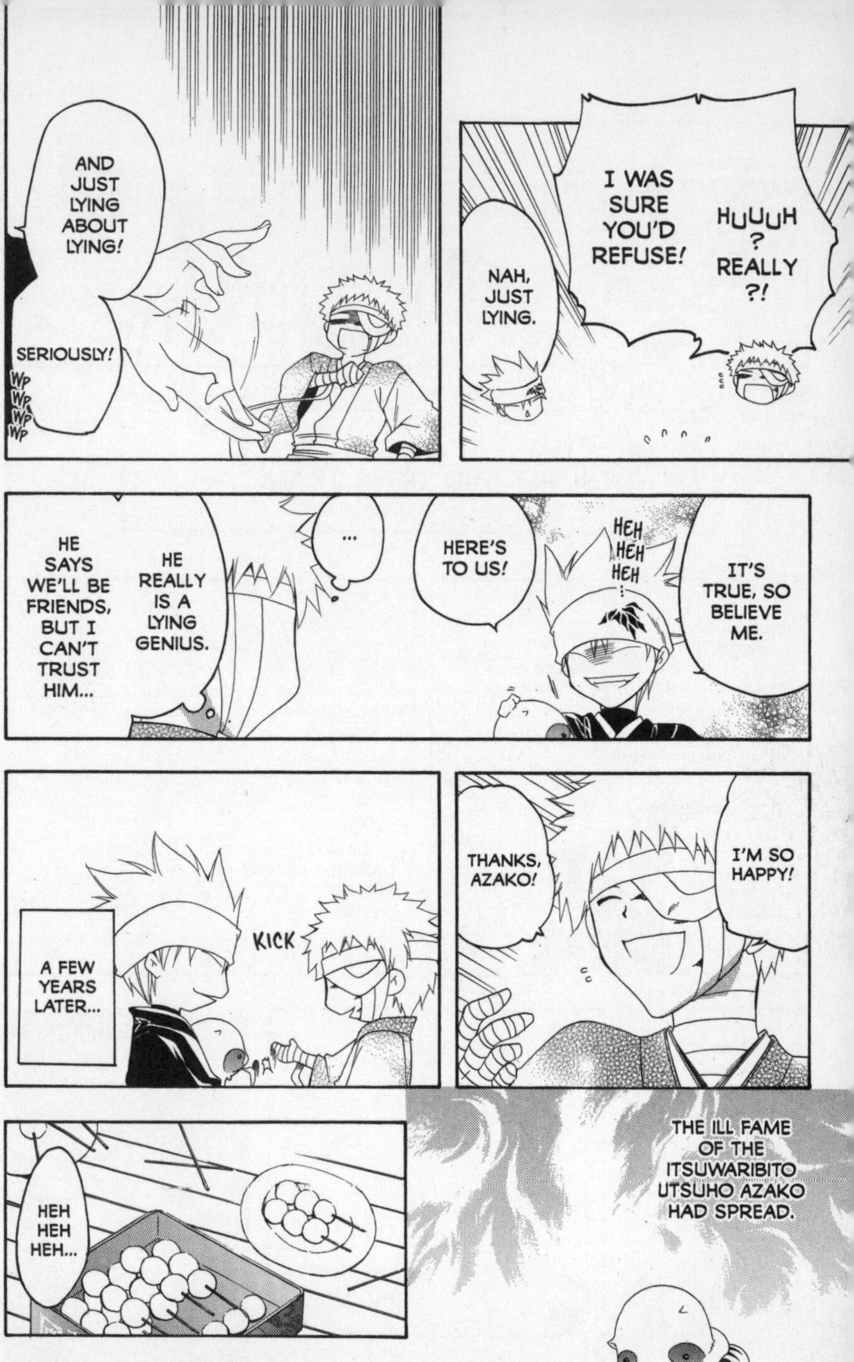
HUUUH? REALLY?!
I WAS SURE YOU'D REFUSE!
NAH, JUST LYING.
AND JUST LYING ABOUT LYING!
SERIOUSLY!
WP WP WP WP
IT'S TRUE, SO BELIEVE ME.
HEH HEH HEH
HERE'S TO US!
...
HE REALLY IS A LYING GENIUS.
HE SAYS WE'LL BE FRIENDS, BUT I CAN'T TRUST HIM...
I'M SO HAPPY!
THANKS, AZAKO!
KICK
A FEW YEARS LATER...
THE ILL FAME OF THE ITSUWARIBITO UTSUHO AZAKO HAD SPREAD.
HEH HEH HEH...

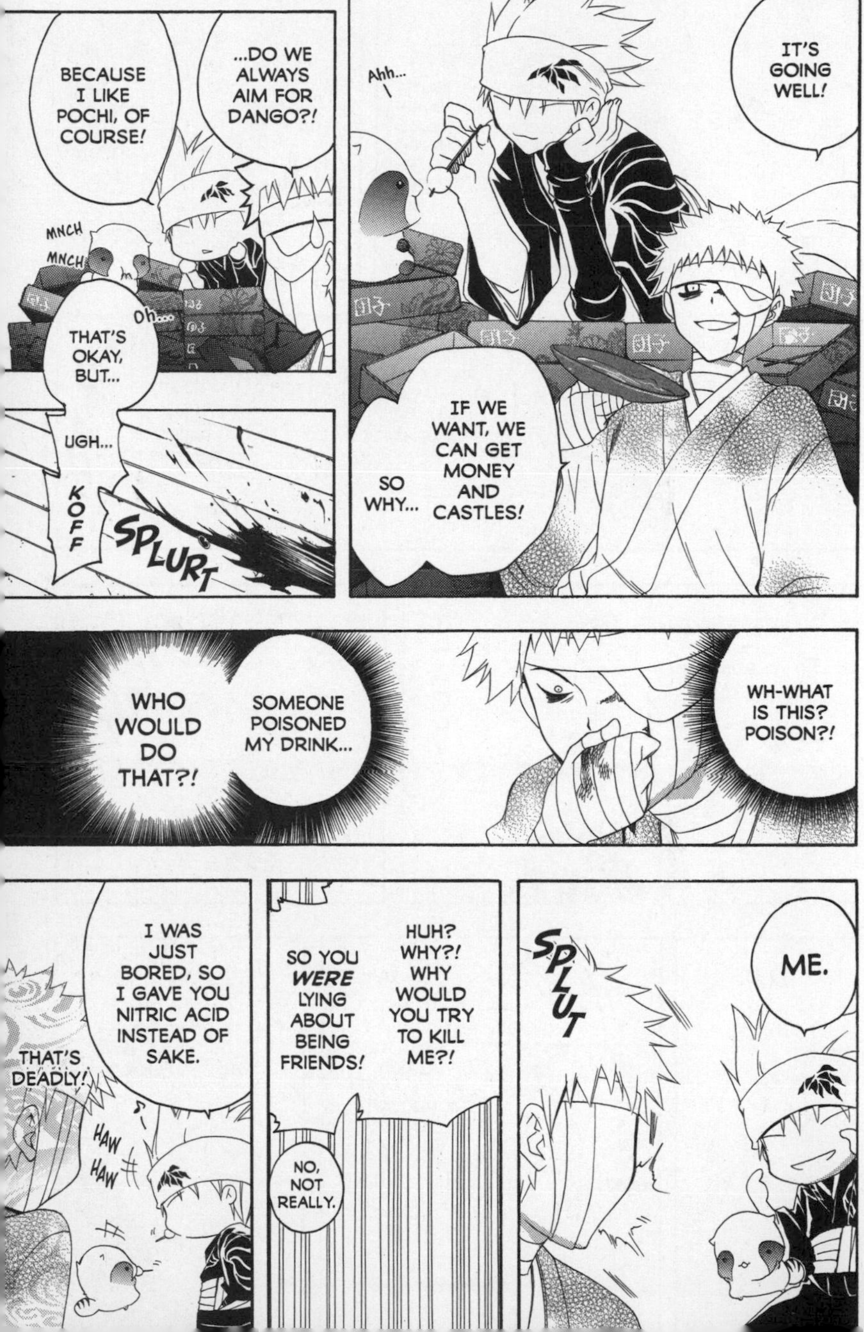
IT'S GOING WELL!
Ahh...
IF WE WANT, WE CAN GET MONEY AND CASTLES!
SO WHY...
...DO WE ALWAYS AIM FOR DANGO?!
BECAUSE I LIKE POCHI, OF COURSE!
MNCH MNCH
Oh...
THAT'S OKAY, BUT...
UGH...
KOFF
SPLURT
WH-WHAT IS THIS? POISON?!
SOMEONE POISONED MY DRINK...
WHO WOULD DO THAT?!
ME.
SPLUT
HUH? WHY?! WHY WOULD YOU TRY TO KILL ME?!
SO YOU *WERE* LYING ABOUT BEING FRIENDS!
NO, NOT REALLY.
I WAS JUST BORED, SO I GAVE YOU NITRIC ACID INSTEAD OF SAKE.
THAT'S DEADLY!
HAW HAW

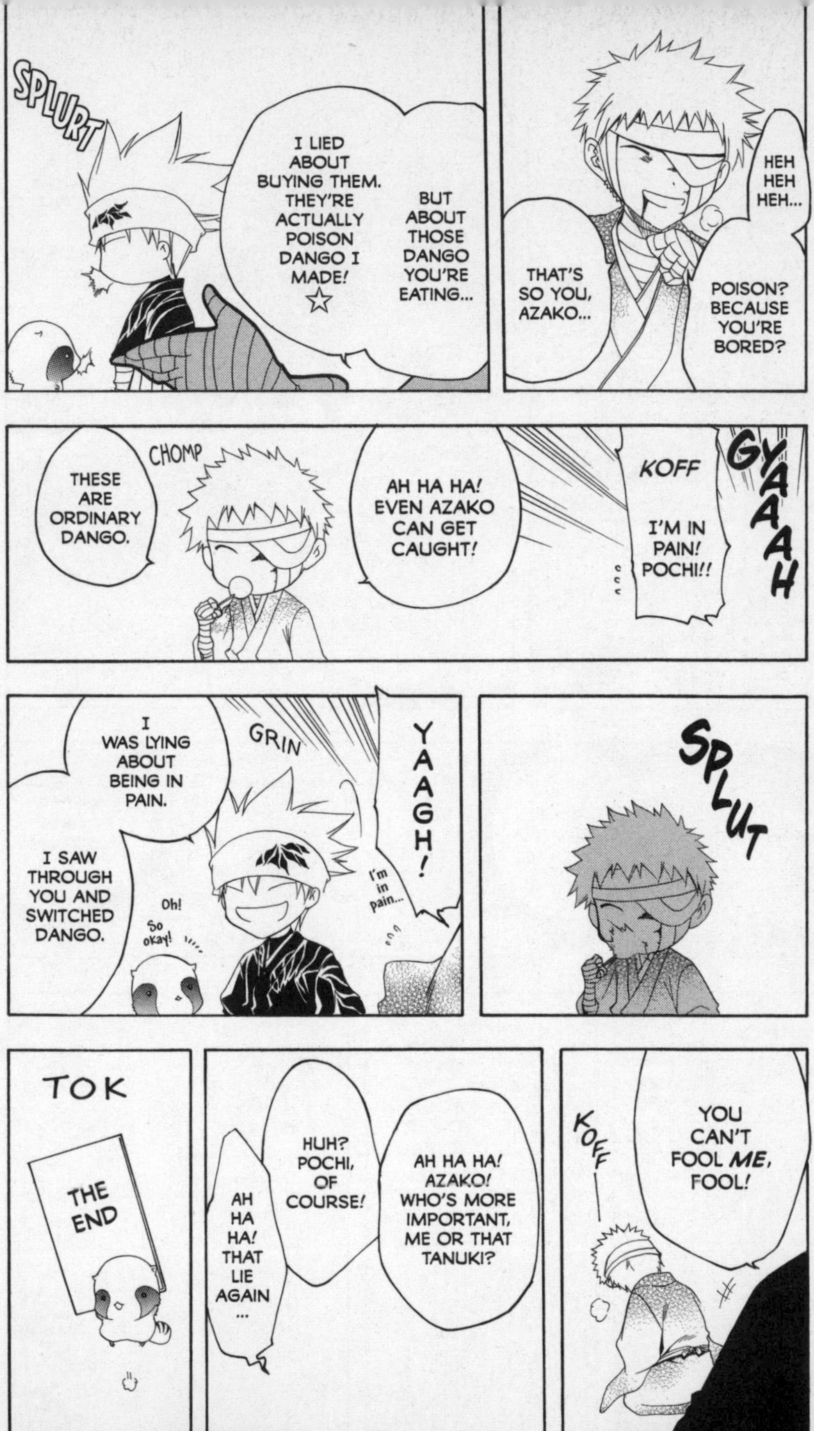
HEH HEH HEH...
POISON? BECAUSE YOU'RE BORED?
THAT'S SO YOU, AZAKO...
BUT ABOUT THOSE DANGO YOU'RE EATING...
I LIED ABOUT BUYING THEM. THEY'RE ACTUALLY POISON DANGO I MADE! ☆
SPLURT
GYAAAH
KOFF
I'M IN PAIN! POCHI!!
AH HA HA! EVEN AZAKO CAN GET CAUGHT!
CHOMP
THESE ARE ORDINARY DANGO.
SPLUT
YAAGH!
I'm in pain...
GRIN
I WAS LYING ABOUT BEING IN PAIN.
I SAW THROUGH YOU AND SWITCHED DANGO.
Oh! So okay!
KOFF
YOU CAN'T FOOL *ME*, FOOL!
AH HA HA! AZAKO! WHO'S MORE IMPORTANT, ME OR THAT TANUKI?
HUH? POCHI, OF COURSE!
AH HA HA! THAT LIE AGAIN...
TOK
THE END

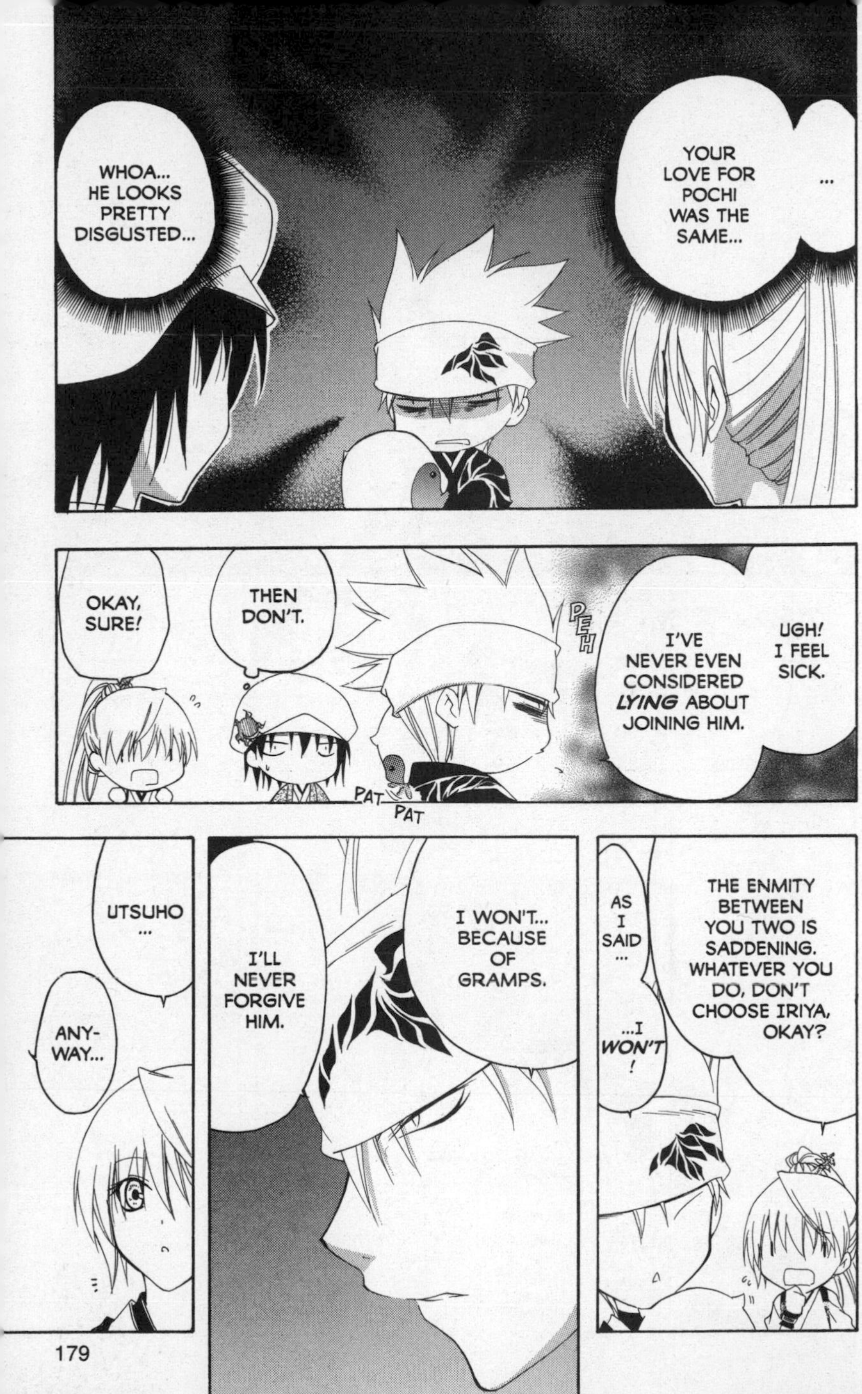

...
YOUR LOVE FOR POCHI WAS THE SAME...
WHOA... HE LOOKS PRETTY DISGUSTED...
UGH! I FEEL SICK.
I'VE NEVER EVEN CONSIDERED *LYING* ABOUT JOINING HIM.
PEH
THEN DON'T.
OKAY, SURE!
PAT PAT
THE ENMITY BETWEEN YOU TWO IS SADDENING. WHATEVER YOU DO, DON'T CHOOSE IRIYA, OKAY?
AS I SAID...
...I *WON'T*!
I WON'T... BECAUSE OF GRAMPS.
I'LL NEVER FORGIVE HIM.
UTSUHO...
ANY-WAY...

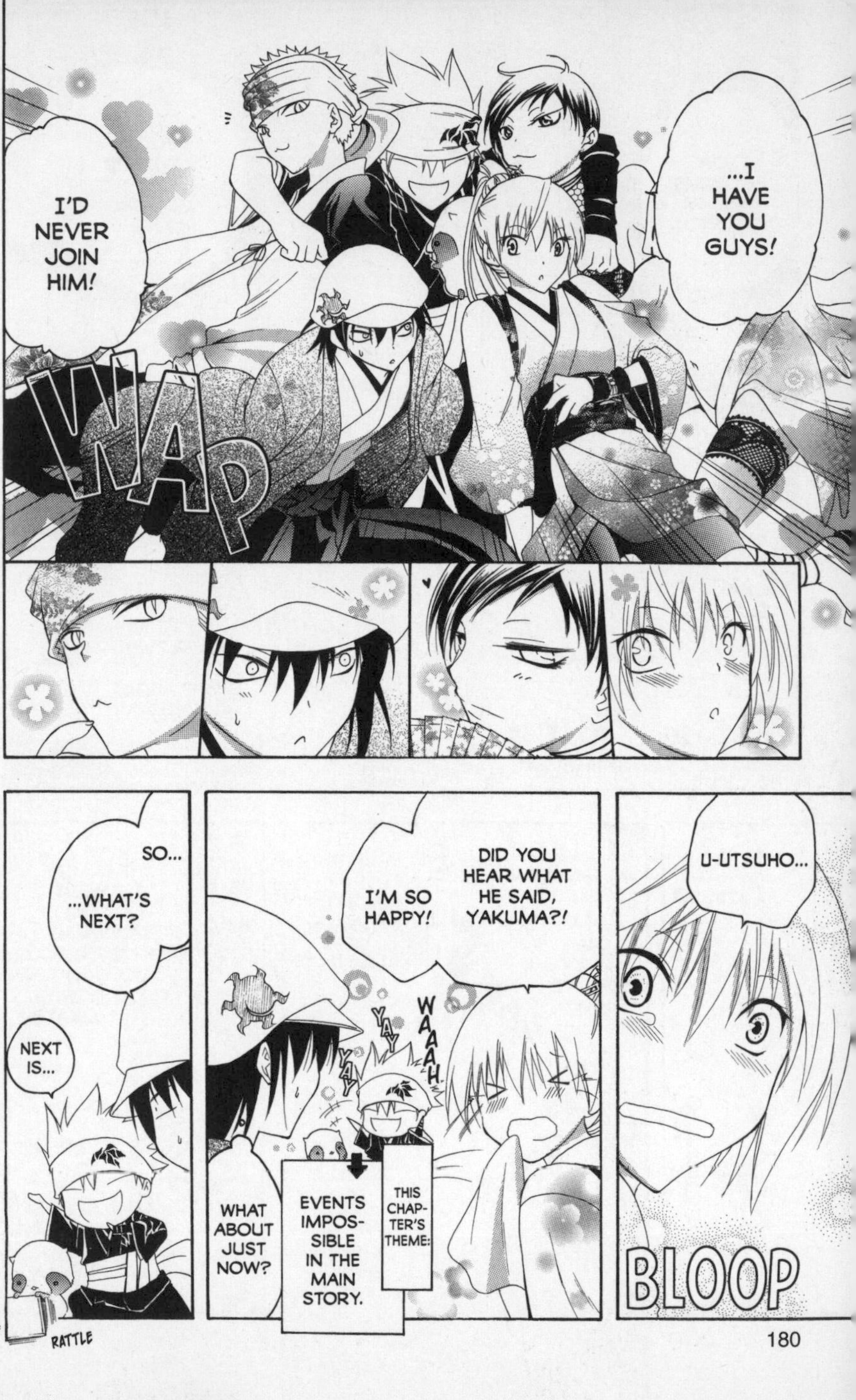
...I HAVE YOU GUYS!
I'D NEVER JOIN HIM!
WAP
U-UTSUHO...
BLOOP
DID YOU HEAR WHAT HE SAID, YAKUMA?!
I'M SO HAPPY!
WAAAH
YAY
YAY
THIS CHAPTER'S THEME:
EVENTS IMPOSSIBLE IN THE MAIN STORY.
WHAT ABOUT JUST NOW?
SO...
...WHAT'S NEXT?
NEXT IS...
RATTLE
RATTLE

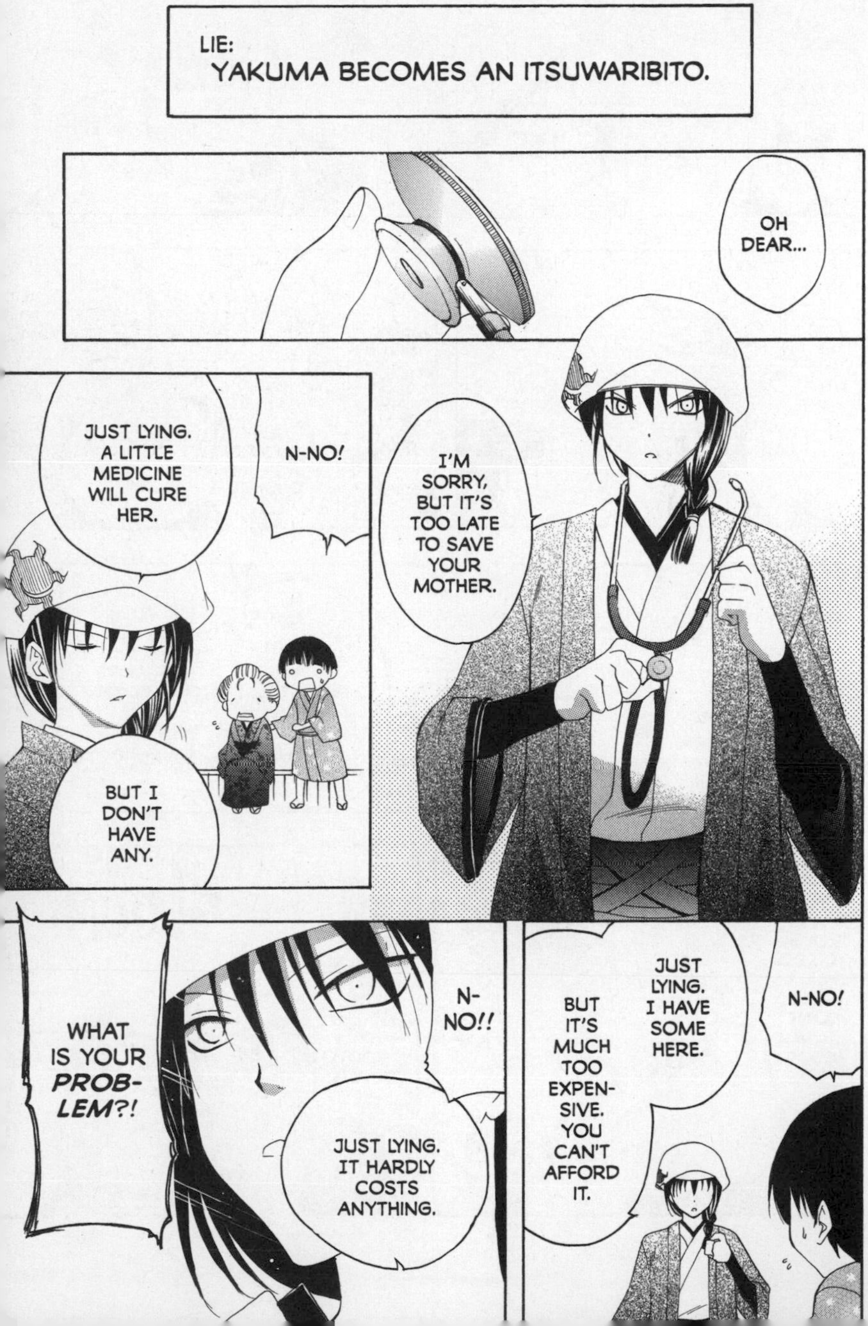
LIE:
YAKUMA BECOMES AN ITSUWARIBITO.
OH DEAR...
I'M SORRY, BUT IT'S TOO LATE TO SAVE YOUR MOTHER.
N-NO!
JUST LYING. A LITTLE MEDICINE WILL CURE HER.
BUT I DON'T HAVE ANY.
N-NO!
JUST LYING. I HAVE SOME HERE.
BUT IT'S MUCH TOO EXPEN-SIVE. YOU CAN'T AFFORD IT.
N-NO!!
JUST LYING. IT HARDLY COSTS ANYTHING.
WHAT IS YOUR *PROB-LEM*?!

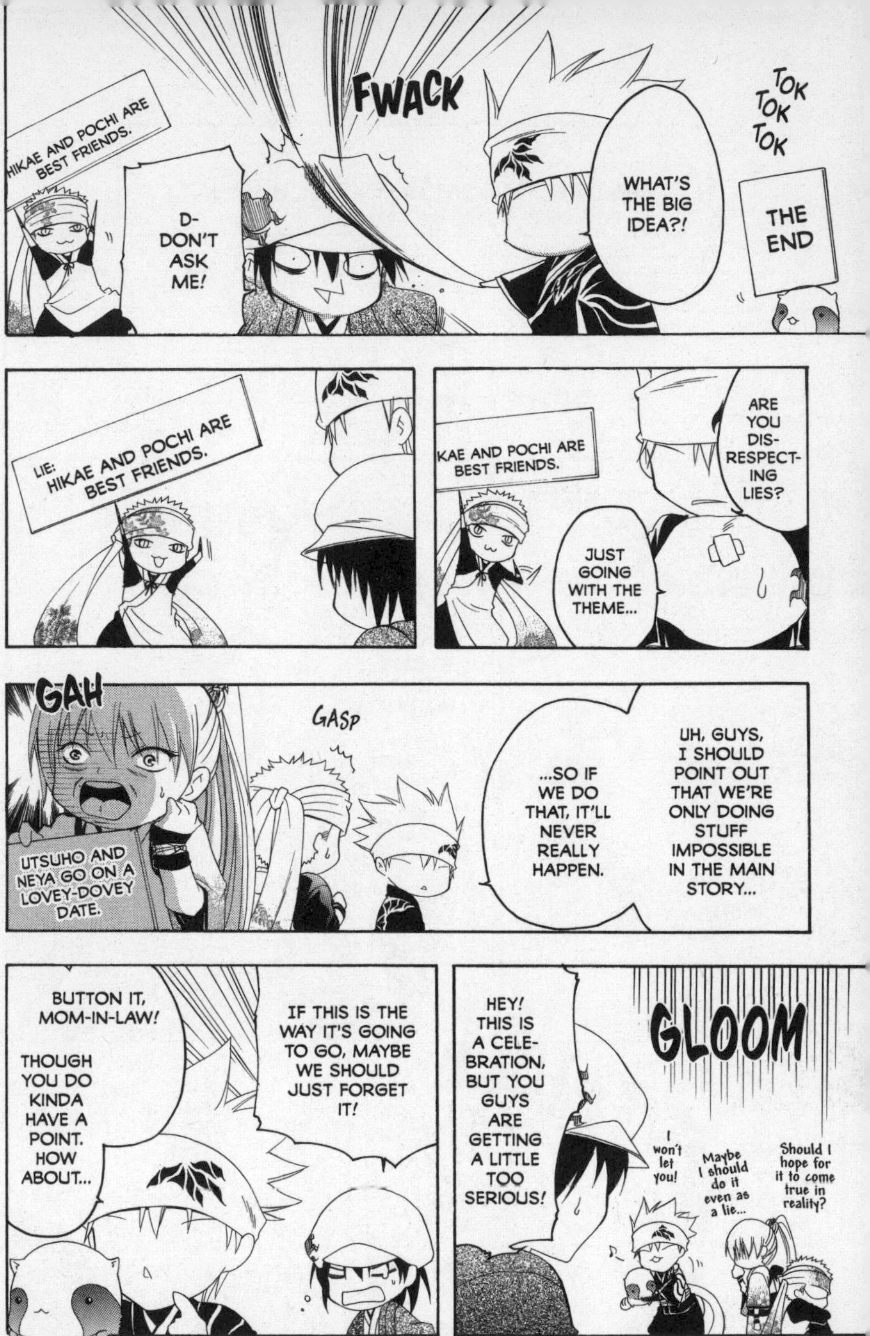
TOK TOK TOK
THE END
WHAT'S THE BIG IDEA?!
FWACK
D-DON'T ASK ME!
HIKAE AND POCHI ARE BEST FRIENDS.
ARE YOU DIS-RESPECTING LIES?
JUST GOING WITH THE THEME...
KAE AND POCHI ARE BEST FRIENDS.
LIE: HIKAE AND POCHI ARE BEST FRIENDS.
UH, GUYS, I SHOULD POINT OUT THAT WE'RE ONLY DOING STUFF IMPOSSIBLE IN THE MAIN STORY...
...SO IF WE DO THAT, IT'LL NEVER REALLY HAPPEN.
GASP
GAH
UTSUHO AND NEYA GO ON A LOVEY-DOVEY DATE.
GLOOM
HEY! THIS IS A CELEBRATION, BUT YOU GUYS ARE GETTING A LITTLE TOO SERIOUS!
Should I hope for it to come true in reality?
Maybe I should do it even as a lie...
I won't let you!
IF THIS IS THE WAY IT'S GOING TO GO, MAYBE WE SHOULD JUST FORGET IT!
BUTTON IT, MOM-IN-LAW!
THOUGH YOU DO KINDA HAVE A POINT. HOW ABOUT...

LIE:
THE ITSUWARIBITO GO TO SCHOOL IN MODERN TIMES.

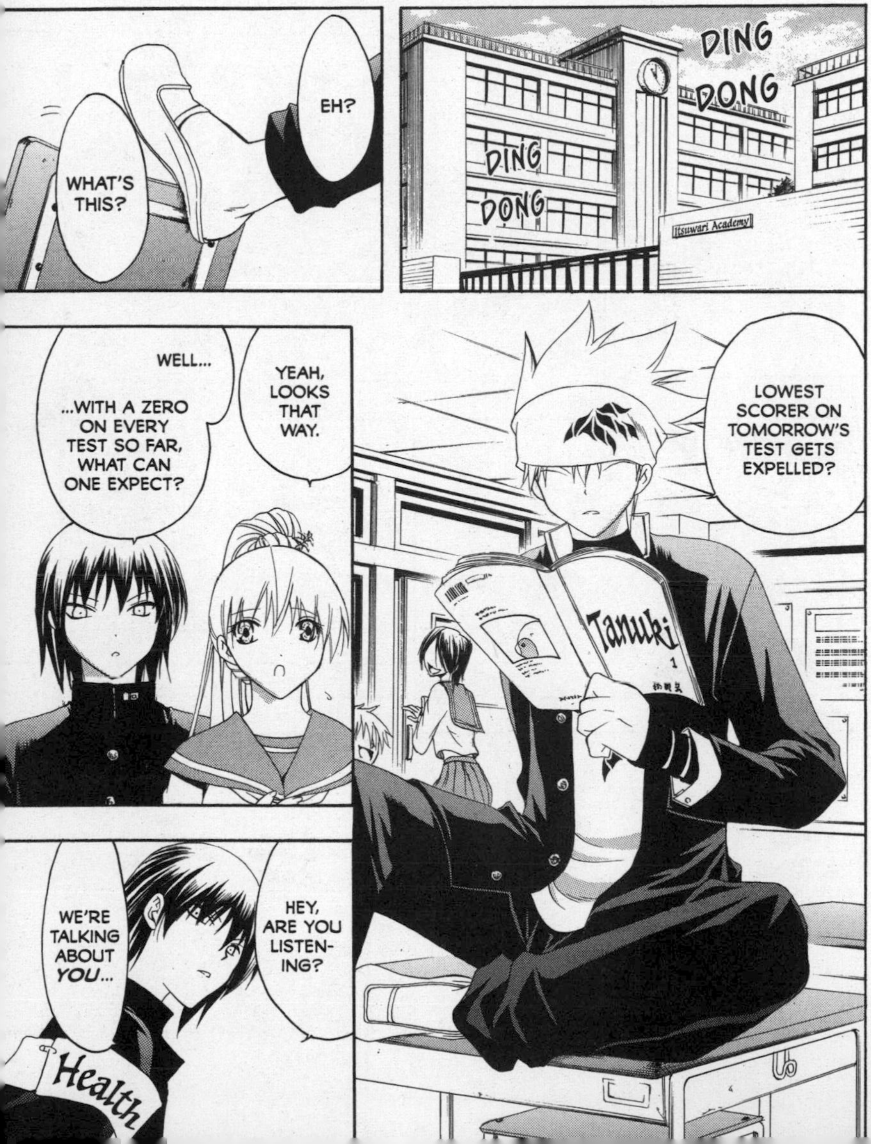
DING DONG
DING DONG
Itsuwari Academy
EH?
WHAT'S THIS?
LOWEST SCORER ON TOMORROW'S TEST GETS EXPELLED?
Tanuki
1
YEAH, LOOKS THAT WAY.
WELL...
...WITH A ZERO ON EVERY TEST SO FAR, WHAT CAN ONE EXPECT?
HEY, ARE YOU LISTEN-ING?
WE'RE TALKING ABOUT *YOU*...
Health

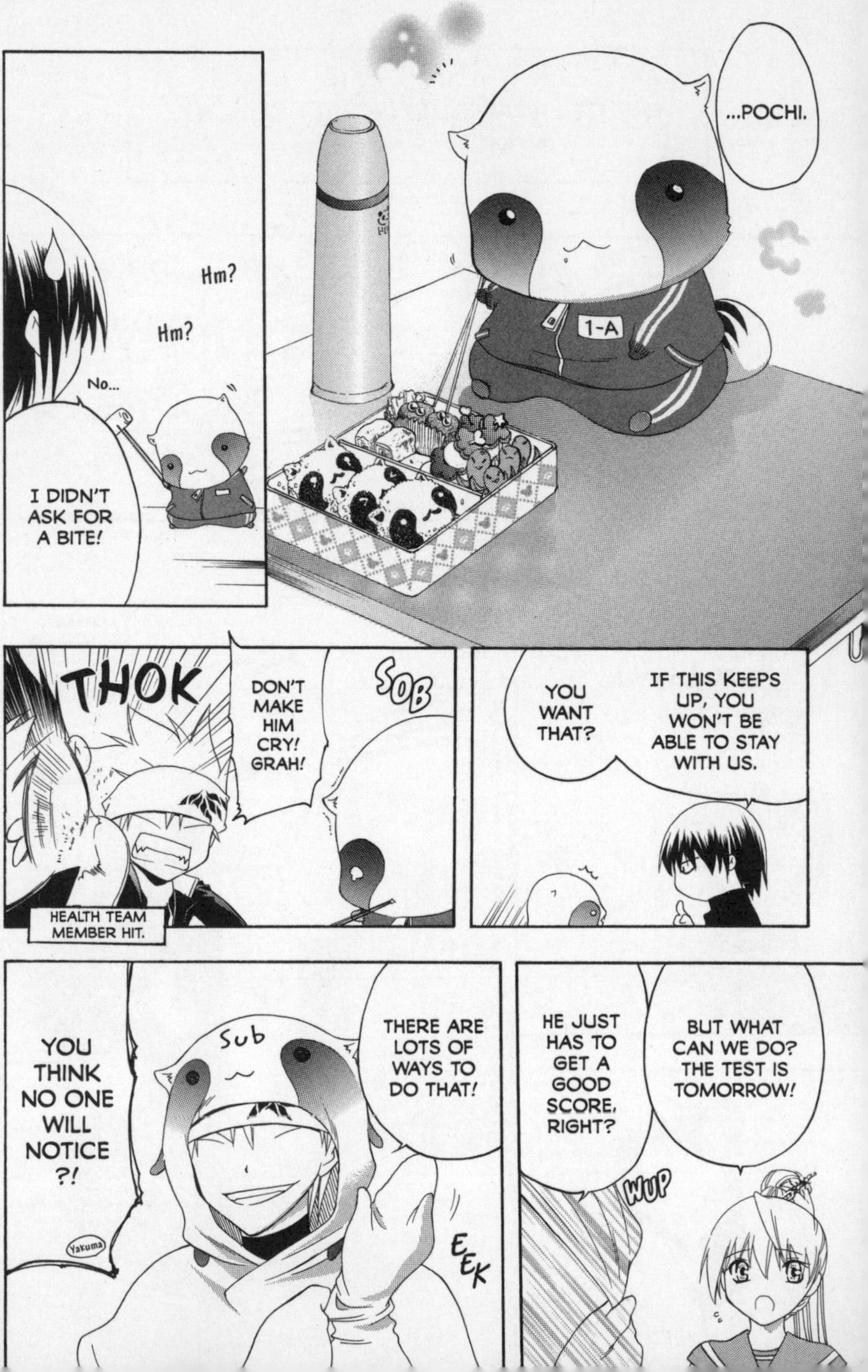
...POCHI.
Hm?
Hm?
No...
I DIDN'T ASK FOR A BITE!
IF THIS KEEPS UP, YOU WON'T BE ABLE TO STAY WITH US.
YOU WANT THAT?
SOB
DON'T MAKE HIM CRY! GRAH!
THOK
HEALTH TEAM MEMBER HIT.
BUT WHAT CAN WE DO? THE TEST IS TOMORROW!
HE JUST HAS TO GET A GOOD SCORE, RIGHT?
WUP
THERE ARE LOTS OF WAYS TO DO THAT!
Sub
EEK
YOU THINK NO ONE WILL NOTICE ?!
Yakuma

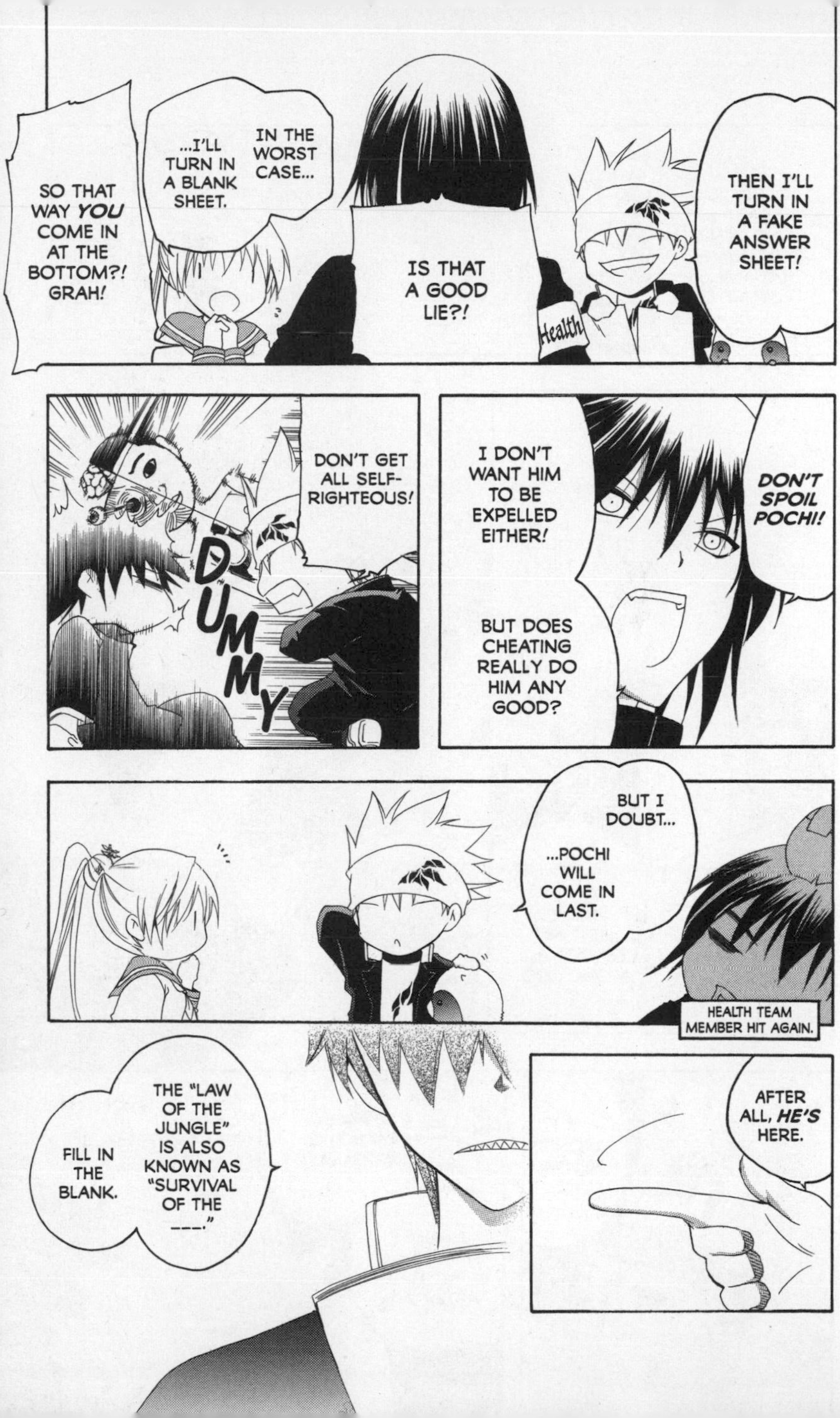
THEN I'LL TURN IN A FAKE ANSWER SHEET!
Health
IS THAT A GOOD LIE?!
IN THE WORST CASE...
...I'LL TURN IN A BLANK SHEET.
SO THAT WAY *YOU* COME IN AT THE BOTTOM?! GRAH!
DON'T SPOIL POCHI!
I DON'T WANT HIM TO BE EXPELLED EITHER!
BUT DOES CHEATING REALLY DO HIM ANY GOOD?
DON'T GET ALL SELF-RIGHTEOUS!
DUMMY
BUT I DOUBT...
...POCHI WILL COME IN LAST.
HEALTH TEAM MEMBER HIT AGAIN.
AFTER ALL, *HE'S* HERE.
THE "LAW OF THE JUNGLE" IS ALSO KNOWN AS "SURVIVAL OF THE ___."
FILL IN THE BLANK.

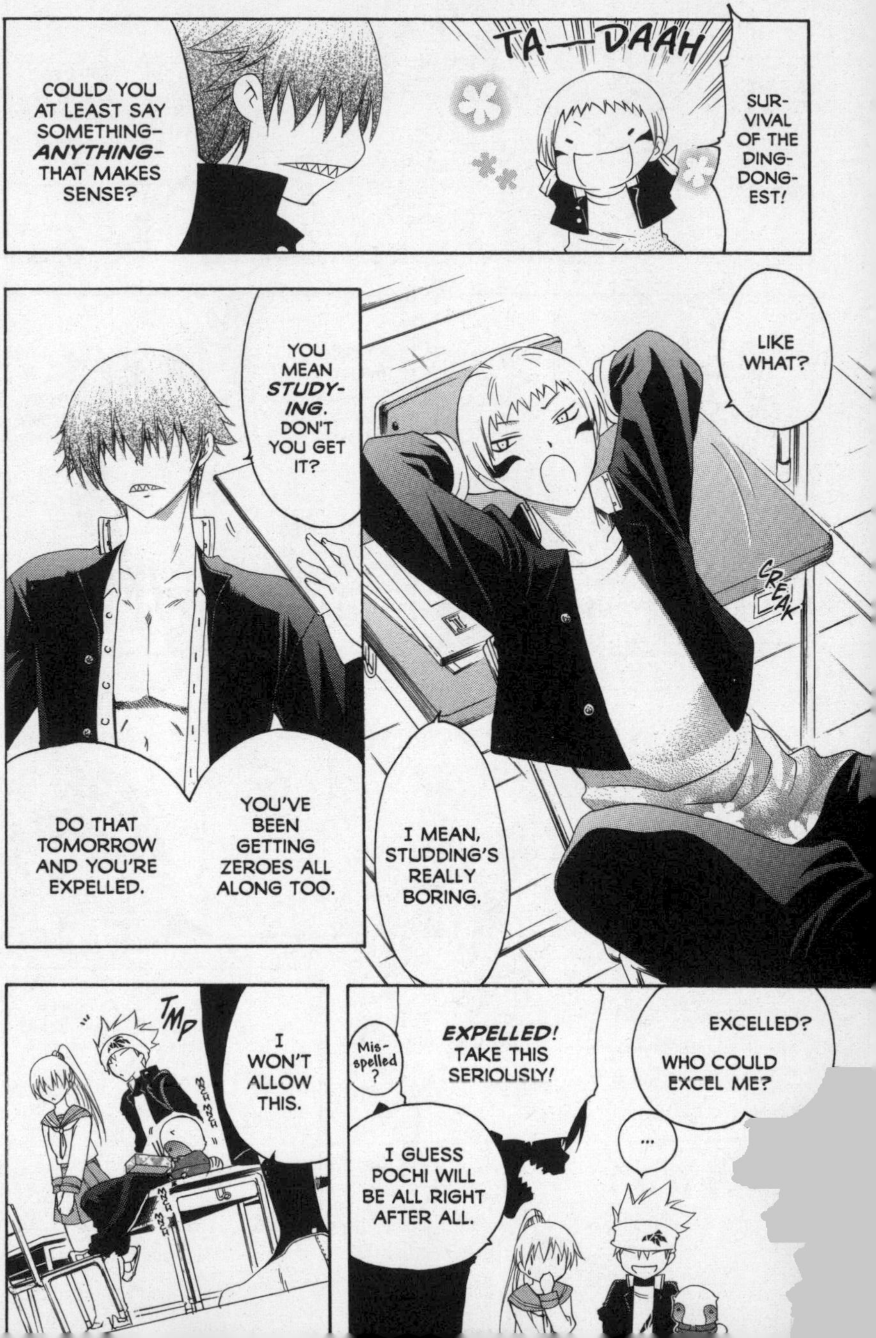
TA—DAAH
SURVIVAL OF THE DING-DONG-EST!
COULD YOU AT LEAST SAY SOMETHING—*ANYTHING*—THAT MAKES SENSE?
LIKE WHAT?
CREAK
I MEAN, STUDDING'S REALLY BORING.
YOU MEAN *STUDYING*. DON'T YOU GET IT?
YOU'VE BEEN GETTING ZEROES ALL ALONG TOO.
DO THAT TOMORROW AND YOU'RE EXPELLED.
EXCELLED?
WHO COULD EXCEL ME?
EXPELLED! TAKE THIS SERIOUSLY!
Mis-spelled?
...
I GUESS POCHI WILL BE ALL RIGHT AFTER ALL.
TMP
I WON'T ALLOW THIS.
MNCH MNCH
MNCH MNCH

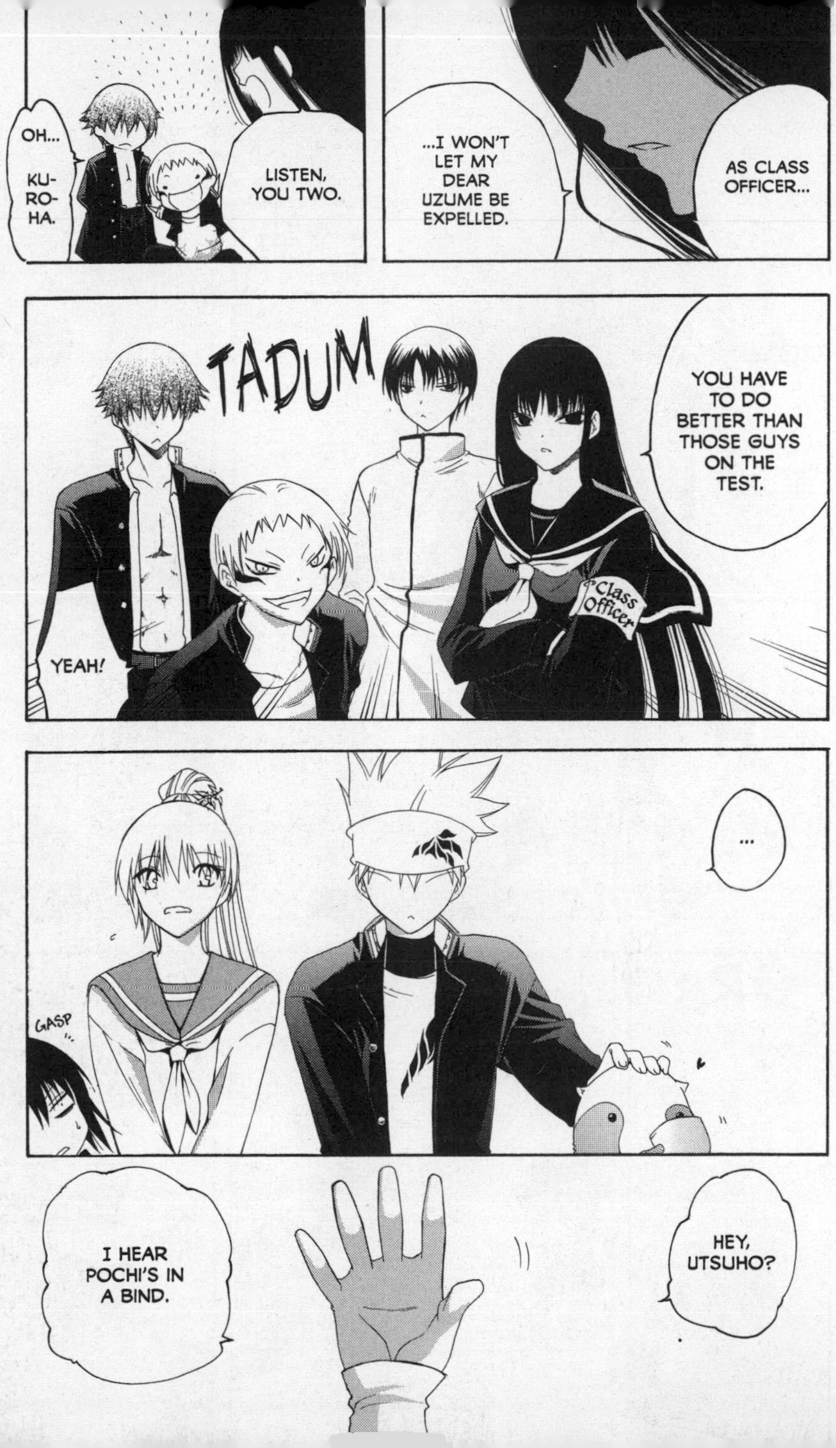
AS CLASS OFFICER...
...I WON'T LET MY DEAR UZUME BE EXPELLED.
LISTEN, YOU TWO.
OH... KU-RO-HA.
YOU HAVE TO DO BETTER THAN THOSE GUYS ON THE TEST.
TADUM
Class Officer
YEAH!
...
GASP
HEY, UTSUHO?
I HEAR POCHI'S IN A BIND.

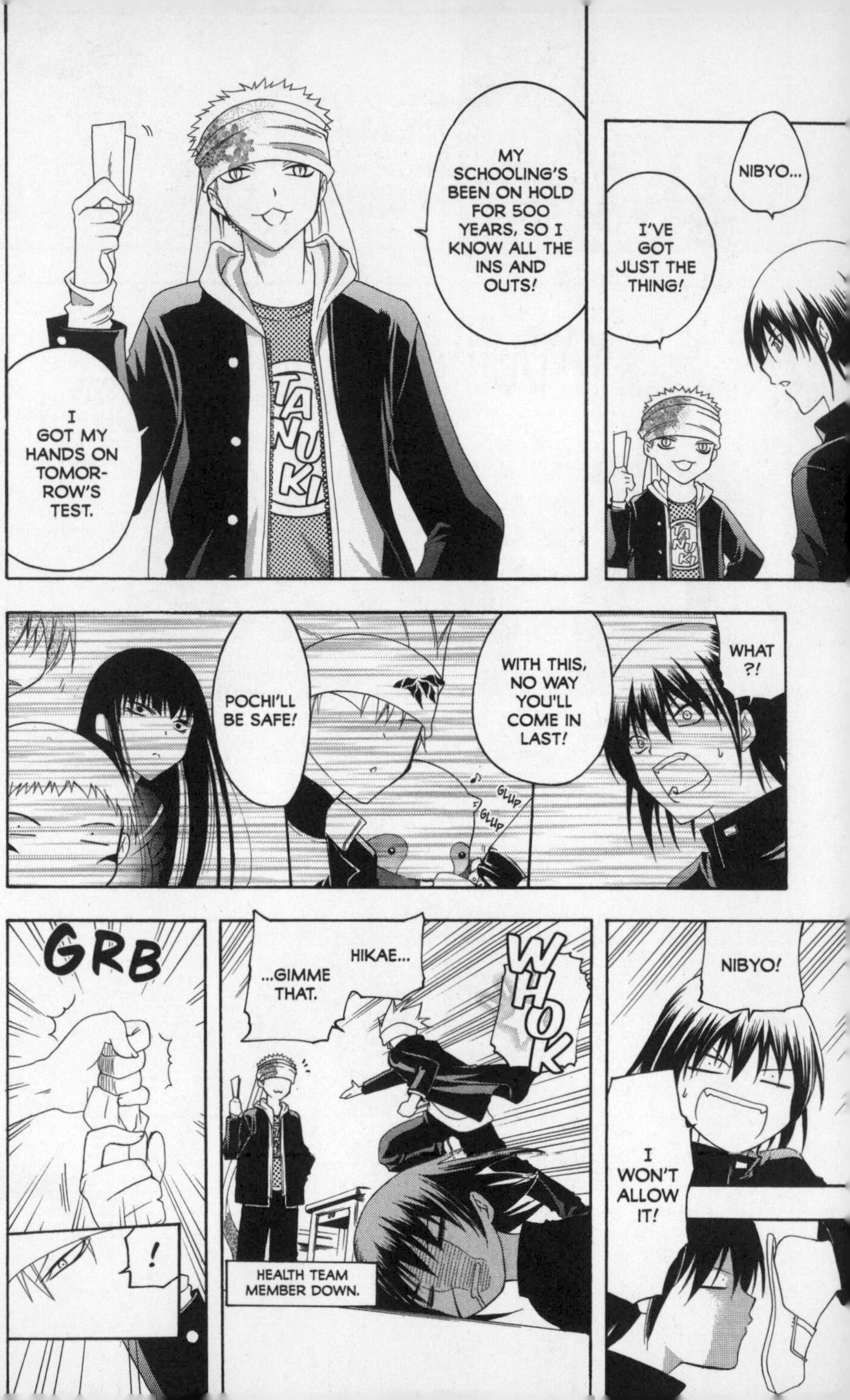
NIBYO...
I'VE GOT JUST THE THING!
MY SCHOOLING'S BEEN ON HOLD FOR 500 YEARS, SO I KNOW ALL THE INS AND OUTS!
I GOT MY HANDS ON TOMORROW'S TEST.
WHAT ?!
WITH THIS, NO WAY YOU'LL COME IN LAST!
GLUP GLUP
POCHI'LL BE SAFE!
NIBYO!
I WON'T ALLOW IT!
HIKAE...
...GIMME THAT.
WHOK
HEALTH TEAM MEMBER DOWN.
GRB
!

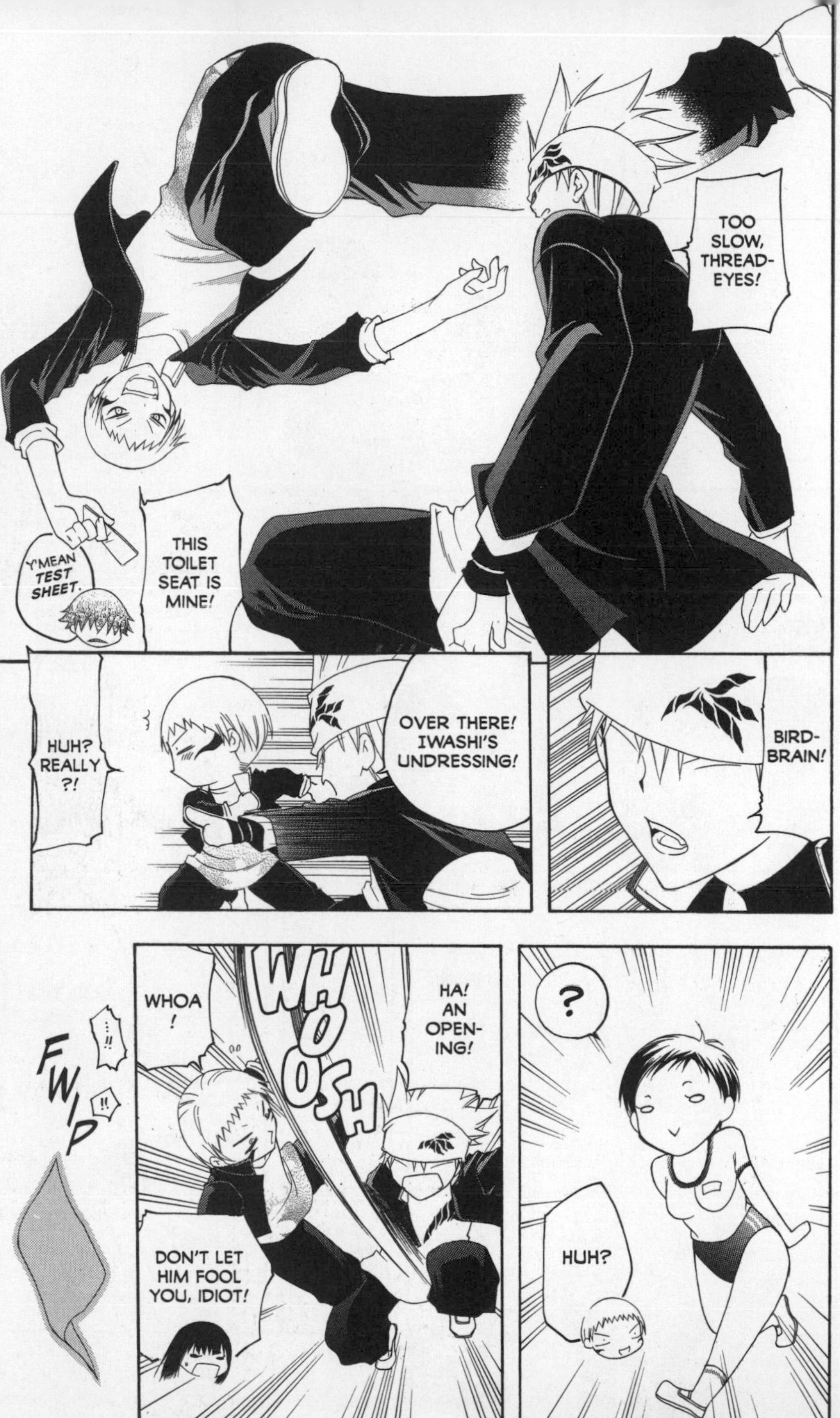
TOO SLOW, THREAD-EYES!
THIS TOILET SEAT IS MINE!
Y'MEAN *TEST SHEET*.
BIRD-BRAIN!
OVER THERE! IWASHI'S UNDRESSING!
HUH? REALLY?!
?
HUH?
HA! AN OPENING!
WHOOSH
WHOA!
...!!
!!
FWIP
DON'T LET HIM FOOL YOU, IDIOT!

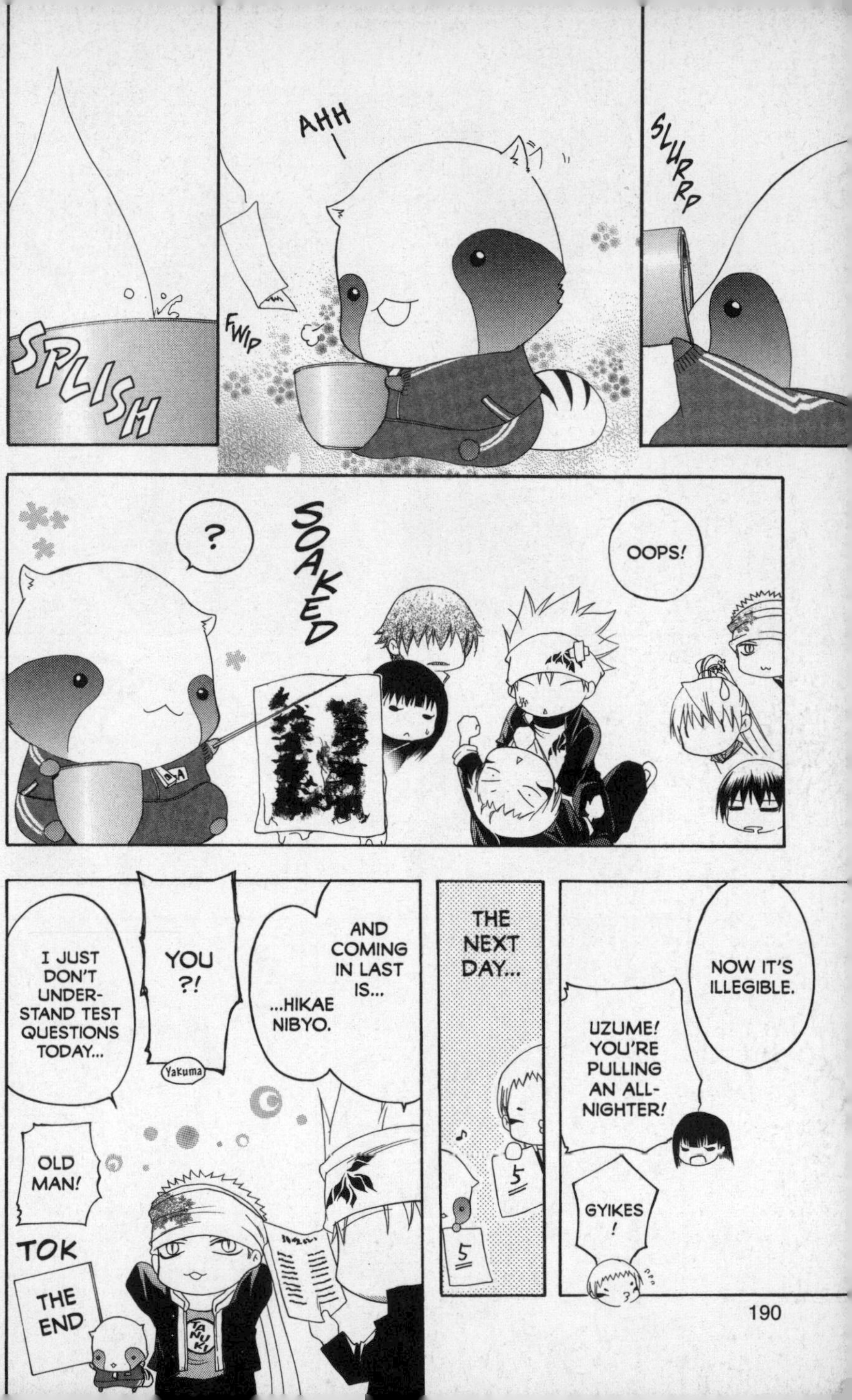
SLURRP
AHH
FWIP
SPLISH
OOPS!
SOAKED
?
NOW IT'S ILLEGIBLE.
UZUME! YOU'RE PULLING AN ALL-NIGHTER!
GYIKES!
THE NEXT DAY...
AND COMING IN LAST IS...
...HIKAE NIBYO.
YOU?!
Yakuma
I JUST DON'T UNDER-STAND TEST QUESTIONS TODAY...
OLD MAN!
TOK
THE END